La Fayette Curry Baker

Spies. Traitors and Conspirators of the late Civil War

La Fayette Curry Baker

Spies. Traitors and Conspirators of the late Civil War

ISBN/EAN: 9783337183165

Printed in Europe, USA, Canada, Australia, Japan

Cover: Foto ©ninafisch / pixelio.de

More available books at **www.hansebooks.com**

Spies. Traitors
and Conspirators
of the Late Civil War

BY GENERAL LA FAYETTE C. BAKER
ORGANIZER AND FIRST CHIEF OF THE
SECRET SERVICE OF THE UNITED
STATES. ILLUSTRATED.

JOHN E. POTTER & COMPANY,
PHILADELPHIA.   MDCCCLXIV.

COPYRIGHT, 1894,
BY
JOHN E. POTTER & CO.

DEDICATION

TO THE AMERICAN PEOPLE.

To the People of this Great Nation,

And more especially

TO THE BRAVE BOYS IN BLUE AND THEIR HEROIC LEADERS,

Who so Gallantly and Valorously bore our Country

Through the Pestilential Ordeal of Secession and the Great Civil War,

And who lifted the dark pall of Slavery from our National Escutcheon, restoring, with new lustre,

A BRIGHTNESS THAT CAN NEVER AGAIN BE SHADOWED,

This Volume of True and Stirring Narrative is

Earnestly, Affectionately and Patriotically Dedicated by their Humble and Devoted Servant,

LA FAYETTE C. BAKER,

Late Chief of the National Secret Service Bureau.

PREFACE.

IN giving to the public this volume, it has been the design to present the operations of the Bureau of the National Detective Police during the war, so far as it is proper to make them known to the people. It is not a book of romantic adventures, but a narrative of facts in the secret history of the conflict, and mainly an exposure of the manifold and gigantic frauds and crimes of both the openly disloyal and the professed friends of the Republic. Many reports are introduced, some of which are lengthy, and portions of them are dry, because they are the official records of the work done, and the verification of the statements made, and the highest vindication of the character and importance of the secret service. Passages occur in them, the propriety of which many readers may question, but their omission would have weakened the strength of the reports, and softened down the enormity of the offenses charged upon certain individuals. The whole volume might have been made up of chapters very similar to those of the first hundred pages or more, but we preferred to sacrifice the peculiar interest, to some extent, of a merely sensational work—sketches of exciting scenes and hair-breadth escapes—for the greater object of an authentic official record of the vast amount of indispensable service rendered to the Government, during nearly four years of bloody strife, with the months of trial and agitation which followed. The plan of the book was, therefore, chosen by the responsible head of the bureau, while the introductory chapters were written by another, whose editoral aid was secured in the general preparation of the annals for the press. No desire or effort has been cherished to wantonly expose or wound in feeling any man, and therefore initials, for the most part, alone appear; but a faithful history of transactions under the authority delegated to the Bureau, will unavoidably reach the sensibilities of persons of distinction, no less than those in humble life.

The volume of war records, the most of which have never before met the public eye, is offered to the people as a part of the veritable history of the most extraordinary and perilous times the Republic has known, or is likely to pass through again.

CONTENTS.

INTRODUCTORY CHAPTER.

GENERAL BAKER AND THE BUREAU OF SECRET SERVICE.

The Ancestry and Birth-place of General Baker—His Early Life—Residence in California—Is a Member of the Vigilance Committee—Returns to New York in 1861—Visits Washington—Interview with General Scott—Enters the Secret Service—The Great Facts established and illustrated by these Annals.. 17

CHAPTER I.

ORIGIN OF THE BUREAU OF DETECTIVE SERVICE.

The first visit to Washington—Interview with General Hiram Walbridge, and Hon. W. D. Kelley—Introduction to General Winfield Scott—Return to New York—Appointed by General Scott to renew the Attempt to visit Richmond—The first Failure—Crossing the Lines—The Arrest—Examinations—Sent to General Beauregard—On to Richmond...................... 41

CHAPTER II.

RESIDENCE IN RICHMOND.

Summoned to an interview with Jeff. Davis—Subsequent Examinations by him—Critical Emergencies—Mr. Brock—"Samuel Munson"—Confidence secured—Mr. "Munson" is appointed Confederate Agent—Original Letters from Davis, Toombs, and Walker—Starts for the North—Unpleasant Delays—A Narrow Escape—Reaches the Potomac—Deceives the Dutch Fishermen and runs the Rebel Gauntlet safely.. 58

CHAPTER III.

NORTHERN EXPERIENCES AS CONFEDERATE AGENT.

Hospitalities by the way—The Report to General Scott—Operations in Baltimore—The Janus-faced Unionist—A rich Development in Philadelphia—The Arrests—Amusing Prison Scene 75

CHAPTER IV.

TREASON AND TRAITORS AT THE NORTH.

Baltimore—The Detective Service and the Arrest of the Maryland Legislature—The Refugee and the Spy—The Pursuit and the Capture—Traitors at Niagara Falls—Acquaintance with them—The Arrest—In Fort Lafayette.......... 89

CHAPTER V.

A KNIGHT OF THE GOLDEN SQUARE.

? H. F., *alias* Carlisle Murray, a Knight of the Golden Square—The Arrest—Release—Papers of F. examined—Secretary Seward's Order for a Second Arrest—On the Track—The Rural Retreat—Mr. Carlisle Murray a Reformer and Lover—The Official Writ—The Astonished Landlord and Landlady—A Scene—Report 99

CHAPTER VI.

DISLOYALTY AMONG THE POSTMASTERS.

A Mystery—The Result of Cabinet Meetings in Washington known in Richmond—The Detectives learn the Reason—A Visit to Lower Maryland—Amusing Scenes—The Mysterious Box—The Reports—A Rebel Letter 108

CHAPTER VII.

FRAUDS—DISLOYALTY IN MARYLAND.

The Freighted Traveler—Treason and Frauds overlooked in the Rising Storm of Rebellion—The Bankers—The Pretty Smuggler—Reliable Character of the Detective Bureau—Disloyalty, and its Punishments in Lower Maryland—The Friends of Hon. Montgomery Blair and the Quinine Traffic—"Chunook" Telegrams... 118

CHAPTER VIII.

OFFICIAL SERVICES AND EMBARRASSMENTS—NEW ORDER OF THINGS.

The Bureau transferred to the War Department—Dr. H., and the Perilous Adventure of which he was the occasion—Report of the Case—Arrest of the Leaders of a great secret Southern Organization—Documents and Letters 133

CHAPTER IX.

THE BUREAU IN CANADA—IN THE ARMY.

Tricks of False Correspondence—Mr. Delisle and the "Secret Secession Legation" 148

CHAPTER X.

WEALTHY TRAITORS—FRUITLESS SCHEMES.

John H. Waring—His Operations—An Efficient Tool—Walter Bowie—A Wild Career—Rebel Mail—Contrabands—Extracts from the Private Journals of Rebel Spies 158

CHAPTER XI.

SLAVERY—PLAYING REBEL GENERAL—FIRST DISTRICT CAVALRY.

The Hostages—Mr. Lincoln—Deceiving the Rebels—A successful Game—Organization of the First District Cavalry—Its Services 167

CHAPTER XII.

FIRST DISTRICT CAVALRY.

Leaving Camp again—"Wilson's Raid"—Battles—The Escape of Kautz—The End of Regimental Service 190

CHAPTER XIII.

THE ANIMUS OF SECESSION.

A Disloyal Pastor and his Friends compelled to "do justly"—The "Peculiar Institution" Dies Hard—Man-Stealers Foiled in their Schemes of Robbery 204

CHAPTER XIV.

ENGLISH SYMPATHY WITH THE SOUTH—NEGRO-HATE IN WASHINGTON.

An English Emissary of the South—He Deceives the Secretary of State—My Acquaintance with Him—The Fruitless Effort to Betray Me—The Journey to the Old Capitol Prison—Negro-hate in the National Capital......... 209

CHAPTER XV.

GIGANTIC VICES OF THE NATIONAL CAPITAL.

Gambling and the Gamblers—The Purpose to Break up the Dens Discouraged—The Midnight Raid—Results—Drinking and Liquor Saloons—The Descent upon them—Broken up—Licentiousness and its Patrons—The Raid on their haunts at Dead of Night—The Arrests.. 217

CHAPTER XVI.

A PERILOUS ADVENTURE.

Pope's Defeat—Banks' Advance—The Importance of communicating wit' him—The Successful Attempt—Rebel Pursuers—The Escape................. 225

CHAPTER XVII.

SPECULATION AND FRAUD.

Devices of Contractors—Detection of Forage Contractor—Appeal to the President—Further Frauds as "Silent Partner"...................................... 233

CHAPTER XVIII.

A FEMALE ADVENTURER.

Woman in the Rebellion—Her Aid indispensable in the worst as well as the best Causes—A Spicy Letter—Miss A. J.—Vidocq's Experience............ 235

CHAPTER XIX.

THE BOUNTY JUMPERS.

Fraudulent Practices of Bounty Brokers and Jumpers—Contrast between English and American Deserters—Plans to check Desertion, and bring Criminals to Justice......... 249

CHAPTER XX.

THE BOUNTY JUMPERS AND BROKERS.

Quotas filled with Falsified Enlistment-Papers—Arrest of Brokers—Amusing and Exciting Scene—The Hoboken Raid—Slanderous Charges—Large Number of Arrests—Incarceration in Fort Lafayette—Other Arrests—Trial before a Military Commission.. 253

CHAPTER XXI.

BOUNTY JUMPING INCIDENTS.

Personal Experience in Bounty Jumping—A Perfect Trump—Detectives Enlisted—Passes obtained for Bounty Jumpers—Arrest and Surprise—Court-Martial and Conviction 262

CHAPTER XXII.

BOUNTY JUMPERS IN ORGANIZED BANDS.

Gipsy-like Bounty Jumpers—Wholesale Bounty Jumping carried on adroitly by a Gang of Operators—Opposition from a Canadian Gang—Thirty-two Thousand Dollars in as many Days—Frauds in Drafting—An Old Man put in as a Substitute—A Boy Decoyed—His Adventures—A Mother of Thirteen Children—Unavailing Efforts of a Mother in search of her Idiotic Son.. 268

CHAPTER XXIII.

THE GREAT CONSPIRACY.

Assassinations—Eglon, King of Moab—Cæsar, Emperor of Rome—James I. of England—Marat, the French Revolutionary Leader—Alexander of Russia—Abraham Lincoln, President of the United States 274

CHAPTER XXIV.

THE ASSASSINS CAPTURED.

Excitement around my Headquarters at Washington—The Chief Conspirator —A Graphic Narrative of his Arrest—His Burial—Desire for Relics from his Body—Hanging of the Conspirators.. 284

CHAPTER XXV.

THE DETECTIVE POLICE—AND THE ARREST OF THE ASSASSINS.

Personal Relations to President Lincoln—His Kindness and Confidence—My Order to Pursue the Conspirators—Results—Statements of Subordinates and Others 342

CHAPTER XXVI.

LETTERS ON THE ASSASSINATION.

Jacob Thompson—Volunteer Suggestions respecting the Assassin's Hiding-Places before his Death, and the Disposal of his Remains afterward—Threats of more Assassinations—A Mysterious Letter—J. H. Suratt........ 371

CHAPTER XXVII.

ATTEMPTED SUICIDE OF WIRZ.

My Connection with the Imprisonment of Wirz and Jeff Davis—Vigilance in Guarding the Prisoner—Mrs. Wirz visits her Husband—He desires a Call—The Interview—Attempted Suicide 394

INTRODUCTORY CHAPTER.

GENERAL BAKER AND THE BUREAU OF SECRET SERVICE.

The Ancestry and Birth-place of General Baker—His Early Life—Residence in California—Is a Member of the Vigilance Committee—Returns to New York in 1861—Visits Washington—Interview with General Scott—Enters the Secret Service—The Great Facts established and illustrated by these Annals.

BRIGADIER-GENERAL LA FAYETTE C. BAKER belongs to a family of New England origin. In an early history of Vermont, entitled the "Green Mountain Boys," the name for two generations is conspicuous among those of the heroic men of the French and Indian wars. About the year 1770, the military organization bearing that name was formed, to resist the arbitrary claims of the colonial government of New York over the settlers and soil of the "New Hampshire Grants." Ethan Allen, Seth Warner, and Remember Baker were acknowledged leaders of the heroic, self-sacrificing band of patriots. We find it recorded, that "previous to 1770, many acts of violence had been committed by both of the belligerent parties. It was at this date that the governor of New York attempted to enforce his authority over the territory in dispute by a resort to military force. The Green Mountain Boys having learned that a military force of seven hundred and fifty men were marching to subjugate them, immediately organized themselves, and appointed Ethan Allen colonel, and Seth Warner, Remember Baker, and others, captains of the several companies under him. The New York force having advanced at night upon the dwelling of a settler, were suddenly surprised by the mountaineers in ambush, and the whole posse ingloriously fled, without a gun being fired on either side. The Green

Mountain Boys were occasionally called out for military exercise and discipline. In 1771, the governor of New York issued a proclamation offering a reward for the arrest of Colonel Allen, and Captains Warner and Baker. Several attempts were made to abduct them, but none were successful."

Subsequently, in the Indian conflicts, Mr. Baker's toes were cut off, and other barbarities inflicted upon members of his family. General Baker's father, who inherited the paternal name, removed to Stafford, New York, in 1815. La Fayette was born there, October 13, 1826. When three years of age, his father removed to Elba, an adjoining town, where he lived till thirteen years of age, when the family started for the wilderness of the Great West. Mr. Remember Baker chose his home within the limits of Michigan, where Lansing, the capital, now stands, then a primeval forest, haunted by the aborigines. Soon the log-house and the clearing around it rewarded the toil of the father and the son.

In the year 1848 he returned to New York, where he remained nearly two years, when he went to the city of Philadelphia, and was engaged in mechanical and mercantile pursuits. Mr. Baker was married December 24, 1852, to Miss Jennie C. Curry, daughter of John Curry, Esq., of Southwark. The next year he went to California. An incident occurred on the Isthmus, illustrative of his bold, fearless, and adventurous character. A native attempted to take advantage of an Irish emigrant, and charge him for the passage of two children the second time. Mr. Baker remonstrated. The party of half a dozen were in a small boat, near Gorgona. The enraged boatman seized one of the children, and threatened to throw him in the water unless the unjust demand were complied with by the father. Mr. Baker told him to stop, but he refused; when a well-directed blow from an oar staggered the man. Recovering himself in a few moments, he drew his knife, and rushed toward Baker, who, raising his revolver, shot him dead, the lifeless body tumbling over the boat's side into the water. He suddenly became conscious of his danger, aware that the native population would, if possible, kill him. Leaping from the small craft, he waded to the opposite shore, the frantic pursuers at his back. Turning, he shot the leader, and crept into the tangled, matted thicket. Here he eluded search, and at length reached the American consul's house, where he was concealed in a subterranean passage for two weeks, and then smuggled on board of a vessel bound for California, and safely landed. The next meeting with one of his traveling companions, where the tragic scene narrated occurred, was in Richmond. He was accosted by him there, but, as it will be seen, having become "Mr. Munson," did not choose to know his friend of California memory.

Mr. Baker engaged in mechanical pursuits on the Pacific coast, when the lawless period of 1856 called into existence the Vigilance Committee. Mr. Baker was immediately enrolled in the army of 2,200 men, every one of whom was known by a number, his own being 208. In the summary work of ridding the country of reckless gamblers and "ballot-box stuffers," for exposing whose crimes James Casey had murdered James King of William, editor of the *San Francisco Bulletin*, Mr. Baker was an active and efficient member, giving unmistakable evidences of that peculiar adaptation to the detective service, which has made him pre-eminent in it, on this continent, since the long struggle for victory over a foe that gloried in treason under a smiling face, and robbery in the name of inalienable rights, called for and received the best men and treasure of the country. With the disbandment of the extraordinary and formidable organization, Mr. Baker returned to his peaceful occupation, in which he continued till 1861, when he came to New York City, intending to remain only a brief period. The appreciation of his services while a member of the Vigilance Committee and engaged in a mercantile agency, was very emphatically and tastefully expressed on New Year's day, the date of his departure, by the merchants of San Francisco. They met at the Bank Exchange, and sent for Mr. Baker. When he entered the room, to his entire surprise, a gentleman presented him with a cane of mansinita wood, found only in California. The head is polished gold quartz from the Ish Mine, Oregon, and around it are nine oval stones of similar material from as many different mines. The whole is richly mounted with solid gold, and cost two hundred and fifty dollars.

At the very moment he was ready to return to the Pacific coast, the tocsin of civil war startled the land. In common with the loyal millions of the North, his patriotic indignation at the treasonable revolt, and the desire to aid in its suppression, made all other purposes and plans of small importance. He immediately decided to abandon his business schemes and serve the imperiled country. How well he succeeded, and his public career from this point in his history, will appear in his story of the National Secret Service.

In General Baker's personal appearance there is nothing, to a casual observer, remarkable. And yet, physically, he is an extraordinary man. Before the exhausting labors of his official position during the war reduced his weight, it averaged one hundred and eighty pounds. His frame is of the firmest texture, and its powers of endurance very great. For days together he has prosecuted his duties without food or sleep, and exposed to winter storms. He is of medium height, lithe, and sinewy, and his movements are quick, and yet having the air of deliberateness natural to a profession in which circumspection and habitual self-control are among the first conditions of success. Around his forehead of intelligent outline lies a profusion of brown hair, and his face is partially covered with a heavy brown beard. His gray eye, in repose, wears a cold expression; in his naturally cheerful mood, and in the unguarded enjoyment of social life, it is changeful and playful; and, engaged in his special duty of detecting crime, it becomes sharply piercing, often making the victim of his vigilance to quail before its steady gaze. Indeed, he was evidently the man for the place he filled during the national struggle. The personal peril to which he exposed himself, and the untiring service performed, at the head of a division, or even a regiment, would have sounded his name over the land as a daring, untiring and heroic leader. He is probably the best "shot" in the country, and also a fine horseman. Some additional and interesting facts in his history will be noticed in the eloquent defense of General Baker by Mr. Riddle, in the "Cobb case."

For nearly twenty years he has not tasted intoxicating drinks, but has been enrolled among the Sons of Temperance; and what seems still more remarkable, when we think of the associations inseparable from his adventurous career, he has never been addicted to the shameless profanity so common in the army and among men of adventurous character. His fidelity and kindness of heart in his domestic relations, and toward kindred less fortunate than himself are well known.

Such are the general characteristics of the first national chief of a Detective Bureau in the war record of this country.

Blackstone's definition of the police is: "The due regulation and domestic order of the kingdom, whereby the individuals of a State, like members of a family, are compelled to conform their general behavior to the rules of propriety and good neighborhood, and good manners, and to be decent, inoffensive individuals in their several stations."

The definition is comprehensive, and certainly gives to this public service both great utility and honorable, dignified character. Another able writer divides the services of policemen into several distinct duties; among which is "giving recent intelligence," the very work of the detective police, when a specialty in time of public perils, and one which awakens the prejudice and hostility of all classes.

The history of the police of the world, would be a most exciting and instructive library of itself. We can only glance at this service in the two leading nations of Europe; one Protestant and the other Catholic. "The office of constable," says a "magistrate," in his annals of the London police, "is as old as the monarchy of England." He writes again, with reference to the unpopular character of the indispensable office: "The best laws are worthless, if the public impression be cherished that it is a matter of infamy to carry them into execution." Doubtless, the principal reason for the general disfavor toward the police department, arises from the *espionage* inseparable from it. People do not like to be *watched*, and are still less willing to have their offenses against law and order reported to the tribunals of justice. Nevertheless, the records of the police, with all that is unworthy of it, are irresistible evidence of its importance in securing public and personal security from the depravity which scorns all restraints but the iron grasp of law. In Britain, the police department has never become a national institution; but, until comparatively a recent date, has been "a hand to mouth affair." About the middle of the eighteenth century, Henry Fielding devoted his energies and influence to the organization of the London police into an efficient and able force under the acting magistrate of the city. And, like the modern defenders of the "constitution," there were not a few who wrote and talked about the dangerous infringement of the rights of citizenship, and predicted the rapid decay of liberty, until the "British lion would slumber ingloriously in the net of captivity." But the reform went forward, and the charter of English freedom remained unshaken by the dreaded power of an omnipresent police. The crimes it exposed and the criminals convicted, for a single year, were tens of thousands.

We turn to France for the most complete and successful system of police service the world has yet seen. Until the latter part of the fifteenth century, the kingdom had no effective police. Even in the streets of Paris, "wolves roamed unmolested," and citizens forsook their habitations. Charles VII. took charge of the criminal business of the realm, to the sudden alarm of the lawless people, who lived on the property and peace of the communities. Francis I., in 1520, appointed a provost-marshal, with thirty constables. The next grand advance in this department of justice, was the creation, by Louis XIV., of a lieutenant-general, which office continued from March, 1667, to the memorable July 14, 1787. The most distinguished officer during this period was De La Renye.

The storm of the French revolution, which swept away the entire order of things, reduced the police organization to sixty petty committees. After the restoration, the prefect was appointed. Through all these changes, the national police of France stood alone in the recognition of its worth, and the mighty power it wielded in securing the public good.

The very vices of the great metropolis are so far regulated and controlled by it, that their ruinous results in Paris are probably not one-half they are in proportion to the population in Protestant London or New York. We shall quote a few passages from Vidocq's memoirs, a man of doubtful character, but the great modern Parisian detective, to illustrate the practical workings of the system there.

M. Henry, to whom Vidocq refers, was "the préfet" of police. He thus describes his entrance upon his official duties:—

"As the secret agent of government, I had duties marked out, and the kind and respectable M. Henry took upon himself to instruct me in their fulfillment; for in his hands were intrusted nearly the entire safety of the capital: to prevent crimes, discover malefactors, and to give them up to justice, were the principal functions confided to me. By thieves, M. Henry was styled the Evil Spirit; and well did he merit the surname, for, with him, cunning and suavity of manners were so conjoined as seldom to fail in their purpose. Among the coadjutors of M. Henry was M. Bertaux, a cross-examiner of great merit. The proofs of his talent may be found in the archives of the court. Next to him, I have great pleasure in naming M. Parisot governor of the prisons. In a word, M. Henry, Bertaux, and Parisot formed a veritable triumvirate, which was incessantly conspiring against the perpetrators of all manner of crimes; to extirpate rogues from Paris, and to procure for the inhabitants of that immense city a perfect security.

"So soon as I was installed in my new office of secret agent, I commenced my rounds, in order to take my measures well for setting effectually to work. These journeys, which occupied me nearly twenty days, furnished me with many useful and important observations, but as yet I was only preparing to act, and studying my ground.

"One morning I was hastily summoned to attend the chief of the division. The matter in hand was to discover a man named Watrin, accused of having fabricated and put in circulation false money and bank notes. The inspectors of the police had already arrested Watrin, but, according to custom, had allowed him to escape. M. Henry gave me every direction which he deemed likely to assist me in the search after him; but, unfortunately, he had only gleaned a few simple particulars of his usual habits and customary haunts: every place he was known to frequent was freely pointed out to me; but it was not very likely he would be found in those resorts which prudence would call upon him carefully to avoid; there remained, therefore, only a chance of reaching him by some by-path. When I learn that he had left his effects in a furnished house, where he once lodged, on the boulevard of Mont Parnasse, I took it for granted that, sooner or later, he would go there in search of his property, or at least that he would send some person to fetch it from thence; consequently, I directed all my vigilance to this spot, and after having reconnoitred the house, I lay in ambush in its vicinity night and day, in order to keep a watchful eye upon all comers and goers. This went on for nearly a week, when, weary of not observing any thing, I determined upon engaging the master of the house in my interest, and to hire an apartment of him, where I accordingly established myself with Annette, certain that my presence could give rise to no suspicion. I ad occupied this post for about fifteen days, when one evening, at leven o'clock, I was informed that Watrin had just come, accompanied by another person. Owing to a slight indisposition, I had retired to bed earlier than usual; however, at this news I rose hastily, and descended the staircase by four stairs at a time; but whatever diligence I might use, I was only just in time to catch Watrin's companion; him I had no right to detain, but I made myself sure that I might, by intimidation, obtain further particulars from him. I therefore seized him, threatened him, and soon drew from him a confession that he was a shoemaker, and that Watrin lived with him, No. 4, Rue des Mauvais Garçons. This was all I wanted to know: I had only had time to slip an old greatcoat over my shirt, and without stopping to put on more garments, I hurried on to the place thus pointed out to me. I reached the house at the very instant that some person was quitting it: persuaded that it was Watrin, I attempted to seize him; he escaped from me, and I darted after him up a staircase; but, at the moment of grasping him, a violent blow which struck my chest, drove me down twenty stairs. I sprang forward again, and that so quickly, that to escape from my pursuit he was compelled to return into the house through a sash window. I then knocked loudly at the door, summoning him to open it without delay. This he refused to do. I then desired Annette (who had followed me) to go in search of the guard, and while she was preparing to obey me, I counterfeited the noise of a man descending the stairs. Watrin, deceived by this feint, was anxious to satisfy himself whether I had actually gone, and softly put his head out of window to observe if all was safe. This was exactly what I wanted. I made a vigorous dart forward, and seized him by the hair of his head: he grasped me in the same manner, and a desperate struggle took place; jammed against the partition wall which separated us, he opposed me with a determined resistance. Nevertheless, I felt that he was growing weaker. I collected all my strength for a last effort; I strained every nerve, and drew him nearly out of the window through which we were struggling: one more trial and the victory was mine; but in the earnestness of my grasp we both rolled on the passage floor, on to which I had pulled him; to rise, snatch from his hands the shoemaker's cutting-knife with which he had armed himself, to bind him, and lead him out of the house, was the work of an instant. Accompanied only by Annette, I conducted him to the prefecture, where I received the congratulations, first of M. Henry, and afterward those of the prefect of police, who bestowed on me a pecuniary recompense. Watrin was a man of unusual address; he followed a coarse, clumsy business, and yet he had given himself up to making counterfeit money, which required extreme delicacy of hand. Condemned to death, he obtained a reprieve the very hour that was destined for his execution; the scaffold was prepared, he was taken down from it, and the lovers of such scenes experienced a disappointment. All Paris remembers it. A report was in circulation that he was about to make some very important discoveries; but as he had nothing to reveal, a few days afterward he underwent his sentence.

"Watrin was my first capture, and an important one too; this successful beginning awoke the jealousy of the peace-officers, as well as of those under my orders; all were exasperated against me, but in vain; they could not forgive me for being more successful than themselves. The superiors, on the contrary, were highly pleased with my conduct; and I redoubled my zeal, to render myself still more worthy their confidence.

"About this period a vast number of counterfeit five-franc pieces had got into general circulation; several of them were shown me while examining them, I fancied I could discover the workmanship of Bouhin (who had informed against me) and of his friend, Dr. Terrier. I resolved to satisfy my mind as to the truth of this; and in consequence of this determination, I set about watching the steps of these two individuals; but as I durst not follow too closely, lest they might recognize me, and mistrust my observation, it was difficult for me to obtain the intelligence I wanted. Nevertheless, by dint of unwearied perseverance, I arrived at the certainty of my not having mistaken the matter, and the two coiners were arrested in the very act of fabricating their base coin; they were shortly after condemned and executed for it."

"In so populous a capital as that of Paris, there are usually a vast many places of bad resort, at which assembled persons of broken fortune and ruined fame; in order to judge of them under my own eye, I frequented every house and street of ill-fame, sometimes unde one disguise and sometimes under another; assuming, indeed, all those rapid changes of dress and manner which indicated a person desirous of concealing himself from the observation of the police, till the rogues and thieves whom I daily met there firmly believed me to be one of themselves; persuaded of my being a runaway, they would have been cut to pieces before I should have been taken; for not only had I acquired their fullest confidence, but their strongest regard; and so much did they respect my situation, as a fugitive galley-slave, that they would not even propose to me to join in any of their daring schemes, lest it might compromise my safety. All, however, did not exercise this delicacy, as will be seen hereafter. Some months had passed since I commenced my secret investigations, when chance threw in my way St. Germain, whose visits had so often filled me with consternation. He had with him a person named Boudin, whom I had formerly seen as a restaurateur in Paris, in the Rue des Prouvaires, and of whom I knew no more than that trifling acquaintance which arose from my occasionally exchanging my money for his dinners. He, however, seemed easily to recollect me, and, addressing me with bold familiarity, which my determined coolness seemed unable to subdue, 'Pray,' said he, 'have I been guilty of any offense toward you, that you seem so resolved upon cutting me?'—'By no means, sir,' replied I; 'but I have been informed that you have been in the service of the police.'—'Oh, oh, is that all,' cried he; 'never mind that, my boy; suppose I have, what then? I had my reasons; and when I tell you what they were, I am quite sure you will not bear m any ill-will for it.'—'Come, come,' said St. Germain,'I must have yo good friends; Boudin is an excellent fellow, and I will answer for hi honor, as I would do for my own. Many a thing happens in life we should never have dreamed of, and if Boudin did accept the situation you mention, it was but to save his brother: besides, you must feel satisfied, that were his principles such as a gentleman ought not to possess, why, you would not find him in my company.' I was much amused with this excellent reasoning, as well as with the pledge given for Boudin's good faith; however, I no longer sought to avoid the conversation of Boudin. It was natural enough that St. Germain should relate to me all that had happened to him since his last disappearance, which had given me such pleasure.

"After complimenting me on my flight, he informed me that after my arrest he had recovered his employment, which he, however, was not fortunate enough to keep; he lost it a second time, and had since been compelled to trust to his wits to procure a subsistence. I requested he would tell me what had become of Blondy and Deluc? 'What,' said he; 'the two who slit the wagoner's throat? Oh, why, the guillotine settled their business at Beauvais.' When I learnt that these two villains had at length reaped the just reward of their crimes, I experienced but one regret, and that was, that the heads of their worthless accomplices had not fallen on the same scaffold.

"After we had sat together long enough to empty several bottles of wine, we separated. At parting, St. Germain having observed that I was but meanly clad, inquired what I was doing, and as I carelessly answered that at present I had no occupation, he promised to do his best for me, and to push my interest the first opportunity that offered. I suggested that, as I very rarely ventured out, for fear of being arrested, we might not possibly meet again for some time. 'You can see me whenever you choose,' said he; 'I shall expect that you will call on me frequently.' Upon my promise to do so, he gave me his address, without once thinking of asking for mine.

"St. Germain was no longer an object of such excessive terror as formerly in my eyes; I even thought it my interest to keep him in sight, for if I applied myself to scrutinizing the actions of suspicious persons, who better than he called for the most vigilant attention? In a word, I resolved upon purging society of such a monster. Meanwhile, I waged a determined war with all the crowd of rogues who infested the capital. About this time, robberies of every species were multiplying to a frightful extent: nothing was talked of but stolen palisades, out-houses broken open, roofs stripped of their lead; more than twenty reflecting lamps were successively stolen from the Rue Fontaine au Roi, without the plunderers being detected. For a whole month the inspectors had been lying in wait in order to surprise them, and the first night of their discontinuing their vigilance the same depredations took place. In this state, which appeared like setting the police at defiance, I accepted the task which none seemed able to accomplish, and in a very short time I was enabled to bring the whole band of these shameless plunderers to public justice, which immediately consigned them to the galleys.

"Each day increased the number of my discoveries. Of the many who were committed to prison, there were none who did not owe their arrest to me, and yet not one of them for a moment suspected my share in the business. I managed so well, that neither within nor without its walls had the slightest suspicion transpired. The thieves of my acquaintance looked upon me as their best friend and true comrade; the others esteemed themselves happy to have an opportunity of initiating me in their secrets, whether from the pleasure of conversing with me, or in the hope of benefiting by my counsels. It was principally beyond the barriers that I met with these unfortunate beings. One day that I was crossing the outer Boulevards, I was accosted by St. Germain, who was still accompanied by Boudin. They invited me to dinner; I accepted the proposition, and over a bottle of wine they did me the honor to propose that I should make a third in an intended murder.

"The matter in hand was to dispatch two old men who lived together in the house which Boudin had formerly occupied in the Rue des Fronçaires. Shuddering at the confidence placed in me by these villains, I yet blessed the invisible hand which had led them to seek my aid. At first I affected some scruples at entering into the plot, but at last feigned to yield to their lively and pressing solicitations, and 't was agreed that we should wait the favorable moment for putting into execution this most execrable project. This resolution taken, I bade farewell to St. Germain and his companion, and (decided upon preventing the meditated crime) hastened to carry a report of the affair to M. Henry, who sent me, without loss of time, to obtain more ample details of the discovery I had just made to him. His intention was to satisfy himself whether I had been really solicited to take part in it, or whether, from a mistaken devotion to the cause of justice, I had endeavored to instigate those unhappy men to an act which would render them amenable to it. I protested that I had adopted no such expedient, and as he discovered marks of truth in my manner and declaration, he expressed himself satisfied. He did not, however, omit to impress on me the following discourse upon instigating agents, which penetrated my very heart. Ah, why was it not also heard by those wretches, who, since the revolution, have made so many victims The renewed era of legitimacy would not then, in some circumstances, have recalled the bloody days of another epoch. 'Remember well,' said M. Henry to me, in conclusion, 'remember that the greatest scourge to society is he who urges another on to the commission of evil. Where there are no instigators to bad practices, they are committed only by the really hardened; because they alone are capable of conceiving and executing them. Weak beings may be drawn away and excited: to precipitate them into the abyss, it frequently requires no more than to call to your aid their passions or self-love; but he who avails himself of their weakness to procure their destruction, is more than a monster—he is the guilty one, and it is on his head that the sword of justice should fall. As to those engaged in the police, they had better remain forever idle, than create matter for employment.'

"Although this lesson was not required in my case, yet I thanked M. Henry for it, who enjoined me not to lose sight of the two assassins, and to use every means in my power to prevent their arriving at the completion of their diabolical plan. 'The police,' said he, 'is instituted as much to correct and punish malefactors, as to prevent their committing crimes; but on every occasion I would wish it to be understood, that we hold ourselves under greater obligations to that person who prevents one crime, than to him who procures the punishment of many.' * * * * * * * *

"At the words 'secret agent,' a feeling almost approaching to suffocation stole over me, but I quickly rallied upon perceiving that however true the report might be, it had obtained but little faith with St. Germain, who was evidently waiting for my explanation or denial of it, without once suspecting its reality. My ever-ready genius quickly flew to my aid, and without hesitation I replied, that I was not much surprised at the charge, and for the simple reason that I myself had been the first to set the rumor afloat. St. Germain stared with wonder. 'My good fellow,' said I, 'you are well aware that I managed to escape from the police while they were transferring me from La Force to Bicêtre. Well! I went to Paris and stayed there till I could go elsewhere. One must live, you know, how and where one can. Unfortunately, I am still compelled to play at hide and seek, and it is only by assuming a variety of disguises that I dare venture abroad, to look about and just see what my old friends are doing; but, in spite of all my precautions, I live in constant dread of many individuals, whose keen eyes quickly penetrate my assumption of other names and habits than my own ; and who, having formerly been upon terms of familiarity with me, pestered me with questions I had no other means of shaking off, than by insinuating that I was in the pay of the police ; and thus I obtained the double advantage of evading, in my character of "spy," both their suspicions and ill-will, should they feel disposed to exercise it in procuring my arrest.'

"'Enough—enough,' interrupted St. Germain ; 'I believe you; and to convince you of the unbroken confidence I place in you, I will let you into the secret of our plans for to-night.'"

We add a single adventure which is illustrative of the shrewdness and success of the ever-active, fearless, self-reliant, and successful Vidocq :—

"I was employed to detect the authors of a nocturnal robbery, committed by climbing and forcible entry into the apartments of the Prince de Condé, in the Palais Bourbon. Glasses of a vast size had disappeared, and their abstraction was effected with so much precaution, that the sleep of two *cerberi*, who supplied the place of a watchman, had not been for a moment disturbed. The frames in which these glasses had been were not at all injured: and I was at first tempted to believe that they had been taken out by looking-glass makers or cabinet-makers ; but in Paris these workmen are so numerous, that I could not pitch on any one of them whom I knew, with any certainty of suspicion. Yet I was resolved to detect the guilty, and to effect this I commenced my inquiries.

"The keeper of a sculpture-gallery, near the Quincaux of the invalids, gave me first the information by which I was guided. About three o'clock in the morning, he had seen near his door several glasses in the care of a young man, who pretended to have been obliged to station them there while waiting for the return of his porters, who had broken their hand-barrow. Two hours afterward, the young man, having found two messengers, had made them carry off the glasses, and had directed them to the side of the Fountain of the Invalids. According to the keeper, the person he saw was about twenty-three years of age, and about five feet and an inch (French measure). He was clothed in an iron-gray greatcoat, and had a very good countenance. This information was not immediately useful to me; but it led me to find the messenger, who, the day after the robbery, had carried some glasses of large size to the Rue Saint-Dominique, and left them at the little Hôtel de Caraman. These were, in all probability, the glasses stolen, and if they were, who could say that they had not changed domicile and owner? I had the person who had received them pointed out to me, and determined on introducing myself to her; and that my presence might not inspire her with fear, it was in the guise of a cook that I introduced myself to her notice. The light jacket and cotton nightcap are the ensigns of the profession; I clothed myself in such attire, and, fully entering into the spirit of my character, went to the little Hôtel de Caraman, where I ascended to the first floor. The door was closed; I knocked, and it was opened to me by a very good-looking young fellow, who asked me what I wanted. I gave him an address, and told him that having learnt that he was in want of a cook, I had taken the liberty of offering my services to him.

"'My dear fellow, you are under a mistake,' he replied, 'the address you have given me is not mine, but as there are two Rues Saint-Dominique, it is most probably to the other that you should go.'

"All Ganymedes had not been carried off to Olympus, and the handsome youth who spoke to me had manners, gestures, and language, which, united to his appearance, convinced me in an instant with whom my business lay. I instantly assumed the tone of an initiate in the mysteries of the ultra philanthropists, and after some signs which he perfectly understood, I told him how very sorry I was that he did not want me.

"'Ah, sir,' I said to him, 'I would rather remain with you, even if you only gave me half what I should get elsewhere; if you only knew how miserable I am; I have been six months out of place, and

I do not get a dinner every day. Would you believe that thirty-six hours have elapsed and I have not taken any thing?'

"'You pain me, my good fellow; what, are you still fasting! Come, come, you shall dine here.'

"I had really an appetite capable of giving the lie I had just uttered all the semblance of truth; a two-pound loaf, half a fowl, cheese and a bottle of wine which he had procured, did not make long sojourn on the table. Once filled, I began again to talk of my unfortunate condition.

"'See, sir,' said I, 'if it be possible to be in a more pitiable situation. I know four trades, and out of the whole four can not get employ in one—tailor, hatter, cook; I know a little of all, and yet can not get on. My first start was as a looking-glass setter.'

"'A looking-glass setter!' said he, abruptly; and without giving him time to reflect on the imprudence of such an exclamation, I went on.

"'Yes, a looking-glass setter, and I know that trade the best of the four; but business is so dead that there is really nothing now stirring in it.'

"'Here, my friend,' said the young man, presenting to me a small glass; 'this is brandy, it will do you good; you know not how much you interest me. I can give you work for several days.'

"'Ah! sir, you are too good, you restore me to life; how, if you please, do you intend to employ me?'

"'As a looking-glass framer.'

"'If you have glasses to fit, pier, Psyche, light-of-day, joy-of-Narcissus, or any others, you have only to intrust me with them, and I will give you a cast of my craft.'

"'I have glasses of great beauty; they were at my country-house, whence I sent for them, lest the gentlemen Cossacks should take a fancy to break them.'

"'You were quite right; but may I see them?'

"'Yes, my friend.'

"He took me into a room, and at the first glance I recognized the glasses of the Palais Bourbon. I was ecstatic in their praise, their size, &c.; and after having examined them with the minute attention of a man who understands what he is about, I praised the skill of the workman who unframed them, without injury to the silvering.

"'The workman, my friend,' said he; 'the workman was myself: I would not allow any other person to touch them, not even to load them in the carriage.'

"'Ah! sir, I am very sorry to give you the lie, but what you tell me is impossible; a man must have been a workman to undertake such work, and even the best of the craft might not have succeeded.'

"In spite of my observation, he persisted in asserting that he had no help, and as it would not have answered my purpose to have contradicted him, I dropped the subject.

"A lie was an accusation at which he might have been angry, but he did not speak with less amenity, and after having given me his instructions, desired me to come early next day, and begin my work as early as possible.

"'Do not forget to bring your diamond, as I wish you to remove those arches, which are no longer fashionable.'

"He had no more to say to me, and I had no more to learn. I left him, and went to join my two agents, to whom I gave the description of the person, and desired them to follow him if he should go out. A warrant was necessary to effect his apprehension, which I procured; and soon afterward, having changed my dress, I returned, with the commissary of police and my agents, to the house of the amateur of glasses, who did not expect me so soon. He did not know me at first, and it was only at the termination of our search, that, examining me more closely, he said to me:—

"'I think I recognize you; are you not a cook?'

"'Yes, sir,' I replied; 'I am cook, tailor, hatter, looking-glass setter, and, moreover, a spy, at your service.'

"My coolness so much disconcerted him, that he could not utter another word.

"This gentleman was named Alexander Paruitte. Besides the two glasses, and two chimeras in gilt bronze, which he had stolen from the Palais Bourbon, many other articles were found in his apartments, the produce of various robberies. The inspectors who had accompanied me in this expedition undertook to conduct Paruitte to the depot but, on the way, were careless enough to allow him to escape, nev

INTRODUCTORY CHAPTER.

was it until ten days afterward that I contrived to get sight of him, at the gate of the embassador of his highness, the Sultan Mahmoud and I apprehended him at the moment he got into the carriage of a Turk, who apparently had sold his odalisques.

"I am still at a loss to explain how, in spite of obstacles which the most expert robbers judged insurmountable, Parnitte effected the robbery which twice compelled me to see him. He was steadfast n his assertion of having no companions; for on his trial, when sentenced to irons and imprisonment, no indication, not even the slightest, could be elicited, encouraging the idea that he had any participators."

The annals of this Bureau, we think, will establish the three following propositions:

I. The Detective Bureau, although contrary to the spirit of our republican institutions in time of peace, is indispensable in time of war.

II. Some of the most important army movements and battles have been made and fought entirely upon information obtained through this Bureau.

III. There is nothing in the Secret Service that demands a violaion of honor, or a sacrifice of principle, beyond the ordinary rules of warfare.

Reference will be made to these statements in connection with the striking and illustrative facts which will be recorded in the progress of the narrative.

There is an important distinction to be made between the service of a scout and that of a detective. The principal qualifications in the scout are courage and daring. He is to ride boldly into the enemy's lines, generally during action, or while the army is in motion. to ascertain the locality and movements of the hostile forces.

The detective must possess ability, shrewdness, great self-reliance and self-control, discretion, courage, and integrity. He will have complicated and important measures to carry forward, requiring no ordinary amount of mental power, and plans and plots to unravel which demand keen discernment and a profound knowledge of men; critical moments, when vacillation, or even hesitation, would be fatal; secrets, which without a complete mastery over feeling and all its forms of expression, will be revealed; delicate questions of procedure and duty, to decide which the nicest prudence will be necessary; dangers to meet, requiring a fearless spirit nothing can alarm or intimidate; and, to crown all, as the servant of the Government in matters of the gravest responsibility, he must have reliability of character to win and hold the unclouded confidence of its officers in his revelations, on which the most momentous operations may depend.

A moment's reflection will convince any mind of the correctness of this estimate of qualifications, among which the last-mentioned has not been generally understood and appreciated. But the fidelity to his trust of the Chief of the Detective Police must be such as to command no ordinary faith in information which may decide the victory or defeat of an army. Not only so, but he must be inapproachable by *bribery*. Striking illustrations of this will be given in the record of official services. Another interesting fact will appear General Baker's impartial justice to the colored race, in contrast with the *animus* of slavery, whose most cruel wrongs he was compelled to meet, and endeavored to remedy.

The detective police has ever been an indispensable institution in the old monarchies of other lands. The throne is apart from the people, and under its shadow watchful eyes must guard the sovereign's life and law, by observing and reporting the first symptom of discontent, or intimations of a treasonable plot.

In a republic the people govern, and in the nature of things an official espionage in the time of peace over their conduct, by some of their own number, is contrary to the genius of the institutions they create and control. But when war, especially its most fearful form, a civil conflict, exists, the unnatural condition of things calls for the detective service, to watch and bring to justice the enemies of the State, who are plotting its ruin.

There are reasons why such needful and valuable service has fallen into dishonor, many regarding it as small and doubtful business in its nature, thoroughly illustrated by the common adage, "It takes a rogue to catch a rogue." In despotic countries, shrewd and unprincipled men have been largely employed to betray their companions in guilt, and, guided by their experiences in vice, to put the police and other officers of justice on the track of criminals.

In this country, the Detective Bureau was entirely new; and there was, for a time, mismanagement of its work in certain quarters. Department commanders, district and post provost-marshals, and post quartermasters, permitted by military law and army regulations to do so, have, in the contingencies of the case, employed detectives. Most of these persons had only a limited knowledge of the detective service. As an inevitable result, the most ignorant, unscrupulous, and worthless characters were sometimes employed by them.

The fact is, the detective business for the war was commenced with no head, system, or regulations, excepting such as were made by those having no knowledge of the peculiar and difficult business.

Had Congress passed a law at the outset of the Rebellion, authorizing the organization of a detective police, with a head responsible only to the War or some other Department, no complaints would ever have been heard against a detective police system.

From the nature of the detective's professional work, he must pre-eminently awaken prejudice at every step, and make bitter enemies, not only among those hostile to the cause with which his special service is connected, but also among its friends.

He must interfere with plans of speculation, and cut off extra rations, which unlawful appropriations might secure. Then, again, his business forbids him to give his authority for certain acts, or assign any reason for his procedure. Hence the clamor was often raised, of rash and lawless abuse of power, when all the time he was acting under the direct orders of Government. These statements will have abundant confirmation in the pages of this history.

And we doubt whether any other officer, not excepting the Lieutenant-General, has more patiently borne misrepresentation and abuse in silence, for the sake of the common cause of the country, than General Baker.

With sublime moral courage, for nearly five years he toiled on, with the crushing weight of public opinion, and prejudice, and peril of death constantly before him, sustained by exalted patriotism, and a laudable desire to excel in his peculiar service or line of duty. While the public press was filled with eulogies upon daring and valor of officers in the field, the Chief of the Detective Bureau, whose deeds are no less heroic, and the importance of whose achievements cannot be over-estimated, if noticed at all by the press, is referred to in a doubtful or contemptuous manner. And even when the chief and his subordinates frequented the presidential mansion, after the execution of the assassins of Mr. Lincoln, because telegrams were received from leading army officers, giving information of a design by friends of the murderers to avenge their death, the object and motives of the protection were unappreciated and, by a member of the cabinet, denounced. The facts will appear in the progress of these annals.

He was not permitted to disclose his authority for the summary work he was required to do. The propriety for such a course by the War Department we do not question, for we know not the reasons back of it—they are not given. The fact, however, presents clearly the offensive position in which he was placed by the difficult and perilous office he held, even while he desired to be transferred to a more pleasant service. He was thus the target of unjust suspicion and bitterest hate, when the true object of the popular and personal displeasure was in reality the Government he was faithfully obeying. We give here a single forcible illustration of the truth of these statements, and of General Baker's uncomplaining endurance of undeserved persecution.

During 1862, an order was issued to arrest a certain prominent Pennsylvanian, on the charge of selling a large quantity of bandages and lint donated by ladies benevolent societies in Philadelphia or the benefit of the Union soldiers.

General Baker knew nothing about the case, having no acquaintance even with the individual, nor the charges brought against him.

It was his official work only to arrest and confine him in the Old Capitol prison. This duty he performed. Within an hour, a whole delegation of friends called at General Baker's headquarters, and, in an excited and boisterous manner, demanded the prisoner's release. He was offered a large amount for bail. To all this outcry and appeal, he calmly replied, that he knew nothing of the charges; was simply executing orders. The same evening, an indignation meeting was held, presided over by Judge B——, a prominent Union man of Pennsylvania. Resolutions were passed, openly denouncing General

Baker as an arbitrary, vindictive man, and appointing a committee to wait on the President and Secretary of War, asking for his dismissal from service. In this instance, which is one among many of a similar character, he was not permitted to show the order of arrest to any citizen. A reporter was never allowed to enter his headquarters, nor any communication allowed to be had by his bureau with the public press. Yet there are not wanting cheering tokens of confidence and esteem. The citizens of Philadelphia presented him with a badge of solid gold, nearly three inches square, surmounted by an eagle carved from the coin, and bearing on a scroll the words "Death to Traitors;" and on the back, "Presented to L. C. Baker, by his friends." Its value was not less than two hundred dollars.

The officers of the First District Cavalry, raised by General Baker, presented to him an elegant saber, with sash of China silk, valued at about the same amount.

He was also the recipient, from officers, of the most elaborately finished saddle and trappings probably in the country. Its value was six hundred and fifty dollars. These and other mementoes of regard confirm the statement, made by prominent officers, that his subordinates in the Bureau, numbering in all about four hundred, were ready to fight for him.

We have received, among other volunteer testimony to his official sagacity and achievements, the following—the first from a chaplain in "Baker's Cavalry," the other from another army chaplain:—

"General Baker, I think, acquitted himself with marvelous tact, energy, and success. He was the terror of all rogues, whether with clean faces or dirty, in broadcloth or rags, with a general's star or a corporal's stripe. I think that, during the most critical period of the war, he was (next to Secretary Stanton) the most important officer of the Government."

Washington, D. C., June 15, 1866.

"In regard to Gen. L. C. Baker, Chief Detective of the War Department, during the late rebellion, I feel it a duty to say : *First.* It is scarcely possible to estimate the *good* he has accomplished in strengthening the armies afield. *Second.* In weeding out the mischievous and the worthless. *Third.* In making copperheads, scoundrels, and traitors feel the secret war power at home. I believe him to have done more during the late war to save the country than any other single power. His name carried with it a dread that made evil-doers tremble. He was always at his post when wanted (a rare trait), and most efficient when active. Booth knew that Baker was in New York, or he would have delayed the tragedy of the 14th of April, 1865! And when he knew that Baker was on his trail, his heart fainted in him, and lost all hope!

"And now about certain facts Baker may state with respect to men high in official relation with the Government or otherwise: The half he will not tell. I know of many things he will not state which I would. I have no mercy on men who will corrupt and contaminate all with whom they come in official contact; and men who, in time of peace, after treason has been put down, again secretly plot the overthrow of a Government at once the best and noblest that the sun of the Eternal ever shone upon.

"I hope to see truth come, let it cut where it may, as I believe the country to be still in danger; and unless some master hand will seize the knife and lay open the festering wound, the disease of the Republic will never heal!   "I am, very respectfully."

It may interest the curious reader to give some illustrative incidents in regard to trivial circumstances which lead to detection, and which would escape the notice of men unaccustomed to the close observation indispensable to success in the secret service.

The clue to a deserter's character was found in his bronzed face while his dress and positive declarations indicated the life of a quiet citizen. In another case, the falsehood was exposed by the *spur-marl in the boot.* A soldier in disguise, and asserting his innocence of battle-service, was detected through an examination of his hand, on the palm of which was a callous spot where the gun-lock had pressed in the march.

The red line on Government stockings and the peculiar style of the shirts have revealed the fact denied by the lips and all the rest of the apparel.

A deserter from the Twelfth New York Battery so well concealed his "soldiering" that nothing about his person confirmed my suspicions

At last General Baker resorted to *strategy*. He watched for an opportunity when he was lazily dozing in his office, and suddenly and loudly shouted: "Fall in, men!" He started up, looked around, and began to prepare for the march. It was plainly useless to deny any longer that he had been in the ranks.

At another time, General Baker was searching for a female spy and had his attention drawn to rather a delicate-looking young man, whom he followed, with some companions, into a saloon. When they stood before the bar, drinking and talking, he noticed that this youth threw up the fingers often to brush aside the hair. The form was shaped like a woman's, and in a sitting posture the hands were crossed just as women are in the habit of placing them.

He called the astonished stranger aside, and desired a private interview, in which he said the game of deception was finished—that he knew both the sex and business in hand. She burst into tears, and confessed all.

Not unfrequently the simplest disguises were entirely successful. The slouched hat drawn down over the forehead; the garb of "butternut," or of an honest farmer; the dress and manner of an itinerant Jew; the face and gait of an inebriate,—each served the purpose of an introduction to the desired company and scenes.

We might multiply illustrations, and make an inventory of disguises in apparel and modes of dressing the hair and face to which the detective is compelled to resort. But, excepting the narratives which will make further revelations of the kind, these will be sufficient to indicate the varied language of moral and professional character and pursuits to a practiced eye.

Mention has already been made of the fact that the detective police of the Government were brought into disrepute, and some reasons assigned for it. His bureau was known as the only regularly organized national police, although, as stated before, there were employed, at the headquarters of every department commander, provost-marshal, and quartermaster, a large number of persons representing themselves as Government detectives. These men had been selected, in many instances, from the most worthless and disreputable characters, and whenever they were found to be receiving bribes, or committing other offenses, they were always denominated "Baker's detectives." The reporters of the press invariably did this. Hence he was held responsible to the public for the acts of these scoundrels, when in fact he knew nothing of their operations, except as he might have occasion, from time to time, to arrest them himself. The provost-marshal of the District of Columbia, appointed under the Enrollment Act, for the recruiting service, had employed at one time a large number of these detectives. Scarcely a day passed but complaints were made at his headquarters respecting these men. There was in the vicinity of Washington a large military force; and a bounty had been offered for the apprehension of deserters. The enrolling provost-marshal at Washington had detailed a number of his detectives and placed them on duty at the Baltimore depot in Washington, for the purpose of apprehending them. A deserter, in citizen's clothes, would repair to the depot, and attempt to enter the cars; these officers would arrest him, and for a small bribe allow him to go at large. This was practiced for many months. Colonel Baker called the attention of the Secretary of War to the fact, but there seemed to be no remedy. Finally, he determined to ascertain who these detectives were. Assuming the garb and dress of a loafer and deserter, he one evening repaired to the depot. He was so completely disguised that his own men did not recognize him. On attempting to pass the gate and enter the cars, he was stopped by an individual who said, "Let me see your ticket." He showed him his railroad ticket, when he charged him with being a deserter. He replied that he was not; that he was a citizen, and did not want to be detained. One or two other detectives approached, and all insisted that he should be arrested. Accordingly, he was taken into a small room, with one or two others, who had also been arrested and searched. They took from him his passage ticket, a valuable gold watch, and some seventy-five dollars in treasury notes, which he had marked for the occasion. He was then placed in charge of a detective, to be taken to the provost-marshal's headquarters. Instead of taking Colonel Baker directly there, the detective took him to a low drinking-saloon on Seventh Street, near the avenue, called the "McClellan House," which was the general rendezvous of these detectives and deserters. He was here asked to take a drink, but he declined, pretending to feel very badly about his arrest. He was then taken into a back room, and in the presence of detectives No. 1

and 2, his watch and money were divided between the two detectives. He was here told that he could go at large, provided he would leave his watch and money. He complained bitterly of this treatment, and threatened to report the facts to Colonel Baker, when they laughed, and remarked that they were not Colonel Baker's detectives, but the detectives of the provost-marshal. He consented to give them the money, but declined to give up his watch, as it was a very valuable one. This refusal induced detective No. 2 to take him to the provost-marshal's headquarters. On the way there, he had a conversation with the detective, who told him it was very foolish for him to go to headquarters; if he went there, he would be locked up for several days, and finally sent back to his regiment, tried, and perhaps shot as a deserter. He persisted, however, in declining to deliver up the watch. On arriving at headquarters, Baker was ushered into a room, where, seated at a table, he saw the provost-marshal, with whom he was well acquainted, and his clerks, none of whom recognized him. The detective remarked to the provost-marshal, "Here is a deserter, captain, that we have taken at the depot. He won't tell what regiment he belongs to, but if we took him up a few days, and put him under the shower-bath, he will probably tell all about it." The provost-marshal said to him, "What regiment do you belong to?" He said, "Sir, I am not a deserter, but a citizen." He remarked, "Oh, that's played out. We know you; we have been looking for you for some time." Some other conversation occurred, and the provost-marshal directed that Baker should be locked up. He took off his old slouched hat, and, standing at the end of the table, said to the provost-marshal, "I am Colonel Baker. I have assumed this disguise for the purpose of detecting your detectives, and ascertaining the *modus operandi* by which deserters are allowed to escape." The aspect of a proud superiority gave place to that of consternation. The detective attempted to leave the room, when Colonel Baker immediately arrested him, took him to his headquarters, searched him, and found a portion of the money he had marked, in his pocket.

It was a standing complaint against the Detective Police Bureau that the force was liable to be corrupted. In no other branch of public service were the opportunities so great for manipulation and bribery as in the police department. It is a well-known fact that nearly every individual arrested, who represented or personated an officer of the Government, was alleged to be one of Colonel Baker's men. At Barnum's Museum, in 1865, a man was arrested who had a forged appointment from him. At Elmira, New York, another was arrested with a similar paper, endorsed by the Secretary of War. These, and hundreds of other instances of a similar character, were heralded through the country as a sufficient reason why the Detective Bureau should be abolished. In New York, two individuals by the names of McNeil and Garvin had for a long time represented themselves as attached to his force. They visited saloons and gambling-houses, threatening to close them up unless certain sums of money were paid. Their operations were principally confined to the arrest of deserters, who were endeavoring to keep out of the way of arrest. In the month of February, these individuals arrested one John H. Harris, who was an omnibus-driver in the city of New York, and demanded from him the sum of one hundred dollars, in consideration of which they would allow him to go at large. The fact was reported to Colonel Baker, and he immediately detailed officers to search for these bogus detectives.

Harris not having the money with him, but having a friend in Maiden Lane, by the name of Depew, he asked McNeil and Garvin to come to his friend's store the following morning and he would give them the one hundred dollars. In the mean time Baker directed a detective to conceal himself in the store. At the appointed time the detectives arrived, received the one hundred dollars, and were immediately arrested, tried, convicted, and sentenced to the penitentiary.

Report in cases of John McNeil and Charles Garvin.

John H. Harris, of No 156 West Thirty-fifth Street, betwee Sixth and Seventh Avenues, stage-driver, states:—

He has been arrested twice before this, on charge of being deserter; both times discharged, and no proof against him.

On February 17, 1865, McNeil and Garvin got into his stage, rode with him to the end of his route, where they arrested him on charge of being a deserter; told him they were Government officers, and proposed to compromise the matter with him. He took them to his house, and arranged to pay them one hundred dollars if they would meet him the next day at the office of a Mr. Depew. They declined; then went together to Depew's hotel, represented themselves to Depew as Government officers, and authorized to make arrests; agreed to let off Harris if Depew would become responsible for the payment of one hundred dollars next day. Depew agreed to do so; parties arranged to meet at Depew's office, No. 53 Cedar Street. Depew then gave information to Colonel Baker, who sent one officer to the place of meeting. The parties met; McNeil professing to have a descriptive list for Harris, which he said he would tear up on receipt of the one hundred dollars. The one hundred dollars were paid by Depew to McNeil and Garvin, when the officer appeared and took them into custody.

The money and certain papers are transmitted to you with this statement. The money will be needed in proof, after which I think it should be returned to Depew.

J. H. HARRIS.

It may be said, that the deception and misstatements resorted to, and inseparable from the detective service, are demoralizing, and prove unsoundness of character in its officers. But it must be borne in mind that, in war, no commander fails to deceive the enemy when possible, to secure the least advantage. Spies, scouts, intercepted correspondence, feints in army movements, misrepresentations of military strength and position, are regarded as honorable means of securing victory over the foe. The work of the detective is simply deception reduced to a science or profession; and whatever objection, on ethical grounds, may lie against the secret service, lies with equal force against the strategy and tactics of Washington, Scott, Grant, and the host of their illustrious associates in the wars of the world. War is a last and terrible resort in the defense of even a righteous cause, and sets at defiance all the ordinary laws and customs of society, overriding the rights of property and the sanctity of the Sabbath. And not until the nations learn war no more, will the work of deception and waste of morals, men, and treasures, cease.

CHAPTER I.

ORIGIN OF THE BUREAU OF DETECTIVE SERVICE.

The first Visit to Washington—Interview with General Hiram Walbridge, and Hon W. D. Kelley—Introduction to General Winfield Scott—Return to New York —Appointed by General Scott to renew the Attempt to visit Richmond—The first Failure—Crossing the Lines—The Arrest—Examinations—Sent to General Beauregard—On to Richmond.

IN April, 1861, I went to Washington, to learn, if possible, in what capacity I could serve the loyal cause. At Willard's Hotel, I met its able and fearless champion, General Hiram Walbridge, of New York, and the Hon. William D. Kelley, of Philadelphia. We conversed freely upon the condition of the country, and the necessity of more reliable information respecting the strength and movements of the enemy.

General Walbridge then said to me, "Baker, you are the man of all others to go into this secret service; you have the ability and courage." General W., with the Hon. Mr. Kelley, strongly urged an interview with General Scott, who was in command of the Army of the United States; accompanied by him and the Hon. George W Wright, of California. I went to his rooms. My father having fought under Gen. Scott in the last war with England, I was introduced as the son of "an old friend, with discretion, ability, and courage to do what was necessary."

After a little general conversation, the venerable commander requested those present to leave the room, when he talked freely of my experiences as a detective, and the services required to ascertain the strength and plans of the enemy, requesting an interview the following day.

At the hour appointed, with a deliberate purpose to accept any service for the country he might desire, I was again closeted with the Lieut.-General. After stating that he had thus far found it impossible to obtain definite information respecting the rebel forces at Manassas, that of the five men who had been sent to Richmond two were known to be killed, and the other three were probably taken prisoners, with patriarchal and patriotic interest, he said to me: "Young man, if you have judgment and discretion, you can be of great service to the country."

I then told him that I could not immediately engage in the service, but must at once return to New York, to arrange unsettled affairs; and left him with the understanding that I should report to him as soon as circumstances would permit The latter part of June, I was again in Washington, and had repeated interviews with the General. The result was, a definite arrangement for a journey toward Richmond, if not *into* the rebel capital. Directions in detail were given me respecting the difficult service I was expected to perform.

Taking from his vest pocket ten double eagles of coin, General Scott handed them to me, expressing the warmest hopes of my success in the excursion to "Dixie."

July 11, 1861, I started for Richmond. Along the route of my travel toward the Confederate Capital, and while there, I was to learn, if possible, the locality and strength of the hostile troops, especially of the dreaded Black-horse cavalry, and also of their fortifications; leaving no opportunity to gather items of information concerning the movements and plans of the enemy which might be of any service to the Government.

To one unacquainted with the nature of the service, it may seem strange that our troops should not know my character and design. But such concealment is not only always practiced in the Secret service, but was pre-eminently needful for us at that time, when we knew not whom to trust, because traitors were in the Government and in the army. To let the Union troops into the secret, would be to send it to Richmond before I had reached Manassas. Guarding the frontier of the Confederacy, the rebel army lay before Washington, stretching from a point three miles below Alexandria, toward the Potomac, eight miles above the capital. At Alexandria, then recently stained with the martyr blood of Ellsworth, Gen. Heintzelman was Provost-marshal. No passes were recognized by either the Union or rebel army, and I must necessarily run the risk equally, in the attempt to pass their lines, of being arrested as a spy. The surreptitious movements would begin, therefore, with the first step from Washington toward the "sacred soil of Virginia."

I went to a daguerrean establishment, and purchased for four dollars an old box which had once contained photographic apparatus, slung it across my back, after the fashion of an itinerant artist, and started for Alexandria. Four miles out of the city I came to the Second Maine Regiment, and proceeded at once to the headquarters of the colonel. He received me politely, and wished me to take a view of the camp, including his tent and the principal officers standing in the foreground. War scenes were new to the people, and the desire was natural enough, to gratify friends at home with pictures of the martial field. After a good dinner, I took my box, and told the colonel I would go to a neighboring hill and take views of the encampment, then return to photograph the headquarters. I was soon in the woods with my hollow box, eluding guards, and pushing forward through the tangled undergrowth, toward the heart of rebeldom. When across the Federal lines as I supposed, I was startled with the shout, "Who goes there?" I looked up, to see sentinel, with lifted gun, standing upon a knoll just before me.

I had no alternative but to surrender, and march with him to the colonel's quarters. This officer was sure he had caught a spy, and, escorted by ten men, I was sent back along the railroad, the same way I came, to General Heintzelman's headquarters. The lieutenant in charge presented me to the commanding officer, with the following flattering and promising introduction : "Here is a spy, general, that we foun lurking about our camp, trying to get through the lines."

"Oh! you villain you, you," said Heintzelman, with hi usual nasal twang and an oath, " trying to get through my lines, are you? I've a good notion to cut your head off. But I'll fix you, you rascal ; I'll send you to General Scott." Another guard, with a message from the brave general, who was evidently gratified with the successful vigilance of his men, was ordered for me, and I was hurried away to Washington. The escort was dismissed by General Scott, and my story told. With an expression that indicated both amusement at the *ruse*, and its failure, and confidence in me, the old veteran said : "Well, try again!"

The uprising North was now sending her legions to the field of civil conflict, and in an almost unbroken line they were marching over Long Bridge into Virginia. That night. I took a position at the end of the bridge, and, when a regiment came down broken into considerable disorder, I stepped into the ranks, hoping to be borne along with the troops. Unfortunately, a lieutenant saw the movement, and, taking me by the collar, put me under guard, and sent me back to the rear. Another night was spent in Washington, but not wholly in sleep. My mind was busy with new plans for a successful visit to the Confederate capital.

With the dawn of the next morning I renewed my journey afoot through the lower counties of Maryland, toward Port Tobacco, traveling thirty-five miles that day, and reaching that town at night. Exhaustion prepared me for sound and refreshing sleep. In the morning I gave a negro a twenty-dollar gold piece to row me across the river, when I was safely in the Confederacy, below Dumfries. The country was wooded, and an unfrequented road, whose general direction was toward Richmond, suggested the line of my advance into the Old Dominion. I pursued my solitary journey through the desolate country, slaking thirst, excited by the heat of the Southern sun, at brooks which at intervals crossed my path. I could necessarily have no settled plan of future movements, but trusted to providential indications of what, under the circumstances, it would be prudent and politic to do. With that entire composure of feeling and self-reliance which attend a purpose, however daring, when once the die is cast, to reach its final issue, I cast my eye over the sparsely-settled country, with its old roads crossed with paths, and studded with oaks, particularly careful to observe the least sign of a human form within its horizon. Four miles of distance lay between me and the banks of the Potomac, when two Confederate soldiers made their appearance, too near me to make an escape possible. I was taken prisoner under an order to arrest as a spy any stranger passing that way, and marched off toward camp, eight miles distant. A beer shop by the roadside tempted the guard, and we all entered it. I was invited to drink. I saw my opportunity, and, although I never indulge in stimulants, accepted the offer of a glass of ale, and in return treated my captors. The generous indulgence was repeated, until my escort were stupidly under the influence of the potations, and fell asleep on the stoop of the beer-house, leaving me to go unmolested on my way.

I went up the road toward Manassas Junction, congratulating myself on my easy escape, when four rebel cavalrymen suddenly came out of the brush and ordered me to halt; then drawing their sabers, commanded me to surrender. I replied to them: "I am a peaceful citizen, unarmed, and on my way to Richmond." One dismounted, proceeded to search me, and succeeded in finding a number of letters introducing me to prominent rebels in Richmond. Among them were two written by the Rev. Mr. Shuck, for many years a missionary in China. He returned to California, where I had formed his acquaintance, and came to the Atlantic States in the same steamer with myself. He was at this time chaplain of a rebel regiment near Richmond. After obtaining possession of all my letters, the boastful chivalry could not read them. They requested me to be seated, while they heard from me the contents of the epistles.

Taking advantage of their ignorance, I read such portions as I chose. They at once directed me to proceed under guard to Brentsville, distant about ten miles—they riding, and keeping me on foot between them, and constantly conversing in a low tone of voice respecting the importance of the arrest. Arriving at Brentsville at ten o'clock, P. M., I was taken to the headquarters of General Bonham, of South Carolina, commanding at that point, ushered into the large tent occupied by General Bonham and staff officers, and ordered to take a seat. In a few minutes, General Bonham, in splendid uniform, took a seat beside me, and commenced conversation, by asking the direct question, "Where did you come from, and where are you going?" I replied: "I came from Washington, and am on my way to Richmond." Apparently unconscious of the deference due to the commanding officer, I sat with my hat on. Observing it he said, "Take off your hat, sir." With the order, I at once complied.

The letters were then handed to General Bonham by one of the captors.

After reading, he said, "How dare you come inside of my lines?"

Exhibiting proper surprise and indignation, I replied, "I am a loyal and peaceful citizen of the United States, engaged in an honorable and legitimate pursuit. I have business in Richmond, and desire to go there."

He replied, "Well, I will see that you *do* go there. I believe you are a Yankee spy, and I'll send you to General Beauregard at once." He gave the necessary order to detail a guard, and, handing a sealed letter to a lieutenant standing by, said, "Put this man in irons, and with this letter take him to General Beauregard's headquarters." Accordingly I left Brentsville at twelve o'clock at night, protesting, however, against being compelled to go on foot. He said, "As you have chosen that mode of conveyance, sir, you ought not now to find fault. Take him away."

We arrived at Manassas Junction about daylight, and went to General Beauregard's headquarters—the Weire House. Completely exhausted by the walk, and the excitement attending the arrest, I laid down in front of the house and went to sleep. At nine o'clock A. M., I was awakened by the warm, bright rays of the sun, shining in my face, and found myself in charge of the guard attached to the headquarters. I called for food, and was informed that General Beauregard desired to see me. I was taken into his presence, with whom were two or three staff officers. Pointing to an open letter (General Bonham's, I supposed), he said: "From this letter I see you have been found within our lines. What explanation have you to make?"

I replied, "I am from Washington, and going to Richmond, on private business. I have not intended to violate any law, regulation, or military rule, of the Confederate army."

"When did you leave Washington?"

"Day before yesterday," I replied.

"Where did you cross the river?"

"In the vicinity of Port Tobacco."
"How did you get across?"
"In a boat."
"Who brought you across?"
"A negro."
"So you are going to Richmond, are you?"
"Yes, if I can get there; but am willing to return if you will permit me to do so."
"No; I prefer that you should go to Richmond. Where do you reside?"
"I have lived in California the last ten years; but formerly lived in the South."
"What part of the South?"
"Knoxville, Tennessee."
"How long since you were in Knoxville?"
"Ten or twelve years."
"What is your name?"
"Samuel Munson."
"Yes, I see from your letters that that is your name; but what was your name before you turned spy?"
"I am no spy."
"I believe you are: and, if I was satisfied of it, I would hang you on that tree," pointing through an open window to an oak-tree in full view. "Orderly," he added, "take this man out and put him in the guard-house."
"I am very hungry; can you give me breakfast?"
"You will find breakfast in the guard-house."

I was taken by the guard to a stockade or pen, inside of which was a log-house. Following the officer in command, I said:

"Sir, I am very hungry—can you give me something to eat?"—taking from my pocket a gold eagle. At sight of the coin, he said—

"What will you have?"

"Send out and get me the worth of that, or the best breakfast you can get."

He soon returned with a good warm breakfast and a bottle of sour wine. The wine I gave to the guard, and ate the breakfast.

Having put myself on good terms with the officer in

command of the guard-house, he asked me what I was there for.

I replied I did not know—but, if not in violation of his orders, would like to go outside in charge of a guard. Whether it would be so or not, the sight of a twenty-dollar gold piece relieved his mind of any doubt on the subject. Handing it to him, he called a soldier and said:

"Take this man out, and walk him around awhile."

I went to the hotel, treated my escort, and then went with him to take a general survey of all the troops in the immediate vicinity of Manassas Junction. One of my instructions from General Scott, and not least in importance, was to ascertain the numbers of the famous, and by the Union army much dreaded, black-horse cavalry. In conversation with my half-drunken guard, I referred to this cavalry, and inquired where they were.

He replied, "Down on the railroad."

I expressed a wish to see them.

He said, "Certainly—them's the boys to whip the Yankees!"

We went down the line of the railroad half a mile, and there found the cavalry in camp. I asked him how many men there were in that command.

He said, "Two hundred."

I made a thorough inspection of these troops. My accommodating guard then took me to all the camps, pointed out the different intrenchments in course of erection, the names of the several regiments and brigades, who commanded them, their strength, &c. When I had obtained this information, my guard met drunken friends, and left me to go where I pleased. Fearing I should be missed, I immediately returned to the guard-house. I was not locked up, but allowed to remain in the stockade, where I met two fellow-prisoners, as I then supposed, who at once began asking me questions. It did not take me long, however, to decide that they were decoys placed there for the purpose of eliciting from me, if possible, my real character. They complained bitterly of their treatment, and one even requested me to take a letter to his wife in Washington.

I consented to take the letter. It was written in a way well

calculated to mislead me. I went to the guard-house, called the lieutenant on guard, and said: "You have a spy in the stockade"—handing him the letter. He said, "I will send it up to headquarters." A few minutes later I saw the same man in private confidential conversation with the lieutenant, at the same time pointing to me across the yard.

This satisfied me of the truth of my suspicions. Repeated efforts were afterward made, during my stay in the stockade, to ascertain who I was, and my intentions. To all inquiries, however, I had but one answer, and that was: "That they had made a great mistake in arresting me." My next questioner was a woman, assuming the calling of a colporteur, or tract distributer. I was standing by the pump—she approached me and said:

"Sir, will you read one of my tracts?"

"Certainly, thank you, madam."

Handing me two or three tracts, she remarked, "This war is a terrible thing. How long have you been here?"

"Came here this morning."

She said—"Read those tracts, and then give them to your fellow-prisoners."

"What are you here for?"

"I do not know, madam, but hope nothing very serious."

"Do you live in the South?"

"No, I am from the North—was arrested yesterday down on the river."

"Oh, you are from the other side, are you—from Washington?"

"Yes, I left there three days ago."

"Are you going back?"

"Well, that depends upon General Beauregard."

"Oh! he is a very kind man, and certainly would not keep you here a moment without some good reason. Were ou born in the North?"

"Yes, I suppose I am a Yankee."

"Is the North really going to fight the South?"

"I think it will."

She then left me, to continue her mission, distributing acts to the prisoners and guards.

Returning soon afterward, she said in a low tone of voice. "I am trying to do all the good I can. Are you a Christian?"

I answered, "I thought I was once, but now have very serious doubts on the subject."

She then added: "The lieutenant thinks you are a spy: if you are, be very careful what you say. I was born at the North, but have lived among these people seven years. My sympathies are all with the Northern people. I am trying now to get a pass from General Beauregard, that I may visit my sister in New York, who is a teacher in one of the public schools. I will gladly take any message you may want to send to your friends. I think I shall get my pass to-morrow."

The only reply I made was, "I think I shall see my friends before you do."

With this she shook my hand cordially, and left me. Two years and a half later, I met my tract friend, who was the famous "Belle Boyd," under very different circumstances, which will be recorded in the order of their occurrence.

At eleven o'clock that night, the sergeant, with four men, came to the guard-house, and took me to General Beauregard's headquarters, where I again caught a glimpse of the attentive colporteur. After waiting in silence a brief time, the sergeant ordered me to follow him.

"Where am I going?" I asked.

"To Richmond. Fall in, men."

I was at once marched to the dépôt, and put into a freight car which had been used for the conveyance of troops, having the sides knocked off near the top, and started off at half-past one o'clock, P. M. The train moved very slowly, and Gordonsville was not reached until the next night. This otherwise irksome delay afforded me an excellent opportunity to observe the number of troops moving toward Manassas.

At Gordonsville, I was turned over to another guard, put into a passenger car, and entered Richmond at eight o'clock the succeeding evening.

The tidings of my capture had gone before, and the value of it to the Confederacy discussed and of course magnified, as was everything by distance, on both sides, at that early period of the war.

Instead of giving me a cell in Libby prison, I was conveyed to the third story of an engine-house, an open, airy loft, with a clean bed, and in all respects more comfortable quarters than I anticipated. A guard of two soldiers were my keepers.

I retired to rest, and reflected on the course to be followed from this crisis in the enterprise. I was in the rebel capital, must survey its military resources, and get back to Washington, or die as a spy

CHAPTER II.

RESIDENCE IN RICHMOND.

Summoned to an interview with Jeff. Davis—Subsequent Examinations by him—Critical Emergencies—Mr. Brock—"Samuel Munson"—Confidence secured—Mr "Munson" is appointed Confederate Agent—Original Letters from Davis, Toombs, and Walker—Starts for the North—Unpleasant Delays—A Narrow Escape—Reaches the Potomac—Deceives the Dutch Fishermen and runs the Robel Gauntlet safely.

On the fourth or fifth day of my confinement, a commissioned officer, attended by a guard, entered the apartment and said the President wished to see me. I obeyed the summons, and after reaching his room waited nearly two hours before I was presented to Mr. Davis with the simple expression, "This is the man, sir!" The room occupied by him in the Spottswood House was a front parlor connecting with a bedroom. The weather was warm, and he wore simply a light linen coat, without vest, collar, or cravat. He then said, "You have been sent here from Manassas as a spy! what have you to say?" I related the circumstances of my capture, complaining bitterly of my treatment, to which he listened with perfect indifference. He then asked substantially the same questions Beauregard had proposed, and which were answered as nearly as possible in the words used during the interview with him. I was taken back to the engine-loft, and at the expiration of three days was once more escorted to the executive apartment. The Confederate President was out, engaged in the inspection of troops who had just arrived from the South, and I returned to my quarters without an interview. At the expiration of a week, I was ordered for the third time into the presence of Jefferson Davis. The following inquiries were made by him:

"How many troops do you suppose there are in Washington and its vicinity?"

I answered, "I have no means of knowing; probably 75,000 or 100,000, with more daily arriving."
"Who commands the Yankee troops?"
"I suppose, General Scott."
"Where are his headquarters?"
"In Washington."
"Then he is not with the troops?"
"No; General McDowell is in immediate command."
I was then marched back to my prison-chamber.
At the next interview the arch-traitor determined to mak a thorough and satisfactory examination of his prisoner.
He began: "What is your name, sir?"
"Samuel Munson."
"Where were you born?"
"In Knoxville, Tennessee."
"What is your business here?"
"The settlement of certain land-claims in California for a man whose agent I am."
"Who is the man?"
"Rev. Mr. S——, of Barnwell Court-House; now I believe a chaplain in the army."
Having brought with me from the Pacific Coast land-claims in behalf of a minister, who returned to Barnwell Court-House, his former place of residence, and whose name as chaplain was on the Army Roll, my statement had certainly an air of plausibility.
"How long have you resided North?"
"I have been in California eight years."
"When did you leave California?"
"On the first day of January, 1861."
"Were you in Washington?"
"I was."
"Did you come directly here from Washington?"
"Yes, sir."
"Were there many troops in Washington?"
"Yes, sir, a great many."
"How many?"
"It is impossible to say, as they were constantly arriving and departing."
"Where were they concentrating?"

"In Virginia, opposite Washington."
"Throwing up fortifications, are they ?"
"Yes, sir ; I believe so."
"Are they fortifying Arlington Heights ?"
"I do not know."
"Or in the vicinity of Long Bridge ?"
"I do not know."
"Are they fortifying about Alexandria ?"
"I can not say, I have not been there."
"Can you tell me the names of any of the regiments now in Washington ?"

I mentioned the names of a few of which he could not have failed to know something through the press and rumors afloat.

He continued, "Where is General Scott ?"
"I do not know. He is said to be in Washington.'
"Do you consider yourself a Southern man ?"
"Yes, sir, I do."
"Do you sympathize with the Southern people ?"
"I do."
"Are you willing to fight with them ?"
"Yes, sir."
"Will you enlist ?"
"No, sir."
"Why not ?"
"Because I am here on business which I ought first to accomplish."

The guard was summoned to take "Mr. Munson" to his prison again. Before leaving, I stepped forward to a table on which stood a pitcher of ice-water, and, turning to the rebel chief, said:

"Will you allow me to take a drink of ice-water ? I get none where I am."

"Certainly," he replied.

I was soon in my upper room reflecting upon the difficulties in my way, and the probability that they would yet thwart my plans, and leave me undisguised at the mercy of exasperated enemies.

Three additional days of monotonous life in my loft were passed, when I was summoned once more into the presence of Davis. He sat by his table writing, with his back toward the door, while nearly opposite, reclining upon a lounge half asleep, and looking much like a man who had imbibed strong drink too freely, was Robert Toombs. He roused himself as I entered, to listen to my examination by the President, who, laying down his pen, turned to me and said:

"Have you any other way of proving that your name is Munson, excepting the letters found in your pocket?"

"I am not acquainted here, sir, and do not know any one."

Davis resumed his writing for a few moments, then said:

"Do you know how far they are running the cars on the Alexandria and Orange Railroad?"

"I don't know. I have not been on that side."

"Do you know whether they are running the cars on the Leesburg road?"

"I do not."

"How many Yankee troops do you think there are in the vicinity of Washington?"

"I have heard that there are one hundred and twenty thousand, but have no means of knowing whether it is true."

"I suppose you know who commands them?"

"I believe General McDowell does."

"You say you are originally from Knoxville. Can you give me the name of any persons whom you know there?"

"It has been a good many years since I lived in Knoxville, but I remember some persons who were there when I left."

I gave the names of several men whom I knew resided in that city.

"Would they know you?"

"I think so, though a residence of eight years in California has, no doubt, changed me very much. If I should see them, I think I could make them remember me."

I had taken the name of Munson, because I had learned that several families of that name belonged in Knoxville, and the son of a Judge Munson had been in California, whom I could represent.

Davis rang a bell, a messenger appeared, and, taking a

name, left the room. I suspected at once his errand. He was dispatched for somebody from Knoxville, to identify me, if my story were true. The crisis in my affairs had come. I concluded the game was up, and my vocation gone. It was a moment of great anxiety, and my thoughts were intensely active with the possibilities of escape from the snare in which I seemed to be caught. Davis continued writing, and Toombs closed his eyes. The messenger left the door ajar, and, unobserved, I drew my chair nearly in front of it, to gain a view of the outer hall. In it, on a small table, were blank cards on which those who called to see the Confederate President wrote their names, and sent them by an orderly, before they were admitted to an audience with him.

Soon the messenger with a stranger entered the hall. The latter wrote his name, and handed it to the orderly, who came in where I was sitting. I raised my hand to take the card, and he stopped to give it to me, when I glanced at the name, and made a motion to have it laid on Davis's table. The rebel Executive did not observe this, and Toombs was apparently asleep. The orderly put the card before him, was directed to admit the visitor, and retired. The Knoxville man came in, and, turning toward him with a look of sudden recognition, I rose, grasped his hand, and exclaimed:

"Why, how do you do, Brock?"

Toombs raised himself up and nodded to Davis, who said:

"Be seated, sir. Do you know this man?"

Brock was taken by surprise, but, not to appear ignorant before the President, replied:

"Yes, I know him, but I can't call his name now."

"My name is Munson, of Knoxville. Don't you remember Judge Munson's son who went to California?"

"What, Sam Munson?"

"That's my name."

"Oh yes," said Brock, turning to Davis, "now I remember him. Yes, I know him very well."

"Do you know his people there?" asked Davis.

"I know his father, Judge Munson, very well."

Toombs stood up and said, "That will do, sir, that will do," and Brock walked out of the room.

Toombs then drew a chair close to Davis, and they conversed in whispers for a few moments, when the guard escorted me to my quarters. I fancied that I had made some progress at this interview.

The next morning brought Mr. Brock to my loft, evidently sent to satisfy himself fully that I was Sam Munson. A delicate and difficult task was before me, and the result to my own mind very doubtful. Brock, however, was talkative, willing to carry on the conversation, and evidently quite sure that he was not mistaken in his man. I knew something of the Munsons, and localities in Knoxville, and, by the aid of imagination, could fill any pauses in Brock's conversation; eight years of absence excusing failures in memory. Brock asked leading questions, saying, for illustration, "You know so-and-so." "Oh, yes," I responded, though I had not the remotest knowledge of the person. Then Brock would refer to something very ludicrous, and I would burst into laughter, as though at the recollection, while Brock, greatly enjoying it, would unconsciously tell the whole story, so that I could put in a fitting remark here and there, which seemed to come naturally from recollection. Brock went away entirely satisfied, and reported to Jeff. Davis. Two days later, a commissioned officer entered the room with a parole, pledging myself not to leave the city of Richmond without orders from the provost-marshal. I signed it, and was released from confinement. With the freedom of the city, I continued my observations.

Walking through a street one Sunday morning, by a high board fence covered with posters concerning regiments being organized and other military announcements, from which I gleaned additional information, a man came up and slapped me on the shoulder with,—

"Hallo, Baker! What are you doing here?"

The name sounding strangely, under the circumstances, I was startled, but, looking around, calmly said:

"I guess you are mistaken, sir. My name is Munson."

"Ain't your name Baker?"

"No, sir."

"Didn't you go to California in 1850?"

"No, sir. I have lived in California, but I did not go there till '52."

"Why, didn't you go across the isthmus with me in April, 1850, when we had the fight with the natives?"

"No, sir. I guess you have mistaken the man."

"Well, I would have sworn that you were Baker. Didn't you have a brother there!"

"I had a brother there, but he came home in '53."

"Well," said he, turning away, "it's all right, I suppose; but I never saw two men look so much alike in my life!"

In the mean time I had obtained information of military movements and plans, learned where the enemy had stationed troops, or were building fortifications, and what they were doing at the Tredegar works. I had obtained the knowledge for which I came, and was anxious to return North. Through the influence of Hayes, I got from the provost-marshal, a pass to visit Fredericksburg, making an appointment to meet the former, which, of course, I did not keep. Arriving in Fredericksburg, I made three or four ineffectual attempts to get into the country, and finally, by the aid of a negro, crossed the Rappahannock one morning four miles below the city. To reach the Potomac would tax all my powers to the utmost, but the case was desperate and I must go forward. As, when entering upon my Southern tour, it was indispensable to success that I should even among friends be *incog.*, so now I must return with the precious epistles in my pocket, through the Confederate lines, on my own account, having only the chances of escape which any wanderer at large might have.

My face was toward Washington, and the only question remaining was, whether the success in the attempt to reach it would equal that of my journey to Richmond.

The Potomac was the goal of my solitary travel through forest and over open fields; for on its northern banks lay the Union Army, and, once across its waters, I was safe. My appearance was that of a common citizen, and I hoped to pass unnoticed any persons with whom a meeting was unavoidable. Scarcely two miles were traveled, when, by the side of woods which bordered the road, an officer and soldier on horseback appeared, and too near to give me time to seek concealment in the forest.

The officer reined up before me, and inquired: "Have you got a pass, sir:"

"Yes, sir."

"Let me see it."

With the promptness of assurance, I drew forth and handed him the pass from Richmond to Fredericksburg. If able to read, I hoped he might be satisfied with a glance at the paper, and let me proceed. He studied it awhile, till his eye caught the word "Fredericksburg;" he then said:—

"I don't think this will do, sir!"

"'Tis all right."

"Well, it may be, but you'll have to go back with me to Fredericksburg."

My locomotion had not been observed, and, with a pitiful limp, I remarked that it was hard for a lame man to be compelled to walk that distance; and that, if I attempted it, I must necessarily defer my journey till another day. I made a painful effort to walk, and so far moved the compassion of the officer, that he offered to take the pass to the commanding general, and leave me in charge of the soldier. When he was gone, after a little pleasant conversation, the day being warm, I proposed to my guard that we go into the shade of the woods. Tying his horse to a small tree, he threw himself down on the grass. Half an hour was spent in pleasant chat, and the officer did not make his appearance.

"Ugh!" said the guard stretching, "How sleepy I am, I didn't sleep a wink last night."

This fact, with the inviting greensward and shade, disposed him to snatch a nap; and soon he was oblivious to everything around him. It was no pleasure to me to subject him to punishment or even censure on my account; but the law of self-protection necessarily overruled my regard for the unwatchful guard, and, carefully appropriating his revolver, I unloosed and mounted his horse. Riding leisurely along the path a short time, I turned suddenly into the woods; but the ground was rough, and the bushes almost impenetrable, making progress distressingly slow. As the sun was sinking behind the trees, having traveled half a dozen miles, I emerged into a clearing, where a white-haired

old man, who evidently had reached his threescore years and
ten, was making shingles.

With a respectful salutation, I inquired:

"Will you tell me the shortest road to the Potomac?"

This Southern patriarch looked at me with surprise. I
said again :

"The river—the Potomac river—which way is it?"

"I never heard of it in my life."

"How long have you lived here?"

"Always; was born here."

"And don't know where the Potomac river is?"

"I never heard about such a river."

He was equally ignorant of the existence of Aquia Creek,
or any of the streams or places along the river.

"Did you know that the South had seceded?" I inquired.

"Well, well! I've heard suthing was going on, but
hain't taken much interest in politics no how since Jackson's
time. 'Spose they are all the time getting up suthing new.'

With a cup of water from the unsuspecting Jacksonian
democrat, who was enjoying Cowper's lodge in the wilderness, undisturbed by the alarms of war, I rode away, to try
the next turn in the wheel of fortune. At length a house
was visible in the distance, and toward it I directed my
course.

Dismounting near it, I hitched my horse, and commenced
observations. Two negroes only were in sight, in an out-
house. I went to them with a plausible story, and for ten
cents obtained some bread and milk, which broke the day's
fast, with refreshment for the night's adventure before me.
Darkness was setting upon the forest, and, unable to discern
the mire and stones ahead, I became entangled among the
branches, and found I must abandon my horse, and plunge
into the thicket alone. After wandering about bewildered
for an hour, I unconsciously returned to the very house I
had left. I decided to risk a rest here till morning, and
working my body feet foremost under a haystack, until completely hidden, fell into a sound sleep. Just before the
dawn of the next day, I was startled from slumber, and, listening, soon learned that rebel cavalry were in search of me,
and had surrounded the house. A dozen horsemen could be

seen through the lattice-work of hay, moving about in the darkness. From the dwelling they went to the outhouses, and finally came to the haystack. I prepared for the worst. With my head thinly covered, I could watch my foes, unseen by them; while my revolver lay before me. If discovered, I resolved to shoot the successful man, and run for dear life toward the woods. Several times the cavalry rode around the stack; then one of the number, dismounting, began a sword examination of my lodgings. I could hear the thrust of the blade into the hay, until it grazed my coat, and I grasped my six-shooter to spring; but he passed on, saying:

"He ain't in there, boys."

Remounting, with his comrades, he rode off.

Watching them till out of sight, I crept cautiously into the deepening light, and started for the woods. The sun rose gloriously over the near horizon; but whether to light me toward safety or capture, was entirely uncertain.

Without breakfast or dinner, I hastened on, having not even a glimpse of a human being, and avoiding every indication of his habitation. At two o'clock in the afternoon, when emerging from a clump of bushes, I came in full view of a man hauling timber. I could not retreat, and, changing the coat hanging on one arm to the other, I put my hand on my pocket, and stood in thinking posture. I saw that I had an Irishman to deal with, and not a remarkably bright specimen of his race.

With the air of one interested, I asked:

"What is this timber for?"

"It's fur the batthery down here, in course."

This answer settled the question of the proximity of the Potomac, and also apprised me that fortifications and plenty of rebels were not far off. I walked along a stick of timber, measuring it by paces, and then said:

"Tell these men they are getting this timber four feet too short, will you?"

"Yes, sur, I will sur. It's only haulin, I am, meself."

"Well," I replied, leaving him, "tell them to cut it four feet longer, will you? Tell them I say so."

"I will, sur."

Into the woods again, and, making as good time as possible, I walked on two hours longer. Hunger began to gnaw, and create that desperation which disregards the cooler prudence of a full stomach. Striking a small creek or bayou, running into the Potomac, I resolved to follow it till it decided my fortunes for the night. No sign of anything in reach to appease hunger appeared, nor of a boat in which to get across the river. The very first sight of human existence was in a form to excite fear—a white tent, snugly pitched on the sloping point of a hill, by the water-side, and surrounded with bushes. I paused to watch for further intimations of what was there.

At length a soldier came up the bank with fish, and entered the tent. Soon after, with another man, he reappeared outside, and they sat down, lighted their pipes, and chatted, after the fashion of good-natured Dutchmen. The imperious demands of hunger urged me to join them, and, advancing, I accosted them. It turned out that they belonged to a battery on the hill above, and had moved to the bank to catch fish for the officers. I told them I lived up the creek, and had come down to see how things were getting on; then inquired:

"Have you got anything to eat in the tent?"

"We got not much here to eat."

"Boys, I am very hungry. I hain't had anything to eat since I came from home, and I'll pay you for something."

"Vell, dat ish tifferent matter. If you pays, dat ish tifferent matter."

"Can't you cook some fish?"

"Oh, ersh, I spose we get you some fish."

In a few minutes they set before me a supper simply of fish, cooked in their primitive style, and yet no luxury was ever so grateful to the taste. After it was finished, I asked for a pipe, and began to puff away, entirely at home; but all the while revolving in my mind the chances and expedients for a final parting with my Dutch friends. Finally, my eye fell upon a small boat lying in the bushes below; and the conviction followed the discovery, that it was my only hope of crossing the Potomac. Learning that the fishermen owned it, I said to them:

"I want to buy that boat. What will you take for it?"

"I no sells dat poat," replied one.

"I'll give you twenty dollars for it, in gold."

"It's worth more as that to us. The Yankees ish breaking up all poats on the Potomac."

There was an end to the prospect of a purchase; and a new plan must be devised. The sun sank behind the trees, and in the pleasant shade we smoked and talked away the hours. I found, in the course of conversation, that the battery was not over two hundred yards from us, and the Potomac few rods below.

The evening advanced, and I begged the privilege of sleeping in the tent, as I was too tired to think of returning home before morning. Permission was reluctantly granted; and, spreading their blanket, they "turned in," while I continued without, smoking, till the moon rose. I had practical business on hand, which excluded contemplation of the romantic scene—the silver light tipping and then flooding the hills, and creeping down to the quiet spot of anxious wakefulness. For the illumination was to aid me in my design to escape. I could now watch the movements of my companions in the tent sufficiently to see when they were apparently asleep, depending on the ear for the further evidence of the desirable fact. When all was still, indicating profound slumber, suddenly a change of position. a grunt, and a look outside, would dispel the illusion.

Toward midnight, I heard a shout:

"Hello, there! you come to ped to-night?"

"Yes, I am coming in."

Soon after entering the tent, I found that room for me had been left between the men, and the effort to get on an outer edge of the blanket was fruitless.

A suspicion evidently crossed the mind of the one who had just spoken to me, respecting the stranger, and there was a design to guard against any unpleasant results from the visit.

The day's fatigue made my own inclination to sleep almost irresistible; but I watched anxiously for the favoring moment to leave the bed unobserved. Repeated trials found the distrustful soldier sufficiently wakeful to look after his guest. Overcome by the slumberous influences of fatigue, my comfortable quarters, and the "stilly night," I sank into a restless repose. Scarcely an hour had passed, when I suddenly awoke, starting with alarm lest the opportunity to escape was lost. On the contrary, I found my companions were thoroughly asleep, their loud breathing the only sign of life. I carefully crawled from between them, till half my body was out of the tent. The suspicious man, with a sound of unrest, turned over. I remained perfectly still till he made another turn and stretched out his arm to see if all was right in the middle. I drew back to my old place, and he laid his hand upon me several times, before he seemed satisfied that I was there. Several attempts to leave the tent ended in a similar failure. Daylight began to steal into the tent, and the night of suspense must end in some decisive effort to secure the boat and cross the Potomac. The soldier-fishermen were sleeping quite as soundly as at any time before, and in another moment I stood before the door watching the effect of my movement. There was a little stir, and I stood mechanically poking the embers of our evening fire, as if looking out to see the breaking day; but with my pistol in one hand ready for service. Returning it to my pocket muzzle down, I hastened to the bank. To my great disappointment, there were no oars in the boat. Upon making search among the willows, I found a short one, partially decayed. Noiselessly as possible I launched the frail bark, fearing each sound on the sand or in the water would bring my Dutch friends down the bank. In a few moments, which suspense made oppressively long, I floated away into the stream, at this point, not over thirty feet in width. Taking the middle of the current, I pulled off my coat, and began to row for life. The tide favored me, and I was congratulating myself upon the prospect of an unmolested voyage when a shout drew my attention to the vigilant Dutchman, whose gesticulations could not be misunderstood. He called loudly to his bedfellow: "Meyer! Meyer! the poat ish gone! the poat ish gone!"

He seized his musket and made for the bank, not more than a dozen feet from me, shouting:

"Come pack here! Come pack mit that poat!"

My only answer was a more vigorous use of the oar

Placing my right hand upon the pistol, and watching the soldier, I propelled the boat with my left.

"Come pack!" he continued, following me along the bank. He then paused, leveled his musket, and was about to fire. I did not want to kill "mine host," but the law of self-defense again demanded a sacrifice. With quick and sudden aim, I fired—with a cry of distress, he staggered and fell lifeless beside his musket. His comrade was running down the hill, when, seeing what had happened, he turned back to the tent. He soon returned with a double-barreled shot gun, and stole along cautiously, through the bushes, till within forty yards of the boat, and then fired. The shot fell around me, in the water. Catching a glimpse of my enemy in the thicket, I discharged my revolver. He ran away, evidently unhurt. The reports had given the alarm, and several soldiers soon came in sight. An instant later, a bullet whistled over my shoulder. I had reached the decisive moments of my last effort to get out of "Dixie." Again getting sight of the Dutchman in the bushes, I once more took deliberate aim and fired. He threw up one arm, gave a yell, and fell to the ground. In a moment he rose again, and, groaning, staggered away. Then two or three shots saluted me unceremoniously, striking and splintering the side of the boat. I was now at the mouth of the creek, and rapidly left the shore behind me. A squad of soldiers, by this time, stood on the brow and at the base of the hill, firing their muskets. The *chug* of the bullets in the water reminded me that my transit to loyal soil was not yet certain. Both hands were laid to the oar, and, striking the broad current of the Potomac, which was here four miles wide, I rapidly receded from musket range. A high wind swept the waters, and, while rounding a bluff, a sudden gust carried away my hat, and lifted my coat lying in the bow of the boat, dropping it into the river. But it was no time to look backward to those articles of apparel, floating between me and my foes, whose bullets still came unpleasantly near. Their shots continued until they fell far in the wake of my boat. The sun had risen above the horizon, warm and bright, while, for two hours and a half, I worked with a single oar, and, aided by the drifting tide, approached the Maryland shore. With an inexpressible sense of relief, I heard the boat's bow touch the sand. I was near Chapel Point, ten miles below the creek on which I embarked, and so exhausted, that with difficulty I reached the bank. On its green carpet, and under the cooling shade of its trees, I laid down to rest, leaving the boat to which I owed my deliverance to the winds and waves of the Potomac.

CHAPTER III.

NORTHERN EXPERIENCES AS CONFEDERATE AGENT.

Hospitalities by the way—The Report to General Scott—Operations in Baltimore—The Janus-faced Unionist—A rich Development in Philadelphia—The Arrests—Amusing Prison Scene.

REFRESHED by an hour of rest sufficiently to renew my journey toward Washington, I soon came to a small and poor habitation, in whose door stood a coarse and dirty female. I asked her for something to eat.

"I have nothing to spare: can't give you a mouthful."

Whether meanness, destitution, or my dilapidated appearance were the exciting cause of her rudeness, I can not tell. But to my plea for a crust, or inquiries where I might find even a partial supply of the lost apparel, she closed the door in my face. I wandered on, a solitary country mocking my hunger. Toward noon a noble mansion, surrounded by a large plantation, arrested my eye, and on its porch an elderly woman sitting alone amid the rural quiet. Entering the gate, I approached her with a morning salutation. She returned it, with a suspicious glance at my unusual appearance. I inquired:

"Can I get a drink of water here, madam?"

"Certainly," calling a colored girl to bring it.

The roar of the cannon at Matthias Point, where the rebels were practicing with the battery, could be distinctly heard. I said:

"We are getting ready for the Yankees there pretty fast."

"Yes."

"They won't be able to sail up and down the river much more."

"No, that they won't."

The peculiar animation with which she made this reply

showed me that I had not mistaken her character. While I was drinking, she inquired from what place I had come.

I told her from Richmond, to see what the Yankees were doing, and report to Jeff. Davis and Beauregard. She then inquired how I lost my hat and coat. I told her they were blown off while crossing the river, and that I had just left the shore, with nothing to eat since the night before.

"Our dinner will be ready soon," she said, "and I shall be very glad to have you stay and dine with us."

The invitation was accepted, and extra preparation made for me. An excellent meal, many inquiries from my hostess concerning the progress of the "holy cause," and predictions of its speedy triumph followed. When I was ready to leave, she supplied me with a second-hand hat and coat, and, with a cordial good-bye, expressed the hope that I should be prospered in my good work, and do much for the independence of the South.

With no incidents of remarkable interest, I passed through the counties of Maryland, reaching Washington after an absence of three eventful weeks.

I at once reported to General Scott, giving him all the information desired respecting Manassas, Fredericksburg, and Richmond, the resources and plans of the rebel chiefs, and the blockade running of the Potomac.

He read, with a smile, the letters from the Confederate Government, when I expressed my design to use them in tracking northern traitors in their treasonable alliance with the South. Expressing his gratification, he recommended my name to Mr. Cameron for permanent service as a secret agent of the War Department.

I commenced, without delay, ferreting out these sympathizers with secession. Two brothers named A., one of them within the rebel lines, were engaged in supplying munitions of war to the Confederacy.

The apparently loyal man who lived in Baltimore had a contract to furnish the regiment of Col. ———, then on the Potomac, with forage. He owned a small vessel on the river, whose captain shared with him the profits of their secret treachery. Filling the hold with small-arms, ammunition, and other light *matériel* of war, they were covered with hay and oats for the Union troops. Upon reaching Matthias Point, the captain signaled A., who was watching for him, and the contraband goods were landed, when the vessel proceeded to Washington with its light freight of forage. This shrewd operation had been carried on a considerable time, with no suspicion attaching to the Baltimore brother from his loyal neighbors, of the illegitimate traffic.

I proceeded to Barnum's Hotel in Baltimore, and dispatched a note to A., informing him that Mr. Munson, from Richmond, would like to see him, and designating a time for our interview. A. promptly called.

He entered the room, when the following conversation passed between us.

"This is Mr. A., I presume."

"Yes, sir."

"I am glad to see you, sir. Take a seat."

A. sat down.

"Mr. A., I am a man of very few words. I came here on business, and I want to get through with it as soon as I can conveniently. I am an agent of the Confederate Government. I understand that you are willing to help us, and have been doing so. I want to purchase goods, and I have the gold to pay for them."

A., who was a short, impulsive man, with a German accent, was thrown entirely off his guard.

"I'm your man. I'm just the person you ought to have come to. I help the South, and I make a little money out of the North. I'll show you how easy it is."

From his coat pocket he drew an envelope, containing two contracts—one of them to send goods to Richmond, and the other to furnish a Union regiment with certain supplies. His eye twinkled with delight, while he watched my perusal of the documents. The delivery of the goods was a subject of considerable discussion, and A. was very particular in his inquiries about the pay. I replied:—

"Mr. A., I do not come here to make money out of my government. I came here purely from patriotic motives. While I am willing to pay you a fair percentage on any goods you may buy, and a liberal allowance for your services, I of course can not submit to any extortion, or to any exorbitant charges. I am working for the interests of my people. I, myself, do not want to make a cent out of this business."

"That is all right—it is honorable and patriotic. But it is not safe to buy the goods here, because men in this trade have been detected, and the police watch us all the time. We can do better in Philadelphia, where I have friends to help us."

We agreed to start in the 4:20 train the same afternoon for Philadelphia. While standing in the depot waiting for the train, talking with A., I saw Senator McDougal, whom I had known in California, and George Wilkes, coming toward me. I tried in vain to avoid their recognition, but McDougal, taking my arm, exclaimed:

"Why, how d'ye do, Baker?"

With a look of strange surprise, I said:

"You've got the advantage of me, sir. I don't know you."

"Well, that's a good joke," replied McDougal, laughing.

"It may be, but I don't know you, sir. My name is Munson."

Suddenly McDougal seemed to fathom the mystery sufficiently to relieve me of farther embarrassment, by remarking, as he turned away:

"Well, upon my soul, I believe I am mistaken. Excuse me, sir; you look very much like a friend of mine." The incident made but slight if any impression upon the mind of A., for he made no allusion to it during the ride to Philadelphia.

I stopped at the American Hotel, when A. left me to find B., who was connected with a large hardware house in the city, and bring him to the hotel. Meanwhile, by a circuitous route, I reached the headquarters of the police and had an interview with Ben. Franklin, the chief of the department. Acquainting him thoroughly with the business in hand, his assistance was secured to make the arrests at the proper time. He suggested that it might be well to have the conference with my disloyal friends. To this I assented, and, accompanying me to the hotel, he was concealed under the bed. Soon after A. and B. entered—the latter a tall, gaunt, shrewd, and taciturn man. A. opened the conversation, and talked on, while B. stroked his whiskers and said nothing. I repeated the assurance that my object was to serve the South and not speculation. I urged the risk of delay in completing my arrangements, as a reason for prompt action. In conclusion, I remarked to B. : "I learn from Mr. A. that you are friendly to our people and willing to assist us."

"Yes, sir, my sympathies are with the South, and possibly I may be able to aid you."

B. desired to know the kind of goods that were needed, and repeated the assurance that Philadelphia was a safer place than Baltimore or New York for the purchase of them. I then produced my letters, which B. read carefully and with evident satisfaction ; but preferred to defer any further negotiations for the present. As he rose to leave, he requested me to call at his place of business that afternoon. A. remained and suggested another gentleman, who would be glad to take hold of the business—a Mr. C., of Commerce Street. I gratefully accepted the proposal, and we left the room, releasing Franklin from his close confinement under the bed. We found C. in his office, but disinclined to talk. He inquired where I stopped, and I returned to the hotel. Shortly after, C. made his appearance and commenced conversation in a very confidential way. He went for the South, but did not like A., who, he affirmed, was simply a money-making Jew. I told him I knew nothing of A., but supposed him to be a reliable friend of our cause. The result of the interview was a plan to keep A. interested in the transaction, but ignorant of its most important particulars. In the afternoon I called upon Mr. B., whose confidence was now unreserved, and stated to him my conversation with C. He then said :

"Now, Mr. Munson, you and I are actuated by the same motives in this thing. These men, A. and C., are engaged in it simply for the percentage they can make. I think you had better get rid of them."

I replied, that this could not well be done, but that I might withhold any further information than was absolutely necessary.

The conversation closed with an invitation to dine with

him that afternoon. I expressed a fear that it would give offense to A., if I should go alone.

"Well," said B., "You had better bring him along."

I went with A., at the appointed hour, and sat down to a sumptuous dinner. Wine was abundant, and the health of Davis, Beauregard, and other leading rebels was not forgotten. B. became exhilarated, and his secession songs were sung so loudly that we were obliged to hint that possibly he might be heard in the streets. The party broke up at a late hour in fine spirits. I made arrangements with one of the banks by which I would appear to have plenty of money at my command. I went to a tinner's and had several canvas bags full of pieces of zinc cut the size of gold coin, and these were deposited in the vaults. I began to make my purchases. I bought two hundred thousand cannon-primers, two hundred Colt's revolvers, a million friction caps, and other similar goods. I also ascertained that these parties were carrying on systematically contraband trade with the South. Franklin, Chief of Police, was informed of my operations, and we concluded it was time to begin making arrests. On a subsequent day, having an invitation to dine with A. at the house of B., I told Franklin to watch us when we came away, and if, when we were opposite the City Hall, I raised my hand, he was to arrest them—otherwise to make no demonstration. As we stepped from the house into a street car, Franklin got on to the platform. When the designated point was reached, A. got off first, and I immediately gave the signal. Franklin, laying his hand upon A.'s shoulder, said:

"I want you, sir."

I was making off across the street, when Franklin shouted:

"Here, sir, I want you, too."

I, of course, returned, looking somewhat alarmed.

Said Franklin:

"You will have to come with me, gentlemen, I have a little private business with you."

A. and myself were soon in the station-house together. Franklin, turning to me, remarked:

"I've been looking after you, sir, for some time. Your

name is Munson, isn't it? You came here from the South to buy goods, didn't you? You were very bold about it; a little too bold, as you have just discovered. I've been looking after you, too, A. You're a Baltimorean, ain't you? You came here to get rebel supplies, too, didn't you? I shall have to search you both."

We were searched, and, of course, the two contracts to supply both the rebel and Union troops were found in A.'s possession.

"Take this man to the Sixth Precinct station-house, and lock him up by himself," said Franklin to an officer, "and then come back after this man," pointing to me.

"Now, Ben," I said, when A. had gone, "we must gobble up those other two men the best way we can, as soon as possible."

"All right," said Franklin.

I had an appointment to meet C. the next morning, to examine some caps which he had received from New York. When we met according to this arrangement, C. inquired for A.

I replied:

"He got a dispatch that his brother was in Baltimore, and he has gone on to see him. He will be back to-morrow."

The caps were satisfactory, but C. stated that he must go to New York, to get some telegraphic material, which he was to furnish—some small wires to wind the battery, and asked me if I could not advance money.

"I haven't any with me now, but, if you will meet me at the corner of Third and Market Streets, at half-past one, I can let you have some, and you will be in time then to get the two o'clock train for New York."

I left and went to Franklin's office, requesting him to arrest us when we met on the corner. C. and myself arrived a little before the time, and I made some preliminary conversation on that account. At the moment he was anticipating the transfer of the funds, Franklin came up, and suspended operations by saying:

"I am the chief of police here, and I want you two gentlemen."

C. laughed, and said:

"I guess you don't know who I am."

"Oh, yes, I do, and I know this other man, too. He's a blockade runner, from Richmond, and you're not much better."

We went to a station-house, and Franklin apparently searched me, while another officer attended to C. He was then taken to the Sixth Precinct station-house, and locked in a cell by himself.

B. only remained to be arrested. But he was the most important one of the number, and Marshal Milwood, of that district, was to assist in his arrest. I called on Mr. B., who said:

"I think we have both got about tired of A. and C., and I think you had better meet me to-morrow, and bring them with you, so that we can settle up with them, pay them their commission, and tell them that you have bought all you require. Then we can go into New York, to-morrow, in the two o'clock train, and make arrangements for all the goods you want, without the heavy commission you are obliged to pay them."

I promised to come to his office, at twelve o'clock, the next day. Franklin and Marshal Milwood were duly informed of this appointment.

Mr. B.'s store was in a long, narrow building, and in the rear were two or three small offices, with desks for writing. I was with Mr. B. in one of these.

After the usual salutations, B. asked:

"Where are A. and C.?"

"They are running about town, somewhere. I didn't want to bring them here. I will sit down and write them a letter, stating that my business is nearly done in Philadelphia, and that I am about to leave."

Mr. B. furnished me with paper, and I took a seat at one of the desks, to write. The time passed on, and I became restless, for Franklin and Milwood should already have arrived.

If they should fail me, I thought I should be in a very disagreeable dilemma, having promised to go with B. to New York

I was thus meditating, when I heard two men coming down the store from the front. In a moment more Marshal Milwood—a large, strong man, with a gold-headed cane and a gold badge—entered the next office, and said:

"Is this Mr. B.?"

"That is my name, sir," responded B.

"I am the United States marshal of this district, and I arrest you, sir."

B. turned pale.

Meanwhile, Franklin, who had also entered, turned and said:

"Here's another man that we want. This is that man Munson."

I tore off the paper I had written, and commenced rolling it up, as though secretly. Taking my black silk hat in my hand, I quietly put the paper under the leather lining inside, and placed the hat on my head. B. was watching me, and conjectured that I had written something in the letter which could criminate them. If he had any doubt before that I was what I represented myself to be, this action would have removed his suspicions.

"I guess you are mistaken, gentlemen," said I.

"Oh, no, not at all," said Franklin; "you can't fool us. You are the man that came here from the South, to buy goods. Let me see the letter you were writing."

"I haven't written any letter," said I.

"Oh, none of that!" said Franklin, knocking my hat from my head as roughly as though he had been in earnest. "You thought I didn't see that little sleight-of-hand performance, didn't you?" he continued, taking the paper from the hat. He read it, and handed it to Milwood.

B. was walking up and down, stroking his beard, having regained his composure.

"We want both of you," said Milwood. "Mr. Marshal," said B., "I think you are entirely too fast in this matter. I am an old citizen here, well known, and a partner in this house. This gentleman is from the South, it is true. He inquired me out and visited me, but I cannot believe he is here for any improper purpose. So far as I am concerned I shall be able to show who and what I am very easily."

B. was searched, and quite important papers for evidence were found on him. He was then sent to the Sixth Precinct station-house.

That evening Marshal Milwood, Ben. Franklin, and I, went down to see the prisoners, I keeping carefully out of their sight.

"Let us see what they will say to each other," said one of the party. An officer took A. into C.'s room.

"My G—d! what are you doing here?" exclaimed A.

"Doing here?" answered C., angrily. "I'm arrested."

"Why, when were you arrested?"

"I was standing on the corner of Market and Third Streets with Munson, and Ben. Franklin took us both."

"My G—d, I was arrested with Munson," said A.

"You can't play that on me. You're a —— Jew, and it's you who have brought all this trouble on me."

A. was enraged at this, and conversation followed of the roughest sort.

When the excitement subsided, B. was put into the same room with them, Milwood, Franklin, and myself, still out of sight, listening.

"My G—d, B., you arrested too?" said A.

B. stroked his whiskers and looked sternly.

"I understand it all," said he. "You are two scoundrels, and one or the other of you either betrayed this matter or let it out by your cursed carelessness. I believe A., that that you came from Baltimore with Munson to beat him out of his money and get him arrested."

They abused each other for nearly an hour, and A. wanted to fight the rest. Each declared that he was arrested with Munson, and not one would believe a word the other said.

"Come, you're making too much noise," said the officer, finally. "We'll have to separate you again."

Early in the morning they were taken to a prison out of town, and in the afternoon Milwood and Franklin went with me to visit them again. I was put into a cell, and A. brought and locked in with me.

"Mein Got, Munson, what a troubles this is!" said A., his German accent more noticeable in his dejection. "Mein

Got, when we got out of that cars and that man Franklin came up, I thought I should have died. And B. and C. are arrested too."

"Well, we're all in the same boat," said I: "I suppose they'll hang me."

In a short time A. was told to come out and get his dinner, and B. was locked in with me; I putting on the aspect of chief mourner over our fate.

"Well, I'm sorry for you, Munson," said B. "I suppose my friends will have me out this afternoon or to-morrow, and if I can do anything for you I shall be glad to. I never liked that Jew, and I am convinced that this is all his doing."

After a while B. was removed, and C. put in the cell. He came in with a knowing leer on his face. He had suspected the truth.

"I'm glad to see you, Munson," said he; "that was a splendid thing we played on them fellows, wasn't it? Oh, that's the way to catch them!"

"What do you mean?" said I.

"Why, I knew who you were all the time. You couldn't fool me; I wanted to help you catch the scoundrels."

"Who do you think I am?"

"You are a detective from Washington. I knew you well enough. I was just going up to Marshal Milwood, to tell him what we had done."

"C., it is too late to tell that story now. It won't do."

A statement of the cases was forwarded to Washington and A., B. and C. were sent to Fort Warren. A., probably from the excitement and mortification attending his arrest and imprisonment, became insane, and was sent to Blackwell's Island, and afterward to the asylum near Baltimore, where he still remains. Before A. left, in a fit of passion, he struck C. in the face, breaking his nose. B. and C. were released on bail for trial.

A leading New York daily paper contained the very correct account of the case as quoted below:—

"The most important arrests that have been made during the rebellion came to light in this city to-day. Most of those previously incarcerated in Fort Lafayette had been devoting their influences to treason; but the parties here arrested were contributing arms and munitions of war daily, bribing officers of the United States Army to further their designs, and had organized a system of treason so skillful and so complete, that only after the utmost vigilance, and when the detectives had tested all means to entrap and decoy them, the full proofs came to light.

"The names of these men are J. M. H., F. W., and W. G.—H. is a Baltimore Israelite, whose business is the making of military trimmings, epaulettes, sword-handles, &c. He had obtained a hay contract from the United States Government, to more effectually conceal his plans, and was armed with numerous letters from Federal functionaries, that he intended to produce in emergencies. This man conducted contraband trade from Baltimore until General Dix and the provost-marshal showed him up. He was first observed in this wise:—A package, containing several thousand friction tubes and cannon-primers, had been left at Adams's Express office in this city, addressed to a well-known firm n Baltimore. Being threatened with arrest, the latter firm confessed that they were the agents of J. M. H., and it was further educed that the same was shipped under a fictitious name by W. G.

"Detective Benjamin Franklin, a sagacious and fertile Philadelphia officer, now determined to seduce H. to this city; for which purpose he resorted to certain ingenious means, not now ripe for publication. Convinced that heavy orders awaited him here, and that Philadelphia was less under espionage than Baltimore, H. came on. A celebrated Lincoln detective now took part in the matter, and the means by which they inveigled all the parties constitute the richest item in the history of criminal surveillance. The Israelite was so played upon that he is not yet aware of the enemies who ruined him, and when the matter was ripe the whole party were taken up, their goods and papers seized, and they are now in Fort Lafayette, having gone forward on Sunday night.

"W. G. is a razor and cutlery importer, whose establishment is situated at Fifth and Commerce Streets. He has never taken the oath of allegiance, being an Englishman. His game was to pretend himself a Federal agent until the worst came, when he was to claim the privileges of a British subject. In his establishment were found surgical instruments, caps, pistols, bowie-knives, &c., packed and directed to go southward. The property amounts to $10,000 in value.

"F. W. is a Virginian, formerly in partnership with C. B. C., 205 North Water Street. He has always been a rabid traitor, and his wife has been six times to Richmond and back within as many weeks, taking each time trunks heavily filled with weapons and goods contraband. She passed our lines by bribing an officer of the army, who obtained passes for the purpose. Said officer has been arrested, and will probably be shot. At W.'s house an extensive correspondence with parties in the South was found, and his complicity with the rebels was proved by his papers, even in the absence of any other evidence. Among other articles seized, there was a pair of epaulettes, marked with the name of Captain R., an officer in the rebel army. There were also a photographic group of worthies, of which W. was the center. A gentleman, who is familiar with the likenesses, says that they represent Captain R., Captain J. A. C., Lieutenant C. D. F., of Georgia, and B., mayor of Savannah, all decided rebels.

"The hay contract in which H. was engaged was to have been worked to good advantage. Two vessels, one loaded with bales of hay, and the other with bales containing war munitions, were to have been dispatched up the Potomac, and at Aquia Creek, at a given signal, the bogus hay would have been run under the Rebel batteries. All this was proved by seized letters, and also the fact that the late captures of Federal sloops and small craft by the Rebels, off the Potomac and Rappahannock Rivers, were the work of design and not of accident, the same containing contraband matters. New York, Philadelphia, and Baltimore merchants are thus implicated, and the proofs are too plain and startling to be set aside. These three men were leagued together, and among their several correspondence were late letters from Rebel contractors, acknowledging the receipt of pistols and side-arms.

"After being arrested, they were shifted from station houses to prison, being one night taken out of town to stave off judicial decisions, writs of habeas corpus, &c. Finally, on Sunday, Marshals Jenkins and Steele drove them to the New York boat—W. defiant, G. cowed and sullen, and the Israelite trembling like a leaf.

"A part of the correspondence implicating them was obtained from the wife of a lieutenant in the Federal army, who had been rather delicately implicated with N. H. W., now in Fort Lafayette. She has been arrested in Newark, New Jersey, where she resides.

"The Government decoy who assisted detective Franklin in these labors is said to be a daring Californian, full of nerve and fertile in expedients, who has been twice in Charleston and thrice in Richmond since the battle of Bull Run. His manner of making the arrest cannot now be disclosed, although it rivals in interest and danger the exploits of the best Bow Street officers."

CHAPTER IV.

TREASON AND TRAITORS AT THE NORTH.

Baltimore—The Detective Service and the Arrest of the Maryland Legislature—The Refugee and the Spy—The Pursuit and the Capture—Traitors at Niagara Falls- Acquaintance with them—The Arrest—In Fort Lafayette.

OF all places north of Mason and Dixon's line, Baltimore had the pre-eminence in the early development of treason, and its defiant audacity. It is doubtful whether any other city furnished as largely and promptly for the rebel army the sons of aristocratic families. Here originated, practically, armed resistance to the Government.

The blood of the Massachusetts Sixth was the first martyr-blood of the war, and it stained the pavements of Baltimore. From that city was sent the first expedition to destroy a railroad—that to Gunpowder River.

Whatever Baltimore may have done since to redeem her name from treason's darkest hue, at the beginning of the civil conflict it was a hot-bed of crime, and its manifold products served well the garner of all its harvest—Richmond.

To make the most of the information obtained in Richmond, and of my letters from the authorities, I sought the acquaintance of leading secessionists, and was soon on excellent terms with them; indeed, I was admitted into their secret councils. This was more readily done at this time, when any representative of the South was cordially welcomed to the traitorous circles of that city. And my commission from the Confederate government gave me distinction among the friends of the revolt.

So determined and persistent were the people in their opposition to the Government, that a well-devised and deeply-laid plan was nearly consummated to carry the State out of the Union and to link its destinies with the South

This was to be accomplished through the secret assembling of the Legislature of Maryland. So dark, disloyal, and unknown to the public had been the meetings of this Legislature, that none (or very few) of the most prominent rebels were apprised of its movements. As a confidential and trusted friend of the authorities at Richmond, there could be no objection to revealing to me the plot.

At many of the private meetings which I was invited to attend, I was shocked and amazed at the cool and deliberate manner in which they declared their intentions to meet at Frederick, pass the ordinance of secession, and by it make and proclaim Maryland a Confederate State. These facts, as fast as they were obtained, were forwarded to Washington.

The rebel legislators arrived in Frederick, in accordance with a previous understanding, at different times, and from various directions, to avoid suspicion in loyal minds as to their real object. This was about the middle of September, 1861. Those that did reach Frederick were quietly arrested, and others *en route*, or just ready to leave Baltimore to meet their fellow-conspirators, were taken with so little demonstration, scarcely any one of the number knew of the arrest of his fellow-traitor.

The prompt action taken by the Government and its importance, I believe, have never been appreciated by the people of the loyal States.

It is startling to contemplate for a moment the result which must have followed the vote of this body of treasonable men.

It would have been taken at once as the signal for the immediate organization of a large rebel force in the State; and, instead of Washington having been the capital of the Union in the civil war, it would have been the capital of the Confederacy.

Instead of the Potomac river being the picket line between the hostile armies, that line would probably have been somewhere on the borders of Pennsylvania.

Whatever may be the estimate put upon the military or civil *status* of Benjamin F. Butler, to his energy, courage, and executive power in an emergency, the country is indebted for the position which Maryland occupied during the war

Had he faltered on his arrival in the State, or even hesitated a moment, Maryland would have been a Confederate State. Had he done nothing more, the country would have owed General Butler a lasting debt of gratitude.

September 28, 1861, while stopping at French's Hotel, in New York, I made the acquaintance of Mr. C., the book-keeper. Having had occasion to make inquiries of the character of his guests, I was compelled to disclose my office.

While conversing with him on one occasion about the hardships of the loyal people of the South, he called my attention to a man stopping there, who said he was a refugee from Mobile, and wished me to hear his story of wrongs.

I consented, and was introduced to an apparently respectable and honest mechanic, who stated that he was a Northern man, and had been South for some time, as locomotive engineer.

When the rebellion began, he inadvertently declared his sentiments, and the vigilance committee ordered him to go North.

He owned a small house, worth a few thousand dollars, and wished to stay long enough to sell it and take his family with him. But he was required to start at once, leaving his family behind.

An intimation to him by Mr. C. that I might influence the authorities at Washington and get a pass, induced him to apply to me for assistance.

I took a deep interest in the case, gave him my address in Washington, and asked him to call upon me there. Subsequently, when the incident had passed from my mind, one day my refugee friend came rushing into my apartment at Washington, and excitedly said:

"I have just met B. on the avenue, a young man from Montgomery, Alabama, where I was once employed, elegantly dressed in female attire, and accompanied by a man whom I do not know. I believe he is a spy."

"Why did you not follow him?"

"I was so much excited, I did not think of it."

My informant then gave me some account of B., when I requested him to go with one of my assistants through the principal streets in search of the mysterious strangers.

The search was continued for six days.

One morning he came with the haste of great excitement into my quarters again, saying:

"Well, I met B. and his friend just now, and followed them to the National Hotel."

I went there with my informant, procured two tickets for dinner, and we were soon seated at the table, where I found the couple. They were registered in the book as "Dr. McC. and wife, Harper's Ferry, Va." I did not lose sight of them again.

On Saturday they left Washington. I followed them to Philadelphia. They stopped at the Continental Hotel, registering their names "Dr. McC. and wife, Washington, D. C." Under their names I put my own as "John Brown." After some further disclosures, which we shall not here detail, on Sunday night they started for the West.

I was dressed in the garb of a farmer, and managed without suspicion to sit near them and hear much of their conversation; all of which proved clearly their treasonable character.

Monday night we reached the Burnett House, Cincinnati, Ohio. I saw them safely domiciled in the fourth story, and waited until after one o'clock at night, when I knocked at the door. It was cautiously opened, when I said:

"Doctor, I want to see you privately a moment."

His wife was sitting with her feet on the mantel-piece, smoking a cigar, and her dress unhooked.

I said, "Doctor, I have followed you from Washington; I know the character of this young man in female dress."

At this moment I noticed a revolver on the mantel-piece, and remarked:

"This might be dangerous in the hands of an ill-minded person; I guess I will take possession of it."

The doctor was boisterous and threatening. I told him I did not wish to make him notorious there, and alarm the house; that I knew all about them, and resistance would not help the matter. McC. commenced pulling on his boots, when I noticed the glitter of the handle of a bowie-knife which was thrust into a pocket in the side of his boot. I added, reaching out my hand:

ARREST OF REBEL AGENTS. 93

"Doctor, I think I will take this also; you might hurt yourself."

With a slight resistance on his part, I secured it The search of his baggage revealed, drawn on tissue paper, elaborately prepared plans of the fortifications and number of troops in and around Washington, with a large number of letters of great importance to the Government.

All of these were put into the trunks, again locked up, and with the keys in my possession, at four o'clock A. M., I was on my way to Washington with the travelers and their precious freight. They were safely quartered in the Old Capitol prison, and the maps, &c., delivered to Mr. Seward.

As an evidence that the great rebellion had long been premeditated by the prominent politicians of the South, it is only necessary to observe how completely they seemed to have the machinery of their treason in operation. For, before the roar of the cannon around Sumter had ceased to echo in the bay of Charleston, the secret emissaries of the cause had received their instructions, and each knew distinctly the part he was to play in the great drama.

From Floyd to the lowest traitor, the certainty of success, and the matured plans, had so emboldened them, that but little discretion or concealment was deemed important. And while Breckinridge was daring the North in Congress to oppose the right of the South to secede, its traitorous agents were boasting in the streets of Washington what they intended to do.

With a view to the arrest of these rebel agents, October 18, 1861, I went to Canada, as the subjoined letter will show:

WASHINGTON, *October 25,* 1861.

Hon. SECRETARY OF STATE:

DEAR SIR—I returned from Canada this morning. I found at the Clifton House, Niagara Falls, a large number of prominent secessionists, who have just returned from Europe.

I would like an order for the arrest and conveyance to Fort Lafayette of S. W. A. and O. B. C., the first-named being a member of the so-called Confederate Congress at this time. These traitors are waiting an opportunity to go South. They have very important correspondence in their possession, some of which I have seen. I am confident I shall succeed in inducing them to visit our side of the river, which of course will be the only opportunity for arresting them. Yours, very respectfully,

L. C. BAKER.

Having obtained the desired order from the Secretary of State, I immediately started for Niagara Falls. At Rochester I employed a colored servant, for I had determined to play the part of some prominent rebel from the South, and wrote three letters, all addressed to the name at the Clifton House which I had assumed.

One of these letters was mailed in New York, one in St. Louis, and the third in Washington. On my arrival at the Clifton House, where my secession friends alluded to were stopping, I registered my assumed name, and put on the airs of a Southern gentleman. I secured two of the most spacious rooms in the house.

The obliging landlord brought to me my letters, and in view of the honor conferred upon him he was more than ordinarily civil.

He remarked that he had often heard my name mentioned by his Southern friends. Upon my adding that I desired to live in perfect quiet, he said that it would be impossible for one so distinguished to do this; especially would my acquaintance be sought by fellow-exiles from the "sunny South."

I was allowed to pass that evening in seclusion; but early the next morning a servant handed me the card of S. W. Ashley, with his compliments, and expressing a desire to see me.

I graciously granted Mr. A.'s request, and told the servant to show him up.

I may here remark that the chances or risks so often taken of being detected in the assumed name by some acquaintance of the real person, sometimes do prove fatal to the plan; but even a defeat by the discovery of the real object by those I am seeking to entrap is only the failure of that particular plot, leaving a hundred others open for farther experiment.

Fortune favored me, however, in this case, as Mr. A. had no personal acquaintance with the traitor whose name I had assumed.

Our aims and purposes apparently being alike, we were soon on the most familiar terms. We talked over the prospect of glorious successes by our gallant troops, and laughed

CAPTURE OF A REBEL CONGRESSMAN ON SUSPENSION BRIDGE AT NIAGARA FALLS.

at the absurdity of the attempt of the Yankees to resist the valor of the chivalric South.

Mr. A., having preceded me several days in the visit to the Falls, had become acquainted with the interesting localities, and politely invited me to accompany him on a tour of observation. I gladly accepted, and spent a day among the wonders of the great cataract.

The following morning he called again, to repeat the kind attention.

At my suggestion, we decided to visit that marvelous monument of engineering skill, the Suspension Bridge. I was enthusiastic in praise of the designer, and tried to explain how the first wires were thrown over the chasm; and, to have a farther inspection, proposed that we should buy tickets to cross, intimating to my friend that we had better not go over, but simply advance a sufficient distance to make an examination of the structure.

I entertained my friend with remarks upon the scenery, the cables, &c.; and, to go into the scientific observation of the different parts of the bridge, I went over the national line a hundred feet perhaps, toward the American shore. While deeply interested in conversation, we were suddenly accosted by a mild, gentlemanly man, who said to my friend, Mr. A.:

"Your name is A., sir? I have an order from the Secretary of State for your arrest. In your admiration of this structure, I think you have ventured a little too far. You will please accompany me with your friend."

I replied: "Sir, certainly you can not have an order for my arrest; if so, will you produce it?"

He then took from his pocket the order for the arrest of Philip Herbert, my assumed name.

I suggested to Mr. A. that we should accompany the officer, quite sure that, upon the proper explanation, we should be at once released.

Our protestations were of no avail. He said: "I have been watching this bridge for you three weeks; quite sure you could not resist the temptation to examine it. You must go with me." We started immediately for New York.

Mr. A. had been quite thoughtful and sombre on the way to Rochester, and there remarked to me that his mind was not perfectly *clear* in regard to the part I was playing, he had his suspicions that he had mistaken his man. Philip Herbert, it will be recollected, while in Congress, killed a waiter in Willard's Hotel, and after the date of this affair was himself killed in the war while colonel of a regiment.

We were taken from New York to Fort Lafayette, where I remained an hour and my less fortunate friend eight months

CHAPTER V.

A KNIGHT OF THE GOLDEN SQUARE.

P H F., *alias* Carlisle Murray, a Knight of the Golden Square—The Arrest—Release—Papers of F. examined—Secretary Seward's Order for a Second Arrest—On the Track—The Rural Retreat—Mr. Carlisle Murray a Reformer and Lover—The Official Writ—The Astonished Landlord and Landlady—A Scene-Report.

It was during the month of November, 1861, that the existence of certain treasonable organizations, having for their object the overthrow of the Government, began to attract attention. October 17, 1861, a communication was received by the Hon. Secretary of State, purporting to give the history of a secret society in Texas, known as Knights of the Golden Circle. The particular objects of this organization were not, however, fully explained. A few days later, another letter was received at the State Department, giving similar information. On the 24th of October, Benjamin Franklin, Chief of the Philadelphia Police, arrested, on a telegraphic dispatch, a one-armed man, named Carlisle Murray, and confined him in the station-house of that city. On searching his person, mysterious papers were found, apparently containing the constitution and by-laws of the Knights of the Golden Square. Franklin sent a dispatch to me, informing me of the arrest.

I came to Philadelphia, compared the documents with the original records of the Knights of the Golden Circle in the State Department, and found them to agree—the two societies were clearly essentially one in character. In a further conversation with Murray, he claimed to be an intimate friend of a well-known merchant-prince of Boston, for whom he acted as agent. At this stage of the war so little was known of the Knights of the Golden Circle, no great importance was attached to Murray's papers, and he was released.

Before this, however, I recognized him as a somewhat distinguished individual. His name was P. H. F., who figured as Fillibuster Walker's minister from Nicaragua in 1848. A subsequent examination of the papers in Murray's possession, taken in connection with those before referred to, satisfied me that he was really a member of the Knights of the Golden Circle.

Clothed with the authority conferred by the following order, I entered upon the search after F. :—

DEPARTMENT OF STATE,
WASHINGTON, November 2, 1861.

To L. C. BAKER, Esq., Washington, D. C.:—

You will please arrest P. H. F., *alias* Carlisle Murray, and convey him to Fort Warren, Boston, Massachusetts. Examine his person and baggage, and send all papers found in his possession to this Department.

I am, sir, your obedient servant,

(Signed)   WILLIAM H. SEWARD,
Secretary of State.

He had been released some weeks before his real character was discovered. To find him then seemed a hopeless task. By intercepted letters postmarked Branford, Conn., I was soon on his track. Assuming another name, he had selected this quiet town as his temporary residence. His assumed name there I did not know; consequently must devise some plan which would lead to the knowledge of his locality. Accompanied by Franklin, I proceeded to Branford. To avoid suspicion on the part of the citizens, it was necessary that Mr. Franklin and myself should appear under an assumed character. We represented ourselves to be gun manufacturers in behalf of the Government, seeking for an eligible spot and building in which to carry forward our business. An old machine shop, not then used, answered my purpose.

When it was known that two intelligent men were about establishing business for the loyal cause, the good people of course were very anxious to serve us. The only hotel in Branford was a quiet inn, kept by a venerable couple. Here we found ourselves, strangers to all and in pursuit of a stranger, with no tangible clew to his person or place of abode. To get on good terms with "mine host" and hostess it was only necessary to state prospective plans, and that their house would be my headquarters. The old man talked freely of the facilities for my contemplated business, and of the moral and social condition of the people; inviting Franklin and myself to dine with them. Up to this time we had made no inquiry for the object of our visit, trusting to circumstances for farther developments. We soon sat down to an excellent dinner. While at the table, the old lady inquired of her husband, "Is Mr. Jackson coming down to dinner? You had better ask him." This question satisfied me that we had a distinguished guest. Who was that Mr. Jackson? I immediately rose, giving Franklin the cue, and, to the astonishment of the honest pair presiding at the table, rushed up stairs to search the house. Hurrying from room to room, at length I found the strange boarder occupying the only bedroom and parlor in the house. I said, extending my hand:

"How are you, F?"

He arose, and, politely taking my hand, said:

"You have the advantage of me."

I replied: "I believe I have; for I have a warrant for your arrest; and I don't think you have one for me."

"Oh, yes," he replied; "I recollect you now. You are from California?"

And in the coolest and most off-hand manner said:

"Why, I am glad to see anybody from California. Here is some good brandy. Well, how are my friends, McDougal and Tillford?"

He then added: "Why, Baker, this is a good joke. How did you find out where I was? I thought I had got beyond the reach of detectives. Now, the people here think me a very good man. I have lectured on temperance and religion; have a class in the Sabbath-school; and am courting one of the prettiest girls in Connecticut. This is too bad."

By this time the landlord and his wife had entered the room, having learned from Franklin French's real character, when she said:

"Why, Mr. Jackson, how could you be so wicked? These gentlemen say you are a rebel spy. To think that a secessionist has even slept under our roof. I'll have to air the bed and purify the whole house."

Then, looking at her hands and crying bitterly, she added:

"And I have washed your clothes! May the Lord forgive you, for I can't."

The scene was a mixture of the pathetic and comic rarely witnessed. The unsuspecting landlord, who had nearly reached his threescore and ten years, stood trembling with the palsy, and with a most woebegone expression, while his more demonstrative companion seemed beyond the reach of a comforting word. Then followed a hasty packing up of French's effects, and sending them down stairs, when he paid his weekly bill, and said to the landlady:

"I will return and explain this whole thing to you."

In less time than it has taken to tell the story the news had spread through the village. The pastor whose pulpit French had occupied, the postmaster and blacksmith were at the hotel. But one person could be found who objected to the proceedings, and he was a newly arrived M.D. from Texas, who at once declared his purpose to resist the order of arrest, and called upon the people to assist in rescuing the prisoner. The display of a six-shooter immediately quieted his rebellious spirit. F. was taken to New Haven, thence to Fort Warren. After a brief incarceration he was paroled by Secretary Seward; and so the matter ended. The disloyal order of the Knights of the Golden Circle was so vaguely understood that it was thought, after all, harmless to the Government.

The subjoined report to the Secretary of State will shed more light upon the character and career of F., and illustrate further the necessity of a detective police when traitors in arms and in the disguise of loyal citizens are plotting with unscrupulous hate against the Government:

WASHINGTON, *November 17, 1861.*

To the Hon. W. H. SEWARD:—

DEAR SIR—On the 2d of November I received an order from the State Department to arrest and convey to Fort Warren one P. H. F., *alias* Carlisle Murray. From an intercepted letter found in the Philadelphia post-office I had reason to believe that F. was at or near Branford, Connecticut. On the fifth instant I took officer Ben. Franklin and proceeded to the above named place. After some delay I succeeded in finding F. at a small hotel, where he had been stopping for some months. I immediately placed him under arrest, searched his person and effects, and found a number of letters, most of which seem to be a correspondence between him (F.) and a distinguished merchant, relating to the sale of certain steamboats to the United States Government belonging to this merchant. F. had represented himself to the confiding gentleman as one Carlisle Murray, who had been driven out of the South because of his Union sentiments. He also exhibited what purported to be genuine letters from the Hon. Mr. Etheridge, Andrew Johnson, Parson Brownlow and others, authorizing him to collect moneys from loyal people of the North, for the support of Parson Brownlow's paper (the *Knoxville Whig*). I have ascertained that he did collect, from the merchant already mentioned and others, about four thousand dollars. A careful perusal of the correspondence between these parties shows that the latter did make an engagement with Mr. F. to sell two steamers to our Government, and that he was to receive a certain commission for the same. During the time he was trying to sell or negotiate for the steamboats he visited the merchant at his country residence, was invited to spend the Sabbath and dine with him (which invitation F. accepted), receiving letters of introduction to prominent and wealthy citizens of Boston, New York, Brooklyn and other places. There can be no doubt but that F. is one of the most accomplished villians in America; nor that the merchant did *bona fide* enter into a contract or agreement with F. to sell certain steamboats to the United States; nor that his patron was informed of the true character of F. long before he took any steps for his arrest. The correspondence and all the facts in the case go to show: First, that F., by forged letters and misrepresentations, deceived his patron; second, that the merchant, finding F. a very shrewd, intelligent man, did employ him to sell the steamers; and third, that when he learned the real character of F., the authorities were not immediately notified by him; and when said merchant ascertained that F. could not, or would not, make a sale of the boats, he telegraphed to the authorities in Philadelphia to arrest Carlisle Murray for swindling. These are, in my opinion, about the facts relating to the matter, as far as the merchant is concerned.

Among the papers found in F.'s possession was a manuscript purporting to be the constitution and by-laws of a secret order or association, known as the Knights of the Golden Square. This document is copied almost verbatim from the constitution and by-laws of the Knights of the Golden Circle, an order that originated in Texas some two years since, the object of which was, the overthrow of the United States Government. By an ingenious wording of these papers—that is, whenever the name and objects of the order occur—the terms have been used, evidently intending to convey the impression that it was a Union order, designed to be secret in its nature, but the object of which was to be the maintenance of the cause of the North.

I am satisfied that F. is a member of the Knights of the Golden Circle; that he has copied their constitution and by-laws; that the papers found in his possession have been altered or worded differently from the original, so that, if he should at any time be suspected or arrested, these papers could not be used as evidence against him. All the letters and papers found in F.'s *possession* are forwarded to your Department.

Yours, very truly,
L. C. BAKER.

In the early stages of the war, before any police organization of the Government had been perfected or set in operation, and before blockade restrictions had been established, the whole North was flooded by a class of southern spies, correspondents, and incendiaries. That the spying and detective business was not confined to those who had made it a profession would seem to be indicated by the following letter. The writer of this precious document was an Episcopalian minister from the South, who had been employed by the rebel government to visit the North, with a view to ascertain the movements then on foot toward the organization of the army. It was written to Bishop General P. The "Joe" spoken of, was a sergeant in one of the Federal regiments, with whom an arrangement had been made by the writer to convey through the lines to the rebels any documents that might be forwarded to him for that purpose. "Joe" was ferreted out and arrested, and made a confession of the whole scheme which is referred to in the communication; to wit, the organization of a force in Philadelphia, New Jersey, and Delaware, to seize the Arsenal, Navy Yard, and public property at Philadelphia. The "friend Bob" spoken of was Bob B. (ex-senator B.), of Delaware. When the ringleaders of this conspiracy discovered that I was on their track, they immediately abandoned the scheme, or transferred their field of operations to the West, where an organization was perfected, but broken up by the arrest of Dr. D. at Indianapolis, in 1864.

PHILADELPHIA, *December* 26, 1861.

WORTHY SIR—Various good and sufficient reasons have detained me north of this point several days beyond the time specified in your instructions. First of these, I, in a room in Boston, was expatiating, as usual, upon the horrors and sin of slavery, as a matter of course, and misrepresenting, in a blundering way, its real condition. One of the chaps took up the cudgel in good earnest. He had sailed South, been in Southern ports, knew Southern people well, they were kind to the nigger, &c., &c. I invited talk, solicited conversation and information—gained his confidence, finding how freely he let himself out. I had several interviews, and finally threw off the mask, and told my real object was to gain information, in which he aided me to the extent of his utmost ability. He is a man about sixty years of age, but strong and active; and although a native-born New Englander, he hates, with a perfect ferociousness, the name of New England. Several reasons conspire to produce this. First, he has been swindled by a pious deacon, his brother-in-law, who induced his wife to forsake him; then he has mingled, to a great extent, with our people South, and cherishes a fond recollection of many of our citizens. Oh, how he swears at the Yankees. I soon ascertained that I might place implicit reliance upon his word. My respect and confidence were confirmed by the opinions entertained and freely expressed here by all classes. They represent him as a bold, outspoken secessionist. Being a man of tried and sterling bravery, the people know well that it would never do to trifle with him; and, added to this, he is worth some twenty or twenty-five thousand dollars; being quite judiciously invested, enables him to realize an income of at least three or four thousand a year, at least three-fourths of which he gives away—not in the form of common charities altogether, but gifts in the shape of loans to deserving beginners. In this way his popularity among a great many is solid, not only with those whom he has benefited, but others, whose respect for such unostentatious nobleness is challenged and secured.

Well, he is the man we need. He will go into the scheme with heart and soul. His plan is, receive orders for a stanch, swift sea-steamer from a South American power, have her quietly and expeditiously built, manned with the right kind of a crew, give out that he is going with her, let her take in a cargo of just such articles as we need at present—boots, shoes, &c.—sail, and enter the first Southern port that looks clear. I would here remark, that his plan is to have three just such steamers under way at the same time. Either this, or he will buy—each, however, from different points. Marine signal No. 8 (eight) of the Confederate States of America will be used upon entrance of our port. This, you remember, is the plan agreed upon to deceive the blockade fleet.

The day after my arrival in this place I was accosted by a venerable old beggar, who stood at a corner soliciting alms. His touching tone of voice, coupled with his meek yet respectful appearance, although in rags, attracted and interested me. I gave him a dime, and asked him carelessly where he lived, with no intention, however, of paying him a visit, but hardly knowing what to say, and feeling I ought to say something.

He replied, "You aint got any Jeames River tobacky, I reckon, to give a fellow a chaw."

Imagine my surprise when my beggar friend proved to be our old Nebo. Cute as ever, he plies his artful game. He tells me that he was in Washington last week; says old —— is drunk one-half his time. —— and —— are aying up big piles of United States money both for themselves and friends, though —— is the sharpest in the way of money. That old stupid fool, ——, is completely under the thumb of ——, —— ditto.

Nebo says that, unsuspectingly, he has been permitted to enter both the civil and military department in Washington and Alexandria. As his means of communicating with head-quarters is so very expeditious and complete, I deem it both impolitic and unnecessary to detail, in this communication, the vast amount of useful information which he is enabled to pick up. One thing I must mention. He says that in less than three months we will have Philadelphia and Baltimore. He says that as soon as the advance is made upon the .ines at W., a party here, now numbering over five thousand, in this city, together with thrice that number in the adjoining counties, will seize the Navy Yard, Arsenal, &c. His experience tallies with mine, that is, that New Jersey is sound to the back-bone for us: yes, far more so than Delaware, although a Southern State.

I am afraid to advise you to take *that* trip, for, notwithstanding the clerical cut of my coat, I am watched very closely, as are all strangers, by the Government spies. The people are heartily sick and tired of this war, but are afraid to utter such sentiments, it being treason, or so ruled by that drunken thief, ——.

Nebo says that whenever —— needs money he sends ahead some startling telegraph communications, manufactured, as a matter of course. Soon the streets of Philadelphia and New York ring with the cry of extras: "Glorious news (in big letters). Fifty thousand secessionists routed by a Union force of only one hundred and fifty. We took thirty thousand prisoners, two hundred and seventy-five thousand stand of arms, one thousand four hundred cannon, and an immense stock of ammunition. The rebel general shot in the mouth by a Buck-tail, which would have proved fatal, but just as the ball hit him he spit out a quid of tobacco, which turned the ball aside. It, however, glanced from the quid and killed a colonel and eleven privates. Our loss (Union)—two killed, three wounded, one missing."

Such, my dear general, is the windy stuff which —— uses to draw money out of the Wall Street kings. Verily, this is a humbuggy age. To my mind it is past my comprehension how the two sections can ever meet together, even in ordinary intercourse. You can form no conception of the bitter feeling of hostility entertained by all classes here. An instance or two will suffice. An interesting *pious* family, whose *savory* discourse did my *soul much good in its* growth in grace, &c., &c., whose hospitality I often enjoyed, one day last week, in making a call, I found them much excited. Upon inquiring the cause, Miss Annie informed me that they had just learned that the bonnet-maker was a vile secessionist. I straightened my eye-brows, turned up my whites, and made an appropriate pious ejaculation, and inquired how she had made the discovery. By accident, sir. Well, to sift the testimony from their verbiage, Mrs. ——, a poor widow, who makes a living for herself and children in the bonnet business, had been so imprudent as to say to my friend, "Well, I hope if they do liberate the negroes, they will make some provision for their support, for they will no longer have their owners to look to." Now, for this vile secession (!!!), my pious friends are determined not to pay their bonnet-bills until the war is over. Don't you admire their spunk? The other instance is this:—A pious elder in one of the Presbyterian churches here has a daughter married to a Southern elder, who is in the Southern army; and so bitter is his feeling, that neither daughter, child, nor husband is ever alluded to, even [in] his prayers. Indeed, my dear sir, the spirit of the wolf, the hyena, ay, rattlesnake, and all vicious animals, are let loose in the hearts of this people. There is no language sufficiently strong to describe the malignity of their feelings. Ages hence will this feeling burn. I thought some of our Hotspurs went far in their expressions of hatred and contempt, but it don't begin to touch bottom with Philadelphians. But with all this, I understand that we have a goodly heritage in this city and its vicinity. Old Nebo tells me that there is now in process of completion a scheme to be inaugurated soon upon a grand scale. It contemplates the seizure of Philadelphia. He says there is over three millions of dollars invested. He could not make me acquainted with the particulars. They are called the "Regulators." He says that several prominent military men have it [in] charge. It embraces New Jersey and Delaware. I find, however, I am repeating what I have already written in this letter.

Dr. ——'s church, during the week, is turned into a tailor shop. The Doctor is a strong coercionist in the pulpit; in the parlor he is a secessionist, or, I should say, an apologist for that *vile heresy*, Dr. ——, ditto, Dr. ——, ditto, and many others, who were converted during the days of terror last April, when our friend Bob escaped the halter in Philadelphia. Thousands here entertain earnest and anxious desires for peace, but dare not utter their thoughts even to their nearest kin. In my clerical capacity I say, that this people is given over not only to believe a lie, but lies. The truth is too tame and commonplace. They are confident that ten of their men can beat and put to rout one hundred of the South. I then ask them why their Army of the Potomac, which outnumbers the South, don't move, and crush Beauregard. They say, "Oh, that is the fault of politicians." As an Englishman, some avoid and wheedle me.   Your obedient servant,

THOMAS, the D. D.

I will be in Cleveland ten days from time first noted.

The following is a copy from a letter which accompanied the former, in similar handwriting:—

PHILADELPHIA, *December* 27, 1861.

DEAR PHIL—Joe tells me that you are about *Sin sin naughty*, as he draws it out. I detained this to say a word about the M. and G. difficulty; but you see the papers—all bosh. Send word by this, if you choose, that it will end in smoke—a flash in the pan. You can read and remember as much of the inclosed as you can. Be sure to note the figures, as they mark the name of the Sea Dog. Burn the letter unless you can safely carry, and then get in your hole and skeet for Dixie. It ought to have gone before, but I was far away when F. was here, and did not see him. Oh, how these Northern papers lie about us. Joe is a sergeant in a company of one of the regiments here—will start for Washington soon. If he gets on picket duty he will communicate. Direct your letters to Rev. ——, D. D. (be sure to put the D. D.), of Bath, England. Good-by, and G. B. Y.

TOM.

CHAPTER VI.

DISLOYALTY AMONG THE POSTMASTERS.

A Mystery—The Result of Cabinet Meetings in Washington known in Richmond—The Detectives learn the Reason—A Visit to Lower Maryland—Amusing Scenes—The Mysterious Box—The Reports—A Rebel Letter.

IT was a surprising fact during the first six or eight months after the war began, that the result of every Cabinet meeting at Washington was reported in Richmond within twenty-four hours after it was held. The secret was, that every postmaster in Lower Maryland, comprising the counties of St. Charles, St. George, and St. Mary's, with three exceptions, were disloyal. It had been taken for granted that the State was true to the Government, while rebel emissaries were constantly conveying information from Washington to the post-offices along the Potomac, from which it was transmitted to Fredericksburg by blockade-runners and spies, and thence telegraphed to Richmond. By this arrangement, uninterrupted and unrestrained communication was kept open between the rebels North and South until November 20. 1861, when I decided, if possible, to break up the treasonable correspondence. Accordingly, the Secretary of War directed that three companies, of one hundred men each, from the Third Indiana Cavalry, then in General Hooker's division at Budd's Ferry, be detached, and report to me for the purpose of visiting and, if necessary, permanently occupying Lower Maryland.

The first post-office upon which I called was at Chaptico, a small village at the head of a bay of the Potomac, bearing the same name, and about sixty miles from Washington. I reached the village late one afternoon, when an amusing incident occurred, illustrating the ignorance in the country generally, more profound, perhaps, in some portions of it respecting military affairs, resulting from the peaceful pursuits of the people during a long period of declining martial spirit and demonstrations.

The first military seen in Chaptico was my advent with three hundred of "Uncle Sam's boys," which naturally created intense excitement among this rural people.

My force was composed principally of Germans, who became brave soldiers subsequently in the western battlefields. They were addicted, of course, to the use of intoxicating drinks; hence it was necessary to encamp apart from places where liquors were sold. I entered the town with my orderly, to notify all vendors of strong drink to close their bars, and under no circumstances to sell to the soldiers under my command.

In the evening, to my surprise, when passing one of the drinking-houses, I found it full of troops who, with the landlord, were having a jolly time over their potations.

I immediately stepped in and inquired of the host:

"Did I not give you an order not to sell liquor to my men?"

"Why, Colonel," he said, "these ain't no soldiers; they are officers. They have got swords on."

Officers generally wearing swords, the cavalrymen thus armed deceived the benighted dealer in poor whisky and beer. He was sure that he was honored with men quite above common soldiering.

I proceeded to the post-office, and found the postmaster sick and all the family in about the same plight, excepting a bright little girl, twelve years of age.

I rapped at the door, when she raised the window and said:

"Father told me I must not let any of the Yankee soldiers in."

I replied: "I am not a Yankee soldier, but an agent of the Post-office Department."

I was then admitted; and asked where the office was kept. She pointed to a box of pigeon holes. While examining it, I accidentally observed a rough pine box with iron hasp and hinges and a United States mail lock. It was partitioned through the center, with a hole for letters in each division. Over one part was "Southern Letters;" over the other, "Northern Letters."

I said: "What is this box for?"

She innocently answered, pointing to the inscriptions:

"Why, the letters put in that hole (the Southern) go to Richmond; and those in the other go to Washington."

The postmaster, who was in bed, overhearing her, spoke somewhat excitedly:

"No, that ain't so; why do you tell the gentleman such a story?"

I answered: "I guess the girl tells the truth."

Taking the box, which, upon examination, was found to contain letters from rebels on the way to the Confederacy, and those whose hearts, if not their faces, were toward rebeldom, I placed it in the Post-office Department at Washington as a curiosity, where it still remains.

At L., the largest village in all that part of Lower Maryland, another amusing incident occurred. It had long been the residence of aristocratic families. A weekly newspaper was published there—a paper which was pre-eminent in fanning the fires of rebellion throughout that region.

Arriving within two miles of the town at evening, I encamped in a grove of pines. With a captain, sergeant, and two orderlies I rode into the village, and found the people had heard of our arrival. The principal men of the place waited upon me and protested in the most violent manner against Yankee troops disturbing their peace; for they were "State-rights people, who only wished to be let alone." They made threats of personal violence if my soldiers were brought into Leonardtown.

I replied: "I am here under orders of the Secretary of War, on a peaceful investigation, and not as charged, to steal your slaves, to burn your houses and barns, or to molest the inhabitants. I have money to pay for forage and rations if you will sell them; if not, shall take them."

By this time the editor of the paper had become boisterous in his condemnation of the Government and its officers. I quietly directed a guard to be placed around his printing-office. Selecting from my command Judge L. of

Cleveland, Ohio, an officer who had some experience as an editor, I directed him to write an article for the paper, in which the rebel editor was made to recant his secession heresy and declare for the Union, advising all his subscribers to do the same. The compositors were compelled to set it up, and then the pressmen reluctantly struck off the paper. The subscription book was consulted, and to each name a copy of the paper was mailed. The excitement and indignation which followed the distribution of the suddenly loyal sheet, and the discovery of the serious joke, made one of the most ludicrous incidents in my official experience. The further results of this expedition are presented in the subjoined note and reports:

WASHINGTON, *November* 25, 1861.

Brigadier-General HOOKER, Commanding at Budd's Ferry:

DEAR SIR—The expedition under my command to the lower coast of Maryland has proved successful. We captured four mounted traitors and one rebel *spy*. Mr. Seward is much gratified at the promptness with which you responded to the orders given to me. Also obtained many valuable letters and documents, from which important results will follow. To Captain Keister and Lieutenant Lemon, I am under many obligations; I found them very prompt and ready to act at all times. The men under their command conducted themselves with the greatest propriety. A detachment of sixteen men, as a guard, accompanied me by steamer *via* Baltimore to this city. I return them to their quarters to-day. Allow me to return you my thanks for your extreme kindness to me during my short stay at your headquarters.

Yours, truly,

L. C. BAKER.

WASHINGTON, *November* 27, 1861.

To the Hon. WILLIAM H. SEWARD, Secretary of State:

DEAR SIR—In compliance with orders issued from your Department, under date of November 18th, I repaired to the headquarters of Brigadier-General Hooker, at or near Budd's Ferry, and was promptly furnished with one hundred men from the Third Indiana Cavalry, under command of Captain Keister. The object of the expedition was to arrest parties suspected of rendering aid to Virginia rebels, to discover the channel through which contraband correspondence was being carried on, and, if necessary, to take into custody any persons found in arms against the United States Government. On my arrival at Port Tobacco, the headquarters of Colonel Graham's regiment, I found the inhabitants complaining bitterly at their alleged ill-treatment, and depredations committed by the soldiers under his command. In justice to Colonel G., however, I found, on inquiring, that the inhabitants had been the first aggressors. There are residing at this place but four or five Union men—the balance either being sympathizers with secessionists, or open and avowed aiders and abettors of treason. The postmaster at this place is secretly doing all in his power to further the interests of the Confederacy. Eight miles from the above-named locality is a small town, known as Allen's Fresh. There are but two Union men at this place. I found in the post-office here five letters, addressed to fictitious names; on opening them, I discovered that they contained sealed letters, addressed to well-known secessionists in Virginia. The postmaster was one of those who assisted and contributed to organize and equip Confederate soldiers now in Virginia. At the Newport post-office, some two miles from Allen's Fresh, I found a package of thirty-four letters, post-marked "Newport P. O., Maryland," all ready to be forwarded to different localities at the North. On examining these letters, I found that they were all written in Virginia, and had all been dropped into the office by one person. At Chaptico, a place of about two or three hundred inhabitants, located at the head of a small inlet opening into the Potomac, I found but four Union men, the traitors at this point having threatened to hang and burn the property of any man who dares to avow Union sentiments. At this point, there has been carried on for months a regular communication with Virginia. The postmaster here openly declares himself a traitor; I should have placed him under arrest, but found him confined in his bed with chills and fever, besides having a large family depending on him for their daily support. I next stopped at Leonardtown. This is the largest and by far the most prosperous village in Lower Maryland. I do not consider it safe to say that there is one Union man in the town or vicinity, although many declare themselves *State Rights Men*, which is but a milder term for secessionists. At this place has been enlisted, equipped, and conveyed to Virginia, a very large number of men for the Confederate army. But very few hesitate to declare openly their secession sentiments; I think this is attributable almost wholly to the publication of a bitter and uncompromising secession paper, published in this place. I found in the post-office a large number of letters going to and coming from Virginia. The postmaster, a Mr. Yates, declared himself to me a good Union man; I, however, afterward obtained the most undeniable proof of his disloyalty to the Government and sympathy with the rebels. I think that Leonardtown should be at once placed under martial law, and a provost-marshal appointed, in order that the few Union men residing there may have some kind of protection against these traitors. From Leonardtown I went to Great Mills, a distance of twelve miles. There are but few inhabitants residing directly on the road, the population being mostly on the Potomac and Pawtuxent rivers. Daily steamboat communication from Baltimore to Millstone Landing (a point on the Pawtuxent river, near its mout) has, in my opinion, made this the most important point in Lower Maryland That you may more readily understand with what facilities correspondence and goods of all descriptions have and are being transported into Virginia by this route, I annex a map of the country. The distance from Millstone Landing, on the Pawtuxent, to Redmond's Landing, at the head of St. Mary's river (four miles from the Potomac), is but eight miles, the road being excellent at all seasons of the year. There are but four or five Union men in this vicinity; most of those who have declared themselves as such have either been driven from the county, or dare not avow themselves in favor of the Government. A number are now residing in the neighborhood who hold commissions in the rebel army. It is, however, exceedingly difficult to arrest them; the approach of any considerable number of troops is a signal for these cheats to leave their houses, or secrete themselves, and it can only be accomplished by the most shrewd and well-laid plans. I made the following arrests, viz.: E. H. J., W. M. A., E. M. S., and R. L. H. These men were a part of an organization known as the Lower Maryland Vigilance Committee.

Mr. E. H. J. resides at what is known as the Old Factory, St. Mary's County, is engaged in merchandising, farming, &c. When the present difficulties broke out, J. went to Baltimore, and was there during the riot of April 19th. On his return hence, he brought not less than four hundred stands of arms from Baltimore, which afterward were sent to Virginia. He has had wagons for hauling contraband goods from the Potomac to the Patuxent, during the greater part of the summer and fall. He made his house the headquarters of secession spies, passing to and from Virginia; has enlisted, equipped, and forwarded a large number of men for the Confederacy; has notified Union men to leave the county; and has, on all occasions, cursed and abused the Government.

D. W. M. A. resides about one mile from J., openly defies the Government, was a co-operator with J. in all his treasonable operations; is said to be the secretary of the Vigilance Committee, and stated to me, after his arrest, that he would yet kill a Yankee for every day that he was imprisoned by the Government.

E. M. S. is a Confederate spy. He was indicted by the Baltimore grand jury for engaging in the riot of the 19th of April, but made his escape into Virginia, and, up to the time of his arrest, had kept out of the way. Some memorandums of importance were found in his possession.

The arrest of B. L. H. will prove of the greatest importance to the Government. H. resided at the landing on the Patuxent River, and made his hotel the rendezvous for all the secessionists in the county. At his house were held all their meetings and deliberations. He had two teams constantly running from the landing to the Potomac River. I have the most positive proof that, the night before his arrest, he took three hundred Colt revolvers to Virginia; I found two large boxes buried in the sand, about two hundred yards from his house, from which he took these revolvers. Mrs. H. informed me that she had frequently cautioned her husband that he would yet be caught and imprisoned by the Government, but he disregarded her advice, and told her that he was determined to make money in some way. Some letters were found in his possession of the strongest secession character, also Confederate envelopes, stamps, circulars, &c. H. was the master spirit, and the worst man in the county.

Much difficulty was experienced in making these arrests. The county is wild and unsettled; a complete set of signals had been established among the inhabitants, and notice of our arrival had been given to the entire country making it necessary to move only at night-time. I endeavored, stating that, as soon as the troops left, their building would be burned, and they themselves assassinated or hung by the Committee.

I am much indebted for my success to Brigadier-General Hooker, for his promptness in furnishing men; to Captain Keister, for the energy, patience, and promptness with which he aided me at all times; to A. G. Lawrence, Esq., who accompanied me from this city, for the very efficient aid and advice he gave at all times. Some small-arms, two kegs of rifle powder, secession flags, and other articles were seized.

Since my return, I have had some conversation with the Postmaster-General in relation to mail matters. When I go down again, he has authorized me to displace all disloyal postmasters, and if safe and reliable Union men can be found, to recommend them for appointment; if such can not be found, discontinue the offices altogether. This course, I have no doubt, will induce them to better regard and appreciate the favors they have and are still receiving from the Government. In order that the channels of communication with the South may be effectually broken up, and protection afforded to Union men in Charles and St. Mary's counties, I would most respectfully recommend that a military force be sent there at once. Two or three hundred men could subsist themselves and horses, without being compelled to transport forage. Should you deem it proper or advisable to send such a force, I would gladly go with them, and render all the assistance in my power. Asking pardon for this my lengthy communication,

I remain, dear Sir, most respectfully,

Your obedient servant,

L. C. BAKER.

WASHINGTON, *January* 14, 1862.

To the Honorable POSTMASTER-GENERAL:—

DEAR SIR—At your request, I herewith send report of the condition in which I found the several post-offices located in Charles and St. Mary's counties, Maryland. At Port Tobacco, numerous and repeated complaints have been forwarded to me by detective agents of the Government, concerning the loyalty of the postmaster at this place. Charges of the most grave and aggravated character have been made by the few Union men residing in this vicinity. On investigation, I found that he has, on three different occasions, received packages of letters, post-marked at Baltimore, and forwarded same to Virginia. On or about the 15th October, a Confederate spy mailed at this office one hundred and forty letters, which he (the spy) brought direct from Virginia. This was done with the full knowledge and consent of the postmaster. In addition to this, he has aided and advised a number of young men in the neighborhood to cross the river and join the Confederate army.

Allen's Fresh.—The postmaster at this place seldom if ever attends personally to the duties of the office, but leaves the business in the hands of a young boy, some twelve or fourteen years old. I found in this office nine

MARYLAND POSTMASTERS.   115

uncalled-for letters, having been addressed to fictitious names, on opening them, I found they were addressed to individuals in the so-called Confederate States. The postmaster in this place is disloyal and can not be trusted.

Newport.—In this office, I found a package of fifty-two letters, written by parties now residing in the rebel States, addressed to persons in Baltimore. The postmaster is a first-class rebel. In my opinion, this office could be discontinued, it being located but two miles from Allen's Fresh.

Charlotte's Hall.—But one contraband letter was found in this office. The postmaster assures me that he is a good Union man, and is doing all he can to assist and forward the interests of the Government. I think him a highly intelligent gentleman, but hardly *sound*.

Oakville.—This office is located in a thrifty, settled community, and is but of little importance; being some distance from the Potomac, has less facilities than other offices for conducting contraband mail matter. I consider the postmaster a loyal, good, and reliable man.

Chaptico.—From the peculiar location of this office (being situated at the head of Chaptico Bay), the postmaster has very superior facilities for conducting a large contraband business, which he has not failed to improve to a greater extent than any other officer in Lower Maryland. Indeed, he openly boasts that he holds two appointments as postmaster—one from Washington, and one from Richmond. A large number of contraband letters were found in his office. In addition to this, he is an habitual drunkard, neglecting the duties of his office; he has repeatedly neglected to lock the mail-bag; has often left the key in the bag, and often refused to open the mail at all. From the importance of this office, it could hardly be discontinued without a positive injury to a large number of good and loyal citizens.

Leonardtown.—This is the largest village or town in Lower Maryland. Charges of disloyalty have repeatedly been made against the postmaster of this place, many of which I have thoroughly investigated. He (Yates) styles himself a State Rights man, which is but a mild term for secession. A number of contraband letters were found in his office, but he positively denies knowing the writers, or the parties to whom they are addressed. The citizens generally speak in the highest terms of him, and, so far as I can judge, the office was well managed. Everything seems to be conducted with a great deal of system and regularity. As no better man could be induced to take the office, I should think a change not advisable at present.

Great Mills.—This is an office of some importance, being located midway between the Pawtuxent river and the head of St. Mary's, by opening directly into the Potomac. In September last, acting under an order from your department, I seized the entire contents of the office. About one-fourth of the mail was directed (under cover) to the Confederate States. I think, however, the postmaster is a loyal citizen, but has been very negligent in his duties. Not desiring to incur the hatred of the secession community in which he resided, he has allowed letters to be received at his office from the rebel States, addressed to well-known traitors, without reporting the same to the proper authorities. I think a change should be made at this office at once.

Saint Inagoes.—This office is of but little importance; but few letters received or mailed. I have heard no complaints against the postmaster here, hence I conclude he is loyal.

From the very meager amount realized, I have found it exceedingly difficult to find good, reliable, loyal men, who would accept the appointment of postmaster. Many who are competent will not devote the necessary time required to perform the duties of the office. I have, however, obtained the names and consent of loyal citizens who will accept an appointment at a number of the offices mentioned in this report, and, as soon as I can complete the list, I shall forward the same to your department. I consider it a matter of the greatest importance to the Government, at this time, that our postmasters should be loyal and true to the Union, particularly when their offices can by any possibility be used in any manner as a medium to convey information to the Confederate States. To discontinue altogether our mail facilities in Lower Maryland, at present time, would result in a great inconvenience and injury to the few loyal people residing in that section, as well as our military forces, which, at my suggestion, have been stationed along the Potomac, to break up the contraband trade so successfully carried on during the past summer.

I am, most respectfully,
Your obedient servant,
(Signed) L. O. BAKER,
Special Agent P. O. Depart., and Government Detective.

A letter which was intercepted about this time will reveal the demoniac spirit of the rebellion, which, I regret to know, exists still to an alarming extent in the conquered South:—

NANJEMOY, *December* 19, 1862.

Dr. HATLING:—

I expect to go from home soon, under another permit, to Nanjemoy, and want to make a good thing of it—*better than before*. What I say about the permit, is confidential; don't forget.

I suppose you have heard but little of the truth of the *little* skirmish before Fredericksburg. Abolition, with *Burnside* at its head, was somewhat scorched. At least thirty thousand were made to bite the dust. The *strangled* newspapers on this side *dare not* tell half the truth. I have my information from officers and men who were on the field, and in the battle. They say the slaughter can never be described or forgotten by those who saw it. They lay by thousands upon a single acre. The Southern blood was fully up; they spared nothing, but slew the *cringing, cowardly,* wiglish *Abolitionists* with an unspar'ng hand.

The Southern loss was comparatively small, it is thought not over fifteen hundred, though nothing can be definitely known, yet awhile, on the subject. It was doubtless the greatest slaughter ever made on this continent. But will it teach the *fools* at Washington wisdom? I hope so. Report reached here yesterday, that Burnside, Stanton, and Halleck have resigned. Lincoln, Seward, &c., ought to follow suit. And then commence and hang every Abolitionist and Black Republican, and the balance may have some peace The sooner this is done the better.

Your friend,

(Signed) A. W. O.

CHAPTER VII.

FRAUDS—DISLOYALTY IN MARYLAND.

The Freighted Traveler—Treason and Frauds overlooked in the Rising Storm of Rebellion—The Bankers—The Pretty Smuggler—Reliable Character of the Detective Bureau—Disloyalty, and its Punishments in Lower Maryland—The Friends of Hon. Montgomery Blair and the Quinine Traffic—"Chinook" Telegrams.

THERE was about this time a rather marked illustration of a common means of transporting contraband goods across the lines. The extent to which such methods of deception were resorted to by both men and women shows the stringency of the blockade at which the rebels sneered for a while, and the mania for speculation amid the horrors of war.

I went to the wharf at Baltimore to watch the movements of a suspicious passenger who had gone just before me to embark.

He succeeded in passing the scrutiny of Provost-Marshal McPhail, and went on board the steamer bound South. I followed him, and became satisfied that I had tracked an old offender. I accordingly addressed him, when he denied any disloyal designs. His hat had a peculiar appearance—seemed heavier than it ought to be. Removing it, I saw that the interior was conical in form, the base fitting his head. I struck the top of the crown upon the rail of the boat, when a cloud of quinine dust rose in the air. The rogue stood disclosed; and my first business was to secure his weapons of defense, if he had any. A pistol was found and seized. This weapon and the knife are the universal means of protection, and used in ways unknown to any but villains and their captors. On one occasion a man had his Deringer in his pantaloons pocket, and with his hand was turning it to fire at me *through his pocket*, when I sprang upon him and took it.

The brief report, which will give further particulars in Wilson's case, alludes to the search for him in Maryland, where, to escape the detectives, he sprang from a window in the second story of a dwelling and got away:—

WASHINGTON, *December* 30, 1861.

To the Honorable SECRETARY OF STATE:—

DEAR SIR—On the morning of the 19th instant, I arrested, on board the steamer *Mary Washington*, in Baltimore, one William Wilson. Upon searching his person, I found concealed in his overcoat pocket a large druggist's jar, containing three ounces of quinine, a package of letters addressed to parties in Europe, and a number of photographs. I also found in Wilson's hat, very ingeniously concealed, twenty ounces of quinine. From reliable information received since the arrest, I am satisfied that Wilson is the notorious "Bill Wilson," of St. Mary's county, Maryland, and the individual for whose arrest the Government lately offered a large reward. Wilson had on his person British papers, showing that he had traveled in Europe as an Englishman.

He is now confined in Fort McHenry, awaiting the orders of the State Department.

I consider him a very dangerous man to be at large.

Yours, very respectfully,

L. C. BAKER.

The storm of civil war came so suddenly upon us, that how to meet it was the great, absorbing question. The Cabinet, Congress, and the loyal masses at the North were intensely aroused to the need of men and money to beat back the wanton assault of treason upon our nationality.

Consequently, scarcely a thought was given to the possibility of disloyalty and frauds at home. The eye was fixed upon the dark horizon of Southern revolt; while within our own brighter one were plots and robberies of the public treasury, whose disclosure was as startling as it was sickening to every patriotic heart.

An example of rebel perfidy and disregard of oaths in the highest class of capitalists was discovered toward the close of 1861. The house of J., Bros. & Co., bankers, in Baltimore, whose business previous to the rebellion was principally with Southern banks, applied to the Hon. Simon Cameron for a permit to visit friends at the South. Mr. Cameron had known the members of this firm to be of the first respectability, and gave the desired pass.

After this was used, another was obtained, until a large number had been obtained and had served well the purpose of the enterprising bankers.

I received information that one of the firm was engaged in conveying large amounts back and forth in connection with the banking house of P. M., Richmond; and that this means was resorted to for the transaction of business which months before had been pronounced contraband.

I determined to detect the offenders in the act, and expose their disloyalty.

Mr. J. was arrested at the Relay House, with his servant, and upon examination of his baggage a large amount of exchange and rebel correspondence was found.

When the pass taken from Mr. J. and all the facts were presented to Mr. Seward, he directed the seizure of the bank. It was decided to make a thorough examination of the vaults. The firm refusing to give up the keys of them, they were broken open, and revealed the shameful truth that the house had been for months acting contrary to a well-known order of the President prohibiting trade with the South.

The next day I was directed by Mr. Seward to visit the War Department by eleven o'clock A. M. I repaired accordingly to his office, and was ushered into the presence of President Lincoln, Secretaries Seward and Cameron, and Thomas A. Scott, and requested to identify the passes issued to J. I cannot pretend to say how far Mr. Cameron was imposed upon by his banking friends, or to what extent the disclosure subsequently influenced his course. Mr. J. was sent to Fort McHenry, and the bank remained for a long time closed.

Not far removed in date of occurrence, another form of fraudulent speculation, of which an instance among the male traitors has been recorded in the experience of "Billy Wilson," presented itself under a new and very amusing aspect.

I was standing on the steamboat wharf at the foot of Seventh Street, Washington, with some of my assistants, when a pretty and tastefully dressed woman stepped from a carriage and cast a restless, inquiring glance upon the miscellaneous crowd around her. This little peculiarity attracted my attention. For, not unfrequently, the clew to a crime and its perpetrator is given by such signals, of both which only a detective of some experience would observe. An anxious look, a passing expression of the face, a confused manner or answer to a question, becomes the key to unlock a great and dark mystery of wrong.

I closely watched the fair traveler as she walked upon the narrow, *springy* plank to the boat, and saw that the foot-bridge yielded to her step quite too much for her natural weight. I was satisfied, upon a nearer observation, that under her light outer dress there was a heavier garment than anything in the usual contents of the female wardrobe.

I politely accosted her in the saloon, and said:

"Madam, what have you concealed under your dress?"

"Nothing, sir," she sharply replied, "that I have not a right to carry."

"See here, my lady; just step into that state-room, and relieve yourself of the contraband goods without further ceremony or trouble."

She disappeared, and a moment later, from the partially opened door spitefully threw a skirt, in which was quilted *forty pounds* of sewing silk, saying:

"I suppose you think that you are very smart."

I quietly replied: "Smart enough for you, madam;" rolled up the valuable garment, and left her to her own reflections.

In the introduction to this volume, I said that it was the aim, and to some extent a successful one, I think, to give to the Detective Bureau a character second to no other part of the national service in reliability. No man, however successful in his particular work, was allowed to remain in my employment if found to be wanting in integrity. I quote one case from several on this point.

Mr. M., in accordance with the subjoined order, was arrested and confined in the Old Capitol Prison:

WASHINGTON, *March* 12, 1862.

To the Honorable P. H. WATSON, Assistant Secretary of War:

DEAR SIR—In compliance with your order of the 6th, I herewith forward report in the case of S. M. M., a detective agent of the United States Government, charged by John Evans, John Bradshaw, and others, captains of schooners engaged on the Potomac, with having at sundry times blackmailed or extorted money illegally from them.

1st. Mr. S. M. M. is not, nor has been at any time, in my employ. On or about the 12th of January, 1862, Mr. M. was appointed by the State Department as a detective agent, and was ordered to report to me. I immediately sent him to Alexandria, Virginia, for the purpose of watching all suspected persons; giving him no authority to arrest or seize property of any description without first obtaining, through me, the proper order from the State Department.

On the 10th instant, I applied to Mr. Allen, before and by whom the affidavits forwarded to your department were acknowledged, and ascertained that the charges were *true*, except as to date, and some other minor discrepancies, which do not in any manner alter the charges or affect the matter. So far as Mr. M. is concerned, I consider the charges made in the affidavits proved, and deeply regret that any officer with whom I have had any connection should be guilty of such conduct.

If any class of men in the employ of the Government at this time should be honest and trustworthy, it is its confidential agents.

I respectfully suggest that you order me officially to discharge Mr. S. M. M. immediately.

I am, Sir, your obedient servant,
(Signed) L. C. BAKER,
Government Detective, War Department.

Several weeks before the occurrences which will soon be narrated, information had been conveyed to the War Department, from Lower Maryland, of treasonable designs and operations of the people residing there. The loyal few entered their complaint in words which I shall quote:—

GREAT MILLS P. O.,
ST. MARY'S COUNTY, *November* 18, 1861.

Hon. SIMON CAMERON, Secretary of War:—

DEAR SIR—Being a loyal citizen of Maryland, I regard it an imperative duty to inform the Government of some facts which I hope the Government may recognize.

There is a set of men here who have done, and are still doing, all in their power to aid the rebel army. They have used the most treasonable language toward the Government; they have harbored, fed, and equipped, in every sense of the word, a great many men, and then have conveyed them to Virginia. I also firmly believe they have arms buried in a churchyard, ready to use upon the Union people here, should the opportunity offer. These men have done much against the Union cause here. At the recent election, they tried to have men vote who acknowledged they had been to Virginia to bear arms against the Government, and did finally succeed in regard to some who had been to the rebels, in the face of all I could do. We polled many more votes than they anticipated, and they now threaten our lives and property, and say they will drive us from our homes.

They organized a vigilance committee, and waited upon many Union men, and even forced one citizen to leave the county; this, sir, would be confirmed by all the Union men in the district. I shall take here the liberty to append the names of these men. As I have said before, if the chance offers itself, our lives and property are in danger. Since the election, their hatred has become bitter, since they see the majority in the State for the Government.

I now beg to say a few words in regard to the gentlemen who have been elected by the disunionists to serve in the Legislature. They have publicly said they owe no allegiance to the Government, and they further say they are not citizens of the United States, and also say they had rather see the Government sink to hell, than to see the Southern Confederacy lose the slightest victory.

These, sir, are the men elected as our guardians in the two branches of the Legislature. We, the Union men of St. Mary's county, do solemnly protest against these men, and contend, as the true and loyal citizens of Maryland they do in no wise represent our views, and believe that these men will not defend our rights, and redress our grievances in the both Houses. We sir, believe that a Camanche has as much right, and would as soon recognize one, as *the* men forced upon us by the rebels. We beg protection in our county, and in the Legislature, by the *removal* of these men from our midst. They are still carrying a great many goods, and I believe some ammunition and arms to the rebels.

Captain Gray, of one the cutters in the Potomac, I much fear will have trouble by his gentlemanly conduct and courtesy toward the rebels here. I heard from them that they intended a party of them, sufficient in number, to go aboard to *dine* or exchange courtesies, and seize the vessel and crew, and run them into Virginia. This is from these men whom I shall give the names of. We beg that these men may be taken out of our midst, and sent away from us. They threaten us in the most unmeasured terms. I beg to know if we are recognized, that I may appease the fears of our people here. Many of them are much frightened, as the rebels are largely in the ascendency, and they threaten desolation. Take the men whose names I here append, and all will be well with us—as loyal people.

Your obedient servant,

JOHN R. BISCOE,
Great Mills P. O.,
St. Mary's County, Maryland.

To HON. SIMON CAMERON, Secretary of War.

Those elected to the Legislature: for Senate, L. B.; House delegates, B. G. Harris, Esq., J. F. D.; Aiders and abettors: H. J. C. and son, J. D. F. and son, B. K., B. H., Dr. F. S., Dr. A. L., I. A., and J. A., E. H. J., S. H., M. H.

F. O., T. S., J. G., Dr. A., W. O. A., B. H., and in fact every rebel here, have done something to contribute to the rebel forces.

Yours,

J. B.

The paper had this indorsement:—

Hon. WILLIAM H. SEWARD:—

Inclosed is a list of candidates that I think are fair subjects for Fort Warren.

THOMAS A. SCOTT, Asst. Sec. of War.

Before leaving Washington, I was directed by Mr. Seward to exercise my own judgment and discretion as to the arrest of these persons, furnished with the following order:—

DEPARTMENT OF STATE,
WASHINGTON, *November* 19, 1861.

To Brigadier-General DANIEL E. SICKLES, &c., &c., &c., or General HOOKER:—

GENERAL—The bearer of this is Mr. I. C. Baker, a detective in the employ of this department, whom I have requested to look after some disloyal persons in St. Mary's county, Maryland. I will thank you to render him any assistance in the discharge of his duty that he may require.

I am, General, very respectfully,

Your obedient servant,

F. W. SEWARD,

Assistant Secretary.

Further facts, in addition to those already in my possession, determined my action in this matter.

I selected the names of eight persons to be arrested; among them, one H., residing on Patuxent river, near its mouth, at a place called Millstone Landing.

H., aside from his secession heresy, was a man of notoriously bad character, and the terror of his neighborhood. An old resident, he had become familiar with all the streams, bays, inlets, &c., of that region, including the Potomac and Patuxent rivers, and Chesapeake bay. The character of the man, and this knowledge of the country, made him a fit tool, and valuable member of the band of blockade runners and spies, who resorted to his house as their place of rendezvous.

For ten days before I was on his track, he had slept in the woods, from fear of being taken.

As an evidence of rebel zeal, they had arranged a system

of signals, to give the alarm whenever a detective or Government agent appeared in the vicinity.

During the day, strips of white cotton cloth were carelessly suspended from the windows of their residences, or from a tree or shrub, to give notice of the arrival. In the night, the signal was the blowing of tin horns.

In view of these facts, and to accomplish the purpose of arresting the traitors, the greatest caution was necessary.

I therefore divided my force of a hundred men into eight or ten parties, giving each officer a minute description of the residence of the man to be arrested. Aware that the arrest of any one of the band before the others would immediately alarm them, these squads all left camp at the same time, with the understanding that, whether the arrests were made or not, the whole company should rendezvous at a certain point the next morning at eight o'clock. A more inclement and a wilder night I have rarely known.

The streams were swollen by rains, and the darkness great, which tended to make the expedition very uncertain and uncomfortable.

With the thirteen men who accompanied me, at two o'clock A. M., I surrounded the house of H. On knocking at the door, I gained no response. Forcing my entrance into the house, I was confronted by H. with a loaded pistol who desired to know my errand. I replied:

"H., your house is surrounded, and I have come to take you prisoner. Give me that pistol." He did so reluctantly.

Upon searching the house, I found six notorious blockade runners in the upper story. Two were on their way to "Dixie" with mail, and four returning, and conveying letters of more or less importance North.

Naturally enough, the company were greatly disconcerted.

I put these under arrest, and, while searching outhouses, found the "intelligent contraband." Upon questioning him, I learned where a large number of pistols and sabers, which he had *carted* to their place of interment, on their way South, were buried. From him I also ascertained that a large square box, containing Sharp's rifles, was buried in a Catholic church-yard three miles from the river.

Upon application to the Rev. Mr. ——, pastor of the flock worshiping there, he treated my statements with ridicule, and refused to let me desecrate the "hallowed ground," pronouncing the act wanton sacrilege. He denounced the Government for permitting it.

I proceeded to the burial-place with the contraband, who pointed out the grave. When my men commenced throwing out the dirt, the priest approached, and with uplifted hands exclaimed : " Is it possible that, in this enlightened age, men can be found who will willfully desecrate the resting-place of the dead !"

I continued the work of exhuming the treasure until a new and large pine box was found and raised to the surface. It contained fifty-six Sharp's rifles, with fifty rounds of ammunition each.

My clerical friend exclaimed, with apparent surprise, "I wonder how those arms could have got there !"

It may be well to state here, that one of the fondest dreams of the people of Lower Maryland was, that at some future day the rebel army would cross the Potomac, and have on the nearer shore to Washington a base of operations against the capital. Therefore these people had long been secreting arms and ammunition, to be ready for this grand movement.

My plan, which has been before referred to, but partially succeeded, owing to the fact that the arrival of the military was known.

Dr. S., a prominent rebel, had left his home on the first intimation of our approach. His house was visited the next day, but he was not at home.

My squad were hungry, and asked for dinner. The women at once began to prepare it. Among the inviting dishes was a roasted opossum. We all ate heartily, and, besides paying liberally for the meal, we kindly thanked our fair hostess for the satisfactory repast.

Upon reaching camp we were taken ill, and in a few hours three out of the five were in a dangerous condition.

A physician was called, who said : "These men have been poisoned. What have they been eating ?"

No explanation could be then given ; but it was afterward ascertained that the opossum had *extra dressing* for our special benefit.

H., with seven of his comparions, was confined in Fort Lafayette a year.

The name will again appear in the record of a later period, in a light no more flattering.

I learned about this time that persons connected with distinguished politicians were engaged in suspicious business in Washington. The names were Mrs. T., Miss L. B. B., and M. B. B., a Baptist minister.

I also learned that Mrs. T. was the mother of Miss B., the sister-in-law of Hon. Montgomery Blair, Postmaster-General, and that Mrs. T. and her friends resided in Fauquier County, Virginia. The passes had been procured on the recommendation of Postmaster Blair, to give these persons the opportunity to get a few of the "necessaries of life."

An espionage of the visitors disclosed a traffic in quinine of considerable extent.

They had visited three drug stores, and purchased *six hundred* ounces. This was taken to the house of Mr. Gallagher, brother of Miss B. To ascertain in what way the quinine was to be conveyed, resort was had again to the contraband.

A negro servant at Mr. Gallagher's house soon reported that Miss B. was engaged in making a skirt formed of sections, or long pockets, lined with oiled silk.

The smugglers were so closely watched that every movement in the purchase was known within half an hour after it occurred.

I had decided not to arrest them until they were over our lines. After they left Washington, I called on the Hon. Mr. Blair, and told him the particulars in regard to his friends; when and where the medicine was obtained; the manufacture of the skirt for its transportation, &c. I further apprised him that they had that morning started for home. Mr. Blair listened to my story, and then pleasantly remarked: "Why, Baker, those persons are as loyal as you are, and I loaned them the money."

Then taking his bank book from his drawer, he added:

"See; I have just had my note for five hundred dollars discounted to help these poor people."

I replied: "Mr. Blair, I cannot be mistaken about this."

Exhibiting much impatience at my positiveness, he said: "Well, arrest them; and if you find the quinine, put them in the Old Capitol."

Three miles over the lines, I stopped the travelers, and informed Miss B. that I wanted to examine the skirt. She immediately went into a farm-house, took off the garment, and threw it down indignantly, saying: "So this is the way you treat Southern ladies."

The whole party were then escorted to Washington.

Miss B. and Mr. B. were lodged in the Old Capitol prison. Upon reporting the facts to the Secretary of War, he directed me turn the quinine over to the medical director, the horse and wagon to the quartermaster, and the groceries to the hospitals.

The next morning the Hon. Montgomery Blair and Miss B. called, and demanded the restoration of the property.

I informed them of its disposal.

On the afternoon of that day, Mr. Blair came back with written order from Mr. Lincoln to deliver up the goods.

I told him that this was impossible, for it had already been handed over to the Government by authority of the Secretary of War.

He then demanded my removal from office.

Mr. Lincoln did not see that I had disobeyed any order, and failed to appreciate his Postmaster's regard for law and his Southern friends.

The parties were kept in prison several weeks, and then paroled.

We add Mr. B.'s statement, made under oath:—

M. B. B. makes the following statement:—

I was born in Loudon County, Virginia. Aged twenty-three years. Reside in Fauquier County, Virginia. On or about the 27th of October, 1862, Mrs. T., her daughter (Miss L. B. B.), and myself, came to Washington city, in a buggy or carriage, which was owned by Mrs. T.—the horse belonged to me. Mrs. T. also had in her employ a wagon and team, which, I believe, were the property of the driver, and which were engaged by her to convey groceries to her home, for family use.

My visit to Washington, at the time referred to, was at the written request of Mrs. T., desiring me to accompany her to Washington. After making her purchases, she (Mrs. T.) obtained the necessary passes for our return; we started for home, and arrived in Alexandria, Virginia. The weather being rainy, Miss B. and myself commenced the preliminaries for taking medicines through the lines, on a speculation. After the agreement to do so, I ordered some of the medicines in Alexandria, when our party (Mrs. T., Miss B., and myself) concluded to return to Washington, D. C.; but Mrs. T., to my knowledge, knew nothing of the contraband arrangement between Miss B. and myself.

The purchases were all made by me, both in Alexandria and in Washington. Miss B. and myself jointly expended about five hundred dollars in the enterprise.

Miss B.'s arrangements for the conveyance were completed at Mr. Gallagher's residence on Fifteenth Street; mine were completed in Alexandria. After taking every precaution for success, we started for home in the same conveyance that brought us, and the same parties, viz.: Mrs. T., Miss B., and myself.

We proceeded homeward until stopped by the pickets, near Chantilly, and were then taken to Centreville, Fairfax County, Virginia, where we were searched, and the contraband medicines found and taken from us. I had but two letters, which were taken from me when arrested—one was given me by Miss B. H. (who, I believe, boards on Four-and-a-Half Street), remarking at the time, that it was from her mother to her sister; Mr. McV., of Alexandria, handed me the other, requesting me to send it to his father, remarking that there was nothing treasonable in it.

I did not know of any letters on the person of Miss B., previous to our arrest. When arrested, Miss B. and myself regretted the cause thereof, as we imagined Postmaster-General Montgomery Blair might be censured for aiding and assisting us in obtaining passes, our actions, as detected, having the appearance of disloyalty. It is but justice to that gentleman to say, that he knew nothing of the matter between Miss B. and myself.

Besides the contraband medicines taken from me, I had two carpet-bags, which contained my clothing. I also hold a receipt from detective officer Lee, for "forty dollars in treasury notes, thirty dollars in Virginia State notes, twenty-four dollars in Confederate notes, and two dollars on broken bank," together with my horse, which was in the buggy when arrested. I believe all these are in the possession of Mr. L. O. Baker, Provost-Marshal of the War Department, and, being my individual property, I respectfully ask their return on the disposal of my case.

Having thus truthfully stated my case, and my lady companion (Miss B.) having been discharged, I presume that justice and punishment should be administered without partiality. I, therefore, respectfully ask my discharge from confinement on the same conditions and privileges as were conceded to

Miss L. B B., my companion in the unfortunate matter which caused my arrest and confinement.

M. B. B.

Personally appeared before me, this eleventh day of December, A. D. 1862 the above-named Marcus B. B., and, being sworn according to law, declares the above statement to be true.

L. O. TURNER,
Judge-Advocate.

Witness my hand and seal the day and year aforesaid.

    The telegraph lines were especially guarded after the war commenced. Great failures in army movements were caused by the improper use of the telegraph.

    When battles were impending, guards and censors to watch it were sent by the Government to the offices, for two reasons: first, to prevent intelligence from reaching the enemy; secondly, to keep it out of the hands of unscrupulous persons, who would use it for speculation. Two millions of dollars were made in Wall Street in an hour by a single telegram. The business of that money market was governed by the army movements. Various tricks and expedients were resorted to for the concealment of the traffic in blood and gold.

    Very few exceptions, however, were made to this general rule. The commanding general, chief quartermaster, and a few others, were permitted to send dispatches not subject to the usual censorship. A prominent officer attached to headquarters, who had spent his early life in Oregon, with the army, had become familiar with an Indian jargon called *Chunook*, introduced by cast-away sailors, seventy-five years ago. No trade but that of whale-ships was then carried on along that coast. The sailors taught the Indians certain expressions, pretending them to be English, which remain in use among them.

    A prominent Oregon politician, then in Washington—a friend of the army officer before referred to—had also learned this "Chunook." Presuming that the knowledge of this jargon was confined to themselves at the East, they had arranged a system of telegrams, to speculate in gold.

    December 12, 1862, after a temporary repulse of the Union Army, I was sent for by the Secretary of War, who said:

"Colonel, can you tell me what this means?" handing me a telegram, which I recognized at once as Chunook. The dispatch was signed "—— ——," and sent to —— ——

I replied: "Oregon Indian jargon."

He added: "What is jargon?"

I explained.

He asked me to write out a translation of it.

The Secretary did not seem fully to appreciate my nowledge of the language.

He inquired if there were others who understood it.

I replied: "Yes, several."

Retaining the telegram, he sent for Mr. D., clerk in the Department of the Interior, who had also been in Oregon.

He translated it substantially as I had done. The Secretary, still incredulous, sent for General ——, who is a fine linguist.

He said: "Mr. Secretary, why, this is Hungarian:" a reply which was for some time a standing joke at the general's expense.

The dispatches continued to arrive that and the next day. They were altered, transposed, &c., then forwarded, to the great wonder and bewilderment of the recipients.

We copy the original telegrams with the two translations, intimating that the Chunook system of telegraphing was rejected by the Government.

The expressions, apparently so disconnected, had each a significance well understood by the army speculators:—

NESIKA ISCUM FREDERICKSBURG.

Ilin nesika pooh cononay okok sun copa hin hias guns. Wake hin tilicum mameloos. Tomolloh tenas sun nesika puck puck copa musket pe cononay pire ictas. Nahnitka clunas silenm nesika mameloos kata wake chaco ole nez.

Where is S. Where H. S. Come here to-day. My soldiers come as you told me. Now tell me, old N., suppose you want to see one big firing. All well, you make haste here now. News why mad, yes, to-morrow.

Where is S. Tell H. S. to come here to-day. The soldiers come as you told me. Now tell old N., suppose he wants to see one big firing, all right, make haste here. They will be mad to-morrow

UNITED STATES SECRET SERVICE.

UNITED STATES MILITARY TELEGRAPH, WAR DEPARTMENT,
WASHINGTON, D. C., *December* 12, 1862.

Wake siyah cultus mitlike nesika conoway okok sun nika tumtum claska rebels puck puck nesika tomallah kagna pilitin divils klash nanitch conoway sun tomallah klark aiyum mika.

We have come to Fredericksburg. A great many we shoot all this day, with a great many big guns. A great many of your people are killed. To-morrow morning we shoot with muskets and all fire-arms. Yes, probably half of us will be dead. Why don't you come.

We have come to Fredericksburg. We have killed a great many to-day, with big guns. A great many of their people are killed. To-morrow morning we shoot with muskets, and all kinds of fire-arms. Probably half of us will be dead. Why don't old N. come.

It appears to patriotic "outsiders" incredible that such a morbid spirit of speculation could exist amid the tragedies of civil war; but those who escaped the contamination in the arena of tempting opportunities were the select and incorruptible few at whose head was Abraham Lincoln.

CHAPTER VIII.

OFFICIAL SERVICES AND EMBARRASSMENTS—NEW ORDER OF THINGS

The Bureau transferred to the War Department—Dr. H., and the Perilous Adventure of which he was the occasion—Report of the Case—Arrest of the Leader of a great secret Southern Organization—Documents and Letters.

DEPARTMENT OF STATE,
WASHINGTON, *February* 15, 1862.

SIR—Permit me to introduce Mr. L. C. Baker, who has been employed by the State Department in the detective service, and who, so far as known, has discharged his duties in a manner entirely acceptable. In consequence of Executive Order No. 1, dated February 14, this department has no further use of his services. He is commended to your consideration as a capable and efficient officer.

I have the honor to be, very respectfully,

Your obedient servant,

W. H. SEWARD.

Hon. EDWIN M. STANTON, Secretary of War.

Some interesting adventures soon after followed.

Dr. G. H. was from Leesburg, Va.; graduated in the Medical College of Philadelphia, and became engaged, while attending lectures, to the daughter of a prominent citizen, and subsequently married her.

Immediately after the rebellion broke out, he took sides with the South, and became so obnoxious to the people of Germantown, by the declaration of his secession sentiments, that a committee waited upon him requesting him to leave, which he refused to do. This so exasperated the citizens, that they warned him to take a peaceful farewell of the community. He decided, at length, to go South. Removing to Baltimore, with others of similar character, among them Captain Wardell, of the *Shenandoah*, he entered into the exciting but lucrative business of blockade-running. In the selection of his associates, as will appear, he took one of my detectives, and gave the details of the plan, dates of intended operations, and the kind of goods to be sold. The schooner chartered by them was the *James Buchanan*—a fitting name.

Having learned all the facts, I provided a tug, and was lying off Annapolis two days and nights, expecting every moment the appearance of the schooner; whose departure was delayed by a terrible snow-storm.

And here I was obliged to resort to one of the subterfuges which were employed afterward so successfully by my assistants.

Putting on the old oily clothes of an engineer, and with an oil can in my hand, I went to the store where the excursionists were getting supplies.

While there, I found the entire company engaged in the purchase.

I was in no hurry to leave the place, but managed to get close to one of the company who belonged to my force, and was admitted to the circle in disguise, trying, by *nudging* him and pulling his coat, to let him know who I was. It was all in vain: so complete was my transformation into a common and greasy engineer.

Captain Wardell asked me on what boat I was engineer I said of a tug-boat.

Wardell, then turning to one of his companions, remarked: "Why, here's a man who can tow us out." Then again addressing me, he inquired:

"What will you ask to tow a small schooner out into the bay?"

I replied: "On moderate terms. If you are all ready, for ten dollars. Where is your schooner?"

"At the wharf."

"Well, if you are ready in an hour I'll do the job. My tug is at the end of the pier."

I went on board and told my twelve assistants to go into a small cabin aft, and not to show themselves till signaled by me.

Soon after the blockade-runners came down, stepped aboard the schooner, threw me a line, bade adieu to their friends on shore, and we started down the bay.

Their vessel being small, with little room under the deck, they remained above.

Six miles from Annapolis, where they could sail their vessel, they hailed me, and told me to cast off the line.

CAPTURE OF A REBEL BLOCKADE RUNNER

THE CAPTURE.

I invited them on the tug to take a glass of good cheer before leaving. They came on board, and, while gathered around the bottle, I gave the signal; my men rushed up the hatchway. I told my guests who I was, and that they were my prisoners. Among them was one of my detectives, who, to be distinguished readily, wore a red shirt and black belt. He had been three weeks with these blockade-runners. A little warlike demonstration was soon quieted by the display of a carbine. I took them to Fort McHenry, in a snow-storm of great severity; and, having let my subordinates return with the boat while I adjusted business details, found the walk of nearly three miles, in the night, no pleasure walk after the excitement and fatigue of the day.

My report recounts the official course of events partially narrated:—

WASHINGTON, *February* 24, 1862.

To the Hon. E. M. STANTON, Secretary of War:—

DEAR SIR—Herewith please find my report in the case of Dr. H. H., arrested at Annapolis, on the 18th instant. The doctor is a resident of Germantown, Pennsylvania. During the excitement last summer, the doctor made himself particularly obnoxious to the Union people in his vicinity by his open denunciations of the Government and his avowed sympathy with the so-called Confederate States; so distasteful had he become, at one time, that the police authorities in Philadelphia were compelled to interfere to protect his person and property. Dr. H. was, until the last two years, a resident of Winchester, Virginia; he married the daughter of F. B., Esq., of Philadelphia (a good Union man and a worthy citizen). On or about the first of the present month, the Doctor began making arrangements for going South, for the purpose of joining the Confederate army as a surgeon. He came on to Baltimore, Maryland, mingled freely with the secession element in that city. On the 10th instant, an organization or party of rebels, in Baltimore (of which the Doctor was one), chartered the sloop *James Buchanan* to carry them to Virginia. Being advised of their intended movements, I chartered (by order of Major-General Dix) a steam tug, with a view to intercept them, it being understood that the party, consisting of thirteen persons, were to embark at Annapolis. The day fixed upon for their departure being very stormy, the sloop did not leave Baltimore. I, however, went to Annapolis on Tuesday last, and found the expedition ready to sail. Having no boat at my disposal, I immediately arrested Dr. H. I searched his baggage, and found letters which settle the question as to his guilt and intentions to join the Confederates. A quantity of gold coin and Confederate bank-bills were found in his possession, also pistols, rubber blankets, ready-made clothing, &c., &c. The prisoner, with the letters, papers, money, and all other effects belonging to him, were turned over to General Dix, at Baltimore. The prisoner is now confined in Fort McHenry, subject to the disposal of your Department.

I am, sir, your obedient servant,
(Signed) L. C. BAKER.

Alexandria notwithstanding its proximity to Washington, became headquarters of secession councils. This state of things culminated, early in the struggle, in the death of Ellsworth.

At Baltimore, while I was apparently in sympathy with the rebels, I learned of a secret organization at Alexandria. It was formed ostensibly for the benefit of the families of both Union and Confederate soldiers. This will account for the connection of Mr. Louis McKenzie with its proceedings. He became a member, unaware of its real character; and when its disloyal spirit was apparent, he absented himself from the meetings of the society. The seizure of the records put me in possession of its entire history. There was "a wheel within a wheel" in this organized benevolence, designed to bring out all the sympathy available for the cause of treason. The Peel correspondence will be found especially rich in expressions of feeling; while the rebel poetry, which graced one of the meetings of the association, presents very forcibly its ruling animus. In this report, as in other narratives I shall quote, sometimes uninteresting details occur, because inseparable from the record:—

WASHINGTON, March 4, 1862.

To the Hon. E. M. STANTON, Secretary of War:—

SIR—I have the honor herewith to transmit my report in the following cases, arrested at Alexandria by myself and assistants, February 26th and 27th, 1862. Accompanying this report are two books—one containing the proceedings of a secret organization, or society, for the benefit of the families of soldiers now in the Confederate army, also the manufacture of uniforms, clothing, &c., which have from time to time been forwarded to the so-called Confederate States. This association was organized in June last, and, as appears from the minutes of their proceedings, the Ladies' Relief Association, composed of the wives and daughters of its members, were admitted, in order, as it is alleged, to extend the usefulness of their operations.

Repeated complaints have been made to me, during the past fall and winter, concerning the meetings and treasonable transactions of this society

CITIZENS OF ALEXANDRIA ARRESTED. 139

Owing to the high social standing and position of these traitors, and the extreme secrecy with which all their operations were carried on, I found it very difficult to ascertain, with any degree of certainty, their places of meeting, their number, or the names of the parties comprising the organization.

During the past four months, large numbers of cards were picked up in the streets and bar-rooms at Alexandria, on which were printed words and sentences, disconnected, which (since the arrests were made) I have ascertained were intended as a notice to the members of the society to meet at a certain time and place. So dark and secret were all their proceedings, that it was with the utmost difficulty, and after months of patient and constant surveillance, that this board of secret plotters against the Government were brought to light.

The book containing the minutes of these meetings was found in the possession of Henry Peel, who, at the time of the arrests, was secretary of the association. This book, fortunately, contained the names of all the officers, which subsequently led to their arrest. The book marked "Dangerfield" was found in his (Dangerfield's) possession. It contains a statement of the object of the association, the names of its contributors, names of subscribers, amount subscribed, and how disbursed.

There can be no question as to the real object of this association. Letters, papers, and memorandums, found in possession of nearly all the parties arrested, show most conclusively that these individuals were engaged in a treasonable conspiracy to levy war against the United States Government, and all have refused to take the oath of allegiance. Much of the proof on which I rely to convict, under the act of 1861, is verbal conversations with and between these rebels, which have been overheard by many of the most reliable citizens of Alexandria, and, I am satisfied, will convince any jury in the land of their guilt.

On or about the 4th of March, 1861, Mr. Louis McKenzie (now Mayor of Alexandria) was called upon for consultation with J. B. Dangerfield, W. F. Booth, W. H. Taylor, W. H. Marburg, General Johnston (now in the Confederate army), James Green, and J. W. Burke, for the purpose of devising some plan for the seizure of Washington, the seizure of steamers running on the Potomac, and destroying the buoys marking the channel up the Potomac. They also gave information and personally assisted in the seizure of the steamer *Paige*, now in possession of the Confederates. All the facts causing this meeting can be proved by a number of reliable witnesses now residing in Alexandria. All the above-named parties (except the rebel General Johnston) are now confined at the Old Capitol prison.

Owing to the recent arrests, and seizure of contraband correspondence, but few letters directly implicating the parties were found.

HENRY PEEL.

The following letter was written to Henry Peel by his brother now in Richmond:—

RICHMOND, *November* 30, 1861.

MY DEAR BROTHER—You can not imagine the source of pleasure your letter gave us. It was the first line I had received from Alexandria since I left. The letter you wrote me in answer to mine I have never received, but hope it may come along in time. Since I came to Richmond I have been busily engaged selling off the goods I shipped to the country, and have been operating in other articles out of my usual line, and have succeeded very well so far. The truth is, almost anything you could buy can be sold at a profit and for cash. Money is more abundant than I ever knew in all my business life. Richmond is the center of trade; it is the point from which the army draw most of their supplies. The supplies are abundant and coming in from every quarter. The noble sons of the South have just laid down their all upon the altar of patriotism, determining to maintain their rights against such a nation of Yankee myrmidons, as are in fact the Northern States. When the South determined to separate from so vile a community, they have to confess that they did not know that they were so much like land pirates as they have shown themselves to be in their effort to crush the Southern people. Of all civilized nations known, a more brutal, despicable crusade against the South is not recorded. They (the South) now fully know with whom they are dealing, and will act accordingly—an eye for an eye—and all prepare to meet them any and everywhere. Whenever a contest has taken place, the Southern soldiers have proven successful. This is true; their papers to the contrary. The whole purpose is to deceive the people, and their papers are under such surveillance that they can not dare to give any other report. The actual loss in the Leesburg fight say prisoners, killed, wounded, drowned, and missing, was thirty-three hundred. Your papers state no such result. Every few days a large batch of prisoners are brought here. Yesterday, twenty-three cavalry were brought down; their horses and all captured Sent off two hundred and fifty to Alabama on Wednesday; about fifteen hundred still remain here. If they attempt to hang those taken as privateers, their rank will be hung here. Already lots have been drawn, and each unhappy man is confined in the cell for criminals prepared for the condemned. In no way can the North get ahead of the South. Plenty of stout hearts, abundance of provisions, full supply of ammunition, army well equipped. The finest long-range rifle cannon and columbiad, that strikes terror whenever fired. The whole South, with a united voice and solemn resolve, have willed to be free from the North or perish in the effort. All feel hopeful and sanguine of success, willing to endure any and all privations, even to life itself. If the North could only know how vain their efforts to conquer the South, or subdue the rebels, they would give it up. If they do know the fact, their acts are only to damage the South, to gratify an intense hatred for losing so good a customer as the South has been; but in carrying on the war, every blow they give strikes back with redoubled force, in loss of life and building up a debt which they will never see paid. As for the Union must be preserved, it is all a farce; the old Union is broken, never again to be united. This is a fixed fact. Every day the blockade lasts only tends to make the South more independent of the North.

as every variety of manufacture is springing up. Just think of it: a few months since there was no Government whatever here; now it is fully organized, and every department is in successful operation. A large army has been organized and well sustained, and can whip three times their weight in Yankee flesh or foreigners either. The crops have been abundant, money is plentiful, and confidence between man and man, all standing shoulder to shoulder, determined to undergo extermination before subjugation. The women and children uniting in the one common effort, besides the slaves all at home laboring to sustain our army with provisions to repel the common foe against us. To conquer such a people, relying upon the God of battles to sustain them, is simply ridiculous. In all our struggles, the hand of the Almighty is plainly visible; for our many sins we may be scourged and have to suffer much, but putting our trust in Him, though many be slain, yet He intends all for our good. It is a source of no little gratification to feel that God is with us in this struggle, and to expect some reverses is natural enough, but the result is only a question of time: the longer we are persecuted, the greater loss of life and money the North will sustain, and accomplish nothing at last. In one thing the Yankees have been mistaken: that was, to incite the negroes to insurrection; but be it said to their advantage when the struggle is over, that where one black face with a true heart has turned against us, ten white faces with black and false hearts have done so; and I regret so many in A'exandria are of that class, but most of foreign-born or Yankees, who never had any sympathy with the institutions of the South. Amidst all the horrors of the war, Richmond is increasing in population and realizing great and un paralleled prosperity. Nearly every branch of business is a success. Manufactories are doing well. We have a very large number of Alexandrians here, and most of them have profitable employment. John McC. J. is here in office at one thousand dollars salary; Wells A. Lockwood is in a bank at one thousand dollars salary. I could extend the list of friends here. Mr. E. K. Witmer and child arrived safely; all of them will keep house together. Tell H. P. I received a letter from his partner, S., and he sent me a letter for H., which I will forward with this, hoping it may reach him, as I trust all our letters, safely. As you all have both piano and melodeon, we would like for Lu. to send round and get F.'s piano and melodeon and take care of it for me, using both as much as they please. If not inconvenient, we would like them to send and get them. I have never heard one word from Mr. B. since I left. I hope he will be able to get along without trouble and meet with no reverses. It is a sad state of things that friends should thus be separated, and for no fault of ours, the fault being at the door of demagogues and politicians. Awful will be the account to settle at the Day of Judgment for so much cruelty wantonly inflicted upon innocent men, women, and children. Surely their cup is fast filling up, and vengeance will overtake them. We have been disappointed in sending this as I expected, but now have a chance in a day or two. Our General Assembly met in Augusta, Georgia, last Wednesday, to organize anew for the South. They expect to get along without large boards to manage their affairs—only a small committee responsible to the Assembly. Theresa

goes over to Petersburg next Thursday, to spend a week or so. Our Congress
and Legislature are in session. The State Convention has adjourned. We
have seen Lincoln's message—a poor thing. How vastly he is mistaken about
Tennessee and North Carolina. He will find both Kentucky and Missouri
going with the South. He may well recommend the fortifying of Northern
cities, fearing European intervention or aid from that quarter. It is all for
no purpose this detestable land-pirate war is carried on; they never can conquer the South We are getting stronger every day. Men enlisting and
implements of warfare increasing weekly. Some new engines of warfare have
been invented that will be used in the next battle, that will carry death and
destruction to any army coming in contact with it. Of this I can not speak
further; but only an opportunity offer to use them, and they will rue the day
they ever thought of subjugating a free and enlightened people. We all
unite in affectionate love to you all, praying a merciful Providence may watch
over and keep you.

I am, affectionately, your brother, S.

It will always be an historical fact, over which the loyal heart will sadly wonder, that, while the cause of treason was rarely betrayed by its professed friends, the most threatening danger at the North was the treachery of those who lived under and and even hurrahed for the old flag.

No future historian of the civil war will probably ever attempt, nor will the records of the quartermasters' department ever show the vast amount of public stores and other property wantonly abandoned and destroyed by its faithless servants.

All over the boundless arena of conflict were scattered the best *materiel* of war—its most abundant supplies—in fragments and decaying masses; a spectacle not beheld, and therefore unappreciated, by the people at home.

It is, however, no new thing under the sun, and peculiar to no party in power.

The Mexican war was, perhaps, never surpassed in this aspect of national conflicts. The speculations were so remote from the great commercial centers of the country, the people knew but little of the manifold and lawless speculations.

The late war offered opportunities of every possible sort for unprincipled traffic; some of them lawful, and many more unmitigated robbery. "Uncle Sam" was the victim of this sharp practice, and therefore it flourished with the air of respectability and comparative impunity.

In one instance, a telegraph operator retained important official messages, and even charged for Government dispatches. Death itself has no barrier to the mercenary trade. The embalming of the dead, and the transportation of the bodies to friends at a distance, were occasions for unblushing extortion.

As we have suggested, the atmosphere of war is petrifying to the moral sensibilities of men who yield to its demoralizing influence, and they will do deeds in the presence of death, and with their own threatened every moment, which, in the purer, calmer air of their domestic and social life, would be utterly repulsive and unthought of by them

CLERKS and employees of the Government, whose business it was to make returns of the amount of forage and supplies received from the contractors, it was found were bribed by the latter to make false entries, and thus increase the weight fraudulently, to a greater or less figure. My investigation of the transactions disclosed the astounding fact that these employees had increased the amount of supplies furnished by sixteen contractors to the amount in money of over two hundred thousand dollars; which, in compliance with my suggestion, was deducted from the sum to be paid the contractors, on their final settlement with the Government.

All means were resorted to, by men who attracted the notice of the bureau, to escape arrest. When bribery and coaxing failed, threats were used, to secure their immunity from merited exposure and punishment. I was not unfrequently cautioned by a member of the Cabinet, against exposure to personal violence and even assassination. The letter copied below refers to a communication of an attorney. A German, named Volk, who had in his possession a large number of horses, nearly all of which belonged to the Government, was arrested, and the horses taken from him. As usual in similar cases, Volk employed an attorney. After a full and patient hearing of the case, I returned to Volk nine of the horses, which could not be proved to belong to the Government. The attorney, after exhausting legal argument to get the rest of the animals, wrote a letter, in which he intimated that he had possession of certain papers reflecting unfavorably upon my private and official character, and that their presentation to the President would make my immediate dismissal from the service certain. But, if I would recommend the Quartermaster-General to restore the horses, and appoint a friend of his on my police force, he would forward me the papers, and spare me the disgraceful exposure by Mr. Lincoln. In reply, I wrote as follows:—

OFFICE PROVOST-MARSHAL WAR DEPARTMENT,
WASHINGTON, *December* 15, 1862.

T. F. B., Attorney and Counselor at Law,
  Washington, D. C.:—

Sir—Your note of this date is received. Previous to my giving you any order for the payment of the nine horses, I took much pains in investigating the case, and satisfied myself that Volk was entitled to the pay for the said nine horses, *and no more*. I have, as yet, seen no proof or facts that would warrant me in recommending the Quartermaster's Department to pay for any more horses on Volk's account.

If you can produce any satisfactory proof that any person or persons in my employ extorted money from Volk, I will not only cause the amount to be refunded, but will immediately discharge and arrest such person or persons. In relation to certain papers you refer to, which you say you will furnish me with, that might be used greatly to my annoyance, I beg leave to reply, that I am not in the market as a purchaser of any such documents.

The *parties* you speak of as being on my track, and whom you say you will exercise your skill to keep off, I have no fears of; therefore you are at liberty (so far as I am concerned) to let them loose as soon as you may think proper.

In the latter part of 1862. I was sent for by Mr. Lincoln to make an investigation respecting the brutal treatment of slaves in Lower Maryland. This whole section had been visited by the Union troops, and, as a natural consequence, the slaves were escaping. There seemed to be something so fascinating to the ignorant bondmen, that they would follow them, as if charmed by the glittering bayonet and blue uniform, which never failed to awaken a strange longing for liberty. It is not military ambition, but an inspiration, which seizes them. They are ready to fall in and keep step to the martial airs of freedom.

An illustration of the interesting peculiarity of the race came under my observation during one of the well-known raids by General Kurtz, from Suffolk, on the Weldon railroad. The First District Cavalry, a regiment I had raised, and of which further mention will be made, was divided into front and rear guard. The advance of the forces was the first appearance of Union troops among these patient "servants" of the region. To be informed that we were "Yankees," was enough, without the slightest hint of our plans or destination, to stir the most stupid toiler like a trumpet-call. The hoe was dropped, the plow and cart abandoned. Even the women, moved by the same wild impulse, deserted their cabins, and all together rushed to the rear of the army, and stepped to the music of the march for days, and sometimes for weeks. They dreaded more than death the return to their owners, or recapture by them.

When it became necessary to leave several hundred at Reams's Station, in our hurried movement backward, they lingered about instead of going forward, and their frantic agony was heart-rending.

A very cruel instance of the welcome given to a recaptured slave, occurs to me in this connection. One Carpenter, a notorious secessionist, was a ruffian and a terror to all Union men. To frighten the slaves, and prevent them from running away, he tied a captured man to a tree, in a nude condition, whipped him with a board til exhausted, then set his slaves at work. When this master and fiend was rested, he returned to the beating, until death closed the scene. There was a formal arrest, but the majority of his "fellow-citizens" were in sympathy with him, and he was soon at liberty. Subsequently, however, he was arrested for treason, and confined in the Old Capitol prison.

It is a matter of history, that at this period of the National struggle for existence, the *cause* of the war was ignored by the North. Not so with the South; there, the "cornerstone" was brought forth to the world's admiring view, and the flag of treason waved proudly over it. There *was then* some excuse for England's sneer at our unbroken loyalty to the South in her defense of the aristocratic claim of superiority over all other American races.

I have never had the honor of being called a reformer, or an "*abolitionist*," but I do not deny that my sense of justice, and my sympathies, have been with the injured and oppressed, irrespective of color, or position in society. I have, therefore, during the entire period my bureau has served the loyal cause, unhesitatingly given the whole power of the department to the protection of the defenseless negro, whenever he was the victim of prejudice or passion.

In common with thousands who were brought to face the practical effect of the slave system during the war, I have seen the soul of tyranny in it, whose lust of power spared not the blood-bought Union, but longed to crack the whip over the hated "Yankee."

Necessarily "behind the scenes," I saw the *demon* disguised by the bland expression of the "chivalry," and learned that the "kind, Christian masters" were so *in spite* of the system which they sustained—they were naturally magnanimous men, or governed by genuine religious principle, modified by a wrong education to the approval of gigantic wrong.

I could fill pages with the narratives of fiendish scorn of the "nigger," while he was docile and unresisting as the lamb led to the slaughter. Nor has the *spirit* of the peculiar institution died with the formal existence of slavery and the defeat of its sworn friends—a fact the country may realize when the retributive storm evoked by the countless mounds of starved prisoners of the loyal North, and the nameless graves of the murdered bondmen, shall again, though in a new aspect, bewilder with darkest fears our wisest statesmen.

Fairfax Court-House was for two years within our lines, and occupied as an outpost by our army. Here lived a citizen by the name of F., with whom boarded several of the staff officers. His daughter, Miss F., was a young and decidedly good-looking woman, with pleasing, insinuating manners. She discoursed fluently, and with enthusiasm, of the Union cause, impressing her admiring guests with her loyalty and intelligence. Meanwhile, she carried her commission as a rebel spy. This document, in its original form, was found through the confidence reposed by Miss F. in a female subordinate in my bureau, who played the part of a Southern lady going to her friends. Miss F. opened her heart to the young adventurer, and also her bed, in which, between the mattress and its nether companion, was concealed the prized and useful paper. It was found there when the fair spy was arrested by my order.

The public have not forgotten the capture of General Stoughton and staff, at Fairfax Court-House, by Moseby, which drew from Mr. Lincoln the remark, when he was told that a hundred horses were captured with the officer: "Well, I am sorry for that—for I can make brigadier-generals, but can't make horses."

It turned out that Miss F. was accustomed to go out at night and meet Moseby, the famous guerrilla, and impart whatever information might be of service to the enemy. Indeed, one day she was invited by a staff officer to take a horseback ride into the country, and met Moseby, whom she introduced to her escort under an assumed name, and passed along. with loyal words upon her traitorous lips.

CHAPTER IX.

THE BUREAU IN CANADA—IN THE ARMY.

Tricks of False Correspondence—Mr. Delisle and the "Secret Secession Legation

THE operations of the bureau were embarrassed unavoidably by the transmission of false intelligence through unreliable persons for mercenary ends, of the gravest importance to this or some other department of the Government. Bogus correspondence was sometimes thrown into my hands to mislead me, and secure to the writers some personal advantages.
For illustration: Early in 1863, a man, who signed himself "C. M. Delisle," wrote to the State Department, expressing an earnest desire to forward important information, dating from Prescott, Canada East, but post-marked at Ogdensburg, New York. Delisle claimed to be the agent of the "Secret Secession Legation, Canada," through whose hands passed all the correspondence between the province and Richmond. The letter below is from this gentleman:—

OGDENSBURG, *May* 4, 1863.

To the Honorable W. H. SEWARD, Secretary of State, Washington:—

SIR—Certain facts having of late come to my knowledge, of the existence of a secret Southern society, the object of which is most detrimental to the Federal Government of the United States; and although a British subject, and residing in the States but for a few months, I deem it my duty to inform you of the fact. Having myself been engaged, in 1837 and '38, in quelling the Canadian rebellion, when I had the honor of holding a commission in a British troop of cavalry, besides having since held several commissions and appointments under the Canadian Government, I can understand the very great injury caused by it to a well-constituted Government as yours. However, I am one of those who are strongly in favor of the Union, and would consider it a very great misfortune if such a promising republic should ever be broken up. Being unwilling that it should be known that I have addressed you on this subject, I trust that the confidence reposed by me in you will be strictly private and confidential; and should your Government think proper to furnish me the means of going to Washington, I shall then be most happy to substantiate my assertions by undeniable evidence. Had I had the means at my disposal, I should certainly have lost no time in seeing you personally. As to my character, it is beyond censure, and with regard to my family connections, they are of the highest standing in Canada, where I was born and brought up. As it might occur to you that this is a ruse to obtain money, I can assure you that it is not so; and I am confident that when I shall have made you acquainted with the whole of the facts connected with my information, it will put you in a position to discover and reap invaluable information for the good of your Government. I may also state that I shall have no objections in offering my services in bringing the whole thing to light, as some one would have to be employed by you on the frontiers and in Canada, every inch of which is most familiar to me.

I have the honor to be, sir, your obedient, &c.,

C. M. DELISLE.

Four or five letters more, of a similar character, were forwarded to me by Mr. Seward, with the indorsement that he believed much valuable information could be procured from Delisle respecting persons in connection with whom he professed to be acquainted.

Accordingly I met him, when he unfolded to me one of the grandest and most skillfully arranged plans ever devised, the great importance of which had rendered it necessary that an organization should be formed, with the sounding title already quoted, whose secretary was "Wm. Sibbald." So completely had these villains made out their programme, the single object of which was to obtain large sums of money, that it was with much difficulty that their plot was finally discovered. The letters which follow were well calculated to deceive the most vigilant servants of the Government:—

MONTREAL, *April* 27, 1862.

SIR—The president of the "Secret Secession Legation in Canada," being desirous to appoint an agent on the border of the United States and Canada for the purpose of facilitating the conveyance of the secret mails, &c., from Richmond, Va., to Europe *via* Canada, and your name having been transmitted to him by a friend of yours in the United States, as a person in whom all confidence can be placed, for your intelligence, integrity, and forbearance, I therefore, sir, beg, at his request, to make you the following offer, for your acceptance or refusal, viz.:—

First. That you will consent to *become* "*Secret Agent*" in the United States for the above Legation.

Second. That you will endeavor, by *secret means*, to forward in packages, so made up and of such size as to avoid detection at the hands of the United States Government, all the letters, &c., delivered to you monthly by persons from Richmond, Va., and who will have been previously instructed in New York of the nature of their mission toward you.

You will also give them any information they may require to make a *silent and secret* entrance in Canada, by indicating to them the roads by which the crossing of the boundary lines can be more easily effected and with less danger.

It will also be your duty to deliver to them, on their making themselves known to you by means of countersigns, which in all cases will be given to you in time by the Legation in Canada, any letters, papers, money, &c., that will have been secretly given to you for them, either from here or from other *secret agents* serving in Canada or the United States.

Also, that you will find means to carefully conceal any documents, &c., from the vigilance of the United States Government police, till such documents, &c., are safely delivered into the hands of the "emissary" it may please our worthy *President, Mr. Jefferson Davis*, to send to us.

Third. That you will be willing and ready to move from one place to the other, at six hours' notice from the Legation here, at any time the said Legation may order such a move, and everywhere act as *secret agent* to them, seeking and gathering any information they may require, and then faithfully transmitting the same to the President here.

Should this offer meet your approbation, your remuneration will be as follows, viz.: two dollars and fifty cents for every letter, paper, &c., not bearing an official stamp; ten dollars for any document, letter, paper, &c., bearing our official Government stamp, and which in both cases you will succeed in forwarding safely to the Legation in Canada.

On the other hand, should you be ordered to move from one city to another, twenty-five cents per mile will be allowed you on journeys performed by rail or by boat; and fifty cents per mile for distances crossed in vehicles drawn by horses—*all payments to be made to you in gold*. In conclusion, I hope, sir, that the confidence the President of the Legation here has placed in you, based upon the recommendation of your recommender, will never be betrayed, and the *strictest secrecy* will be kept by you, should you accept or reject this proposition.

Awaiting your early reply, which, sir, please address to *Wm. Sibbald, simply, General Post, Montreal,*

I remain, sir, your most obedient servant,

WM. SIBBALD,
Secretary to the Secret Secession Legation, Canada.

To O. M. DELISLE, Esq., Ogdensburg, New York.

MONTREAL, *May* 1, 1863.

SIR—I beg to acknowledge the receipt of your answer to my communication of the 27th ultimo, and I avail myself of this opportunity to tender you the thanks of our President.

"LEGATION" SCHEMES. 151

I am aware that the Agency, should you accept it, might become a little annoying in case of detection; but no such accident can happen, if secrecy be your course of conduct, and much will depend upon yourself whether the police agents of the United States seize the dispatches.

The character your benefactor in the United States, who has desired us to suppress his name, has given you, has induced us to broach such a subject to you. Suffice to say, that his motive is one prompted by the personal esteem he entertains for you, and also to have the felicity of withdrawing you from your present embarrassing position.

The post cannot of course be one except of great lucrativeness, as the arrangements made here are very complete, and on a large scale, although *strictly ignored by any stranger to the "Legation."*

To state positively what you might derive monthly from the agency, is a mere impossibility, as no one here is aware of the number of packages the "emissary" may be able to convey; but you can rest assured that a very large income must unavoidably be drawn from it.

The letters and official dispatches will be in all cases written upon the thinnest paper manufactured, to make concealment easier, and in many cases will be mere press copies.

Your remuneration will be paid you by the "emissary" himself, on delivery of the documents, by draft on New York, to an amount equal to gold, or, if more convenient and suited to you, in specie.

When ordered to move, sufficient money will be sent you from here, with the orders to take you, all expenses paid, to any place chosen and back to Ogdensburg, as the latter place will be your headquarters, except you think another spot would facilitate the entrance of mails in Canada: this point, however, is entirely left to your suggestion.

The President, in thanking you, wishes me to say that he is well pleased with the character he has of you, and that no person is better suited than you for the fulfillment of his object; and that, from your honesty, genteel and gentlemanlike bearing, you will manage to initiate yourself into the American agents' favors, and acquire from them valuable information regarding the "lookout parties" on the frontier and outlets around Richmond.

I remain, sir, your obedient servant,

WM. SIBBALD,
Secretary to the Secret Secession Legation in Canada.

To C. M. DELISLE, Esq., Ogdensburg, New York.

I will be glad to hear your answer on receipt of this, whether the proposition is accepted or rejected.

No pains were spared by these conspirators to impress the officers of the Government with the reality of their lying scheme to rob its Treasury. In harmony with this cool purpose and policy, communications were forwarded to individuals anticipating that they would ultimately reach my hands. On this point I shall quote certain correspondence with

Captain H. B. Todd, provost-marshal of the District of Columbia:—

HEADQUARTERS PROVOST-MARSHAL'S OFFICE,
WASHINGTON, D. C., *May* 20, 1863.

Colonel L. C. BAKER:—

I am credibly informed that one Charles Michael Delisle, now living in Ogdensburg, New York, has made arrangements with the Secret Secession Legation, in Montreal, Canada, or with their secretary, William Sibbald, to convey the rebel mails and dispatches into Canada, as soon as the emissaries from Richmond deliver them to him.

Delisle is paid by this Secret Legation, and now stops at Johnson's Hotel, Ogdensburg; of late he has entered his name as F. A. Delisle, instead of C. M. My informant has seen his correspondence with said Legation, and read his (Delisle's) proposition.

He has already sent dispatches to Montreal, undetected, which have been forwarded to Messrs. Mason and Slidell, through the mails of the Montreal Ocean Steamship Company, and others are very soon expected to go through.

I am, sir, your obedient servant,

HENRY B. TODD,
Captain and Provost-Marshal

It is only necessary to add that, on the arrest of Delisle, he confessed that there was no "Secret Secession Legation" in Canada, so far as he knew, but that the design of the parties engaged in the transaction was simply to defraud the United States Government; and, had it not been defeated by the vigilance of this bureau, it would have proved, of course, a very handsome speculation for them.

CHAPTER X.

WEALTHY TRAITORS—FRUITLESS SCHEMES.

John H. Waring—His Operations—An Efficient Tool—Walter Bowie—A Wild Career—Rebel Mail—Contrabands—Extracts from the Private Journals of Rebel Spies.

THE insane treason of the Marylanders revealed itself very strikingly in an incident which now occurred.

Mr. John H. Waring, a wealthy and respectable planter, residing on the banks of the Patuxent River, had long been suspected of assisting the enemy, and devoting his dwelling to the secret service of the blockade-runners, spies, and mail-carriers of the Confederacy. His family had ever been known as the most scornful haters of the Federal Government, outspoken, and fearless. The female members of it, by their connection with disloyal friends of high standing in Baltimore, had special facilities for communicating with the South. He, individually, did not enter into the bitter denunciations of the Government, owing partly to his advanced age, and partly to his occupation of time on the plantation.

Walter Bowie, whose family resided in Maryland, and whose uncle gave the name to the favorite weapon of the chivalry, had early in the struggle cast in his lot with the traitors.

A reckless, unprincipled, and daring young man, with considerable culture, he was selected by the Secretary of War to act as a spy. Born and brought up in Lower Maryland, he was thoroughly acquainted with the country.

To him are many families there indebted for the loss of fathers and sons. He raised, at different times, squads for the rebel service, ran across the Potomac and sold on speculation; now with Moseby's guerrillas, then with the authorities at Richmond, and soon, perhaps, in Washington. I decided, if it were possible, to capture him. Aware that he was assisted and concealed by the Waring ladies, I directed my attention to that quarter. Sending four detectives to the house, I ordered them to surround it on a certain night. They secreted themselves accordingly, waiting for the dawn, the usual way of detour movements. The proximity of the men somehow became known to the inmates of the house, but every precaution had been taken to prevent escape.

As the light of day appeared, an aged negro servant left the dwelling with a washtub upon her head, and walked toward a spring near by for water. Upon her approach, an officer stopped her, and inquired about the family. She could give no information, and was allowed to pass. When sufficient time had elapsed for her return, the detective suspected that he had been deceived, and taking the path to the spring, discovered the tub, and just beyond a horse saddled and bridled, tied to a tree. The whole *ruse* at once flashed upon his mind. The venerable negress was no other than Walter Bowie. He saw that the horse was watched, and went on afoot.

Chagrined at the defeat of his plan, the officer returned to the house, and found, on searching it, the spy's uniform, sash, and sabre. It was ascertained later that a daughter of Mr. W., Mrs. Ducket, had blackened and dressed Bowie for the occasion. A more careful examination of the premises led to the discovery of several suits of rebel uniform.

From this time till autumn he was successfully engaged in raids upon defenseless sutlers and unarmed citizens, until at last, crossing the Potomac with a company of his associates, went to Sandy Hill, broke open a store, and pillaged it. I dispatched a squad in pursuit, and surrounded his camp next morning at Booneville. A skirmish ensued, and Bowie was shot with a double charge, and instantly killed.

The following episode in the darkly romantic history flings a lurid light into the "habitations of cruelty" which have been protected by the "starry flag" of freedom, revealing their domestic scenes:—

OFFICE PROVOST-MARSHAL WAR DEPARTMENT,
WASHINGTON, *July* 9, 1863.

Honorable E. M. STANTON, Secretary of War:—

SIR—I respectfully submit the following statement, and request further directions in the matter.

DEATH OF A REBEL SPY.

CRUELTY TO NEGROES.

On Monday last, having received information that Walter Bowie, a notorious rebel and spy, had been on a recent visit to the house of Mrs. Lizzie Bowie, in Prince George County, Maryland, and also, that subsequent to said visit, on Sunday night last, a loaded wagon containing clothing had been sent from Mrs. Bowie's house to the house of a Mr. Worthington, near the Potomac, for transmission to Virginia, I detailed a force from this office to investigate the matter, and arrest the said Walter Bowie and any other parties engaged in disloyal practices.

Walter Bowie succeeded in evading the search made for him, but it was ascertained that on Sunday night a two-horse wagon was sent from Mrs. Bowie's house, driven by a colored man named Daniel Grant, and in charge of Mr. Contee Warren; that two large trunks were in said wagon, and that the same were taken some miles from Mrs. Bowie's, and then taken from the wagon and deposited by the side of the road, and there left, the driver, Daniel Grant, stating to the said officers that he understood that said trunks contained clothing, &c., and were intended for Walter Bowie. My officers then visited the house of Mr. Worthington, charged with forwarding clothing, goods, &c., from Mrs. Bowie's into Virginia. A full examination of his house and premises was made, but nothing found of a contraband nature. In the process of such examination, my officers, on reaching the garret of Mr. Worthington's house, found the entrance closed and fastened with a padlock. Upon being refused admission, the door was forced open, and, to their surprise and horror, found there two almost naked negro girls, chained together by the wrists, and exhibiting upon their persons evidences of a most brutal and bloody punishment. Their backs were covered with blood, and gashed, as with a sharp knife, from the shoulders to the loins, presenting a spectacle of horrid cruelty and suffering which words cannot describe.

One of these girls was owned by Mrs. Lizzie Bowie, and the other by Mrs. Worthington; and it is understood that they had been beaten with a *trace chain* by three men, namely, Mr. Worthington, Contee Warren, and Mr. Hall, overseer of Mrs. Bowie, and that Mrs. Bowie had ordered the punishment on the girl, who was her slave. I do not understand that any law, human or divine, confers the right to inflict upon helpless women, black or white, the frightful torture borne by these poor and defenseless negro girls. Moved by pity, and the hope that speedy justice from the strong arm of the Government would be visited upon the cowardly miscreants who have dared to commit so infamous a crime, my officers arrested Mr. Worthington and Contee Warren, and brought them to this city, and they are now in the custody of this office until further orders of the War Department are received. I regret to say that the officers, not feeling authorized to act as liberators, left the negro girls chained and bleeding in the garret of Worthington's house.

Respectfully yours,

L. C. BAKER,
Provost-Marshal of the War Department

The captives were released, and, with an expression of the deepest gratitude upon their sad faces, they crawled out of the garret, in which they had not room to stand erect, only to suffer again. I was informed that one of them was soon afterward found in the woods, dead, with marks of the terrible scourge upon her body. The only crime of the poor girls was, obeying the instinctive love of freedom, fired into an irresistible impulse at the sight of the " boys in blue."

A large rebel mail was found between the beds of Mrs. Ducket's room, and specimen packages of blockade goods *in transitu* from Europe were secreted in different parts of the house. Opening the mail, we ascertained that Mr. Waring's mansion had long been the rendezvous of all who served the Southern cause, and a post-office for their correspondence.

Waring was conveyed to Washington, and tried by military commission, and sentenced to two years in Fort Delaware. On his trial it was shown, that for months he had used his horses and wagons to carry rebel recruits to the Potomac; and, even the very night of his arrest, he had brought Bowie, in his Confederate dress, to his house for concealment. After his conviction, the Secretary of War directed that all of his animals and other property should be confiscated and sent to Washington. Accordingly, I repaired to the plantation, and found one hundred and ten slaves, impatient to be free. Unwilling to act without instructions, no proclamation of emancipation having then appeared in behalf of the millions in bondage, and in sympathy with our cause, upon appealing to Mr. Lincoln, with a detailed account of the case, and saying to him, "I did not like to assume the responsibility of their liberation," he characteristically replied : "Baker, let them alone, and they will free themselves!" I took the hint, and returned to the plantation, whither 1 had sent forty Government wagons to transport to the capital the confiscated property.

The more intelligent slaves appointed a committee to wait on me, to inquire what action I intended to take in their case. I reported my interview with "Massa Linkum," as they always called him, and his significant remark. It was quite sufficient for them.

The next morning, with my train, I started, but refused to recognize their escape by affording Government conveyance; when, in a surprisingly brief time, each family was seen with the humble stock of domestic furniture packed, and ready to follow the wagons of "Massa Linkum."

Such patient endurance of fatigue, and uncomplaining toil, to secure the coveted boon of liberty, I never before saw; patience in the pursuit of freedom did "its perfect work."

It was soon known to the neighbors of Waring that his "servants" were *en route* to Washington, who gathered in large numbers, and, fully armed, demanded from me the return of the caravan of laden fugitives. I, of course, refused to do it. The conviction of Waring, and the taking of his property, in my opinion, released the slaves—morally, if not legally.

They then threatened violence, and even attempted to stop the train. The arrest of the ringleaders quieted the mob, and the refugees arrived safely in Washington.

Waring's arrest, and the consequences to him, have been much criticised, and regarded by the South as an arbitrary act; but when we consider that he, with his entire family, were engaged directly in the rebel service, the evidence of which was overwhelming, it must appear to all loyal minds that the proceeding was justifiable, and even necessary.

I copy extracts from the pages of a private journal of the rebel spies captured on the Potomac, which afford a glimpse of life in such adventurous service, that will interest, I am sure, many of my readers:—

JAMES R. MILBURN.

July 23d, 1863. Crossed the Potomac River, from Md. to Va.

24th. Virginia House, Heatharville, Northumberland County, Va.; arrived at Union Wharf, Rap River, 8 P. M.

25th. Miller's Hotel, south side of Rapidan; started for Richmond in company with Captain Cox, of North Va.; walked to Princes, thirty-five miles from Rap.

26th. Breakfasted at Old Church. Arrived in Richmond 4 P. M., Powhatan Hotel · wrote home.

27th. Called on Mr. Barton.

28th. In Richmond. "Disconsolate."

29th. Richmond.

30th. Left Richmond for Buffalo Springs, Mecklenburg County, Va . passed through Petersburg, Va., and Weldon, N. C.

31st. Buffalo Springs, 2 P. M. Room 49, Rowdy Row.
August 1st. First impressions of Springs not very pleasing.
2d. Formed the acquaintance of several pleasant gentlemen.
3d. Found more agreeable company.
4th. Took a long walk in company with Mr. Frank Hobbs, of Md.; talked of dear old Maryland.
5th. Large arrivals; unlimited scope for the study of human nature; to me a look, word, or mere motion of body, hand, or head, will often analyze a person's character; first impressions are often lasting, and generally correct.
6th. Each trying to outwit the other. Grouping of nature.
7th. Wrote to Captain Carlisle, Moseby's Cavalry, and to my friend E. N. Spiller, Atlanta, Ga.
8th. Introduced to Mrs. Paxon, wife of the proprietor of Springs. I have closely observed her; think she is well suited to make married life—yes—painfully disagreeable. Some talk of the freedom and bliss of persons before marriage. If this be true, what is the state of one coupled to a disagreeable person; concentrated hell surely.
9th. Tried to meditate on a portion of the Bible; mind unsettled; thoughts like chaff before the wind. Left cottage for a walk to compose myself.
10th. Drinking the oozings of human nature.
11th. Nothing to do; yet not like Miss Flora McFlimsey, nothing to wear.
12th. Enjoyed myself by dancing; find very little intellectual conversation; thus far during my visit have not heard a solid subject discussed.
13th. Like a butterfly on the wing, pursuing pleasure.
14th. How various are the classifications of the mind; some appear to be guided by reason, others by a species of brutal instinct.
15th. As a general thing the visitors seem to be friendly.
16th. Ladies very agreeable; endeavor to repay their kindness.
19th. Modesty is a polite accomplishment, and often an attendant upon merit; it wins the hearts of all. None are more disgusting in company than the impudent and presuming.
20th. What a fine place to show a person's breeding. Train up a child, &c., &c.
21st. This day to me is a memorial one, no one can tell my feelings, perhaps the thoughts of another one the same; whether it is a day of folly or happiness, the future will show. My intention was honest, howsoever this affair may terminate, perhaps sympathy was the cause of my action and words. I must say, I do not understand myself in this case. Wrote a long letter to my friend Spiller.
22d. Miss Lucy A. Merritt, of Brunswick County, Va., returned to Buffalo; a long walk and confidential talk with her. Having noticed my letter to Mr. Spiller, asked to see it. Miss Merritt had no evil intentions when she made this request, this I firmly believe; I complied with her wish, as it seemed to be a test of friendship.
23d. Placid as a lake, nothing unusual transpired.
24th. In some young people the milk of human kindness seems long since to have curdled· I would advise a little soda to correct the acidity of their

nature. A lady should at all times command her tongue, especially in a public assembly, where a word is an index to intellect and character.

25th. Nothing extraordinary to-day.
26th Preparing to leave Buffalo Springs.
27th. Good-bye, all friends. Confusion to my enemies, if any.
28th. Left Buffalo for Richmond, Va.; at Linwood House.
29th to 31st. Richmond, Va.
September 1st. Enlisted in the Confederate States Navy.
2d. Left Richmond, with Captain John W. Hebb, of Louisiana, for a cruise in the Chesapeake and its tributaries. Left the cars at Milford Station; dined at Lloyd's, Caroline County, Virginia; camped at Central Point, Caroline County.
3d. Camped on the Rapidan River, at Mr. Warren's; one meal at 11 P. M.
4th. Lighton's Ferry, Essex County; breakfast, dinner, supper, 9 P. M.
5th. Crossed the Rap. 3½ P. M.; one meal, 9 P. M.; camped in the woods, Camp Rust, Westmoreland County, five miles from Rap. River.
6th. Camp Rust; two meals.
7th. Received a new supply of arms from Richmond; visited Miss Rust; two meals.
8th. Detailed to go on special duty; arrested William Hammond, a half-breed Indian, for boating Confederate deserters across the Potomac. In camp, 11 P. M., tired and hungry.
9th. Camp Rust.
10th. Broke camp, 10 A. M., for Nomoni River, twenty-five miles dined in the road; camped in Richmond County.
11th. Marched all day; camped, 9 A. M.; one meal.
12th. Dined at 8 P. M.; rained all night, half drowned next morning.
13th. Roasted corn early this morning; went out gunning for something to eat, hog, calf, or any thing; nothing procured.
15th. Went to Nomoni Ferry, 5 P. M.; duck, crab, corn bread, butter, and milk.
16th. Dined with Miss Arnest.
17th. Fight between Manning and Fitzgerald; drew my pistol to shoot Fitzgerald, who threatened to strike me, while in charge of camp, with a sword. I wisely desisted from the intended blow. Nothing to eat.
18th. No provisions; sent out a party to forage, no success.
19th. Killed a hog early this morning.
20th. All quiet; truly a placid state. Strolled about e woods as if I had no home. Home is the dearest place on earth, especially when it is impossible to be there.
21st. Killed another hog.
22d. On picket, fork of road.
23d About to break camp.
24tl Yanks attacked our forces, at Mathias Point, with infantry and gunboats; shelled us out.
25th. Moved camp.
26th. Sick all day.

27th. On Nomoni again; off on an expedition.
28th. Unwell.
29th. Feel better.
30th. Sick.
October 1st. Still sick.
2d. Headache.
3d. In hospital at Bethel M. E. Church.
4th and 5th. Chill.
6th to 11th. Sick at Mr. Ames's.
12th. Colonel Blackwell's, on Potomac.
13th. Crossed to St. Mary's County, last night.
14th. Patuxent River.
15th to 17th. Calvert County, Maryland.
18th. Sharp's Island.
19th to 28th. Tilligman's Island.
31st. Chills.
November 1st. Tilligman's Island.
3d. Tilligman's Island. Captain Hebb captured last night.
4th. Yankee cavalry crossed the bay to Fair Haven, A. A. County.
30th. Cove Point. Cast away.
December 1st. Cove Point. Boat repaired.
2d. On the way to the Confederate States.
22d. Calvert County. Slept in an unoccupied house.
23d.   do.   do.   do.   Nothing to eat.
29th. St. Mary's County. Went to Rob. Thompson's, cold and hungry, would not let me warm myself, or give me any thing to eat. Slept near Point No point.
30th. Took to the woods; afraid of the Yanks.
31st. In a hogpen; wet and cold.
January 1st, 1864. Live in hope that I may safely reach my destination, confident of ultimate success, though every thing seems to oppose.
12th. Pasquith's. Yankee raid from Point Lookout.
14th.   do.   Yankees gone.
17th. Corinth Church.
18th and 19th. Heathsville. (18th. Boat stolen.)
25th. Heathsville. Went to Machota Creek, in woods.
February 1st and 2d. Heathsville. Yankees about.
12th. Attempted to cross the Potomac last night in company with two ladies and Charley; wind fair from S. W., but too heavy; compelled to turn back. Slept at Mr. Bailey G. Haynie's.
13th. Wind S.S.E.; at B. G. Haynie's; crossed the Potomac; rowed from Precher' Creek, Va., to Point Lookout; sailed to Patuxent River; landed ladies, 7 A. M. Sunday, 14th.
15th. Plum Point, Calvert County, Md. Slept in an unoccupied house on shore.

CHARLES W. MILBURN.

July 23d, 1863. Ran the blockade across the Potomac; a little cloudy landed at Cone River; slept on the beach the remainder of the night; mosquitoes very thick, and large enough to bite through my coat.

24th. Arrived at Heathsville; dined at Virginia House; started at 3 P. M. for Union Wharf, on the Rap. River; arrived too late to get across the river, remained all night.

25th. Crossed the river; started for Bowler's; procured conveyance from the ferryman to Millar's; dined at Brown's Hotel; impossible to obtain conveyance to Richmond; after finding a berth in a market-wagon for my baggage, I came to the conclusion to walk; started at 4 P. M.; walked to Mr. Princess's, seventeen miles; remained all night.

26th. Started at daybreak for Old Church, 10 miles; arrived at 8.30 A. M. breakfasted; arrived at Richmond, 4 P. M.; Powhatan Hotel; wrote home.

27th. Obtained a pass from General Winder, to pass unmolested in the city for thirty days; called to see Mr. Barton.

30th. Left Richmond for Buffalo Springs, Mecklenburg County, Va.; passed through Petersburg, Va., and Weldon, N. C., and arrived at my destination, 31st, at 2 P. M.

31st. Occupying room No. 49; prospect very pleasing.

August 7th. Still at Buffalo, enjoying myself wonderfully; wrote to Captain Carlisle, C. S. A., and Mr. Spiller.

22d. Wrote to Mr. Spiller, Atlanta, Ga.; Miss Lucy A. Merritt returned to Buffalo, stayed till Sunday; had a very pleasant time during her visit.

31st. A beautiful day. Received orders from Captain H. to prepare to leave Richmond to-morrow morning, under command of Captain Walter Bowie, C. S. N.

September 1st. After arriving at the depot, received another order, to wait until Wednesday. Went to new R. Theatre; a splendid plot, though not well acted.

2d. Left Richmond on the Fred. train, with Captain Walter Bowie, twenty-two men in all; dined at Lloyd's in Caroline County, Va.; encamped at Center Point, Caroline County, Va.

3d. Got something to eat at Sparta, about 11 P. M.; camped on the Rappahannock River, at Mr. Warren's.

4th. Camped at Leighton's Ferry, Essex Co., Rappahannock River; got some cabbage and bacon about 9 A. M.

5th. Acting cook under difficulties; crossed the Rap. River, 3.30 P. M.; supped in Westmoreland County, 9 P. M.; camped in the woods, on Mr. Rust's plantation, five miles from Rap. River.

6th. Breakfasted about 9; corn bread and crackers, commonly called "short cakes;" amused myself by gathering fox-grapes near the camp; constructed a chebang in the new camp. Captain Hebb arrived with arms and a guard of eight men; went to sleep at 9 o'clock.

7th. Breakfast sent to me by Miss Lizzie Rust; accepted an invitation to dine at Mr. Rust's; had quite a pleasant time with ladies.

8th. Jim, with thirteen others, detailed, at 3 A. M., to go from camp on special duty; they arrived in camp about 11 P. M., with one prisoner, named William Hammond, who seemed to be very uneasy; on guard from 12 P. M. to 2 o'clock. Beautiful night.

9th. Left camp with Captain Bowie, to make a reconnoissance; breakfasted in camp; returned to camp, about 11 P. M., tired and hungry; "scone on the road."

10th. H. H., a prisoner, started for Richmond in charge of Private Rusloe, broke up camp at 10 A. M.; started with Captain Bowie for banks of Potomac, Mathias Point; another party, under Captain H., started for Nomoni River; marched all day, without any thing to eat; slept at Mr. McClannahan's, Machota Creek.

11th. Marched till about 4 P. M.; slept at Dr. Hooes'; Captain Band and myself had quite a pleasant time with the ladies.

12th. Captain B. sent me to Waterloo, and orders to Lieutenant K., C. S. S. O.; started from W. about dusk, for Mathias Point.

12th. Raining very hard; slept in rain all night without a blanket.

13th. Capt. B. left about dark, with eight men, for Maryland (beautiful night for crossing), leaving me in charge of camp.

14th. Nothing unusual transpired; short of rations; mosquitoes a great plague; no sleeping for them.

15th. Sent out a foraging party; nothing procured.

16th. Impossible to get provisions; prepared to go into Maryland after some.

17th. Wind high; no prospect of crossing to-night; dined with Mr. Washington; sent Phil. Key out to get something to eat; obtained very little.

18th. A slight supper last night; nothing since, except some green corn.

19th. All quiet on the Potomac; nothing to eat; 8 P. M. crossed the Potomac (men in full uniform and arms); landed in Charles County, Md.

20th. Went, in company with P. K., to visit Dr. O.; kindly treated. How glad I am to be once more in old Maryland.

21st. This morning two men missing; supposed to have deserted.

22d. Heard from Captain B.; a slight skirmish with the Yanks; prepare to return to Virginia.

23d. Two Confederate prisoners escaped from Point Lookout and came to us to-day. Having procured what we desired, we returned to Virginia. Wrote home before leaving Maryland.

November 20th. Left Baltimore, 1 A. M., on the steamer *John Pentz*, for West River.

21st. Fair Haven, Herring Bay, A. A. County, Md., Medley House.

22d. Fair Haven. Set out on my journey.

23d. Plum Point, Calvert County, Md. Breakfasted at a negro hut; slept at S. Y. Dorsey's; rained all night.

29th. Mr. Bowers. Started for Virginia at dark; wind overblew me; forced to beach my boat near Cove Point; slept in woods.

30th. Cove Point Calvert County, Md.

I will close this chapter of treason and oppression's crimes, with a letter to the President, which, I need not say, elicited all the sympathy and aid the great heart and high position of the President could extend:—

OFFICE PROVOST-MARSHAL WAR DEPARTMENT,
WASHINGTON, *September* 80, 1863.

ABRAHAM LINCOLN, President of the United States:—

SIR—I beg leave respectfully to call your attention to the facts set forth below.

The colored people, slave and free, of this District and the adjoining counties of Maryland, are daily subjected to a more ferocious despotism, and more flagrant and shameless outrages, than were ever before tolerated by any Government claiming to be either wise or humane.

It is well known to you, sir, that large numbers, owned in Maryland, actuated by a supreme desire to participate in the blessings of freedom enjoyed by their fellows in this District, are daily, almost hourly, making attempts to escape from their masters, and fly to this city.

The slave-owners of Maryland, whose plantations are becoming desolate by this constant exodus of their chattels, no longer relying on the protection of their own laws and legally constituted authorities, have, in many cases, formed themselves into armed bands for the purpose of pursuing and recapturing escaped slaves.

Parties of slaves, men, women, and children, have been pursued within the bounds of this District, have been fiercely assailed and shot down, or remorselessly beaten, and the survivors shut up in prison, or conveyed across the Potomac, within the protecting arms of the rebel Confederacy.

Not less than forty slaves (human beings), by these lawless encounters, were killed; and I have information, that no less than three dead bodies of slaves, thus cruelly slaughtered, are now lying in the woods almost within sight of your own homes.

Not a month since, an armed band of Maryland slave-owners surrounded the house of a free negro woman, less than three miles from the Capitol, broke open the door, presented loaded pistols to the heads of its frightened inmates, and, after exercising all their powers of abuse and insult, took away by violence three free negroes.

Visiting this city, and protected by the assumed authority of Mr. Commissioner Cox, these depredators break into the houses of colored citizens, thrust loaded pistols into the faces of terrified women and screaming children, and, *protected by legal papers*, bear off their victims to the tender mercies of the lash and prison, or the hopeless martyrdom of Southern slavery.

Along the borders of the Potomac, below this city, male slaves are now being mustered in gangs, and sent to Virginia, as contributions by their masters to the cause of rebellion; and if these men make an effort to escape, they are pursued and shot down by their unmerciful owners.

There is now in Marlborough jail, a negro man, whose eyes have been utterly destroyed by a charge of shot fired wantonly into his face; and, not long since, two colored girls were found chained in the garret of a private house, in the neighborhood of this city, who, after having been cruelly beaten by three men, one of them using a trace chain to inflict the blows, were left, with their backs one mass of festering wounds, to the further horrors of chains and darkness.

An instance has just come to my knowledge, of a negro woman and three daughters, owned by a citizen of this city still resident here, who were sent to Baltimore a few days before the late Emancipation Act was passed, for the sole purpose of evading its provisions. One of these daughters, an intelligent woman, has succeeded in returning to Washington, and is now claimed as a slave and threatened with seizure through the agency of Mr. Commissioner Ocr's summary and illegal writs.

It can not be that such atrocities will be longer permitted, and that men, whose every sympathy is with slavery, and its legitimate offspring, treason, shall be longer suffered to visit upon the poor slave the hatred they feel to freedom and the Union.

I respectfully ask for such instructions as shall enable me effectually to protect the now helpless victims of the slave-masters' vengeance, and the perjured oaths of their friends, official and otherwise, in this city and District.

I am, sir, your obedient servant,

L. C. BAKER,
Colonel and Provost-Marshal War Department.

CHAPTER XI.

SLAVERY—PLAYING REBEL GENERAL—FIRST DISTRICT CAVALRY.

The Hostages—Mr. Lincoln—Deceiving the Rebels—A Successful Game—Organization of the First District Cavalry—Its Services.

ABOUT this time, one hundred rebel citizens, in Lower Maryland, took possession of two contraband teamsters in my employ, and refused to give any account of the reclaimed property. I immediately arrested and confined two of the leaders, and put them in the Central guard-house, Washington, as hostages, till the former were returned. The indignation, at my assumption that a negro was equal to a white man—especially to one of the chivalry—was intense. An appeal was made to Mr. Lincoln, and I was summoned to report in person to him, which I cheerfully did.

He said: "Well, Baker, you think a white man is as good as a colored man?"

I assured him that in this case, at least, I did; and proposed to keep the gentlemen in prison till the free negroes were returned.

The President acquiesced in the justice of the arrangement, and, soon after, the contrabands were restored, and the insulted, excited prisoners set at liberty, to the great relief of their friends, and amusement of the irreverent "Yankees," who could not see the superiority of Southern blood.

I shall notice here some incidents which will forcibly show the self-sacrifice of the Maryland secessionists, who were vastly in the majority, along with the more important and melancholy truth, that the rebellion could never have succeeded without the sympathy and assistance of "Northern friends." In addition to these facts, the means sometimes necessary to ascertain who were disloyal, will also be apparent.

A few days previous to the rebel Generals Stuart and

Early's raid into Pennsylvania, I had the following paper prepared:—

To THE FRIENDS OF THE SOUTH:—
The Confederate army is now on your border. The Stars and Bars can be seen from your hills. The hirelings of the North are fleeing before us! We want your aid. We want horses, mules, and wagons. Seventy artillery horses are needed for our batteries. The bearers of this appeal are authorized by me to accept of contributions. If I receive the required aid, I will pledge myself that our flag shall float, within ten days, from the Capitol in Washington.
(Signed) J. E. B. STUART,
C. S. Cavalry.

With this sounding proclamation in my pocket, I reached that garden of Maryland, "Middletown Valley," a few miles north of Harper's Ferry. Upon making application to the leading—to the principal secessionists, and exhibiting the paper, the highest expressions of patriotism greeted it. Property and life were at my disposal. And it was suggested to me that a secret meeting be called, to afford all the opportunity to contribute.

The hour came; and I was introduced to those present as a Confederate officer who had ventured over the Potomac. By this means a correct list of all those who were openly or secretly the emissaries of Jeff. Davis, with the names of those who contributed horses, was made out, and the next day I called at their residences. After selecting the best, I left the animals in the hands of the owners, to be called for subsequently. Meanwhile, during the few days I continued in the valley, I learned the strength, resources, and condition of the rebel cause there. I then went around and gathered up the horses, and, with many warm benedictions upon my head, left with sixteen of the choicest horses the region afforded. That night I started for Washington, and the succeeding day I turned them over to the quartermaster's department. They afterward did good service on the battlefield for the Union cause.

The information I obtained, respecting the forward movement of the enemy, was followed by General Hooker's celebrated march toward Gettysburg, during which he was relieved by General Meade; and the inference is legitimate,

REBEL CONTRIBUTION TO THE LOYAL CAUSE.

that it had no unimportant bearing upon the great and decisive struggle, which saved us from a disastrous if not a fatal invasion.

Some two months later, several of the former owners of the horses appeared in Washington, and demanded the restoration of their property. Of course, the animals themselves were comparatively of no consequence, but the intelligence, of which they were made the occasion, was invaluable. The claimants were pointed to the proclamation, their prompt response to which, was no less the evidence of disloyalty because it was a lure instead of treason's actual demand.

The importance of the bureau, and its rapidly accumulating business, rendered a military force, exclusively under my control, a necessity. Scarcely a day passed without some occurrence calling for cavalry troops to execute orders. Accordingly, the Secretary of War issued an order creating me colonel, and authorizing me to raise a regiment of cavalry.

WAR DEPARTMENT, WASHINGTON, *June* 29, 1863.

SIR—You are hereby informed that the President of the United States has appointed you colonel of the First Regiment District of Columbia Cavalry, in the service of the United States, to rank as such from the twenty-ninth day of June, one thousand eight hundred and sixty-three.

Immediately on receipt hereof, please to communicate to this department, through the Adjutant-General of the army, your acceptance or non-acceptance; and, with your letter of acceptance, return the *oath* herewith inclosed, properly filled up, *subscribed*, and *attested*, and report your age, birthplace, and the State of which you were a permanent resident. You will report for duty to—

EDWIN M. STANTON,
Secretary of War.

Colonel L. C. BAKER,
First Regiment District Columbia Cavalry.

Previous to this, being only a citizen, I was viewed in the light of no more than a civil agent. To obviate the hinderance in official service the fact interposed, I received the commission. Immediately I had thousands of applications from men who desired to serve in my battalion. It was my desire to organize a corps of intelligent, moral, and worthy men. So common had it become, in raising regiments, to sell commissions to the highest bidders, that it was a matter of regular traffic. This did more to demoralize and bring into disrepute our whole volunteer service than any other single wrong.

At the outset of the war, morality and fitness were seldom considerations in the selection of officers. I have seen volunteer companies, and even regiments, under the command of those whose capacity and character were inferior to the majority of the privates in the ranks. For illustration of this method of getting commissions, I add the subjoined communication, in answer to an offer of one hundred dollars for a place in my regiment:—

OFFICE PROVOST-MARSHAL WAR DEPARTMENT,
WASHINGTON, *May* 18, 1863.

Mr. J. F. SINGHI, Company D, Fourth Maine Regiment,
Army of the Potomac:—

SIR—Your letter, offering one hundred dollars in gold for a commission in my battalion of cavalry, has been received. It is my intention to recruit *honest men*, and *not rogues*. With this explanation, you will at once perceive that you are entirely ineligible for service under my command, either as officer or private. (Signed) L. C. BAKER,
Provost-Marshal War Department.

The regiment was a splendid body of troops, and achieved all that was anticipated from it; and its services will appear at intervals during the progress of the war.

Much of the service performed for the country will never be written. The detachments of men moving stealthily over the lines of encampment and battle; guarding me or my subordinates in perilous adventures; and other quiet, unheralded, and unreported duties, will have no record but the pages of memory, and, with the death of the actors in the varied scenes of such a life, be forgotten.

But since this volume has been in progress of preparation for the press, a history of the troops whom, I may be permitted to say here, I was proud to command, has been published by their former chaplain, the Rev. S. H. Merrill, of Portland, Maine.

The chaplain states, correctly, that this regiment was organized to remain on duty within the limits of the District of Columbia. The entire military force of the District had failed to check the operations of Mosby's band. I pledged myself to the Secretary of War that, if he would give me permission to raise a battalion of cavalry, I would drive from the region the rebel chief.

After the troops were raised, and armed with six-shooters, they became the object of intense and unjust suspicion on the part of the commanding officer of the Department of Washington and West Virginia, founded on the apprehension that his military honors would be periled by the successes of the brave men who were to range freely through Western Virginia.

The Secretary of War had so much confidence in the battalion, that he authorized the purchase of the best horses that could be procured in the country, and remarked that the Government could afford to pay the expense of maintaining the force, if for no other reason than the powerfully restraining influence upon disloyalty and crime in the District.

The legitimate duties of the battalion were so constantly embarrassed by orders emanating from the department commander, that I decided to ask the Secretary of War to increase it to a full regiment of twelve hundred men. The request was granted, and eight additional companies were raised in the State of Maine, under the direction of its patriotic Governor Coney, whose services during the rebellion will always be gratefully remembered by the loyal North.

On the completion of the organization of the regiment, I requested that it should be sent to some distant field of action. The deeply seated prejudice in the minds of the officers of the Potomac army against my bureau, convinced me that my troops would there have small opportunity to display their ability and heroism. When I had occasion to scrutinize some of their acts, a major-general remarked to me, during a visit to the front, in regard to the injustice of which I had complained, "Your men are a set of d——d spies, and ought to be killed; and the officers of the regiment are detectives in disguise, reporting to you whatever is said by the army commanders." Even the long raids, the fights with Mosby's men in Northern Virginia and Maryland, have scarcely an allusion made to them by any of the army officers or reporters. For nearly two years the regi ment accompanied nearly every raid made by the cavalry along the front of the Potomac army.

It formed the advanced guard of General Kautz's raid from Norfolk to the Weldon Railroad. At Notaway Bridge, Reams' Station, and other points, it is a matter of official record, that this body of troops did three-fourths of all the fighting. My urgent request to be relieved from duty in Washington, and allowed to lead my regiment to the arena of battle, was refused by the Secretary of War, and the active command was given to Lieutenant-Colonel E. J. Conger, who had no superior in the qualities of a brave chieftain.

Before he assumed his duties, he had been wounded three times, and twice left on the field for dead. At the time of Wilson's celebrated raid, he was again shot through the body, and carried from the scene of carnage by his orderly.

Major J. S. Baker, next in rank, commanded the regiment until the close of the war. A more brilliant record than his has never fallen to the lot of a young officer. He entered the service, with the organization of the regiment, as Captain of Company A, which he commanded, until the addition of the Maine companies, in all the celebrated scouts and raids. While a student at Madison University, in Wisconsin, at the beginning of the rebellion, he left his books for his country's service. He was the first Federal officer that entered Lynchburg, after its surrender by Lee.

Major D. S. Curtis, of the same State, next in command, was also a truly brave, discreet, and worthy officer. His coolness in battle was the theme of general remark among the officers of the entire brigade.

A more complete and interesting history of the regiment has been written while this volume has been in press, by the Rev. S. H. Merrill, chaplain of the regiment. From these annals I shall quote the history of the regiment in its general outline of achievement—the more freely, because written by another, who gives to the brave troopers the honors which they so richly won. I shall give the condensed narrative uniform with my own records, with this credit for it awarded to the worthy chaplain:

The First District of Columbia Cavalry was composed of a fine body of men. A single battalion, raised in the District of Columbia, for special duty at the seat of Government, under command of Colonel L. C. Baker (Provost-Marshal of the War Department), and familiarly known as "Baker's Mounted Rangers," formed the nucleus of this regiment.

Long will "Baker's Cavalry" be remembered in Washington, and through a wide region around, as the "terror of evil-doers."

To this command eight companies were added in 1863, embracing about eight hundred men enlisted in Maine, so that it became, to this extent, a Maine organization.

No charge of bad faith is intended, nor is it known who was responsible for the change of the original destination of the regiment, if any change there was; but it is due to the men from Maine, and due to historic truth, to record the fact that they enlisted under the distinct assurance that they would never be required to serve outside the District of Columbia; and if the command was in no degree demoralized by the subsequent disappointment of the men, in being sent to the front, and being placed in the most perilous positions there, it is all the more to their credit.

Company D, numbering one hundred and forty men, under command of Captain J. W. Cloudman, left Augusta on the 22d day of October, 1863, and arrived at Camp Baker, in Washington, on the 25th.

The three officers of this company were commissioned by the President of the United States, while those of the other companies from Maine were commissioned by the Governor of Maine.

A few days after its arrival in Washington, the company was ordered to Anandale, ten miles west of Alexandria, where it remained on duty, under command of Lieutenant Howe, till the 27th of January, when it was ordered with the battalion to Yorktown.

Embarking on board the steamer *Conqueror*, it arrived at Yorktown on the 28th, and went into camp about two miles from the city, on the bank of the beautiful York River. A morning so summer-like and scenery so charming, few of our men had ever seen before in mid-winter.

The next day they moved about eight miles west, and went into camp about three miles from Williamsburg.

January 30th, at daybreak, the bugle sounded "boots and saddles," and in half an hour they were off on a raid.

If the reader should ask what this means, the answer would be, it means an armed expedition into the enemy's country, for the purpose of gaining information, or of capturing or destroying public property, or both, always respecting private property, excepting so far as "military necessity" requires its capture.

In the raid just referred to, the men marched about twelve miles, and returned to camp with nothing of special interest to report.

An expedition was made to Bottom Bridge, on the Chickahominy, twelve miles from Richmond, on the 5th, 6th, 7th, and 8th of February, which will not soon be forgotten by the men who participated in it. They did little fighting, but much hard work. From the time they left camp, on the 5th, till they returned, on the 8th, they were hardly out of the saddle.

This regiment was distinguished by the superiority of the carbines with which it was armed. It was the only regiment in the army of the Potomac armed with "Henry's Repeating Rifle." The peculiarity of this gun is, that it will fire sixteen shots without reloading. It is cocked by the same movement of the guard that opens and closes the breech— the exploded cartridge being withdrawn and a fresh one supplied at the same time and by the same movements. The copper cartridges are placed in a tube, extending the entire length of the barrel, on the under side. From this they are fed into the gun by the operation of the lever guard ; meantime a spiral spring forces down the cartridges as fast as they are discharged. The whole device is of the simplest nature. The work is strong, and the whole thing is so nearly perfect, that it is difficult to conceive of any improvement. The subsequent history of this regiment proves it to be a terribly effective weapon. Fifteen shots can be given with it in ten seconds. Thus, a regiment of one thousand men would fire fifteen thousand shots in ten seconds. After having witnessed the effectiveness of this weapon, one is not surprised at the remark, said to have been made by the guerrilla chief, Mosby, after an encounter with some of our men, that "he did not care for the common gun, or for Spencer's seven-shooter, but as for these guns, that they could wind up on Sunday and shoot all the week, it was useless to fight against them."

On the 16th of February, Company F was mounted, and remained at Camp Baker, engaged in daily drilling until the 7th of April. At that date it left Washington for Norfolk, and the next day joined a squadron of the old battalion on picket at Great Bridge.

On the 14th the company marched to Deep Creek, where 't was joined by three companies of the old battalion, already referred to as having been on picket duty at Newport News.

These companies remained here on picket duty until the organization of the cavalry division, under General Kautz, two weeks later.

On the 5th of May they marched with the cavalry division under Kautz, on his first raid. The object of these raids was twofold, viz.: to weaken the enemy by destroying public property, and by drawing off detachments in pursuit. A successful raid requires a judicious selection of routes, rapid marches, short halts, and sudden and unexpected blows. In this service, General Kautz was "the right man in the right place."

In this movement he had passed through Suffolk and crossed the Black Water (where his march could have been easily arrested by destroying the bridge), before the enemy became aware of his purpose. At half-past two o'clock on the afternoon of the 7th, he had marched a distance of seventy miles, and struck the Weldon Railroad just in time to intercept a body of rebel troops on their way to Petersburg. A thunderbolt from a clear sky could hardly have been more astounding to the enemy. Instantly he was attacked. In an incredibly short time the action was over, the enemy was whipped, the railroad was cut, the public buildings were in flames, and the gallant Kautz was again on his march, with some sixty prisoners in his train.

Turning southward, the march was continued to the point where the railroad crosses the Notaway River. Here an obstinately contested fight took place in which the callant Lieutenant Jackson, of Company E, fell mortally wounded. Here, too, fell a brave private, Samuel de Laite.

In this engagement, as in others, the bravery of the men, and the efficiency of their sixteen-shooters, were put to the proof.

Major Curtis was ordered to deploy his battalion as skirmishers, and charge a much larger force of the enemy, along the railroad, near the bridge. It was a covered bridge, and the rebels soon ran to it for shelter. Our brave boys charged boldly after them, driving them through and into their fortifications on the other side, killing some and taking several prisoners, with small loss on our side. Some of the prisoners said they "thought we must have had a whole army, from the way the bullets flew."

One lieutenant asked if we "loaded up over night and then fired all day." He said "he thought, by the way the bullets came into the bridge, they must have been fired by the basketful."

The result of the affair was that the bridge was burned, and Kautz was again on the march, with forty rebel prisoners added to his train.

The immediate object of the expedition having been accomplished, the command marched to City Point. Crossing the Appomattox on the 10th, they encamped for a day near General Butler's head-quarters. Twenty-four hours, however, had not elapsed, when the division moved again on another raid, which proved to be one of the most hazardous and effective of the war. During the time that General Butler's forces were engaged with the enemy, between Bermuda Hundred and Richmond, General Kautz adroitly slipped through the lines, and again boldly dashed into the heart of Dixie.

He passed rapidly through Chesterfield County, pausing at the court-house only long enough to open the jail and liberate two prisoners.

As we dislike to be laughed at, the reader may pass over the following explanatory statement:—

One of these prisoners was a woman, who refused to leave the jail after the doors were opened, seeming to doubt the authority of the Yankees to discharge her. The other stated that he had been imprisoned on account of his Union sentiments, and seemed very grateful to his deliverers. A few hours later, however, he disappeared from the column, taking with him the horse and equipments with which he had been kindly furnished, and forgetting to give notice of his intended route. The loss of the horse, however, was subsequently made up. A rebel, living not far from our encampment, had a valuable animal, which he was very particular to declare should never be taken from him. Accordingly he armed himself, and took up his lodgings in the stable. But he must needs sleep, and the boys knew it; and it so happened that he opened his eyes one morning on an empty stall. Certain words were spoken, decidedly more energetic than pious, but they did not bring the horse back.

Leaving the court-house, the column moved on to Coalfield Station, on the Danville Railroad, thirteen miles west from Richmond. On the arrival of the troops, at about half-past ten in the evening, the inhabitants were surprised and alarmed quite out of their propriety. That the Yankees should have had the audacity to visit that section, seemed actually incomprehensible. But there was no remedy.

Instantly, guards were posted on all the roads leading to and from Petersburg and Richmond, and the work of the hour was hardly begun before it was ended. No harm was done to persons, or to private property, but the railroad was destroyed, the telegraph came down, and trains of cars, depot buildings, and large quantities of Government stores, went up in smoke.

On the 12th, the "history of this affair" repeated itself at Black's and White's Station, on the Southside Railroad, thirty miles west from Petersburg, and forty from Coalfield Station. The railroad was torn up, and the telegraph torn down, while the depot buildings, together with large quantities of corn, and flour, and meal, and tobacco, and salt, designed for the rebel army, were subjected to the action of fire, and resolved into their original elements.

Wellville Station, five miles east, on the same railroad, a few hours later, shared a similar fate. The column now moved in the direction of Bellefield, on the Weldon Railroad. When within two miles of that place, General Kautz learned that the enemy was in force to receive him. As his object was not so much to fight as to weaken the enemy, by interrupting his communications and destroying his supplies, he avoided an engagement, turning to the left from Bellefield, and marching, *via* Jarratt's Station, to the Notaway River.

When the advance reached Freeman's Bridge, on this river, at ten o'clock P. M., it was discovered that the whole command was in a trap. One span of the bridge, forty feet in length, had been cut out. The river, for a considerable distance, was unfordable. The fords, above and below, were strongly guarded, and the enemy was gathering in force in the rear. The position was not a desirable one. The river must be crossed, or a battle must be fought on the enemy's chosen ground, where little was to be gained, but where every thing must be hazarded. A major of a New York regiment, commanding the advance, declared that the bridge could not be made passable before the afternoon of the next day. But on the assurance of Captain Howe, that it could be done in a much shorter time, Company D was ordered up and told what was wanted. Working parties were instantly organized. In a short time, tall pines in the neighboring woods had fallen before the axes of one party, and stalwart men, by means of the drag-ropes of a battery, had drawn them out. Another party had, in the mean time, crossed the river on a little float they had fortunately found, and stood on the remaining part of the bridge on the other side. The ropes were thrown to them, and the string-pieces were drawn across the chasm and placed in position. To cover them with rails was but the work of a few moments, and in less than three hours from the time the Maine boys began the work it was completed, and the column passed over in safety.

The division reached City Point on the 19th. During the last nine days it marched, on an average, twenty hours out of the twenty-four, leaving only four hours for rest. It will hardly be believed, that in some instances hunger compelled the men to eat raw corn like their horses, but such was the fact.

On this raid they cut the Richmond and Danville and

Southside Railroad in six different places, and inflicted an amount of damage upon the enemy's communications and army stores which told severely upon them afterward.

On their arrival at City Point, both men and horses were much exhausted. On the 20th the command crossed again to Bermuda Hundred, and went into camp about a mile from the river.

On the 7th of April we embarked on board a fine steamer, with a pleasant company, for Fortress Monroe, where we arrived at an early hour next morning. For many years Fortress Monroe had been to us a familiar name, but we were not long in discovering that the descriptions of it and its surroundings as they *were*, conveyed no correct idea of them as they *are*.

Then, there was little to be seen save the formidable walls of the old fort, rising from the sand and rocks, at the distance of a few rods from the water's edge, and the solitary sentry, slowly pacing the lofty parapet; while scarcely a human voice broke the tomb-like silence of the place.

Now, a busy scene was presented. Numerous newly constructed piers had been pushed out into the sparkling waters of the bay, and the grounds outside the walls were occupied with a curious and compact group of buildings of rude architecture, clearly designed for temporary use. The scene on the wharf was one of unusual animation and of picturesque effect. Looking down from the hurricane deck, we beheld a sea of faces, and could not well preserve our gravity as we marked the curious variety it presented.

There was the brown-visaged man in dusky gray, the worse for wear, the seedy representative of an humbled aristocracy, and there was the lean, lank, sallow, dirty, hangdog specimen of the "poor trash" of the South. There were heads adorned with handkerchiefs of many brilliant colors, and heads that had no covering but wool. There were preposterous bonnets and stove-pipe hats, with a "smart sprinkling" of military and naval headgear. There were rich silk dresses and tow frocks. There was crinoline of enormous proportions, and there were flat feet peering from beneath it, perfectly innocent of either shoes or stockings

It was a motley group—big and little, old and young.

civil and military. While all were busy and animated, it was easy to see that the whites of southern blood felt least at home, while the negroes were in their element. They talked the most, made the best show of white teeth, and, of all we could see, seemed decidedly the most comfortable.

There is truth in the old adage, that "it is an ill wind hat blows nobody any good." While the "red tape" business was drawing its "slow length along," some of us took a stroll out to Hampton, or rather to the site of that ancient and once pleasant village.

It was but a short walk, leading, for the most part, through a collection of Government storehouses, and huts and tents so disorderly in their arrangements as to suggest the idea of reading the riot act without delay. On the way we noticed one or two handsome places, among them the residence of the Hon. Mr. Segar, surrounded by venerable trees, and commanding as charming a scene as one could desire, in the beautiful expanse of Hampton Roads, dotted with white sails and stirred by innumerable paddle-wheels. We next came to the McClellan Hospital, with its outlying wards and its broad and beautiful gardens.

Hampton was reached by crossing a bridge about four hundred paces long. Before the rebellion it was a jewel of a village, embosomed in noble trees, which threw their welcome shade over the streets and ample grounds which fronted the tasteful residences.

Hampton was settled ten years after Jamestown, and was, at the time of its destruction, the oldest Anglo-Saxon settlement then inhabited in the United States. Now it is a scene of utter desolation, inhabited almost exclusively by blacks. With the exception of an occasional grocery store, and a very few dwellings of a more respectable appearance, the residences were of the rudest description, nearly all of one room, and situated as if they had been flung out of a great architectural leather apron.

The "Old Church," cruciform in shape, and colonial in date, presented a singularly picturesque appearance, and was almost the only object about the town which indicated its former condition. The tower, from which a noble old bell once pealed out its mellow tones had fallen into a heap of rubbish at the western end of the cross, while massive walls rose aloft in gloomy grandeur. A wilderness of young aspens and willows, with here and there a dense growth of hardy roses, disputed the possession of some once cherished graves, with a savage intrusion of undergrowth. Fragments of tombs, some with armorial blazonry, were scattered about, and the whole place bore sad evidence of the terrible scourge of war. Nor could we resist the conviction that the peopl who have thus felt it will be slow to invoke it again.

Failing of the main object of our expedition, partly, perhaps, from our want of acquaintance with the occult science of "red tape," we returned to Washington, and were there mustered into service, under a special order of the War Department.

On the 12th of May these six companies, still unmounted, and having drilled only on foot, were ordered to Fortress Monroe. Leaving Washington the next afternoon on board of transports, after touching at Fort Monroe, we proceeded to Norfolk, and, reporting to General Shepley, were ordered to Portsmouth, where we disembarked and went into camp in the rear of the town.

On the morning of the 22d we re-embarked on board a transport for James River. Dropping anchor about sunset, opposite Fort Powhattan, we passed the night quietly under the protection of the guns of the *Atlanta*. This craft will be remembered as the strange sea-monster designed by the rebels to destroy the blockading fleet off Charleston harbor, but, by a higher power, to do good service for the Government. One of the boys thought it "looked like the devil." Another could see no such resemblance, but said it "looked like a big sea turtle on a raft, with his '*back up*.'"

A short run of about a dozen miles, the next morning, took us to Bermuda Hundred, where we disembarked, and went into camp about a mile from the landing, beside the other six companies. The regiment was now together for the first time.

At one o'clock A. M. of the 24th, one battalion was ordered to City Point, to take the place of a detachment which had been sent to Fort Powhattan. That fort, manned by colored troops, had been attacked by a considerable force under Fitz

Hugh Lee. They were, however, gallantly repulsed, and, before the arrival of the reinforcements, had retreated, and the battalion returned.

General Butler, commanding the army of the James, consisting of the tenth and eighteenth army corps, had taken possession of City Point and Bermuda Hundred on the 5th instant, greatly to the surprise of the enemy.

His fortifications extended from the Point of Rocks, on the Appomattox, northwardly to near Dutch Gap, on the James River, a distance of about five miles.

General Grant was fighting his way to the south side of the James. The bloody battles of the Wilderness and of Spottsylvania Court-House had been fought, and an order was received by General Butler, for the eighteenth corps to proceed to the White House, to co-operate with the Army of the Potomac.

On the 25th this corps left, and the cavalry, acting as infantry, was ordered to the front to take their places in the intrenchments. The position of this regiment was about midway of the line, between the two rivers, in an open field and on level ground. The tents were pitched a few rods in the rear of the breastworks, and with no protection from the shot and shell of the enemy.

The enemy held a formidable line of works in our front, varying in distance from half a mile to two miles. Directly in front of our camp, at the distance of about forty rods from our main line of works, a thick wood prevented us from seeing the enemy's position. A little to our right, the country was open, and there, on an eminence some eighty rods in advance of our breastworks, we had a small redoubt, known as Fort Pride, defended by a section of a battery, and commanded by Captain Pride, an artillery officer, from whom it took its name.

Company M, Captain Sargent commanding, was stationed in this fort as an artillery support. A portion of the regiment was constantly on picket, in front of our main line of works. We were to hold this line. It was here that the six companies referred to as having recently reached the front, loaded their pieces for action for the first time; and it was here that the pluck of the men and the efficiency of their guns were first put to the test.

The enemy shelled us nearly every day from behind his breastworks, and though we received no damage, still a vivid recollection is retained of the shelling. The guns of the enemy, on a part of his line, were trained on the redoubt and when the shells failed, as they often did, to explode at the point intended, they came directly into our camp, the Whitworth whistling with a sound like that produced by the wing of a pigeon swiftly cutting the air—others screaming over our heads or tearing up the ground. In one instance, the fusee of a shell was blown out and struck a colored boy in the face, but inflicted no serious injury. Some of the boys proposed to wash his face, to see if the fright had not bleached him. The humor of these people is "*irrepressible.*" When the fusee whisked across this fellow's face, he opened his eyes wide, and seeing a friend, exclaimed, "By golly, Bill, did you see dat ar snipe?"

"Yah, yah, yah," exclaimed the other, "you nigger. I reckon you wouldn't like to have dat ar snipe pick you."

At three o'clock A. M. of the 28th, the rebels opened on us with artillery, all along the line, and the whole force was ordered to "fall in." It was supposed they were about to assault our works. Drawn up for the first time in close line of battle, a few paces from the breastworks, in anticipation of a bloody conflict, the whole bearing of the men was such as to make their gallant commander proud of them. When all was ready, as the intrepid Colonel Conger mounted on old "Barney," as his war-horse was called, the inevitable pipe in mouth, puffing as quietly as if sitting at his tent-door, the chaplain passed along in front of the line with words of cheer to the men. As he told them what was expected of them, and that he trusted they would give a good account of themselves in the coming conflict, they answered with the utmost enthusiasm, "We will, Chaplain, we will; that is what we came here for. We will do it." The expected assault, however, was not made, and three hours later they returned to their quarters.

On the picket line the time did not entirely pass without enlivening incidents. An officer, one night, discerned a suspicious looking object moving stealthily toward our fortifications. Making a detour, he got into its rear unperceived, and soon discovered that it was a man, reconnoitering our works. By cautious movements, now stepping behind this tree, and now crouching behind that stump, still when the game was still, and moving quickly when it moved, he succeeded in getting sufficiently near, when, taking deliberate aim, he roared out, "Lay down." Disarmed and brought in, the captive proved to be a lieutenant in the rebel service

On the 30th, the thunder of artillery all day gave us a welcome intimation that General Grant was coming. Beyond incidents like these, nothing occurred worthy of note till the 4th of June.

The part of the picket line which extended along in front of our camp, from left to right, about one mile, was held by our regiment. On our right, the line extending on in front of Fort Pride, and some distance beyond, was manned by another regiment. Before daybreak on the morning of the 4th, the enemy commenced a furious shelling, which was continued till sunrise. Meantime he had thrown out a strong line of skirmishers to attack our pickets on the left, for the purpose, doubtless, of diverting attention from the point at which he intended to strike. The attack was sudden and vigorous, but the reserve rallying promptly, with their superior arms, the enemy was repulsed. The skirmishing continued, however, till about nine o'clock, when a regiment of South Carolina troops left their intrenchments, further to our right, and advanced on Fort Pride with a yell peculiarly their own. The pickets of the regiment referred to left their posts and came in.

Captain Sargent at once sent out twenty-one men, under command of Lieutenant Blethen. This small party, taking advantage of the ground, got a position from which, as the enemy advanced on the fort, they could give him an enfilading fire. The first volley told with terrible effect; another equally destructive instantly followed. Another, another, and another, tore through their thinned and thinning ranks. It seemed as if a whole brigade was on their flank. In the mean time our artillery opened on them with grape and canister. A moment more and the survivors were seeking the shelter of their works, leaving their dead and wounded on the field. Among the dead was the colonel of the regiment. A detachment of our men was sent out to man the picket line. Lieutenant Blethen returned, bringing in thirteen prisoners, among whom was one commissioned officer. It is a singular fact, that we had not a man harmed.

Two hours after the fight, the body of the rebel colonel who fell was sent, under a flag of truce, across the enemy's lines, together with his gold watch, a diamond ring, and various other articles of value found upon his person.

It is a noteworthy fact, that the Sabbath was sometimes remembered" in the army, even in the midst of a vigorous campaign. When the troops were on a march, it was different. But, during the ten months the two great armies confronted each other before Richmond, no instance is remembered in which the religious services of the Sabbath were interrupted by the enemy. As by common consent, aggressive movements on both sides, with rare exceptions, were suspended on that day.

Usually on the Sabbath, "all was quiet along the lines." Especially so were the first Sabbaths we passed at Bermuda Hundred front. At the suggestion of Colonel Mix, of the Third New York Cavalry, that regiment and the First District of Columbia Cavalry attended a united service, while stationed at that point, the chaplains of the two regiments officiating alternately.

At one o'clock on the morning of the 10th, the six mounted companies of the First District of Columbia Cavalry moved with the division under General Kautz, as it afterward appeared, to capture Petersburg. The cavalry was to attack the city on the south, while the tenth corps of infantry, under General Gilmore, was to attack on the north side. The cavalry moved promptly. All the troops did their duty well No further account of the matter, however, can here be given than is necessary to show the part borne by this regiment. As the column, marching by the Jerusalem turnpike, approached the enemy's defenses, Lieutenant-Colonel Conger, commanding, ordered Major Curtis to dismount his battalion and charge the enemy's works. Every fourth man was left in charge of the horses The balance of the battalion moved steadily forward, firing rapidly as they advanced, nor did they pause at all till they were inside the rebel works, securing prisoners and destroying such camp equipage as they could not remove.

It was then discovered that they had done this against three times their own number, fighting behind breastworks With the common arm, this would hardly have been possible. Some of the prisoners said: "Your rapid firing confused our men; they thought the devil helped you, and it was of no use to fight." During the action, Captain Griffin, of Company C, with a small detachment from his own and another company, charged and took a twelve-pound brass howitzer, against large odds of good fighting men. They could not stand the ready-loaded and instant firing arms which our men used against them.

After the defenses had been carried, it was ascertained that the infantry had returned to Bermuda Hundred without striking a blow, and as the enemy was rapidly bringing up reinforcements from Richmond and elsewhere, General Kautz was compelled to retire, which he did without molestation. In the early part of the action, Lieutenant Maguire received a painful wound in the leg. This was our only casualty. While this affair was in progress, a detachment from that portion of the regiment which remained behind reconnoitered the enemy's works in our front, found them deserted, and demolished them.

On the 13th we were relieved from duty in the intrenchments, by a regiment of one hundred days men from Ohio.

The next day the balance of the regiment was mounted, and moved at once with the cavalry division, in concert with the eighteenth corps of infantry, for a second demonstration on Petersburg.

The disadvantage under which they labored will be appreciated, when it is stated that a portion of the District of Columbia men took the saddle that day for the first time in their lives. And yet the regiment was highly complimented for its gallantry in the engagement, which resulted in forcing the enemy back to his inner line of intrenchments.

Lieutenant Parkman, of Company D, a brave and accomplished officer, and an excellent man, was killed.

While at Bermuda Hundred, as well as elsewhere, the kindly ministrations of the Sanitary and Christian Commissions called forth grateful acknowledgments from many a suffering soldier

CHAPTER XII.

FIRST DISTRICT CAVALRY.

Leaving Camp again—"Wilson's Raid"—Battles—The Escape of Kautz—The End of Regimental Service.

HITHERTO one-half the regiment had served as infantry. Now, mounted and released from duty in the intrenchments, they were so far prepared to take the field as cavalry. Probably, however, no other regiment in the service took the field in a condition so unfavorable to success.

Now if (as we shall hereafter see), notwithstanding all the adverse influences, they were distinguished for their bravery and efficiency on every field in which they fought, the fact will prove the sterling qualities of the men.

On the 19th, we broke camp near the breastworks at Bermuda Hundred front, and moved north about five miles, to a point near the James, about two miles below Jones's Landing.

At four o'clock P. M. of the 20th, an order was received to be ready to march at an hour's notice. At nine o'clock our horse equipments arrived from Washington. The different parts of the saddle were in different boxes, and so unacquainted were the men with horse gear, that many of them were unable to adjust the various parts without assistance. Nor was this strange. Before their enlistment they had no occasion to learn, and subsequently, no opportunity, and yet, three hours later, they started on the celebrated "Wilson's Raid."

At one o'clock, on the morning of the 21st of June, the regiment moved with the third division of cavalry, under General Kautz, and joined another division from the Army of the Potomac. The whole force numbered about eight thousand men, with sixteen pieces of artillery, and was commanded by General Wilson.

The object of the movement, like that of similar ones which had preceded it, was not to fight, but to weaken the enemy by cutting his communications, and by destroying army stores and other public property.

The Army of the Potomac was now intrenched on the south side of Richmond. All supplies for the rebel capital must be drawn from the South and West. The question of its reduction was only a question of time, while every interruption of its communications, and every diminution of its supplies, would hasten the time.

On the night of the 21st, the command bivouacked at Blanford, on the Suffolk Railroad, four miles south of Petersburg. Of the use of this road the enemy had already been deprived. Passing on the 22d to Prince George's Court-house, thence marching in a southerly direction, they struck the Weldon Railroad at Reams's Station, twelve miles from Petersburg. The place was guarded by a small body of militia. A portion of them were captured and the remainder dispersed.

Here the sad but necessary work of destruction began. All the buildings at the station, together with a locomotive, and a train of five or six cars, were consigned to the flames.

After tearing up the road for a considerable distance, the command marched to Ford's Station, on the South Side Railroad, eighteen miles southwest from Petersburg. Here the work of destruction was resumed. The public buildings, together with three locomotives and fifteen cars, shared the fate of those at Reams's Station.

On the 23d, they advanced to Black's and White's, fifteen miles southwest, on the same road, destroying the three intervening stations, and tearing up the road along their line of march.

On the morning of the 24th, a march of eight miles led them to Notaway Court-house, where they destroyed a railroad station, together with a large storehouse, filled with cotton.

Resuming the line of march, they advanced to Keysville, on the Richmond and Danville Railroad, leaving behind them a track of smouldering ruins, as far as the public property of the enemy furnished combustible matter. Nor is it to be denied that, within certain limits, a good deal of foraging was done.

In a healthy subject, free exercise in the open air, espe cially on horseback, tends to give an appetite, whose cravings nothing can appease but food. This was the experience of our boys. And if their haversacks were sometimes empty, and they were fain to gnaw the raw corn, "which the horses did eat," their appetites were all the more clamorous when they came within reach of food. At such times, bread, and meat, and butter, and milk, and eggs, and cream, in a word, whatever the smoke-house, or the spring-house, or the field, or garden, or stall, or pasture of a rebel contained, which was capable of being readily con· verted into good food, was remorselessly appropriated, without waiting for either commissary or quartermaster process. These acts of the boys were never denied; and yet, for the life of us, we could never discover any signs of penitence on account of them. It should be stated, however, that the law of magnanimity was not entirely ignored.

The boys were one day in want of meat, and, as they had no other means of getting it, they "confiscated" the contents of a smoke-house on the plantation of a wealthy rebel. While the distribution was going on, the victim demanded, in no very pleasant tones, whether he was to have none for himself.

"Certainly," a quiet Yankee replied. "Now is your time. Pitch in, pitch in, and take your share, while it is going!"

After passing Drake's Depot, eight miles further south, and paying it the same compliments they had paid to others, they approached Roanoke Bridge, which crosses the Staun· ton River, at the mouth of the Little Roanoke. As this was a point of great importance to the enemy, it was fortified and strongly guarded. On this side of the river, at the distance of about three-fourths of a mile, running parallel with it, was a range of hills. Between the hills and the river, the ground was open and level. At the left of the railroad was a broad field of wheat, while on the right a luxuriant growth of grass and weeds, rising nearly to the height of a man's shoulders, covered the ground. The bluff on the opposite side of the river was lined with earthworks, and bristled with cannon, both above and below the bridge, while a strong line of the enemy's skirmishers had been thrown across the bridge, and deployed along the shore.

Wilson's object was to burn the bridge, and Lieutenant-Colonel Conger, of the First District of Columbia Cavalry, was detailed to do it. The regiment was composed of new recruits, with little experience, and had received less instruction than any other regiment in the command. The undertaking was a perilous one. Its wisdom the reader will be likely to question. And yet, when the final order was given to charge across the level ground, in the face of the rebel batteries, the gallant First District of Columbia moved forward in splendid style, dismounted (except the intrepid Conger, who, being lame from previous wounds, was compelled to ride). The advance squadron, commanded by Captain Benson, had not advanced far, when, from the line of the enemy's works in front, a murderous storm of grape and canister was hurled into their ranks with terrible effect. Officers and men went down in large numbers. Still, without the least protection, in the face of that withering fire, and at too great a distance from the enemy to effect much by their own, those brave men pressed on till near the bridge. Efforts were made to burn it, but they were unsuccessful. The regiment did but little actual fighting here, for the simple reason that they could not get at the enemy, but the cannonading was rapid and heavy. The hills presented a line of fire and smoke, and the earth trembled with the terrific concussions. Shells screamed across the horizon, bursting into deadly iron hail—the grim forms of smoke-masked men, the gleam of burnished guns in the wheat field, where the men were not engaged, and the flashing of sabers where they were, with horsemen in the distance, sweeping to and fro, formed a scene of exciting grandeur such as few of our men had ever witnessed before.

When at length it was discovered that the object could not be accomplished but at too great a sacrifice of life, the advance was ordered back, and, as nothing else was to be

done in this direction, the return march was commenced
The enemy followed all day, but made no attack. After a
march of thirty-two miles directly east, through Greensborough, the column halted for the night near Oak Grove.

A march of thirty-eight miles brought them to the Iron
Bridge across Stony Creek, at about ten o'clock on the
morning of the 28th. Here a heavy force of cavalry and
artillery was found in position to dispute the crossing. The
cavalry consisted of Hampton's command, together with that
of Fitz Hugh Lee.

A severe engagement took place, in which this regiment
lost about eighty men in killed, wounded, and missing.
The result was indecisive. The enemy was pressed back,
while our column turned to the left and crossed the creek at
a point above.

General Kautz's division had the advance, this regiment
moving at the head of the column, and the Eleventh Pennsylvania next.

On approaching Reams's Station, which had been supposed to be in our possession, General Kautz found himself
confronted by the enemy, both infantry and artillery.
Mahone's whole division, and one brigade from another
division, had been sent out to intercept Wilson's command,
which was now outnumbered two to one.* The enemy was
drawn up in strong line of battle, extending from the Notaway River, on our right, to a point far out on our left. This
regiment and the Eleventh Pennsylvania charged directly
through. General Wilson, however, instead of following
on, fell back, abandoned his artillery, wagons, and ambulances, and, by making a wide detour, avoided the enemy
and abandoned these two regiments to their fate.

Kautz had marched but a short distance, when he found
himself in a triangle, two sides of which, including his rear
and left front, were held by the enemy in overwhelming
numbers. Extending along his right front was the railroad,
running through a cut from ten to twelve feet in depth.

---

* Stung to madness by the previous daring and destructive raids of Kautz, Lee
is said to have declared that he would crush these raiders, if it cost him his whole
army

Beyond it, and running nearly parallel with it, was a muddy stream of considerable depth, and beyond that, an extensive swamp, supposed to be impassable.

The enemy now thought himself sure of his prey. Under the circumstances, almost any other man would have surrendered. Not so the indomitable Kautz.

It was a wild and exciting scene to see those mounted men slide down that steep embankment to the railroad track, and scramble up the opposite bank, and dash down the next declivity into the stream, and wallow through mire and water, the horses in some instances rolling over, and the men going under, amid the thunder of artillery, and with solid shot plunging, and shells exploding, and grape and canister raining, and musket balls whistling around them, till they reached the opposite shore, and disappeared in the swamp.

Following their indefatigable commander, they pressed their way through, and reached their old camp at Jones's Landing, the next day.*

Lieutenant-Colonel Conger, Major Curtis, and Captain Sanford were severely wounded. Captains Benson and Chase, who had been wounded at Roanoke Bridge, fell into the enemy's hands as prisoners, when the ambulances were abandoned at Stony Creek.

The damage to the enemy by this raid was immense. Besides the destruction of buildings, of cotton, of commissary stores, and rolling stock, Richmond and Petersburg were cut off from all railroad communication for several weeks.

The whole Army of the Potomac was now in front of Petersburg, and was intrenching in the direction of the South Side Railroad.

One of our companies was on duty in Fort Pride. With this exception, the history of the regiment, for the next few weeks, is little else than a history of alternate rest and drill. Once or twice it was ordered out on reconnoissance, and once on foot to repel an expected assault, which, however, was not made.

---

* This swamp had been made passable by a drouth of almost unprecedented severity.

On the 27th, orders were received to be ready to move at six o'clock, P. M., with three days' rations. The whole cavalry force, together with the second corps of infantry, had been ordered to the north side of the James. The object was to draw the enemy from Petersburg, where an assault was to be made in connection with the mine explosion. The head of Sheridan's column arrived from the west side of the Appomattox at nine; P. M. At three o'clock, A. M., the First District of Columbia joined the rear, and, after marching to Jones's Landing, halted for the command to cross the pontoon bridge. Late in the day the crossing was effected, and the regiment bivouacked for the night.

Some skirmishing occurred on the next day, in which Lieutenant McBride, of Company C, was wounded.

On the 30th, the regiment returned to camp, and on the same afternoon marched to the west side of the Appomattox. On the 2d of August, it was ordered on picket near the enemy's lines, on the extreme left of the army.

Our main line of works in front of Petersburg conformed very nearly to that of the enemy on the left, bending southward, so as to face the Weldon Railroad. A picket line extended from the left of our line of fortifications, in an easterly direction, through Prince George's Court-House, Lee's Mills, Sycamore Church, and Cox's Mills. On the 3d of August, the headquarters of the regiment were established at Sycamore Church, Major Baker commanding. This place was about ten miles southeast from City Point.

From the 8th to the 21st of August, the regiment was on picket duty on the Weldon Railroad, four miles from Petersburg.

On the 18th, while a demonstration was made on the north side of the James, in front of Richmond, by Generals Gregg and Harcock, with their respective commands of cavalry and infantry, and while a portion of the rebel troops were withdrawn from our front to meet the emergency, the fifth corps of infantry advanced and took possession of the Weldon Railroad. Desperate but fruitless efforts were made by the enemy to recover it. Severe fighting occurred on the 21st, in which this regiment participated. Dismounted, and deployed as skirmishers on the left of the fifth corps, they participated in the capture of a brigade of rebel troops and three stands of colors.

After picketing again, on the 22d, the regiment became engaged with a body of rebel troops the next morning, and drove them four miles, destroying a quantity of army stores. In the afternoon, Hampton's Legion was encountered. It was "Greek meeting Greek." It was impossible, however, for him to stand against the sixteen-shooters, and he was driven back, leaving his dead and wounded on the field We also took some prisoners. During this last engagement, Captain Sargent, of Company M, was killed while charging the enemy. We lost two men besides.

On the 24th, the fighting was resumed at various points, and at some was severe, but with no decisive results. On the 25th, this regiment met the enemy in three distinct engagements, repulsing him in each.

At four o'clock there were indications that he intended a flank movement, and this regiment was ordered to the extreme left of the line, and dismounted, to fortify against the expected attack at that point. After the hard and almost incessant fighting of the day, the men could hardly have been in the best working condition, and yet, in momentary expectation of an attack, they wrought with a will. Without intrenching tools, their own "hands ministered" to the necessities of the hour. Logs, stumps, brush, roots, whatever movable material the forest afforded, was brought into requisition. The extemporized breastwork was hardly completed, when the enemy opened on us with artillery. Against this our works were no protection. But the men stood firm. Only one man was killed, and one wounded. There was no enemy in sight, but all understood what this shelling boded.

The men had received their orders, and all was silent along the line. Every man was at his post. Every eye was open, and every ear attent. No sound was heard but the roar of the enemy's artillery, and the scream and crash of shells around us. This, however, had continued but a short time, when the enemy was seen in strong line of battle advancing through the woods. No sooner had they discovered our position than they raised a yell and rushed on to the charge. But they paid dearly for their temerity Our men reserved their fire—coolly waiting till the enemy was sufficiently near. Their first volley told with startling effect. Many a poor fellow drew short breath and never breathed again. Another and another volley followed in instantaneous succession, and the enemy was swept from our front. Unfortunately, however, the infantry on our right, pressed by superior numbers, had fallen back, and the enemy was on our flank. The regiment held its position till dark, and was the last to leave the field. The next day it returned to Sycamore Church and resumed picket duty.

While here, our officers formed an acquaintance with some of the "F. F. V.'s." For the most part, the acquaintance was pleasant, but not always. The following incident will illustrate the spirit sometimes encountered: One of our officers, while out on a scouting expedition with a small squad of men, halted near a fine old Virginia mansion, at a considerable distance outside of our lines, while he advanced and politely accosted the lordly proprietor, as he sat puffing his cigar in the cool shade of his piazza. His lordship at once commenced a furious tirade against "Lincoln and his dirty minions." The lieutenant listened patiently, meanwhile observing one of the colored women carrying a fine churning of butter into the house from a building near by, where it seemed to have been just made. At the first pause in the furious tirade, he said, in substance, "Well, sir, the war is a costly thing. It has made it necessary to tax almost every thing, especially luxuries. Now, as this sort of talk seems a luxury to you, it must be taxed. You will please send out to my men a few pounds of your new butter."

Whether from generosity or some other motive, the butter was furnished, but the spirit of the man was not at all improved. He went on to abuse the Government, and all who supported it, in terms more violent than before. At the next pause, his tormentor quietly remarked: "For this fresh indulgence, you will please furnish us with half a dozen of your best hams, and a sack of flour; *and the sooner it is done the better!*"

The negro who executed the order clearly indicated, by an exhibition of his fine white teeth, and a mischievous twinkle of his eye, that he enjoyed the thing much better than "massa" did. The master, in the mean time, was foaming with rage, and venting his feelings in terms of the most intense bitterness.

At length, the imperturbable lieutenant interposed coolly: "Sir, your indulgence has gone far enough. You will square the account by turning out the two beeves I see in yonder lot, and if I hear any more of this abuse of my Government, I will take you along too." With a polite good-by, he was left a sadder, if not a wiser man. For some days after, the boys ate good, new, soft bread and butter, instead of hard-tack, and fresh beef and ham, instead of salt pork.

The portion of the picket-line held by the First District of Columbia, now numbering about four hundred effective men, was nearly five miles in length, extending along a road running nearly east and west, mostly through a wooded country. Major Baker, in immediate command of two battalions, held the right of the line, with the reserve at Sycamore Church, whilst Captain Howe, with one battalion, held the left, with the reserve at Cox's Mills, two miles east.

Such was the position of this little devoted band of four hundred men, on the outer picket-line, five miles from any support, when at daybreak, on the 16th of September, they were suddenly attacked by the whole force of Hampton's cavalry, supported by three brigades of infantry.

In some way, which has never been explained, one detachment of the enemy's force had passed through the picket-line on the right, held by another regiment. Another had gone round our left flank, where there were no pickets. This must have been done hours before the assault, for (as it afterward appeared) they had barricaded the roads three miles in our rear.

If the reader inquires why the enemy threw so formidable a force against a point so remote, so weak, and apparently so unimportant, the answer is, that just in our rear was a herd of twenty-three hundred cattle, and the rebel army wanted meat.

If the position, purpose, and strength of the assaulting

party had been known, any attempt at resistance would have been madness.

The first intimation of an assault at Sycamore Church was given by the charging shout of the enemy. Instantly our men rallied under their intrepid commander, to meet the furious onset. So rapid and terrible was their fire, that three times the enemy fell back in confusion. But the contest was too unequal. This little handful of men was in a few moments surrounded, their horses captured, and they were compelled to succumb.

As illustrations of this sudden, short, wild, and terrible fight, we give one or two incidents. At the first note of alarm, Lieutenant Spaulding, of Company E, mounted his horse, which had been kept saddled all night, and started out to reconnoiter. Meeting a body of cavalry, he mistook them for a party of our own men, and found himself among them before discovering his error. As he was taken by them for one of their own men, he rode along with them till the order was given to charge, when, with stentorian voice, he roared out, "Charge—charge!" and, putting spurs to his horse, he dashed forward, and turning into the bushes made good his escape.

Nearly at the same moment he started down the road to reconnoiter, Lieutenant Mountfort, of Company K, started with a sergeant, W. F. Lunt, and a small squad of men, dismounted, in the same direction. They had gone but a short distance, when they met the enemy charging up the road. Comprehending the situation at once, the lieutenant shouted, "Give it to them, boys, give it to them!" at the same time setting the example. Two men at the head of the column were seen to sway and fall from their saddles, before the unerring aim of the lieutenant. Other saddles were emptied, and the advance fell back. A moment later, however, they came on in line of battle. The lieutenant now ordered his men to fall back to a tree, which had fallen across the road. On reaching it, they found the enemy all around them. Observing a squad of them who had just seized Major Baker, Sergeant Lunt fired on them, when instantly several carbines were leveled on him. Struck in the head and stunned, he fell forward into the thick tree top. Falling between the limbs, they closed over him, their thick foliage concealing him. When consciousness returned, the body of the gallant lieutenant lay within a few feet of him, dead, and the enemy was plundering the camp. Crawling cautiously out, he succeeded in reaching the bushes, where, falling in with a small squad of men who, like himself, had thus far escaped capture, he started with them for the next picket post. But as they were passing through a deep cut in the road, the sergeant, from exhaustion, being somewhat in the rear, as those in advance of him emerged from the cut, they were met by a party of the enemy, and nearly all captured. The sergeant escaped, in consequence of being in the rear. Who would have thought that the exhaustion, which seemed to put him to such a disadvantage, would have been the means of saving him from a horrible captivity? Such are the ways of Providence. Of twenty-five men of Company G, who were captured on that fatal morning, only three are known to have survived the barbarities of their imprisonment.

The attack on Cox's Mills was made at nearly the same moment with that at Sycamore Church.

A little to the left of Captain Howe's position, and at the foot of a very considerable descent, the road crosses a bridge over a small stream. To command this bridge, a slight breastwork had been thrown up upon the high ground on this side. At the first notice of the approach of the enemy, the command rallied just in time to reach this breastwork, behind which they formed. A heavy force of mounted rebels had crossed the bridge, and with wild yells was charging up the hill, outnumbering our men ten to one. On, on they came, expecting an easy victory. Coolly our men waited. Not a shot was fired till they were within easy range. Then a few volleys from the sixteen-shooters sent them back in confusion. A second time they charged, with the same result. This time they did not return. After waiting some time, in expectation of another attack, scouts were sent out to ascertain what they were about. They found a formidable force in front, and a strong force advancing on each flank.

No alternative now remained but to fall back to Sycamore Church, as Captain Howe had been ordered to do, in case a retreat became necessary. The enemy had been so severely punished, that he was careful to keep at a safe distance, and the command fell back in good order, and without the loss of a man. At the church, however, a sad fate awaited them. Ignorant of what had occurred there, they expected to join Major Baker's reserve, and to make a stand. But in the mean time, the enemy, having secured their prisoners, and plundered the camp, had formed in a semicircle across the road, and, dressed in our uniform, were mistaken for our own men. Successful resistance was now impossible, and, having done all that brave men could do, like men they yielded to their fate.

Some men seem to bear a charmed life. Lieutenant E. P. Merrill, of Company M, commanded a squadron under Captain Howe. During a few moments of suspense, anxious to know the position of the enemy, he sprang upon the first horse that came to hand, and, plunging the spurs into his flanks, dashed forward to reconnoiter.

The horse stumbled, and, coming suddenly to the ground, threw his rider over his head, far down the hill. Instantly he rose, made a hasty reconnoissance, and returned to the line in safety.

During the subsequent melee, a rebel officer made his appearance in the edge of the woods, and, taking deliberate aim at the lieutentant, fired three shots in quick succession, neither of which took effect.

Our loss in killed and wounded was small, but in prisoners, large, numbering several hundred. They were among the bravest men Maine had sent to the war, and here their services in the First District of Columbia Cavalry ended.

There was much speculation at the time, as to who was responsible for the exposed position of the cattle-herd which invited this rebel raid. It seems to have been a high officer of the army, who in all other respects has deserved well of his country, and whose name is for this reason withheld.

Shortly after this affair, this officer dined with the commander-in-chief at the headquarters of General Kautz. In the course of conversation, he put this question: "General, how long are we to remain here?" The reticent Grant smoked on a few seconds, then took the inevitable cigar from his lips, and, while dislodging the ashes with his little finger, quietly answered: "I don't know, General; if you keep on feeding Lee's army with beef, we shall have to stay a good while."

The questioner blushed, and Grant resumed his smoking.

CHAPTER XIII

THE ANIMUS OF SECESSION

A Disloyal Pastor and his Friends compelled to "do justly"—The "Peculiar Institution" Dies Hard—Man-Stealers Foiled in their Schemes of Robbery.

ANOTHER phase of disloyalty presented itself with the advent of the autumn of 1863; an example of the conflicting elements in Southern communities during the rebellion, whose sharpest, most unrelenting outbreak was seen in the alliance of religion with treason.

It was notorious that the clergy and women were the "best haters," and loudest talkers, in the ranks of secession. The reason lay, perhaps, in the nature of things. Never is wrong feeling and action so intense as when it takes the sanctions of Christianity; while the strong impulses and the lively sensibilities of woman's nature lend a similar strength and activity to it in a bad cause.

I was making an excursion, in an official way, toward Point Lookout, upon a Sabbath evening. While approaching it with a force of about fifty men of my cavalry, we came to a small church, about twenty-four miles from Washington, which was closed, and a number of people standing before the door. I naturally asked the meaning of the strange scene. It seemed that the majority of the people in the parish were disloyal, and, after permitting the Unionists to occupy the sanctuary a portion of the time, nearly in proportion to their relative numerical strength, had voted to exclude them altogether.

I inquired: "Who has the key to this church?"

"Rev. Mr. P., who lives down the road a quarter of a mile."

I immediately rode away to the parsonage, and knocked at its door. A gentleman with white cravat and dignified demeanor opened it, when I asked him:—

"You preach in the little church up at the Corners, do you not?"

"I do."

"And you keep the key?"

"Yes, sir."

"So you won't let the loyal people serve God there?"

"No; the parish voted to exclude those who didn't agree with us."

"Well, I want you to unlock the church."

"Oh, no; I can't do that."

"Then you will go with me to Washington; and you can have three minutes to decide which you will do."

He reached out his hand to take the key, which was hanging on the wall, near the door.

"That will not do; you must go and unlock the church yourself."

"No, I can't."

"Then start for Washington."

"Of course, you have the power."

"Yes, and I intend to exercise it."

The aggrieved pastor then reluctantly followed me with the key. We approached the church, before which stood the wondering and waiting people, when my clerical friend handed the key to a brother, requesting him to open the door.

I interposed. "Don't you take that key; he must unlock the church."

There being no alternative, he doggedly obeyed; and, one after another, the outsiders went in, till the house was nearly full.

I said to them: "Now you can serve God according to the dictates of your own conscience."

The loyal minister, who had vainly attempted to occupy the pulpit for several successive Sabbaths, entered it, and commenced the usual service. Meanwhile, an officer of my cavalry force reported that the horses were suffering for want of water. I directed them to be taken to a ford four miles distant for watering.

When the rebels found my cavalry were gone, they also went into the church, and commenced a disturbance of the meeting, first by scraping their feet upon the pews, then by audible expressions of their hatred. I rose, and, in no gentle mood, called an orderly, and told him to ride in hot haste after the cavalry, and tell the officer in command to send back ten men as quickly as possible.

In a short time, the force came on the full gallop to the church, when I ordered a halt. The frightened disturbers of loyal worship attempted to get out of the way, when I directed the arrest of about a dozen of them, and told them they must march with us to Washington that night. They begged for mercy, but it was too late.

They certainly didn't play by the way; for we reached the city before daylight the next morning.

After I had risen, in single file, and with drooping heads, and hats in hand, they formed a ring of chop-fallen chivalry around me—a comical and pitiful sight. Upon giving their parole they were released, and no further quarrel interrupted the Union worshipers, who gratefully assembled upon the recurrence of their appointed service in the rural temple.

In every thing and everywhere, it was evident to the casual observer that slavery was the soul of the rebellion—the educator in treason, perverting law, religion, and social order, and laying on its altar, like the idolatry of Hindoostan, unsparingly, human victims.

The determination of the Government, and of the army officers generally, notwithstanding, to save the "peculiar institution" with the Union, in the beginning of the war, was equally apparent. Under the notorious fugitive slave law of 1857, which offered a premium upon the re-enslavement of the refugee from unrequited toil and personal abuse, the commissioner appointed to enforce its provisions in Washington was a secessionist by the name of Cox, who took care to restore every chattel to the claimant, without nicely discriminating between the bond and free. As a consequence, not a few persons, who, by birth or purchase of freedom, were citizens, were seized and forced into bondage I had some very interesting cases of the kind.

A free-born mulatto girl was kidnapped by the slave

catchers, and through perjury the proper order was obtained, and she was taken to her pretended owner. Intelligent, and resolved to be free, she had the facts conveyed to my headquarters. By a military order I compelled the woman-stealer to restore to her friends the captive robbed of her rights in the name of law. The tinge of African hue alone made the outrage a trivial incident to all but the grateful and, I might add, graceful young lady.

Upon my return from an expedition into Lower Maryland, when within a mile from the State line, I met a farmer with a wagon load of slaves, consisting of a father and mother, with their two small children, and a wife's sister, all in charge of a constable and a force of armed citizens. The slaves, tied hand and foot, and thrown upon the straw in an old country wagon, were on their way back to bondage. And this was done in the name of law, to pacify the men who were plotting to destroy the Union!

I was completely exhausted; but, nerved to action by indignation too intense for expression, I demanded the authority for the horrible proceeding. The claimant produced his parchment, bearing the seal of Commissioner Cox. He flourished the precious document before me, and directed my attention to the great seal of the United States.

Upon careful perusal of it, I found that it bore the names of only four slaves, while the load included five. When I pointed the chivalrous and confident owner to the apparently unimportant circumstance, he replied: "We don't count that baby," pointing to an infant three months old, in the arms of a mother, whose feet were tied, while she leaned against the side of the vehicle.

I answered: "The mother was a slave, and the child was born in bondage. You claim the mother, and of course the child is kidnapped; and as you profess to be a law-abiding citizen, and are violating the statute, I arrest the entire company."

He warmly protested, and threatened resistance.

He said, "Take the baby; what in h—ll do we want of the baby? We want grown people."

The mother began to weep. One of my men was touched, and, turning to me with pleading tone, inquired if I would separate the mother and child

The display of a dozen of Colt's revolvers, by myself and assistants, satisfied my excited friend that I was in earnest in expressing my interpretation of the law. I sprang into the wagon, and with my saber's point cut the ropes.

This, I think, was the first practical application of the principle of the famous Emancipation Proclamation of later date.

I directed the horses' heads to be turned toward Washington, when the owner and driver of the load remonstrated, and said, with an oath:

"Let the niggers walk to Washington."

I said, "No. You brought them here, and must carry them back."

The poor captives sank on their knees; the venerable old man exclaiming, with uplifted hands, "Bless God!" and the mother adding, "God bless Colonel Baker!"

I took them to my headquarters and set them at liberty.

This transaction, of course, brought upon my head the curses of the slaveholders of Lower Maryland. But I had violated no law, on account of the fortunate presence of the baby.

A delegation called on Mr. Lincoln the next morning, protesting against the arbitrary act, producing, as before, the sacred parchment. I was summoned to the White House. The President said:

"Baker, a serious charge is preferred against you;" directing my attention to the document, with the inquiry, "What do you know about the case?"

I briefly made my statement, giving prominence to the number of the slaves, and the juvenile supernumerary.

The Chief-Magistrate, worthy of the nation he represented, replied jocosely: "Well, Baker, I guess the baby saves you!" and dismissed the whole affair, leaving the "contrabands" at large, and myself to the prosecution of my thankless profession.

CHAPTER XIV.

ENGLISH SYMPATHY WITH THE SOUTH—NEGRO-HATE IN WASHINGTON.

English Emissary of the South—He Deceives the Secretary of State—My Acquaintance with Him—The Fruitless Effort to Betray Me—The Journey to the Old Capitol Prison—Negro-hate in the National Capital.

MUCH has been said and written about English sympathy and co-operation with the South. Perhaps nothing can give the extent and success of this alliance a more just prominence in the record of the war than some account of its practical operations, involving the highest official position, but without the least intimation of inability or disloyalty. On the contrary, the narrative only reveals the deliberate and skillful conspiracy of the abettors of treason in the "mother country," deceiving the most intelligent statesmanship, because it seemed impossible that the betrayal of confidence could appear in the disguise of culture, friendship, and appreciated courtesies from the most eminent men in the Government.

During the first years of the rebellion, an Englishman made his appearance in Washington, whose apparent interest in the loyal cause, and his open denunciations of the rebel leaders, attracted the attention of our able Secretary of State. He gained ready access to other officers of the Government.

So completely had he won the confidence of Mr. Seward that he received letters to the commander of the Department of the Shenandoah Valley. With them he waited upon that officer, and was shown the usual attentions which follow such an introduction. From the commanding general he received a *carte blanche* to visit the outposts whenever he thought proper. Disregarding the obligations such favors imposed, he passed the Federal lines beyond Winchester, and boldly entered the camp of Stonewall Jackson boasting of his deception, and receiving similar civilities to those shown him by the Union officers. He remained several days on hostile soil, and then returned to Washington, after having received from Jackson permission to cross his lines at any time, day or night.

While he was in Washington, he soon, by his suspicious bearing, his secret meetings with well-known secessionists, awakened my suspicions. Upon inquiry, I learned that he was a sympathizer with the South, and a reputed correspondent of a London paper.

In the prosecution of my inquiries, I ascertained that he *was* an accredited writer for the English press, and was assured that the stranger was a reliable gentleman. But believing that, if my British friend had facilities for passing the lines of both armies, he could give me important intelligence, I decided to cultivate his acquaintance. I accordingly wrote him a friendly note requesting him to call at my headquarters, which he soon after did. He opened the conversation by an effort to impress my mind with his importance as a detective in the Union service, being able to cross both lines at pleasure. He further informed me that he had just returned from Stonewall Jackson's camp, and had given to our General B. valuable information. He claimed to occupy neutral ground, and naturally had but little interest in either side.

Still, if I would employ and pay him, he could render great service to the Republic; and he could obtain a certificate from the British minister which would give him free entry even to the rebel capital. During the interview, I detected in his conduct a revelation of his real character. Notwithstanding his indorsement by Government, I was sure of his treasonable designs. If so, he was clearly a dangerous man, and I determined to know more about him. I desired him to obtain the certificate from the English minister referred to by him. An examination of it convinced me it was a forgery. I applied to the minister, who informed me that he knew of no such man in Washington. At our next meeting, upon the succeeding day, I expressed my regret that I had not the means of getting to rebel camps which he had; adding, that with them, how easily I could get the plans and movements of the enemy. The bait was a success.

He replied: "Nothing is easier. Go with me, and I will pass you along as a friend, and associate correspondent."

He detailed minutely the plan, and we agreed to leave in company the next morning for Harper's Ferry, *en route* to General Jackson's quarters.

About eleven o'clock that night, when leaving my office, I received the following note, handed me by a colored man :—

COLONEL BAKER:—

Beware of that Englishman! He has devised a plot to betray you. For God's sake, don't go with him.

MRS. ———.

The missive was written by a true-hearted Union woman, a seamstress in one of the aristocratic secession families of Washington.

This revelation increased my anxiety to become his traveling companion. I left Washington with him, according to appointment, and reached Winchester in due time, by rail. The rebel picket-line was between that place and Stanton.

Remaining *incog.* myself, my friend proceeded to General B.'s headquarters and procured passes for both. Hiring a horse and buggy, we proceeded toward Stonewall Jackson's headquarters, he suggesting that it would not probably be safe to go directly to them without giving notice of our arrival within the lines. Four miles from them, we halted at a farm-house, where he said he was acquainted, and proposed to send the message to camp. I was introduced properly, and, after an excellent supper, a letter was written and read to me by him, addressed to the rebel chief, announcing our proximity, and that we would report to him in the morning. A trusted house servant was called, and received his instructions in regard to the delivery of the note.

Carelessly sauntering forth into the yard, I followed him by a circuitous route to his shanty, and asked him if he had the letter.

"Yes, massa," he replied; "which of de letters?" handing me two—the one which I had seen, and another to the Chief of Staff, running thus :—

Have just arrived, and am at Mr. ———'s house. Have with me the Yankee detective, Baker. Send and capture us both.

I took these notes, sealed the envelopes, gave them to the bearer, and told him to hurry as fast as possible. He left, and I returned to the dwelling, where my companion was conversing with the lady of the house.

It was seventeen miles to the rebel headquarters, and I knew the servant could not get back until morning. I determined to await the issue. I occupied the same bed with the Englishman; but passed a sleepless night. He was singularly restless toward morning, often going to the window, to catch a glimpse of the expected cavalry, or hear the echo of the hoofs. He complained of being ill. At seven o'clock the messenger arrived; I had detected, from the movements of all around me, some great event was expected.

The servant was eagerly questioned, who said he had delivered the letters according to orders.

Breakfast was dispatched, and nine o'clock came, when I proposed to my associate that we wait no longer for a special invitation, but go forward to General Jackson's camp. He acquiesced; our carriage was brought to the door, the farewell spoken to the family, and we were on our way.

Great surprise was expressed by my friend that no reply had been received to the note. I apologized for the apparent neglect, on the ground of urgent business, and urged that we hasten on.

When about four miles from our hospitable home for the night, we came to four corners, and I inquired:—

"Which road leads to Winchester?"

He pointed with his whip, saying: "That one."

I said: "Stop a moment!" sprang from the buggy, drew and cocked my six-shooter within six inches of his head, exclaiming: "You scoundrel, you are my prisoner. I have only been waiting to see how far you would go, and what shape your base design would take."

He turned deadly pale, and tried to speak, when I added: "Don't open your mouth; if you do, I'll blow your brains out."

CAPTURE OF A CORRESPONDENT OF THE LONDON TIMES.

Directing him to alight, I drew a pair of handcuffs from my pocket, wrapped in a newspaper, which I deliberately unrolled; and with my pistol in my left hand, with my right I clasped the manacles on his wrist, and said:—
"You have attempted to betray me; if you make an effort to alarm any one, or try to indicate who I am, I will shoot you dead. If you go quietly along, you shall not be hurt. Now, get into the buggy."

I took my pistol, put the muzzle under the cushion of the seat, and with my left hand drove the horse. Fortunately, we met no rebel soldiers, and not a word was spoken until we came to within half a mile of the rebel picket-line, when I drove to the side of the fence, told my prisoner to alight, and entered with him a strip of woods, passed safely the picket, and at four o'clock the following morning we were at Winchester.

I handed the traitor temporarily over to the military authorities, and sought repose. A few hours later, I started for Washington, and upon my arrival placed him in the Old Capitol prison, whose records will disclose his name.

In this connection, chronologically, one or two incidents will present in bold relief the unparalleled malignity of feeling cherished by the rebels and their friends toward an unoffending race, because it was the providential occasion of their troubles, and true to the instincts of humanity in its desire for freedom; a malignity intensified by the despotic possession and control of the body, and, so far as possible, of the soul of the enslaved.

One day I was riding toward the railway depot in Washington, when I noticed a crowd, and saw blows descending upon the form of a colored boy. Upon getting nearer, I found that a large and brutal man was amusing himself and the spectators by beating a well-dressed mulatto lad, who was bitterly crying. I sprang from the carriage, and, taking the ruffian by the arm, inquired what he was about. Turning a savage look upon me, he drew back to strike; but it has been my custom, when necessary to use weapons of defense, to get the *first* blow or shot. Before he could take his aim, he was lying on his back under my feet. The injured child ran away, while a comrade, who somehow recognized me, followed, repeating my name. I then re entered the carriage and drove on unmolested.

There was another instance of fiendish hate, in which a woman was the principal actor. I was crossing the street, upon a dismal night, when just before me walked a lady in splendid attire, attended by a gentleman. Further on wa a poor colored girl, clearing the pavement, as well as sh could with her dilapidated broom, from the snow water and mud, for the penny any passer-by might drop into her hand. She stepped back at the approach of the couple referred to, and extended her hand. The Southern lady leaned toward the little mendicant, and, with a spiteful push, laid her flat in the flooded street. She rose again, dripping and shivering. I confess I was angry; and, going before her, I remarked:—

"That was very unladylike; a specimen of the politeness of the chivalry, I suppose?"

She replied excitedly: "How dare you speak thus to me!" adding epithets of scorn toward the abolitionist.

Her escort then took up the gauntlet, and inquired my name, handing me his card. I told him, and invited him to call. Both parties were bound for the post-office, where we again met, and again the lady's friend demanded satisfaction. I gave him a glimpse of my six-shooter, and intimated that he had better drop the subject, which he decided to do, and I heard no more from him.

CHAPTER XV.

GIGANTIC VICES OF THE NATIONAL CAPITAL.

Gambling and the Gamblers—The Purpose to Break up the Dens Discouraged—The Midnight Raid—Results—Drinking and Liquor Saloons—The Descent upon them—Broken up—Licentiousness and its Patrons—The Raid on their Haunts at Dead of Night—The Arrests.

I HAVE made some disclosures respecting the contraband trade in gaming-cards; but it remains now to record the prevalence and ruinous effects of the vice of gambling itself, during the war, pre-eminently in the National capital. I have no desire to exaggerate the evils that lurk in the high or low places of society; to speak of Washington in a carping tone, as if it had been, or is, a Sodom beyond redemption; nor do I wish to magnify my office at the expense of any man's fair fame, whatever his position.

But I can not be true to myself, the bureau I represented, nor yet to the people for whose sake I send forth these annals, and omit a narrative which will surprise and sadden thousands. And may the country we love, the families, the youth of the land, profit by the recital. It is well known, that there have always been in large cities what are called "gambling hells"—costly houses, fitted up with elegance, and furnished with everything to attract the eye, and lend fascination to the destructive pastime. Indeed, many virtuous citizens earnestly defend the existence of this and other unblushing vices as necessary evils; when, there can be no crime which the law should not reach, and will, if fearlessly wielded by its officers, and they, in turn, are sustained by the people.

In Washington, gambling increased naturally and inevitably, with the progress of the war. It is not a pleasant thing to say, that the patronage of the gaming-table had been drawn largely from members of Congress; to whom were added, with the increasing number of officers gathering to the capital, many high in military command. With the demand for such haunts of "sporting men," their number multiplied until I had a list of more than a hundred houses, many of which were gorgeous beyond description. The fitting up of a single place of this kind cost twenty-five thousand dollars.

The terrible fact which drew my attention to the subject was the discovery that nine in every ten of the defalcations by paymasters, and others in the employment of the Government, were occasioned in every instance by losses at the card table. I recovered forty thousand dollars which had passed into the hands of gamblers from those of a trusted and respected official.

I called on the military commander of the district, and was discouraged in my purpose of testing the statute on gaming in the capital. The popular acquiescence in this state of things, the patronage of distinguished men, and the character of the proprietors of the "hells," were the arguments used by that officer. Still, I was not convinced, but the more decided to proceed to business.

I accordingly mustered my entire force of assistants, and detailed to them my plans. We were to move at the same moment, surround the dozen or more gaming-houses on Pennsylvania Avenue, and at the designated time, to prevent any concert of action by the proprietors, or concealment of their business, to enter and break them up. It was half-past two o'clock in the morning, when the dash was made, the gamblers arrested, and their houses closed.

The next morning brought intense excitement among the sporting gentlemen—some denouncing the interference, and others offering bribes. A number of them raised a sum of more than twenty thousand dollars for me, if I would allow them to resume their lucrative calling. It is scarcely necessary to say, that I refused to pause in the reform commenced.

Mr. Lincoln sent for me, and I repaired to the White House, to find him carelessly sitting in shirt-sleeves and slippers, ready to receive me. He said:—

"Well, Baker, what is the trouble between you and the gamblers?"

I told my story. He laughed, and said:—
"I used to play penny-ante when I ran a flat-boat out West, but for many years have not touched a card."

I stated to him the havoc gambling was making with the army, alluded to before, when he approved my course, but reminded me of the difficulties in the way of reform.

I replied: "I can not fight the gamblers and the Government both."

The President replied: "You won't have to fight *me*."

I added: "It *is* a fight; and all I ask is fair play: that the Government will let me alone, and I will break up the business."

And, with this perfect understanding, we parted for the time.

Remarked one of the gamesters to me: "After all, I don't care; it has cost me five thousand dollars a month to keep officers still."

The result was, the business was effectually spoiled in Washington, and some of the leaders in it removed to other cities; the power of wholesome law was vindicated, the offenders punished, and Washington saved, for the time, from one of its greatest curses; men of commanding position exposed, and young men saved from the serpent's charm and fang.

I shall leave this topic with the final report made to the proper authority:—

OFFICE PROVOST-MARSHAL WAR DEPARTMENT,
WASHINGTON, *August* 26, 1863.

Hon. E. A. STANTON, Secretary of War:—

SIR—I have the honor to submit the following statement in relation to certain illegal establishments in this city, and the steps taken by me for their suppression.

I refer to the gambling-houses of Washington. The evils that grow directly out of the unrestrained practice of gambling are too apparent, and have been too often and eloquently described, to require more than the mere mention to awaken the indignation of all honest and true men, and call forth the most strenuous efforts for their suppression. The peculiar character of the population of this city, composed largely of young men removed from the restraints of home, and the influences of the family circle, offers inducements to the gambling fraternity by which they have thus far largely profited. There are more professional gamblers in this city to-day, than in the city of New York, and two weeks since there were more gambling-houses.

I have had reported to me no less than one hundred and sixty-three of these establishments, where games of chance were openly permitted, and where gathered nightly, hundreds, and I might perhaps say with truth, thousands of the young and middle-aged men of this city, including always a large proportion of persons in Government employ. In such dens of ruin could be found almost every night officers of all grades, paymasters and other disbursing officers, clerks in the different departments, and persons whose escape from certain ruin lay in the direction of abusing the public trusts confided to them, and retrieving their losses at the expense of the Government.

I might cite cases of this nature where disgraced officials of prominent standing have openly pointed to gamblers and gambling-houses as the causes of their downfall; and in more than one instance Government money to a large amount has been recovered from parties who knew perfectly well that their plunder was the proceeds of official crime and dishonor.

So gigantic had this evil become, so utterly, through powerful local influences, beyond the control of the civil authorities, so intense the desire for its suppression by those who know its significance as a leading inducement to crime, and the most prominent element in demoralizing both the officers and men of our armies, that I resolved upon the adoption of the only remedy available and sure of success, and that was to peremptorily close every known gambling-house in the city.

About two weeks since I received orders and detailed officers for that purpose, and those orders have been so effectively carried into execution, that public gambling has entirely ceased, and will not be resumed so long as the control of the matter is left to me. It is true that the men who have carried on this infamous business still remain in the city, that they are laboring, by every means that money can purchase or influence command, to procure a reversal of my orders, and recommence their depredations upon Government officials, under the shadow of Government authority.

I am credibly informed that movements are being made, by parties claiming high consideration in official quarters, with the view of protecting the interests of the unemployed gamblers, and reopening the doors of those gambling hells which I have summarily closed, but which, if unlocked, will again be filled with crowds of swindlers and their unhappy victims.

I have thought it my duty, under a full knowledge of all the facts in the case, to thus briefly call your attention to the matter, in the earnest hope that the efforts I have made to rid this city of its greatest pest and nuisance will receive the approbation and earnest support of the War Department and of the Government authorities.

I am, sir, your obedient servant,
(Signed) L. C. BAKER,
Colonel and Provost-Marshal War Department.

Upon reading the above report, my course was fully sustained by the Secretary of War, who, when convinced of the existence of a wrong, was ever ready and prompt to act to the extent of his jurisdiction and influence for its suppression.

Another kindred and gigantic vice was unblushingly doing its work of death, which I could not overlook. The most superficial observer of Washington must have noticed the unusual number of drinking places, in every form and under every possible disguise. Wherever soldiers were stationed, or army work in progress, there was seen at leas the beer barrel and whisky demijohn. Old street corners and vacant lots were occupied with the bar, around which lay the intoxicated victims of their poison—the "boys in blue." In the suburbs, under the shadow of hospitals, and beside bridges, the liquor booth was reared, until it was estimated that not less than *thirty-seven hundred* such fountains of ruin were in active operation. In spite of the most stringent municipal and military regulations, the traffic went on unchecked, and daily increasing. The imposition of a fine, or incarceration for a few hours in a guard-house, was a mere joke to the speculators in the morals and lives of men. But to enter the saloons, and, with the heavy blows of the ax, to crush in the barrel-head, bring decanters in fragments to the floor, and then lay the structure itself in ruins, was too expensive a jest to be often repeated.

In the vicinity of Twenty-second and G Streets were the headquarters of the depot quartermaster. Here were located the Government warehouses, storehouses, workshops, manufactories, and corrals, employing eight thousand men or more.

Two sides of an entire square were occupied by the lowest places of intoxication. In many of them, the entire stock in trade was a cask of lager beer and a gallon of unknown and villainous compound called Bourbon whisky, dealt ou in an old rusty tin cup, at ten cents per drink. In these dens could be seen, at all hours of the day and night, the common soldier, the teamster, and the mechanic. I distinctly recollect, that on the eve of an important battle, when necessary to dispatch to the front, at an hour's notice, a train of one hundred wagons, not five Government teamsters were sufficiently sober to move forward.

When all other means, laws, and agents had failed to

reach and remedy the frightful evil, my aid, it will appear from the correspondence quoted, was invoked. I officially gave notice to the occupants of these saloons, that they must close them by four o'clock, the next day, or take the consequences of a refusal to comply.

They had so often before been warned, that no attention was given to my caution. At the expiration of the appointed time, with my employees, all armed with axes, I proceeded to the dens of Bacchus, and commenced the work of destruction. Soon the long lines of liquor shops were leveled to the ground, and only broken and empty barrels, crushed decanters, and rubbish remained.

In one case, when the demolition began, the proprietor, with pencil and paper, made an inventory of his property. When asked what he proposed to do with it, he replied: "Make a bill," and scratched away.

I replied: "It is hardly worth the while to present to the Government a bill for a few decanters and rattlesnake whisky; I think I will tear down the house over your head, and then you can make out a bill worth your while."

The assembling of a large army at the capital also drew after it those camp-followers who, of all lost humanity, are the most degraded—fallen women. While the gambler and liquor-seller's den sprang up at the first sound of war, as if spontaneously from the earth which echoed the tramp of armies, from every city came the painted wreck of womanhood, and hired the room at the fashionable hotel, the dwelling, the abandoned chamber, or the negro cabin, to traffic in the virtue, health, domestic peace, and highest interests of men. Along the Potomac, in front of Washington, stretching for fifteen miles along the banks, lay the Union troops.

The horses of staff officers, the ambulance, and orderlies, could be seen during the night, and after the sun had risen even, waiting before the kennels of vice, for those who were within them.

Nor are the instances few, where the pretty, vain wife or daughter has been enticed over the lines, to become the member of the domestic military circle. So notorious had this vice become, that I appealed to the Secretary of War, who issued an order that no commissioned officer or private could enter the city without a written pass from his commanding general. A violation of the order would subject the offender to a lodgment in the guard-house.

For a time, the order was partially regarded, but soon set aside, and the corruption seemed to gain strength by the temporary check. At length, for the two-fold purpose of enforcing the order and exposing to public contempt the transgressors, I decided to make a descent upon some of the *representative* houses of this class.

The scenes which transpired at the hour of midnight, in these dens of corruption, beggar language.

At an hour appointed, and with a concerted plan, similar in all its details to that which was sprung upon the gamblers, with my force I made a raid upon the disreputable houses.

The moment came, the signal was given, doors were opened, the windows raised, and a scene of confusion and comico-tragic nature followed, which must have been witnessed to have been appreciated. Faces quite covered to avoid recognition, gas turned off, and a general stampede of gentlemen sporting martial emblems, were some of the incidents attending the onset upon the intrenchments of vice in midnight quiet of the nation's capital. Between sixty and seventy officers and men were arrested and locked up in the guard-house, for reflection upon their suddenly interrupted debauchery.

When General Burnside opened fire upon Fredericksburg, which was the first assault upon the town, the notice of bombardment given to the inhabitants was so short, that their flight from the city was a wild and hasty stampede, leaving the many palatial residences of this ancient seat of Virginia aristocracy in all the completeness of their peaceful occupancy. Among the first troops who crossed the river were those commanded by Brigadier-General ——— Upon reaching the elegant mansion of Commodore G., they immediately tore down the rich curtains, and pillaged the apartments adorned with expensive works of art, brought by members of the family from Europe. The feeling among the troops then seemed to be, that an enemy's house and "chattels personal" were common plunder. Oil paintings, bronze statuary, and family relics, were appropriated by the military visitors to the house of Commodore G., and seized by me upon their arrival at Washington. A few days later, the accomplished and beautiful Mrs. T., sister of Commodore G., came to the capital, and, dreading to meet me, as I afterward learned, on account of the rumors which had reached her, that I was gifted with a special ferocity of nature, applied to Dr. S., a distinguished physician of Washington, whose acquaintance I had formed in a sick-room, who volunteered to accompany her to my office, assuring her of respectful treatment.

With evident trepidation, she entered the room, and stated her errand. An elegant bronze horse, which had ornamented her brother's house, was then standing on my safe. I told her I saw no reason why these domestic treasures, including heavy silver-ware, bearing the family name, should not be restored. The next day she called again, and spent some time looking over the opened boxes of these family relics. She said at length:—

"Can I have these again?"

"Certainly, madam; they are of no use to the Government."

She burst into tears, thanked me, and retired.

CHAPTER XVI.

A PERILOUS ADVENTURE.

Pope's Defeat—Banks's Advance—The Importance of communicating with him—The Successful Attempt—Rebel Pursuers—The Escape.

ONE of the most disastrous defeats of the Union army was that of General Pope, when he was driven through the mountains of the Blue Ridge by General Lee, in the autumn of 1863. General Banks had left the Shenandoah Valley, but knew nothing of the perilous condition of the army he was hastening to join, nor the danger that would attend his advance, with Lee's entire army across his path. To save his battalions, it was necessary to communicate to him the movements of the two armies. Excepting the route from Washington to Centreville, the rebels had full possession, and the road was exceedingly perilous. Innumerable rumors were floating about Washington, to the effect that Banks had met Lee, and was annihilated. The Secretary of War was unable to obtain any information of him. He had dispatched two messengers with instructions to him not to attempt a junction with Pope. One of them was captured, and the other came back, after several fruitless attempts to get beyond Centreville, and refused to risk his life further.

Secretary Stanton, in this emergency, sent for me, and asked me if I had a man on my force daring and sagacious enough to carry the dispatches to Banks.

"If you will prepare your messages," said I, "I will see that they are delivered; or, at any rate, that an attempt is made to deliver them."

I got ready at once for the uncertain excursion, and reported to Mr. Stanton for orders. He gave me the dispatches, which I concealed under my clothes, next to my body, and, mounting the celebrated racehorse "Patchen,' I galloped away from the Capital at six o'clock in the evening, reaching Centreville at ten. I reported to General McDowell, and requested a fresh and fleet horse. I waited an hour, when the black clouds, which had been gathering overhead for some time, began to pour down a steady rain, and the air grew chill and dismal.

The darkness was almost impenetrable to the vision. The roads were in a wretched condition—muddy, broken, and frequently obstructed. No horse, fit for such a journey—a journey requiring one sure of foot, swift, and perfectly trained—could be found at that hour of the night, in the disorder of the army, and "Patchen" had already carried his owner thirty-five miles along a rough and toilsome route.

These were the considerations which urged me to remain at McDowell's head-quarters until the journey might be commenced with better auguries of safety. The darkness, however, in itself was not unfavorable to the enterprise. By its help, I might hope to pass through regions occupied by the rebels, which would be utterly closed to me in daylight or moonlight. I could depend on "Patchen," in every emergency, to the extent of his strength, while a strange horse might give me infinite trouble, and involve me in great danger. But, above all, Banks's army must be saved, and hours were precious.

As the only alternative, I remounted "Patchen," and plunged into the darkness. It was eight miles from Manassas by the direct route, but I took the Gainesville road, which would increase the distance to twenty-four miles. After pursuing my benighted way, often guided solely by the instinct of the noble animal that bore me, at daybreak I came upon traces of the army for which I was searching. An interview with General Banks immediately followed, which conveyed to him the first intelligence of Pope's defeat, with orders to march for Alexandria as rapidly as possible.

Having accomplished the object of my adventure—to the great relief of that officer, who was intensely anxious to hear from Washington—within an hour I was on my way with dispatches to the Secretary of War. I determined, without delay, to risk a daylight journey back, and retraced my way to Bristow Station, from which, to avoid a circuitous course, I started for the rebel lines. After riding two miles, I caught a glimpse of the rebel army, in rapid march eastward, toward the old Bull Run battle-ground. There were infantry, cavalry, and artillery, in detached squads, occupying the entire country ahead, with occasionally a small opening between them. Prudence would have dictated a speedy retreat, and as wide a circuit as would really be necessary for safety; but I was very anxious to save the distance. I rode down to within three hundred yards of the line, and attempted to discover an opportunity for slipping through.

I loitered in the rear for three-quarters of an hour, and finally observed an opening — a break in the train; and, though I should certainly be seen, and must take my chances with the bullets, I determined to make the effort to pass at this point. I took my six-shooter in my right hand, partly concealing it at my side, grasped the reins firmly with my left, and started, at first slowly and cautiously, down the road. Before I had gone far, I was discovered and hailed. I made no answer, and immediately became a target for every soldier within hearing distance. I now nerved myself for a quick and desperate venture, and gave my horse the spurs. It was necessary either to turn back, or to pass within thirty feet of a whole squad of infantry — that being the only opening. I again lay down upon the neck of "Patchen," who shot by like an arrow. As he passed the troops, they fired, and the bullets flew thickly about him; but horse and rider escaped unhurt. I raised myself in the saddle, and, with pistol in hand, waved an adieu to my disappointed foes; then bending again to "Patchen's" neck, he bore me rapidly from their sight. A cavalry force, who had heard the firing, now appeared in the distance, and began to discharge their carbines at me.

The cavalry at first numbered as many as forty. They continued the pursuit for a mile, when, one by one, they began to lag behind, firing generally an ineffectual parting shot. It was not long until only six or eight, who had remarkably good horses, followed me, and they were too far behind to fire with any accuracy of aim. Sometimes, however, I became entangled in brush, or temporarily impeded by mud; and, on two or three occasions, the foremost man rode to within twenty yards and fired.

For nine miles I did not slacken my pace. Only three of the party were now chasing me, the rest having fallen behind. My horse was covered with foam and dust, and began to show signs of failing strength—the necessary result of so long travel, at so rapid a pace. My powers were strained to their utmost capacity. I had ridden almost continuously over a hundred miles, through mud, and rain, and darkness; but this closing excitement called up the latent powers which every man possesses, but which only lend their aid in the direst emergency. I saw a little hill ahead, and spurred on to get fairly over it before the other party reached its foot. I passed over, and was out of sight for the minute. I wheeled sharply round, and turned into a thick clump of pines, a little to the right, and there dismounting, stood holding by the saddle.

I remained perfectly still, and the party rode past. They went on for a considerable distance, when one of them, perceiving that there was nobody ahead, turned his horse about, and rode back. He came toward the pines, glancing eagerly this way and that. He was not more than twenty yards from me, when a movement of "Patchen" revealed his hidden man. My pursuer saw at a glance my position, and raised his carbine to fire.

A crisis had come in the encounter, and, raising the pistol still in my hand, I discharged it at my enemy. The horse sprang forward, and his rider fell. I then leaped into the saddle, gave the wounded man, who was on the point of rising, another shot, and rode out into the beaten path. The other two, hearing the report of the pistol, returned to the pursuit, while I struck off, at a right angle with the path, to pass them unobserved. They saw me, however, and dashed forward with great speed, one of them firing his carbine, in the desperate endeavor to prevent my escape. Each backward glance revealed the frenzied excite-

COL. BAKER CARRYING DISPATCHES TO GENERAL BANKS.

ment of my foes, and their determination, at all hazards, to take me, either dead or alive.

I now came to the banks of Bull Run, where the final struggle for dear life and liberty was at hand. The stream was swollen, and it would require the best exertions of my good steed to swim it. I knew that if the pursuers reached the bank before I reached the other side, I should be at th mercy of their bullets. On the other hand, I knew tha the Union forces occupied the opposite side of the stream— that being the boundary of the picket line—and that if I should succeed in getting across safely, the peril for that day was over.

I spurred my horse to his final effort of speed, and was well ahead when I arrived at the stream. I plunged into it, and "Patchen" bravely breasted the swift current. It was only eight or ten yards wide, and this distance was soon accomplished; but the bank on the north side was almost perpendicular, and the horse made two or three ineffectual efforts to scale it. I heard distinctly the shouts of the two men behind me, and, cheering "Patchen" with encouraging words, which he evidently understood as well as his rider, he sprang forward, and in a moment stood proudly on the top of the bank, while the echo of a shot, intended for me, died away over the waters from which I had just emerged.

I dismounted, and went to the edge of the declivity to watch the movements of my pursuers. The first galloped down to the margin of the stream, and, after considerable urging, his horse commenced swimming across. Before I had occasion to fire, the Union pickets upon the bluff, having heard the enemy's shot, made their appearance. I shouted to them, and told them I was the bearer of dispatches to the Secretary of War, and was chased by rebels. Immediately four or five bullets were on the way to the Confederate horseman, who was midway in the stream. He tumbled from his saddle, and floated down the river, whose current was tinged with his blood. His comrade took the hint and disappeared in the distance.

Relieved from the peril of pursuit, I remounted "Patchen," and moved leisurely toward Washington, where I arrived at three o'clock, P. M., and reported to the Wai

Department. I had ridden one hundred and twenty-four miles since about six o'clock of the preceding afternoon, without a moment's sleep. I went to my quarters utterly prostrated with exhaustion. From the time the pursuit began, to have my pistol ready in my right hand, I had constantly held the rein in my left, which became so badly swollen, it required careful dressing for more than a week. Poor "Patchen" looked more dilapidated than his master, and required good nursing for over a fortnight.

Mr. Stanton expressed his satisfaction at the result in a characteristic manner, by simply saying to me, after reading my dispatches and hearing my story: "Well, go and tell Mr. Lincoln."

CHAPTER XVII.

SPECULATION AND FRAUD.

Devices of Contractors—Detection of Forage Contractor—Appeal to the President—Further Frauds as "Silent Partner".

MANY of the ingenious devices resorted to by contractors, by which, to gain their fraudulent ends without risk of detection have already been disclosed; but I shall here give another illustration, which, on account of its boldness and success, deserves especial notice.

I detected a conspicuous Government contractor in extensive speculations in the delivery of forage. He was arrested and placed in the "Old Capitol prison." His father, very indignant at his son's imprisonment on such an accusation, which he, in simple faith, considered unmerited, and which would inevitably bring disgrace upon his family, applied to the Secretary of War for his release. The father was a prominent politician of Pennsylvania, and, at the time of his interview with the Secretary, was accompanied by Members of Congress, besides other friends.

He appeared to rest in the belief that there would be little or no difficulty in obtaining the acquittal of his son, and strongly urged, as a reason, the absurdity of supposing that a gentleman of character so high, could have designedly defrauded the Government.

But the Secretary of War, having sufficient evidence to be convinced of the guilt of the contractor, was unmoved by his entreaties, and refused to grant his petition.

Not discouraged by the vain attempt, he next made application to President Lincoln. During this interview. the prisoner's cause was not the only topic of conversation but Colonel Baker's discipline and rule constituted also a very important and lengthy one. The patriotic Congressmen denounced the latter in unqualified terms, for having had the audacity to arrest a highly respectable citizen, and confine him within the walls of the American Bastile. They remarked that such outrages, committed by *detectives*, if allowed, would arouse the people, who would hurl from their offices these minions of power.

They seemed to think that, if they could convince the President of the righteousness of their attacks upon the detective system, their work toward the release of the prisoner would be more speedily accomplished.

This, with much more, delivered in a very emphatic manner, made so strong a plea, that Mr. Lincoln thought it necessary to consult me. He accordingly sent for me, and requested me to relate to him all the circumstances connected with the detection and arrest of the contractor.

I gave him as explicit an account as I could, and then asked his permission to hold the prisoner in custody twelve hours longer; adding that if, at the expiration of that time, I should be unable to produce facts sufficiently proving his guilt, and my rightful authority for arresting him, I would consent to his acquittal.

The President approved of this proposition, which was sent to the prisoner's friends; and the next morning, his father, attended by the Congressional delegation, referred to before, called at the War Department, to notify the Secretary that the President had promised to set the prisoner at liberty.

The same morning, I had carried to the Secretary of War an extended and unreserved confession of guilt by the contractor. This was now produced, and read in the presence of the whole company. In it, the writer very minutely related the manner in which he committed the frauds; he also, to prove his sincerity, handed to me thirty-two thousand dollars, one of the items in his speculations at the expense of the Government.

The effect upon so proud a father of the overwhelming intelligence conveyed in this full confession of the contractor, and before so numerous an audience, may be, perhaps, partially, but never fully imagined. The undeniable evidence of his son's guilt, coming so forcibly upon him, at the very moment that he had fondly anticipated would clear him from all suspicions, and place him higher than before in public opinion, on account of his being so unjustly arrested and imprisoned, bowed him down with shame and sorrow.

The distinguished friends who had accompanied him to the Department, and who, with him, had anticipated a far different issue of their proceedings, were speechless with astonishment and chagrin.

The silence was finally disturbed by a melancholy allusion to the natural depravity of man, and soon afterward the uncomfortable parties dispersed.

This short but sad sketch of the fraudulent undertakings of a contractor, is but a solitary instance, among many others of a similar kind, which might be recorded.

The Secretary of War, wisely judging that the criminal had forfeited all just claim to public benefit, passed an order, which took from him the privilege of making any further contracts with the Government. But so steeped in villany was his nature, that he concluded to evade the order, and still, though in a more surreptitious manner, pursue his swindling operations.

He submitted a proposal, through a partner in business, to the department quartermaster at Alexandria, to furnish what is called "mixed grain," or oats and corn, in the proportion of twenty pounds of oats and twelve of corn. It will be well to remark that, in this transaction, he took especial care to keep his name secret, and acted, therefore, as the "silent partner."

Oats were worth ninety, and corn forty cents. Up to this time, no mixed grain had been received by the Government. The contractor, therefore, prepared a glowing statement of the advantages of the grain to the Government. His enthusiastic assertions regarding the advantages to be obtained from the mixed grain were so convincing, that, upon the recommendation of the department quartermaster, the Government authorized a contract for the delivery of it, to the large amount of three million bushels.

I was ignorant of the negotiations until the affair had arrived at its consummation. Then, as confident as if I had been cognizant of the whole development of the transaction, of a fraudulent operation, I immediately commenced the work of its detection.

It is manifest that the difference of price in the two kinds of grain was considerable; and, therefore, it was an advantage, which the contractor would not willingly let slip by, to deliver a greater proportion of oats than of corn, as the price of the former was so much greater than the other.

The profits in this single contract we may safely estimate at not less than the almost incredible sum of five hundred thousand dollars.

At this date, my attention was attracted to a fruitful source of gain at the expense of virtue, and even decency: the traffic in corrupt literature and art. I know of no lower grade of depravity than that of this shameless business. The vile book, photograph, and wood-cut, were scattered by sutlers, mail agents, and others, throughout the army. I found them in large quantities in the mail-bags of the Government. The extent to which the fiendish business of ruining the morals and bodies of men was carried, would scarcely be believed by the good people of the rural districts, or even of the cities.

The art of photography and printing has flooded the country with these cheap and shameless appeals to the lowest and most brutal passions. No quiet hamlet is so sheltered by kindly moral influences, that it is not reached by the poison of this trade. But the absence from home of the many thousands of our volunteers—separated as they were from all the softening and elevating restraints of domestic and social life—afforded an opportunity for these human vampires, who do their work by stealth, unknown before in this country. They appreciated and improved it.

The illegal and infamous source of gain came to my knowledge in various ways and from different quarters. The post-office being the principal channel through which the business was carried on, I made a formal application to the Postmaster-General for aid in reaching the outrage:—

I received all the encouragement I desired, and entered immediately to check, if I could not break up, the disgraceful traffic. I soon got on the track of a large quantity of the vile goods, on their way to the army. They were seized, and their estimated value, according to the purchase-price, was not less than twenty-two thousand dollars. It was decided to make a bonfire of this pile of sensual trash. Our pure-minded President intimated that he would like to see the conflagration. It was kindled in front of the White House, and he enjoyed the sight, with the zest of a noble nature, to which vice was a loathing.

CHAPTER XVIII

A FEMALE ADVENTURER

Woman in the Rebellion—Her Aid indispensable in the worst as well as the best Causes—A Spicy Letter—Miss A. J.—Vidocq's Experience.

"A WOMAN in every plot" is almost a proverb among those who have had much to do with successful conspiracies and treachery.

It will be recollected that Miss Ford, aid-de-camp of the cavalry commander Stuart, betrayed General Stoughton and his staff to guerrilla Moseby's band. I find a spicy epistle on the subject, from a lady of the first standing, among the intercepted correspondence of the war, which is a fair specimen of refined hate to the North, along with a touch of sympathy with a betrayed and captive Union officer:—

GEORGETOWN.

DEAR J.—Ina is sending off a letter, in which, I presume, she tells you the *news of the day*. (You know how much of *that article* there is in Georgetown.) So I will commence at once with my little piece of business, although I presume you have heard that General Stoughton is now a prisoner in Richmond. *Thank Heaven!* He has at last reached the desired haven, but I fear he is rather in a destitute condition. *Three impudent rebels* dashed into Fairfax and took the gentleman out of his bed, with a number of other soldiers, horses, and contrabands; and I hear that some were in a state of nudity. What a grand entrée it must have been into Richmond. But while I rejoice that his little hands are kept from "picking and stealing," and that his noble efforts for crushing this wicked rebellion are now confined within four walls, yet I can't help feeling a little sorry for the discomfort he will necessarily suffer, and which he *richly deserves*—a prisoner among strangers, and he must be without clothing, money, or any of the necessaries of life. Now, Aunt Josie, please ask Colonel Leftrich, or any of the family, if at any time they go to Richmond, wou't they be so kind as to go and see him. You know, Joe, they are people of *much wealth* and standing, and no matter what General Stoughton might want, in the way of money or clothing, would be most cheerfully returned. Probably Colonel Leftrich would write to some friend

In Richmond. His mother and sister, who were with him at the time, are both inclined to be Southern, and would be so grateful for any kindness shown to General Stoughton. When you write to Cousin E., ask him, if he comes to Richmond, which he very often does, to go and see him, and do any thing for him he can. If you can't get any one else, please write to John Hunter, and beg him to go at once, and do what he can. I highly approve of his being kept behind a bolt and bar. But please, Aunt Joe, attend to it at once, and ask Colonel Leftrich if he will not write to some friend. You know, at least Ina told you in her last letter, that after you left, General Stoughton went to Mrs. G. L.'s and got Charley's valise for me; and he has always been so remarkably kind to me, that I am very anxious, in some way, to repay it.

Yours, &c., FANNIE.

One of the most strangely romantic female histories of the war, which came within the investigations of the bureau, was that of Miss A J.

Statements have been already made concerning female visitors to the army. Much of the information communicated to the rebels was given by these irresponsible characters passing through rebel and Union lines. The condition of morals among officers who found congenial companionship in the society of such women, is apparent, and needs no coloring from pen or pencil.

This unfortunate and degraded young woman was arrested, while attempting to pass the Confederate pickets, within three days after giving her solemn parole not to cross the Potomac into Virginia during the rebellion. Upon the earnest request of the Governor and a distinguished Senator of Massachusetts, she was again released from confinement, on parole; after which she made the subjoined confession:—

STATEMENT OF MISS A. J.

My name is A. J. I was born in Cambridge, Massachusetts. Am twenty years of age. I have neither father or mother living. I have two sisters. In August, 1861, I left my home at Cambridge, without the knowledge or consent of my uncle, sisters, or friends, and came direct to Washington, with the intention of offering my services as a hospital-nurse, which was refused, on account of my age. I then procured a pass from General Wool to visit the different camps in and about Baltimore. I had no particular object or business in the army, but went out of mere curiosity. I spent some months in this way. While in the various camps, I was furnished by the commanding officers with a tent, and sometimes occupied quarters with the officers. In the fall of 1862 I went to the Army of the Potomac, with no different object

In view; spent some time at General S.'s headquarters at Fairfax Court House. During this time was the guest of the General and his staff officers. After General S. left Fairfax Court House I went to Centreville. I do not now recollect who was in command at the time. I remained at Centreville but a short time, then went to Falls Church, from there to Fairfax Court House. In June or July last I attempted to pass the Federal pickets, for the purpose of visiting Drainesville, then outside our lines; was arrested, and taken to General S.'s headquarters, and by him sent to General M., who at once released me, and sent me back to General S.'s headquarters, where I remained until the army returned from Maryland. General S. was then relieved, when I joined General K.'s command, and went to the front, as the friends and companions of General O. We made our headquarters near Hartwood Church. Stopping at this point, General K. became very jealous of General O.'s attentions to me, and went to General M.'s headquarters and charged me with being a rebel spy. I was then arrested and sent to General M., Military Governor of Washington, who committed me to the Old Capitol Prison. I have spent two years and a half in the Union army, and during this time have been the guest of different officers, they furnishing me with horses, orderlies, escorts, sentinels at my tent, or quarter rations, &c. I have invariably received passes from these officers, to go and return when and where I pleased. During the time that I was with the Army of the Potomac I invariably wore major straps. I have repeatedly passed the outside pickets of the Federal army, several miles beyond, into the rebel lines; and was once captured by Moseby and taken to Aldie, to the house of a Mrs. Yankee Davis, whose husband is a Federal scout or spy. I was detained one or two days, then allowed to return. I further state, that during no part of the time that I was with the Federal army was I employed as guide, scout, spy, or hospital-nurse, but, as stated before, a companion to the various commanding officers, as a private friend or companion. On the 7th day of November, 1863, I was released from the Old Capitol Prison, by order of the Secretary of War. During the time of my confinement I became intimately acquainted with Captain M., Mr. J. S. L., the superintendent, clerks, and others. On my release Mr. L. advised me to go to the house of a Mrs. McC., where I was at the time of my arrest. In consequence of Mr. L.'s intimacy with me, during my imprisonment, Mr. W. discharged him. I then went to Colonel J. A. H., at the War Department, and informed him that L. had been discharged, and the reason. Colonel H. then directed that L. should be assigned to duty at General A.'s headquarters, on condition that I would leave the city and return to my home at Cambridge. I did go to Boston, as I promised, and Mr. L. obtained his situation at General A.'s headquarters. I remained away about three weeks, when I returned to Mrs. McC.'s house.

On my discharge from prison, I signed a parole, one of the conditions of which was "that I should not enter the State of Virginia" without proper permission, during the rebellion; but, notwithstanding this obligation, I have made several ineffectual attempts to do so. In reference to my present arrest, I desire to state that I informed Mr. G. R. that I had procured a pass, in connection with Major W., of the Treasury Department, and Mrs. Moxen, that on

Saturday afternoon last I proceeded in a carriage, with the two persons referred to, viz., Mr. W. and Mrs. M., to the Aqueduct Bridge, where we were halted by the guard, who informed us that Mr. W. and Mrs. M. could go on, but that Miss J. could not; that I then returned to Mrs. McC.'s. I also informed Mr. R. that said pass was procured for me through the influence of a brigadier-general (not naming him). I also informed others, at Mrs. McC.'s, that I made the attempt to cross, but was turned back by the guard. During the entire time since my leaving home, in 1861, I have led a very roving, and, may be, questionable life. I am now very unwell, owing to my long confinement and other causes, and desire to be released from custody, in order that I may return to my home and friends; and, if released, I pledge myself not to return to Washington during the present rebellion.

The proper officer certified as follows:—

City of Washington, District of Columbia:
Personally appeared before me A. J., who, being by me duly sworn, on her oath said that she had read the foregoing statement, and that she knew the contents thereof; that all the statements therein contained are true, to the best of her knowledge. That said statement is made without fear or compulsion, or promise of reward, but freely on her part.

The great detective, Vidocq, quoted in the first part of this volume, has an instance both of woman's crafty management, and his own, particularly interesting in this connection:—

It is very rare that a fugitive galley-slave escapes with any intention of amendment; most frequently the aim is to gain the capital, and then put in practice the vicious lessons acquired at the Bagnes, which, like most of our prisons, are schools in which they perfect themselves in the art of appropriating to themselves the property of another. Nearly all celebrated robbers only became expert after passing some time at the galleys. Some have undergone five or six sentences before they became thorough scoundrels; such as the famous Victor Desbois, and his comrade, Mongenet, called Le Tambour (Drummer), who, during various visits to Paris, committed a vast many of those robberies on which people love to descant as proofs of boldness and address.

These two men, who, for many years, were sent away with every chain, and as frequently escaped, were once more back again in Paris; the police got information of it, and I received the orders to search for them. All testified that they had acquaintances with other robbers no less formidable than themselves. A music mistress, whose son, called Noel with the Spectacles, a celebrated robber, was suspected of harboring these thieves. Madame Noel was a well-educated woman, and an admirable musician; she was esteemed a most accomplished performer by the middle class of tradespeople, who employed her to give lessons to their daughters. She was well known in the Marias and the Quartier Saint Denis, where the polish of her manners, the elegance of her language, the gentility of her dress, and that indescribable air of superiority, which the reverses of fortune can never entirely destroy, gave rise to the current belief that she was a member of one of those numerous families to whom the Revolution had only left its hauteur and its regrets.

To those who heard and saw her, without being acquainted, Madame Noel was a most interesting little woman; and besides, there was something touching in her situation; it was a mystery, and no one knew what had become of her husband. Some said that she had been early left in a state of widowhood; others, that she had been forsaken; and a third affirmed that she was a victim of seduction. I know not which of these conjectures approaches nearest the truth, but I know very well that Madame Noel was a little brunette, whose sparkling eye and roguish look were softened down by that gentle demeanor, which seemed to increase the sweetness of her smile, and the tone of her voice, which was in the highest degree musical. There was a mixture of the angel and demon in her face, but the latter perhaps preponderated; for time had developed those traits which characterize evil thoughts.

Madame Noel was obliging and good, but only toward those individuals who were at issue with justice; she received them as the mother of a soldier would welcome the comrade of her son. To insure a welcome with her, it was enough to belong to the same "regiment" as Noel with the Spectacles; and then, as much for love of him, and from inclination, perhaps, she would do all in her power to aid, and was constantly looked upon as a "mother of robbers." At her house, they found shelter; it was she who provided for all their wants. She carried her complaisance so far as to seek "jobs of work" for them; and when a passport was indispensably requisite for their safety, she was not quiet until, by some means, she had succeeded in procuring one. Madame Noel had many friends among her own sex, and it was generally in one of their names that the passport was obtained. A powerful mixture of oxygenated muriatic acid obliterated the writing, and the description of the gentleman who required it, as well as the name which it suited his purpose to assume, replaced the feminine description. Madame Noel had generally by her a supply of these accommodating passports, which were filled according to circumstances, and the wants of the party requiring such assistance.

All the galley-slaves were children of Madame Noel, but those were the most in favor who could give her any account of her son; for them her devotion was boundless. Her house was open to all fugitives, who made it their rendezvous; and there must be gratitude even among them, for the police were informed that they came frequently to Mother Noel's, for the pleasure of seeing her only; she was the confidante of all their plans, all their adventures, all their fears; in fact, they communicated all unreservedly, and never had cause to regret their reliance on her fidelity.

Mother Noel had never seen me; my features were quite unknown to her, although she had frequently heard of my name. There was, then, no difficulty in presenting myself before her, without giving her any cause for alarm but to get her to point out to me the hiding-place of the men whom I sought to detect, was the end I aimed at, and I felt that it would be impossible to attain it without much skill and management.

At first, I resolved on passing myself off as a fugitive galley-slave; but it was necessary to borrow the name of some thief, whom her son or his comrades had mentioned to her in advantageous terms. Moreover, a little resemblance was positively requisite, and I endeavored to recollect if there were not one of the galley-slaves whom I knew had been associated with Noel with the Spectacles, and I could not remember one of my age, or whose person and features at all resembled mine. At last, by dint of much effort of memory, I recalled to mind one Germain, alias "the Captain," who had been an intimate acquaintance of Noel's, and although our similarity was very slight, yet I determined on personating him. Germain, as well as myself, had often escaped from the Bagnes, and that was the only point of resemblance between us. He was about my age, but a smaller framed man; he had dark-brown hair, mine was light; he was thin, and I tolerably stout; his complexion was sallow, and mine fair, with a very clear skin; besides, Germain had an excessively long nose, took a vast deal of snuff, which, begriming his nostrils outside, and stuffing them up within, gave him a peculiarly nasal tone of voice. I had much to do in personating Germain; but the difficulty did not deter me. My hair, cut á la mode des bagnes, was dyed black, as well as my beard, after it had attained a growth of eight days; to embrown my countenance, I washed it with white walnut liquor; and to perfect the imitation, I garnished my upper lip thickly with a kind of coffee-grounds, which I plastered on by means of gum arabic, and thus became as nasal in my twang as Germain himself. My feet were doctored with equal care; I made blisters on them by rubbing in a certain composition, of which I had obtained the receipt at Brest. I also made the marks of the fetters; and when all my toilet was finished, dressed myself in the suitable garb. I had neglected nothing which could complete the metamorphosis—neither the shoes nor the marks of those horrid letters G A L. The costume was perfect; and the only thing wanting was a hundred of those companionable insects which people the solitudes of poverty, and which were, I believe, together with locusts and toads, one of the seven plagues of old Egypt. I procured some for money; and as soon as they were a little accustomed to their new domicile, which was speedily the case, I directed my steps toward the residence of Madame Noel, in the Rue Ticquetonne.

I arrived there, and knocking at the door, she opened it: a glance convincing her how matters stood with me, she desired me to enter, and on finding myself alone with her, I told her who I was. "Ah, my poor lad," she cried, "there is no occasion to tell me where you have come from; I am sure you must be dying with hunger!"

"Oh, yes," I answered, "I am indeed hungry; I have tasted nothing for twenty-four hours."

Instantly, without further question, she went out, and returned with a dish of hog's puddings and a bottle of wine, which she placed before me. I did not eat, I actually devoured; I stuffed myself, and all had disappeared without my saying a word between my first mouthful and my last. Mother Noel was delighted at my appetite, and when the cloth was removed she gave me a dram. "Ah, mother," I exclaimed, embracing her, "you restore me to life; Noel told me how good and kind you were:" and I then began to give her a statement of how I had left her son eighteen days before, and gave her information of all the prisoners in whom she felt interested. The details were so true and well known, that she could have no idea that I was an impostor.

"You must have heard of me," I continued; "I have gone through many an enterprise, and experienced many a reverse. I am called Germain, or the captain; you must know my name."

"Yes, yes, my friend," she said, "I know you well; my son and his friends have told me of your misfortunes; welcome, welcome, my dear captain. But heavens! what a state you are in: you must not remain in such a plight. I see you are infested with those wretched tormenting beasts who ——; but I will get you a change of linen, and contrive something as a comfortable dress for you."

I expressed my gratitude to Madame Noel; and when I saw a good opportunity, without giving cause for the slightest suspicion, I asked what had become of Victor Desbois and his comrade Mongenet. "Desbois and Le Tambour? Ah! my dear, do not mention them, I beg of you," she replied; "that rogue Vidocq has given them very great uneasiness; since one Joseph (Joseph Longueville, an old police inspector), whom they have twice met in the streets, told them that there would soon be a search in this quarter, they have been compelled to cut and run, to avoid being taken."

"What," cried I with a disappointed air, "are they no longer in Paris?"

"Oh, they are not very far distant," replied Mother Noel; "they have not quitted the environs of the 'great village' (Paris): I dare say we shall soon see them, for I trust they will speedily pay me a visit. I think they will be delighted to find you here."

"Oh, I assure you," said I "that they will not be more delighted at the meeting than myself; and if you can write to them, I am sure they would eagerly send for me to join them."

"If I knew where they were," replied Mother Noel, "I would go myself and seek for them to please you; but I do not know their retreat, and the best thing for us to do is to be patient and await their arrival."

In my quality of a new-comer, I excited all Madame Noel's compassion and solicitude, and she attended to nothing but me. "Are you known to Vidocq and his two bull-dogs, Levesque and Compère?" she inquired.

"Alas! yes," was my reply; "they have caught me twice."

"In that case, then, be on your guard: Vidocq is often disguised; he assumes characters, costumes, and shapes, to get hold of unfortunates like yourself."

We conversed together for two hours, when Madame Noel offered me a foot-bath, which I accepted; and when it was prepared, I took off my shoes and stockings, on which she discovered my wounded feet, and said, with a most commiserating tone and manner, "How I pity you; what must you suffer! Why did you not tell me of this at first? you deserve to be scolded for it." And whilst thus reproaching me, she examined my feet; and then pricking the blisters, drew a piece of worsted through each, and anointed my feet with a salve, which she assured me would have the effect of speedily curing them.

The bath concluded, she brought me some clean linen; and, as she thought of all that was needful, added a razor, recommending me to shave. "I shall then see," she added, "about buying you some workman's clothes, as that is the best disguise for men who wish to pass unnoticed; and besides, good luck will turn up, and then you will get yourself some new ones."

As soon as I was thoroughly cleansed Mother Noel conducted me to a sleeping-room, a small apartment, which served as the workshop for false keys, the entrance to which was concealed by several gowns hanging from a row of pegs. "Here," said she, "is a bed in which your friends have slept three or four times; and you need not fear that the police will hunt you out; you may sleep secure as a dormouse."

"I am really in want of sleep," I replied, and begged her permission to take some repose, on which she left me to myself. Three hours afterward I awoke, and on getting up we renewed our conference. It was necessary to be armed at all points to deceive Madame Noel; there was not a trick or custom of the Bagnes with which she was not thoroughly informed; she knew not only the names of all the robbers whom she had seen, but was acquainted with every particular of the life of a great many others; and related with enthusiasm anecdotes of the most noted, particularly of her son, for whom she had as much veneration as love.

"The dear boy, you would be delighted to see him!" said I.

"Yes, yes, overjoyed."

"Well, it is a happiness you will soon enjoy; for Noel has made arrangements for an escape, and is now only awaiting the propitious moment."

Madame Noel was happy in the expectation of seeing her son, and shed tears of tenderness at the very thoughts of it.

In the course of conversation, Mother Noel asked me if I had any affair (plan of robbery) in contemplation; and after having offered to procure me one, in case I was not provided, she questioned me on my skill in fabricating keys. I told her I was as adroit as Fossard.

"If that be the case," she rejoined, "I am easy, and you shall be soon furnished; for as you are so clever, I will go and buy at the ironmonger's a key which you can fit to my safety lock, so that you will have ingress and egress whenever you require it."

I expressed my feelings of obligation for so great a proof of her kindness; and as it was growing late, I went to bed reflecting on the mode of getting away from this lair without running the risk of being assassinated, if perchance any of the villains whom I was seeking should arrive before I had taken the necessary precautions.

I did not sleep, and arose as soon as I heard Madame Noel lighting her fire, she said I was an early riser, and that she would go and procure me what I wanted. A moment afterward she brought me a key not cut into wards, and gave me files and a small vice, which I fixed on my bed; and as soon as my tools were in readiness, I began my work in presence of my hostess, who, seeing that I was perfectly conversant with the business complimented me on my skill; and what she most admired was the expedition of my work; for in fact, in less than four hours, I had perfected a most workmanlike key, which I tried and it fitted most accurately. A few touches of the file completed the instrument; and. like the rest, I had the means of unobstructed entrance whenever I wished to visit the house.

I was Madame Noel's boarder; and, after dinner, I told her I was inclined to take a turn in the dusk, that I might find whether "a job" I contemplated was yet feasible, and she approved the suggestion, at the same time recommending me to use all caution. "That thief of a Vidocq," she observed, " is a thorn in one's path; mind him; and, if I were you, before I made any attempts, I would wait until my feet were well."

"I shall not go far," I replied; "nor stay away long." This assurance of a speedy return seemed to quiet her fears.

"Well, then, go," she said; and I went out limping.

So far all succeeded to my most sanguine wishes; it was impossible to stand better with Mother Noel; but, by remaining in her house, who would guarantee that I should not be knocked on the head? Might not two or three galley-slaves arrive together, recognize me, and attack me? Then farewell to all my plottings; and it was incumbent, that, without losing the fruit of my friendship with Mother Noel, I should prepare myself for the contingent danger. It would have been the height of imprudence to have given her cause to think that I had any motives for avoiding contact with her guests, and I consequently endeavored so to lead her on, that she should herself suggest to me the necessity of quitting her house; that is, that she should advise me no longer to think of sleeping in her domicile.

I had observed that Madame Noel was very intimate with a fruitseller who lived in the house; and I sent to this woman one of my agents named Manceau, whom I charged to ask her secretly, and yet with a want of skill, for some accounts of Madame Noel. I had dictated the questions, and was the more certain that the fruit-woman would not fail to communicate the particulars, as I had desired my man to beg her to observe secrecy.

The event proved that I was not deceived; no sooner had my agent fulfilled his mission, than the fruit-woman hastened to Madame Noel with an account of what had passed; who, in her turn, lost no time in telling me. On the look-out at the steps of the door of her officious neighbor, as soon as she saw me, she came to me, and, without further preface, desired me to follow her, which I did; and on reaching the Place des Victoires, she stopped, and looking about her to be assured that no one was in hearing, she told me what had passed. "So," said she, in conclusion, "you see, my poor Germain, that it would not be prudent for you to sleep at my house; you must even be cautious how you approach it by day."

Mother Noel had no idea that this circumstance, which she bewailed so greatly, was of my own planning; and, that I might remove all suspicion from her mind, I pretended to be more vexed at it than she was, and cursed and swore bitterly at that blackguard Vidocq, who would not leave us at peace. I deprecated the necessity to which I was reduced, of finding a shelter out of Paris, and took leave of Madame Noel, who, wishing me good luck and a speedy return, put a thirty-sous piece into my hand.

I knew that Desbois and Mongenet were expected; and I was also aware that there were comers and goers who visited the house, whether Madame Noel was there or not; and she was often absent, giving music-lessons in the city. It was important that I should know these gentry; and to achieve this, I disguised several of my auxiliaries, and stationed them at the corners of the street, where, mixing with the errand-boys and messengers, their presence excited no suspicion.

These precautions taken, that I might testify all due appearance of fear, I allowed two days to pass before I again visited Madame Noel; and this period having elapsed, I went one evening to her house, accompanied by a young man, whom I introduced as the brother of a female with whom I had once lived; and who, having met me accidentally in Paris, had given me an asylum. This young man was a secret agent, but I took care to tell Mother Noel that he had my fullest confidence, and that she might consider him as my second self; and as he was not known to the spies, I had chosen him to be my messenger to her whenever I did not judge it prudent to show myself. "Henceforward," I added, "he will be our go-between, and will come every two or three days, that I may have information of you and your friends."

"I' faith," said Mother Noel, "you have lost a pleasure; for twenty minutes sooner, and you would have seen a lady of your acquaintance here."

"Ah! who was it?"

"Mongenet's sister."

"Oh! indeed; she has often seen me with her brother."

"Yes; when I mentioned you, she described you as exactly as possible: — 'a lanky chap,' said she, 'with his nose always grimed with snuff.'"

Madame Noel deeply regretted that I had not arrived before Mongenet's sister had departed; but certainly not so much as I rejoiced at my narrow escape from an interview which would have destroyed all my projects; for if this woman knew Germain, she also knew Vidocq; and it was impossible that she could have mistaken one for the other, so great was the difference between us! Although I had altered my features so as to deceive, yet the resemblance which, in description, seemed exact, would not stand the test of a critical examination, and particularly the reminiscences of intimacy. Mother Noel then gave me a very useful warning, when she informed me that Mongenet's sister was a very frequent visitor at her house. From thenceforward I resolved that this female should never catch a glimpse of my countenance; and to avoid meeting with her, whenever I visited Madame Noel, I sent my pretended brother-in-law first, who, when she was not there, had instructions to let me know it by sticking a wafer on the window. At this signal I entered, and my aid-de-camp betook himself to his post in the neighborhood, to guard against any disagreeable surprise. Not very far distant were other auxiliaries, to whom I had confided Mother Noel's key, that they might come to my succor in case of danger; for, from one instant to another, I might fall suddenly among a gang of fugitives, or some of the galley-slaves might recognize and attack me, and then a blow of my fist against a square of glass in the window was the signal which was to denote my need of assistance, to equalize the contending parties.

Thus were my schemes concerted, and the finale was at hand. It was on Tuesday, and a letter from the men I was in quest of, announced their intended arrival on the Friday following; a day which I intended should be for them a black Friday. At the first dawn I betook myself to wine-vaults in the vicinity; and, that they might have no motive for watching me, supposing, as was their custom, that they should traverse the street several times up and down before they entered Madame Noel's domicile, I first sent my pretended brother-in-law, who returned soon afterward, and told me that Mongenet's sister was not there, and that I might safely enter.

"You are not deceiving me?" said I to my agent, whose tone appeared altered and embarrassed, and fixing on him one of those looks which penetrated the very heart's core, I thought I observed one of those ill-suppressed contractions of the muscles of the face which accompany a premeditated lie; and then, quick as lightning, the thought came over me that I was betrayed— that my agent was a traitor. We were in a private room, and, without a moment's hesitation, I grasped his throat with violence, and told him, in presence of his comrades, that I was informed of his perfidy, and that if he did not instantly confess all, I would shoot him on the spot. Dismayed at my penetration and determined manner, he stammered out a few words of excuse, and, falling on his knees, confessed that he had discovered all to Mother Noel.

This baseness, had I not thus detected it, would probably have cost me my life, but I did not think of any personal resentment; it was only the interest of society which I cared for, and which I regretted to see wrecked when so near port. The traitor, Manceau, was put in confinement, and, young as he was, having many old offenses to expiate, was sent to Bicêtre, and then to the Isle of Oleron, where he terminated his career. It may be conjectured that the fugitives did not return to the Rue Ticquetonne; but they were, notwithstanding, apprehended a short time afterward.

Mother Noel did not forgive the trick I had played her; and, to satisfy her revenge, she, one day, had all her goods taken away; and when this had been effected, went out without closing her door, and returned, crying out that she had been robbed. The neighbors were made witnesses, a declaration was made before a commissary, and Mother Noel pointed me out as the thief; because, she said, I had a key of her apartments. The accusation was a grave one, and she was instantly sent to the préfecture of police, and the next day I received the information. My justification was not difficult, for the préfet, as well as M. Henry, saw through the imposture; and we managed so well, that Mother Noel's property was discovered, proof was obtained of the falsity of the charge, and, to give her time for repentance, she was sentenced for six months to St. Lazarre. Such were the issue and the consequences of an enterprise, in which I had not failed to use all precaution; and I have often achieved success in affairs, in which arrangements had been made, not so skillfully concerted or so ably executed.

CHAPTER XIX.

THE BOUNTY JUMPERS.

Fraudulent Practices of Bounty Brokers and Jumpers—Contrast between English and American Deserters—Plans to check Desertion, and bring Criminals to Justice.

THE great demand for recruits during the war, the large bounties offered for them, and the manifold facilities for fraudulent transactions, presented temptations of great power, even to reputable citizens, to evade the plain letter of the law, and traffic in substitutes, or, by bribery and deception, personally to keep out of the hands of the recruiting officer.

The majority of the officers assigned to recruiting service were guilty of great dereliction of duty, inasmuch as, instead of endeavoring to check the growing evil, they rather pretended ignorance, or allowed it to pass unnoticed.

On one occasion, being in the presence of the President and a member of the Cabinet, I heard the latter congratulate the President upon the success attending a certain call for troops, which he had issued, remarking:—

"Mr. Lincoln, if recruiting goes forward in this way, your new call for troops will soon be answered."

The President made this reply:—

"Oh, yes; we have a pretty big army already—on paper; but what we want is, men in boots and breeches. This great array of figures, in respect to soldiers, is not going to suppress the rebellion. I want *men*, who can carry muskets, and eat hard-tack.'

It was indeed surprising to observe the apparent sincerity of persons, who, in various ways, were guilty of unlawful and dishonorable acts, finding a sufficient apology in the necessities or peculiarities of the case; while others, and not a few, went into the remunerative dishonesty with the simple purpose, in common with the professional gambler, to make money out of the Government, or individuals serving it, according to the promised reward. And yet it is difficult to see how any man, of ordinary moral perceptions, could fail to appreciate the criminality of the business, whether viewed from the stand-point of the army depletion and peril, or the robbery of the public treasury. Were the loose principles governing bounty brokers and jumpers once allowed, the ranks of no army could be kept full, and the loyalty of the people could not be maintained.

The lenity of our military authorities, in regard to the punishment of offenders against law and loyalty, was a fruitful cause of the boldness with which they acted, and the air of respectability worn by the crime itself.

At this point, I must refer to the suggestive contrast between foreign armies and our own. Deserters from the English troops are rare, on account of the penalty which is inflicted on such offenders. This penalty, which is death, is never set aside, no matter what extenuating circumstances may attach to the desertion, rendering it a lesser crime in the opinion of mankind. The English military law is arbitrary, carrying out its requirements to the utmost; and, as the punishment for desertion is death, no soldier guilty of the crime receives any lighter doom.

During the late war, the execution of deserters was so rare, that no moral effect was produced on the minds of the people. Who can recollect any shadow of guilt and punishment falling upon his thought, during the whole of the war, on account of the deserter's fate?

The desertions were as common as recruiting, but escapes were so frequent, and pardon was so often granted, that no importance seemed to be attached to the shameful disloyalty. Indeed, it was rather considered in the light of a legitimate business than otherwise; the idea of its criminality hardly seemed to be entertained by any, so lightly was it treated by the law.

The Department at Washington was constantly urging upon me the necessity for forming some plan, which, in a summary and successful manner, would frustrate the designs of these dishonest parties, and bring them to justice. Sev eral attempts had been made for this purpose, but had all proved unsuccessful.

A number of plans were submitted to me, each of which I considered objectionable, on certain accounts. The shortest way to catch these deserters, which was tracking them to their haunts, it would have been folly to pursue, as such a course would result in a general alarm and stampede of the guilty.

After some time, I chanced to think of a method, which seemed so suited to the purpose, that I became immediately inspired with the hope of success. I reported it to the Provost-Marshal General, and, after examination, it was accepted, with some slight modifications.

In January, 1865, the War Department determined to check, if possible, the increasing frauds. On investigation, it was found that only one in four of the enlisted men reached the front—a fact which will doubtless astonish my reader, and probably be denied by him, unless accompanied by the most positive proof.

I received my instructions, and immediately repaired to New York, the great rendezvous of gamblers in recruiting, and the centre of their complicated and increasing business. Two or three days devoted to inquiries concerning them, so astounded, discouraged, and disheartened me, that I resolved to abandon the investigation, and return to Washington. When I reported my purpose to the War Department, I was directed to resume and prosecute my work. This investigation, including my action and that of the Provost-Marshal-General, has been the occasion of Congressional and civil examinations, and therefore demands a pretty full and clear narrative.

The means which I employed, and the manner of proceeding, may seem, to superficial observers, to have been extraordinary, and wholly unwarranted.

All the usual methods of procedure in detective service were quite unavailing in this large undertaking. Nearly the entire circle of military and civil officers were found to be, either directly or indirectly, implicated in bounty swindling —from the staff officer to the orderly, and from the judge to the lowest criminal in the haunts of dissipation and vice.

I considered the matter well, in order to reach some plan by which I could become familiar with the fraudulent enterprise and learn its secrets. The result of my meditations was the belief that, in order to gain my ends, I must select for my service some bounty broker who had been connected with the business a considerable length of time, and who was, consequently, familiar with all its details.

CHAPTER XX.

THE BOUNTY JUMPERS AND BROKERS.

Quotas filled with Falsified Enlistment-Papers—Arrest of Brokers—Amusing and Exciting Scene—The Hoboken Raid—Slanderous Charges—Large Number of Arrests—Incarceration in Fort Lafayette—Other Arrests—Trial before a Military Commission.

It is, doubtless, a matter of surprise that forged enlisting-papers could have been so readily manufactured and profitably used. One of the leading brokers arrested was a notary public. Aided by the clerks at the recruiting-office, the necessary blanks were obtained. These were written out with fictitious names, properly certified by the notary public. Each set of the papers represented an enlisted man, and was ready for sale in the market, to any unsuspecting agent from the country having a quota to fill. There were whole towns in the interior of the Empire State filled with these fraudulent credits. In many instances the same false enlistments were credited in different Congressional districts. The matter will be more fully comprehended by a reference to my official report.

I took up my headquarters at the Astor House, and let the brokers know that I was an agent or supervisor for the interior of the State, having several large quotas to fill. I was at once besieged by applications to purchase credits. The third day I purchased sixteen sets of these enlistment papers; and on the fourth, twenty-two, when a proposition was made by a broker to purchase forged papers, saying, those I had were such, and would answer the same purpose; that so skillfully were they prepared detection was impossible. The offer was accepted, and placed me on the most friendly terms with my associates in business. For a number of days I continued the purchase of spurious papers for less than half the price of the genuine documents. This feature of the swindling came near causing a quarrel among the brokers; some of them insisting that I should not have been informed that I bought forged papers, because I might then have paid full price. The other party contended, that by committing me to the forgery I was secured against betrayal of the cause. The former further claimed, that forged papers were worth as much to me as the genuine. These negotiations were carried on four days, when I decided to arrest the whole company. It will be understood, that the arrest of a single broker in the city would create an alarm, and end the investigation. The greatest strategy and concealment were therefore indispensable to success. The knowledge of my presence in the metropolis would have defeated my plans. On a certain day I requested nine brokers, with whom I had business, to come to my room at the same hour, bringing their papers. I had concealed, in an adjoining room, a number of my assistants. I instructed them that the signal I should use to bring them to my aid, would be a knock on the door of the apartment in which they were placed.

The illustrious nine stood around me, forged papers in hand, eagerly waiting for the checks which would bring the reward of their villainy. To fasten the guilt upon the criminals, beyond dispute, I had written receipts for the money to be paid each broker. As they walked up in line, and made their marks, for most of them could not write, I stepped to the folding-doors and gave the signal. Instantly a detective came in, and I said to my broker-friends: "Gentlemen, this joke has gone far enough; you are my prisoners. I am General Baker, the Chief of the Detective Bureau."

't would be futile for tongue or pen to attempt to describe the effect of my words upon the assemblage before me. The change that passed over it was very marked, and to me, who was the cause of it, irresistibly entertaining. The explosion of a bomb-shell in the battle-ranks could not have startled and dismayed the soldiery more suddenly than this unexpected exposure of their crimes. and the powerful grasp of justice, did the discomfited brokers, who had anticipated a very different fate.

Here, a dapper little fellow, in flashy dress and jewelry,

CAPTURE OF BOUNTY JUMPERS AT HOBOKEN.

changed color, looked ghastly, and reeled to the sofa. There, a burly, red-faced fighter put on a defiant air, and, with an oath, said: "I would like to see you arrest me." A display of my six-shooter cooled him off wonderfully, and he stood like a living firebrand, ready to go into a self-consuming flame. Another burst into tears, and pleaded that he was seduced into the crime by artful men. A few more resolved to make a joke of the whole matter, and laugh off the scare. I transferred the interesting company to an apartment in the Astor House, their prison for the time. Two or three of them made written confessions, which revealed in detail the criminality of their companions, and of many others.

The notorious Hoboken raid upon bounty brokers and bounty jumpers, which has been the subject of a great deal of newspaper comment and censure, was never clearly understood. It cannot be denied that the affair was original and peculiar in its character, but it was called for by the unusual and manifold expedients resorted to by the dishonest harpies preying upon the Government.

The late civil war possessed so many extraordinary features, that means were employed to meet them which, although unknown before, were justified by the emergencies; and on becoming possessed of the facts, as they really were, of the Hoboken transaction, every reasonable person, I am confident, will vindicate the action of the bureau, and especially my own position in the service.

The emissaries of the South, and loyal persons prejudiced against me personally, charged me with a financial connection and interest, and consequently represented me as a sharer in substantial pecuniary profits. These slanderous intimations, however, are wholly without foundation. The careful Congressional investigation, and several civil suits that were instituted, failed to bring a particle of reliable evidence to sustain them.

Men can believe what they please, still there is a wide difference between mere opinion and conviction following upon positive testimony. Upon receiving the latter, no person has an honest right to condemn my motives and conduct.

The official correspondence, and orders connected with the opening of a recruiting rendezvous at Hoboken, are given in my report to the Provost-Marshal General.

With the assistance of the bounty brokers referred to therein, I enlisted as many bounty jumpers as possible, with the understanding that no others were to be taken. March 10th, it was given out among the brokers that a "walk away" had been opened in Hoboken. This novel place was understood to be for the escape of enlisted men who could safely walk away.

Perhaps a more ludicrous trap in detective policy was never laid than that which now secured the swindlers. Appreciating the desperate character of the men I was preparing to deal with, I had a body of soldiers stationed in the hall, over the recruiting headquarters. To avoid all disclosure of the plot, it was arranged that no bounty jumper should leave or communicate with those outside. Every man enlisted was taken to the hall above; and here it is proper to state that each company of jumpers had its agent.

If none of those enlisted were known to have escaped, it would naturally awaken suspicion in the minds of their outside friends that something was wrong; that the "walkaway" was not genuine. Any uncertainty on this point would prove fatal to the scheme of detection.

Recruiting commenced at an early hour in the morning, and continued briskly until two or three o'clock in the afternoon, when the discovery was made, that not a single jumper who had entered the hall an enlisted soldier had been seen afterward. I had anticipated this difficulty, and, anxious to keep the plot secret as long as possible, to increase the number of jumpers, I directed those assisting me to put a mark upon the back of each of the brokers engaged in furnishing recruits. This was done in such a manner as to be unnoticed by the brokers themselves, but perfectly understood by me. I then directed my men to station themselves at the ferry, in New York, and arrest the brokers, which could be done with no difficulty, as the white signs of guilt marked upon their shoulders would instantly betray them.

As I had anticipated, the brokers became uneasy respecting the fate of those already enlisted, and, one after another, left the rendezvous, and took the boat for the metropolis.

When they reached the gate of the ferry, the chalk-marks revealed the criminals, and their arrest immediately followed, until eighteen of the brokers and one hundred and eighty of the jumpers were caught.

It would be difficult to imagine the scene in the Odd Fellows' Hall of Hoboken, on the afternoon of that day of arrest. Formed in a ring were many hundred soldiers, armed for any emergency; within it, seated on benches, were nearly two hundred prisoners. With the dawning of the truth upon the minds of the wondering crowd of arrested men, a sudden and amusing change went over the faces of all. They had been especially careful to avoid me, and now, awakened from a dream of security to find themselves in my toils! Some looked blank with amazement and despair; others had an expression of demoniac hate; while a portion of the arrested seemed strongly inclined to treat their imprisonment jocosely, and regard it as a trivial affair. They were caught in the net set by hands most dreaded and carefully avoided.

I could scarcely conceal an expression of mischievous merriment, which, notwithstanding my efforts to the contrary, was apparent at the singular scene presented by the mixed assembly.

The soldiers looked quietly on, while the dandy apparel and gaudy jewelry of the swindling fraternity presented a mocking and cruel contrast to their anxious and crestfallen countenances.

The facts were communicated to the Provost-Marshal General, with the request to be informed what to do with them. After a delay of nearly a day and a half, the Secretary of War ordered them to be removed to Fort Lafayette. Their incarceration for weeks, with no disposal of their case, was a topic of severe animadversion, and the responsibility laid at my door; a responsibility no more my own than any other act of the War Department through my official relation to it.

I repeatedly called the attention of the Department to

these prisoners, urging that they should be tried as deserters, and punished accordingly.

The only reason which can be given for the delay, and which, to many patriotic persons, will be a sufficient one, was the excitement and rejoicing attending the fall of Richmond and the surrender of General Lee, which occurred at this particular time, absorbing the attention of all parties.

Although overlooked for a while, they were by no means designedly neglected.

The final disposal of the brokers arrested, and those engaged in frauds upon the Government, was equally an affair entirely outside of my official authority.

My arrests, independent of the brokers and jumpers at Hoboken, were about forty-six persons, in every case of which a written order was received from the President of the United States, and, by his direction, they were committed to the Old Capitol prison.

I was requested to furnish, and did so, a written synopsis, or memorandum, in respect to each individual arrested. These statements were submitted to the Hon. L. E. C., and Judge B., of New York, two of the most eminent jurists in the country.

A military commission was convened at Washington, by order of the Secretary of War, for the trial of these prisoners. The ones first arrested were first tried. The great array of counsel for the defendants, and the number of witnesses produced by both parties, made the investigations extended and wearisome. But, notwithstanding the precautions taken by the prisoners, and the large number of counsel which they employed, they were all convicted, as will be seen by reference to the records of the Bureau of Military Justice. The Department exacted from me the most persistent activity in the prosecution of these cases.

Not governed by motives of revenge, or personal feeling, it was the simple aim to render justice to the guilty, and carry out the wishes of the Government.

In the midst of the trials, and immediately succeeding the conviction of about a dozen of the prisoners, the rebellion suddenly collapsed. Great changes in popular sentiment, and policy of the Government, awakened the desire, which soon found expression, for the restoration of civil courts. Fully sympathizing with this natural longing, I sent a written request to the Secretary of War, that all prisoners in my custody might be transferred to the proper authorities.

If they were regarded as legitimate recruits, the order discontinuing further enlistments, and discharge of all enlisted men held in barracks and rendezvous, would apply to these bounty jumpers. They could not be tried for desertion, because the President's proclamation of amnesty, which applied to deserters, would reach their case also. In any view that may be taken of the incarceration of the prisoners, complaints against me for the fact fall to the ground; I was not, and could not be, responsible for it, under the circumstances, which need only to be known to make the assertion of innocence clear.

CHAPTER XXI.

BOUNTY JUMPING INCIDENTS.

Personal Experience in Bounty Jumping—A Perfect Trump—Detectives Enlisted—Passes obtained for Bounty Jumpers—Arrest and Surprise—Court-Martial w Conviction.

It has been sufficiently demonstrated, by incidents recorded, that monstrous frauds were perpetrated by the manufacture and sale of enlistment papers.

Indeed, it is very evident, from knowledge thus far obtained, that not a small proportion of all such documents, on which credits were given, were forged.

I shall only add to the record a few incidents, which combine in their character both the comic and tragic qualities.

I had been told that soldiers would receive the bounty, re-enlist the same day, be sent to the Island, and repeat the process the day following. I was, at the time, skeptical respecting such facility in deception and incredible assurance, and to satisfy myself in regard to the truth of the matter, I dressed myself in the garb of a regular jumper and repaired, February 9th, to a recruiting office in the public square near the Astor House, New York. Assuming the air of a veteran in the business, I asked the officer what he was paying for recruits.

Before the question could be answered, the gentlemanly broker, always at hand, inquired of me my name and place of residence, which I gave him. In a low tone of voice, and with a knowing wink, he said: "Have you been through before in New York?" I answered: "Not since last fall." He added: "All right; come inside." And in less time than it has taken to relate the incident, I was one of "Uncle Sam's boys."

My friend gave me one hundred dollars, promising the remainder due me when I should arrive at the Island; then directing me to remain where I was for a while, he left me.

Returning within an hour, he opened the following conversation with me: "Have you ever been on the Island?" I replied, "Yes." Evidently enlightened in regard to the matter, he immediately remarked: "You know how to get off, then? When you *do*, come up to Tammany Hall, and I will put you through up town;" meaning, of course, he would enlist me again. While this conversation was passing between us another broker stepped up, and said: "Gentlemen, let us take a drink." We accepted the invitation, and they conducted me across the Park to a saloon, where I saw, at a glance, they were quite at home. Liquor was called for, and while the vender was getting it, one of the brokers quietly stepped behind the bar and addressed some conversation to him.

We then all drank to the success of the Union, or rather, all of us *appeared* to do so.

I raised the glass to my lips, and, unobserved by the rest, poured its contents into my bosom, as I had done many times before when compelled to join the convivial ring. I was convinced that my potation had been drugged. Next followed a proposition to repair to an adjoining room and engage in a game of cards.

We played until I thought it necessary to affect drowsiness and insensibility. My eyes began to close, until at length my head rested on the table in front of me, and my whole appearance indicated to my betrayers my entire helplessness in their hands.

At this juncture one of them left the room, but soon returning, exclaimed, "All right." Immediately I caught the sound of carriage wheels, and, as I anticipated, was carried to the door, and, supported by broker number one, lifted into a vehicle, and driven rapidly to the Cedar Street rendezvous. My hat was then unceremoniously pushed over my face, and I was hurried into the presence of the recruiting officer in attendance, who asked me, "Do you wish to enlist?" Number two answered, in a tone to represent my own voice, "Ye-e-s."

I was again declared to be one of the volunteers, taken into another room, and laid on a bench, where I remained an hour, in company with three other recruits, who had been drugged in the same manner, my friends the brokers supposing they had disposed of me.

In the mean time broker number one returned, and said: "Well, old fellow, how do you feel?" to which I replied, "Very sick." Then remarking, "You'll be all right by-and-by," he left me.

I looked about me to judge of the possibility of escape. I saw at once that I could not pass out by the door, as a sentry was stationed there, and came to the conclusion that I would have to try my chances at a window.

I opened one which overlooked a back yard, sprang out, and after walking through a long passage-way, which led me into the open street, I went deliberately to my room in the Astor House.

Here I masked my face, disguised myself anew, and proceeded directly to the office of Mr. Blunt, where I offered myself to the army service, to make my third enlistment for that day.

I was hardly seated, when broker number three approached me, saying:

"You want to enlist, do you?"

"Yes, I am thinking of it. What are you paying recruits now?"

"Six hundred dollars. Where are you from?"

"Steuben County. I would like to enlist if I could get a situation as clerk. I can write a pretty good hand, and am hardly able to go into the ranks."

He replied quickly, "Oh, I can fix all that right."

A conversation then followed between him and the recruiting officer, when I was made a soldier of the Union army once more. I was requested to be seated for a few moments. Soon after the broker asked me to take "a glass." I went with him to an old drinking-saloon in Cherry Street, where I found brokers numbers one and two, who immediately recognized me, but expressed no surprise at the meeting. My successful escape from the Cedar Street headquarters convinced my friends that I was an old expert in the tricks of the trade.

Their admiration for me became so great that they received me into full fellowship, regarded me as a shrewd member of the bounty jumping brotherhood, and, after freely discussing their plans and prospects, declared me to be a "perfect trump." Propositions were made to enter into partnership at once.

I was greatly amused while listening to the exploits of each, as he in turn detailed them. One related, that at a certain period he left New York, and having enlisted at Albany, Troy, Utica, Buffalo, and Chicago, returned *via* Elmira, at which place he likewise enlisted. Another had enlisted at every rendezvous from New York to Portland, Maine; while a third boasted of the amounts he had received, and mentioned those paid to recruiting officers, surgeons, brokers, and detectives. The den in which I spent the evening was a favorite haunt of the bounty jumpers. It contained a wardrobe of wearing apparel, consisting of both soldiers' and citizens' outfits. The idea of this I easily comprehended; here the jumpers could assume whatever dress they pleased, to carry out their designs. Three times that night, before two o'clock, I saw the interesting operation performed.

I selected one of my assistants to experiment in this military lottery. He dressed himself in the appropriate apparel, and in one day enlisted three times; he was sent to the Island, bought himself off, and reported for duty the following day.

The scenes described were followed by numberless arrests of bounty brokers, bounty jumpers, and others in the business, and consequently by the disclosures of their crimes, which have since attracted much public attention.

To illustrate the secrecy with which I necessarily pursued my inquiries, I mention the following incident: I had received intelligence of a notorious bounty broker, doing business on State Street, whose specialty seemed to be to secure, for a consideration, desertion and escape after enlistment. Rumor also said that, at any time, he had the power to obtain an enlisted man from Governor's Island. Extremely desirous to test his proficiency in such swindling, I enlisted two of my own detectives, and had them sent to the Island. I then directed another to apply to the broker for his interposition in their behalf. He consented, on the condition that he should receive two hundred dollars for his trouble. The amount was paid him; and my assistant, being curious to know in what manner he would obtain the release of the two detectives, begged leave to accompany him to the Island.

Upon their landing, he observed that the broker was on excellent terms with the officers of different grades who had the recruits in charge.

Two sergeants, being consulted, furnished a pass to the desired recruits, signed in the name of the provost-general of the Island, requiring their return at roll-call the same evening. For this pass the sergeant received fifty dollars. Sergeant number two, at the end of the wharf, whose duty it was to examine the passes, being in collusion with the other, shared the profits. The detective, and his associates who had been recruited, had no difficulty in leaving the Island.

I made arrangements for the arrest of the whole party on their landing in New York. When brought to my headquarters, the broker confessed the crime, seeing no possible means of escape, and embarrassed with surprise and terror.

His arrest was kept secret for several days. The sergeants, his companions in guilt, missing him, became uneasy, and suspicious that he had been murdered, and his body thrown into the river. The following Sunday they applied at the office of the City Police for assistance in discovering the missing man, having been informed beforehand, by the boy in the broker's office, that he had not been seen since he left with the stranger to go to the Island.

The Metropolitan detectives declined to give any assistance, and sent them to me, as the person most likely to be of use to them in solving the mysterious fate of their friend

Accordingly, on Sunday evening, the sergeants came to my office and excitedly told their story, dwelling on the fact that the broker was last seen on Wednesday, upon the Island, in company with a suspicious-looking stranger; that he had a large amount of money; and they gave five hundred dollars for information respecting him.

After a lengthy conversation, I told them I thought I could find their friend. I ordered an officer to bring in the broker. There was, of course, a mutual recognition, and the sergeants were overjoyed that the lost man was found and alive, until they learned that not only the broker was under arrest, but that they also were in the hands of the law.

The scene was a rich and rare one. The glad surprise of the sergeants was soon toned down by the mysterious gravity of their friend, and also my own. I then took out a pair of handcuffs, and said to the young men, "I am very glad you have saved me the trouble of sending for you, as I intended to do to-morrow."

The broker was sent to the penitentiary, and the sergeants were tried by court-martial and convicted.

These statements will probably appear exaggerated to many readers, but they are strictly true, and will be found on official records.

CHAPTER XXII.

BOUNTY JUMPERS IN ORGANIZED BANDS.

Gipsy-like Bounty Jumpers—Wholesale Bounty Jumping carried on adroitly by a Gang of Operators—Opposition from a Canadian Gang—Thirty-two Thousand Dollars in as many Days—Frauds in Drafting—An Old Man put in as a Substitute—A Boy decoyed—His Adventures—A Mother of Thirteen Children—Unavailing Efforts of a Mother in Search of her Idiotic Son.

I SHALL next relate the movements of these speculators in organized gangs. They had a leader, whom they selected chiefly for his insinuating and plausible manner of address, and with whom they acted in the capacity of Gipsies, wandering from one promising field of action to another.

On March 17, 1865, I ordered a detective to join one of these strolling companies, and, by closely watching every movement made by them, ascertain the *modus operandi* of enlistment under this social form of enterprise.

The company left the Hudson River Depot in the half-past eleven o'clock train, and presented a most desperate and villainous appearance. Indeed, a more unmanageable set of desperadoes scarcely ever was seen on the highway of adventure.

The next morning, before noon, they arrived in Poughkeepsie, where eleven of the thirty-six were enlisted, four of whom escaped the same afternoon, two during the night, and the remainder the following morning.

The next day, the whole of the gang appeared at the recruiting-office in Albany, seventeen re-enlisting there, five of whom had enlisted in Troy. Nine of these escaped that evening, and returned to Troy; two pleaded illness, became in consequence inmates of the hospital, effecting their escape during the night, and proceeding immediately to Utica, to meet those who had gone elsewhere. Four others of the company enlisted in Troy, but made their escape the same night.

The whole party then remained five days in Utica, at which place twenty-one enlisted, four of them twice, and one, three times. At Buffalo, owing to the competition in the business by parties in Canada, none of the parties enlisted. At Chicago, eight of the band enlisted, four were recognized as old bounty jumpers and arrested, one other was arrested for picking pockets, while the remainder, frightened at the turn events had taken, hurried from the city. In Detroit the Canadian gang had the field, and would not permit any interference with their operations.

The company next appeared in Rochester, but too many being known there as deserters to make their business promising, they proceeded to Elmira, where six were arrested for desertion, the remainder returning to New York.

These men were absent thirty-two days, and their total profits amounted to thirty-two thousand dollars. The question will be naturally asked, how this handsome profit was made. The bounty broker who was the leader, must first ascertain just how far, and by what means, he can insure the escape of the jumper after enlistment. A hundred dollars paid to the sergeant or corporal in charge at the rendezvous, would secure the liberation of ten men, while the records would show a certain number enlisted on a given day, properly credited to some locality; and the books of the State rendezvous would have the record of but two or three from the same place.

This broker was entitled to receive for every recruit from four to six hundred dollars, and the whole sum, after the expedition closed, was divided among the men. It must be borne in mind that many gangs, the number of which is not known, were moving about in the northern States at the same moment.

On this subject, thus far, I have only narrated frauds committed by the roving military bandits in disguise. There was another way of dishonest speculation, no less remunerative and criminal. The draft requiring men to enter the service, or furnish substitutes, afforded an excellent opportunity to "buy, sell, and get gain." I knew many instances where lads fourteen years of age were enticed into drinking saloons, drugged, and made to perjure themselves, to become the substitutes of some patriotic citizens, the substitutes each receiving, perhaps, one hundred dollars, which was almost invariably stolen from them before reaching the general rendezvous.

A superannuated Frenchman, seventy-two years old, unable to speak English, was taken in an alley at New York, while getting a scanty but honest livelihood, by gathering rags. His hair and whiskers, which were white as snow, were colored by a barber, then he was transferred to the Second Congressional District, Williamsburgh, and enlisted as a substitute for a well-known shipbuilder there. Hearing of the outrage, I sent for the aged man, and, through an interpreter, ascertained the name of the broker. The latter was obliged to disgorge six hundred dollars, which was paid to the victim of the dismayed trader in his fellow-men. The aged stranger thanked me tremulously, and, with eyes suffused with tears, departed from my office, having in his possession a purse which his rag-bag would not have yielded in a long space of time.

The law required that all minors desiring to enlist, should first obtain the consent of their parents. A respectable German, residing in Beaver Street, suddenly missed his son, about fourteen years of age. He searched for him diligently during three weeks, but all attempts to discover him proving fruitless, the anxious father applied to me for counsel and assistance. I made him give me a written description of the boy, promising him that, to discover his whereabouts, I would leave no means in my power untried. I then called a detective and placed in his hand the paper, with directions to use it in tracing the boy. He soon returned, with the information that the lad had enlisted at the Brooklyn rendezvous, in charge of Colonel Fowler.

I sent for the papers, from which I learned that a woman, claiming to be the mother of the boy, had accompanied him to the office and made the required affidavit. Then sending to the front I procured the lad's return, who furnished me with the following particulars. One evening, while passing from his father's store to his house, an elderly man, gentlemanly in appearance, accosted him, inquiring if he did not want a situation. He replied: "No, sir." His venerable friend then left him, and a boy of his own age came up and said, "Come in here and get a glass of lemonade," pointing to a Chatham Street saloon. They went in, and soon after calling for the drink the elderly man entered. He recollected nothing more until the next morning, when he found himself in a drinking saloon in Brooklyn. His hat and boots were gone, and while searching for them an old man entered, whom he recognized as the one he had seen the evening before. He was accompanied by a woman, who exclaimed: "You are a fine-looking boy; would you like to enlist for a bugler?" at the same time taking from under her cloak a small silver bugle, and adding, "Now, my son, if you will enlist you shall have this bugle."

He refused, and immediately was hurried into a carriage, and, in company with this admirable couple, was driven to Colonel Fowler's headquarters.

His papers were here made out, the wretched woman swearing that she was his mother, and giving her full consent to his enlistment. The poor lad's mother had been dead ten years. He was paid twenty-five dollars, while the couple who enlisted him received six hundred and seventy-five dollars.

The boy's description of the two worthies soon led to their arrest, and it turned out that the man was a notorious Jew bounty broker, while the woman was equally well known as a prostitute of the city.

Investigating more deeply, I came to the startling revelation that this vile woman had sworn to be the mother of thirteen other little boys about the same age as this German lad.

I shall select only one additional, very peculiar, and highly interesting narrative, from the mass of fragmentary materials in my possession; that of the kidnapping of the idiot boy Cornelius Garvin, of Troy, New York. Some of the facts found their way into the newspapers at the time of their occurrence.

Mrs. Garvin, the mother of the boy, was a poor, but honest and respectable Irishwoman, who supported her family by hard daily labor. She had placed her imbecile son in the almshouse at Troy, happy in the consciousness of his safety, and being near enough to visit him occasionally. The child, while playing in the grounds, was carried off by bounty brokers, and transported to Albany, where he was enlisted and sent to the front.

The mother, upon receiving the news, became nearly frantic; and, leaving her work, managed to get to Washington, where, through the interest which her story awakened, she gained an interview with the President.

That good man, whose ear was ever open to the appeals of humanity and justice, gave her a note to the Secretary of War, who referred the case to me. I detailed a detective to accompany her to the battle-field. Nearly a month was spent in the fruitless search for the lost boy, notwithstanding it was proved that "poor Con" was somewhere in the army. The disappointed but not discouraged mother went back to her toil again, to get money to bring her once more to the Capital.

Seven months passed over in the search, with no clue to the boy. Officers lent their assistance, and no means were left untried to find the wanderer. The persistency of purpose, the undying hope and affection of the sorrowing mother for her simple "Con," were hardly ever surpassed in human experience.

Unable to read or write, she carried always in her apron a large number of letters, and other memoranda, from prominent officers and others, given to aid her unrewarded search. Yet she could, as if by intuition, or the inspiration of her love, place her hand upon any of the documents she desired to use, and repeat their contents. And whenever she found an interested listener to her mournful story, she would select the particular document she wanted and give its statements.

After exhausting the subject, she would sit in a musing mood, gazing into vacancy for several moments, and then start from her revery, gather up her treasure of manuscripts, and exclaiming: "My poor Con; I must go and find him!" she would start again on her journey among the regiments of the Union army.

When the money which was given her, and earned by the severest toil, was gone, she would get back to Troy, replenish her purse by her daily labor, and return to the hunt for "Con," along a new path of adventure, on which had suddenly fallen a ray of hope from some quarter respecting the absent boy.

Thus month after month passed away, and the undying love of this mother for the imbecile child, over whose unsteady steps and aimless wanderings she had watched with a fondness intensified by his very helplessness, led her along the army lines, and into the camps, at the heart of the great and bloody war.

"Poor Con!" was on her lips when she sought brief and restless sleep, and at the dawn of day, when she resumed the travel, which would have no pause until darkness made it impossible.

While she was roaming at will, followed by the sympathizing interest of the President, and the humblest official in the army, I received the following letter:—

BUREAU OF MILITARY JUSTICE, WAR DEPARTMENT, *June* 1, 1863.

COLONEL:—

The case of Cornelius Garvin, an idiot boy, enlisted into the Fifty-second Regiment of New York Volunteers, has been referred to this bureau for report.

Among the papers in the case, is a letter of yours to the Mayor of the city of Troy, New York, in which you state that Captain Degner—in whose company the boy is supposed to have been—refused, or neglected, to search for him, when ordered to do so, although repeatedly assured that he was in his company, under an assumed name; but, instead of doing so, endeavored to intimidate, by threats, privates of his company who were disposed to aid in the search for the boy.

Be pleased to furnish this bureau with any proof that may be in your possession of the statements referred to, or which may otherwise throw light on the case.

It is desirable that any material information you have in the case should be communicated at your earliest convenience.

Your obedient servant,
W. W. WINTHROP,
Major, and Judge-Advocate, for Judge-Advocate General.

To Col. L. C. BAKER, Special Agent War Department.

Mr. Trott, from this bureau, has twice called at your office on this subject.

But all efforts to find Cornelius Garvin were in vain. Several times the mother seemed to be near him; but the joy at the prospect of meeting him soon faded before cruel disappointment.

It was rumored that he died in the army; which was doubtless true, for no further tidings to this hour, I believe, have been received of his fate. I append a report of my investigations in the case, addressed to the Mayor of Troy.

WASHINGTON, D. C., June 3, 1865.

Mayor THORNE, Troy, New York:—

SIR—Nearly two years since Mrs. Catherine Garvin, the mother of the idiot boy Cornelius Garvin, alleged to have been stolen from the County-House at Troy, applied to my headquarters in this city for assistance to find said boy. With the meagre facts at my disposal, I immediately instituted a search, which has resulted in disclosing the following facts :—

1st. That the idiot boy, C. Garvin, was stolen, or surreptitiously taken from the County Poorhouse at Troy; that he was enlisted, sent to Riker's Island, assigned to the Fifty-second New York Volunteers, and forwarded, with other recruits, to Alexandria, Virginia; that said Garvin was seen and recognized by a number of privates of Company I, at Mitchell's Station, Virginia, afterward at Mine Run, and other places; it is further shown that Captain Degner, Company I, Fifty-second Regiment New York Volunteers, was repeatedly informed that said idiot boy was in his company, under an assumed name; that he, Captain Degner, instead of prosecuting the search for said boy, as directed by his commanding officer, attempted to intimidate, by threats of punishment, those privates of his company who were disposed to assist Mrs. Garvin and others engaged in the investigation.

Some time in the month of May, 1864, by direction of the Hon. Secretary of War, I dispatched a detective officer to your city for the purpose of ascertaining, if possible, whether the boy, Con. Garvin, was sold, taken away, or enlisted by the Superintendent of the County Poorhouse. While the testimony elicited did not directly implicate the said superintendent, enough was shown to satisfy me that said idiot boy could not have escaped without the direct knowledge and connivance of said superintendent. The subsequent conduct of the superintendent toward Mrs. Garvin and those engaged in the investigation, in my opinion, strongly confirms this opinion.

Since the arrival of the Fifty-second New York Volunteers in this city I have placed Captain Degner under arrest, to await a further development of facts. I am exceedingly desirous of probing this matter to the bottom. Our late beloved President, the Hon. Secretary of War, Brigadier-Generals Hardy and Townsend, and in fact all the officers connected with the War Department who have listened to Mrs. Garvin's statements, have taken a deep interest in this case. The enormity of the crime, the affection of the poor mother for her son, her energy, her persistence and determination in following up every visible trace of her poor idiot boy, has awakened, in the minds of all those conversant with the facts and circumstances of the case, a feeling of deep interest and sympathy. I believe that the boy is still living, and will yet be found. I shall neither spare time or means in prosecuting my investigations, with a view to bring to speedy justice all those engaged in this inhuman and diabolical outrage.

I am, sir, your obedient servant,

L. C. BAKER,
Colonel, and Agent War Department.

CHAPTER XXIII.

THE GREAT CONSPIRACY.

Assassinations—Eglon, King of Moab—Cæsar, Emperor of Rome—James I of England—Marat, the French Revolutionary Leader—Alexander of Russia—Abraham Lincoln, President of the United States.

THE history of treason, conspiracy, and assassination, would be a record of awful interest—a revelation of singular contrasts in motive, while the tragical end sought was the same. The desperate determination to secure, at least avenge trampled rights; religious fanaticism; and revengeful passion; these have been the most frequent causes of a resort to treasonable plots and regicide, with its kindred homicides, and attempted murder of representative men in a State.

As introductory to the narrative of the facts respecting the assassination of Mr. Lincoln, which came under my eye and official investigation, with fresh details and documents, I shall cite a few illustrations from the annals of the past, not unfamiliar to intelligent readers, but which, grouped together, will be a suggestive background for the most revolting scene of depravity treason has ever presented to the world. The earliest instance of regicide in the sacred annals is that of Ehud, the left-handed Benjamite. To avenge the tyranny of Eglon, the king of Moab, the invader of his country, he made a two-edged dagger, over a foot and a half in length, and, hiding it under his robe, took in his hand a present to the king. Feigning important intelligence, the ruler ordered the attendants to retire, when Ehud with his left hand drew the dagger from his right side, thrust it into the king's body over the hilt, and, leaving it there, fled, after shutting behind him and locking the "doors of the parlor." He then blew a trumpet, raised an army, drove back the invaders, and delivered the nation from a foreign yoke. It was a successful assassination, because a *dernier resort* in resisting oppressive usurpation, and under the providential sanction of the Almighty.

In old Roman history, the mind turns intuitively to the successful conspiracy of which Brutus was the leader; and who, undoubtedly, was governed by patriotic motives. He sought to restore the Government to the hands of the Senate and the people. This friend of Cæsar very reluctantly consented to become a traitor; and did not, until the persistent and crafty appeals of Cassius and his fellow-conspirators made him feel that he must strike the blow for the people.

Plutarch's description of the assassination is graphic:—

"When Cæsar entered the house, the senate rose to do him honor. Some of Brutus's accomplices came up behind his chair, and others before it, pretending to intercede, along with Metilius Cimbri, for the recall of his brother from exile. They continued their entreaties till he came to his seat. When he was seated, he gave them a positive denial; and as they continued their importunities with an air of compulsion, he grew angry. Cimbri, then, with both hands, pulled his gown off his neck, which was the signal for the attack. Casca gave him the first blow. It was a stroke upon the neck with his sword, but the wound was not dangerous; for in the beginning of so tremendous an enterprise he was probably in some disorder. Cæsar, therefore, turned upon him, and laid hold of his sword. At the same time they both cried out, the one in Latin—'Villain! Casca! what dost thou mean?' and the other in Greek, to his brother—'Brother, help!'

"After such a beginning, those who knew nothing of the conspiracy were seized with consternation and horror, insomuch that they durst neither fly, nor assist, nor even utter a word. All the conspirators now drew their swords, and surrounded him in such a manner, that whatever way he turned he saw nothing but steel gleaming in his face, and met nothing but wounds. Like some savage beast attacked by the hunters, he found every hand lifted against him, for they all agreed to have a share in the sacrifice and a taste of his blood. Therefore Brutus himself gave him a stroke in the groin. Some say, he opposed the rest, and continued struggling and crying out till he perceived the sword of Brutus; then he drew his robe over his face, and yielded to his fate. Either by accident, or pushed thither by the conspirators, he expired on the pedestal of Pompey's statue, and dyed it with his blood: so that Pompey seemed to preside over the work of vengeance, to tread his enemy under his feet, and to enjoy his agonies. Those agonies were great, for he received no less than three-and-twenty wounds; and many of the conspirators wounded each other as they were aiming their blows at him.

"Cæsar thus dispatched, Brutus advanced to speak to the Senate, and to assign his reasons for what he had done; but they could not bear to hear him; they fled out of the house, and filled the people with inexpressible horror and dismay. Some shut up their houses; others left their shops and counters; all were in motion: one was running to see the spectacle; another running back. Antony and Lepidus, Cæsar's principal friends, withdrew, and hid themselves in other people's houses. Meantime, Brutus and his confederates, yet warm from the slaughter, marched in a body, with their bloody swords in their hands, from the senate-house to the capitol, not like men that fled, but with an air of gayety and confidence, calling the people to liberty, and stopping to talk with every man of consequence whom they met. There were some who even joined them, and mingled with their train; desirous of appearing to have had a share in the action, and hoping for one in the glory."

A no less conspicuous, and still more modern conspiracy, although a failure, was the Gunpowder Plot of England, under James I.;—the grandest conspiracy in its scope, and, if successful, in results, on record. Religious fanaticism was its inspiration. The king's growing dislike of the Catholics, and Parliamentary enactments unfavorable to their prosperity, awakened a fierce opposition. This enmity was organized into a conspiracy, under Robert Catesby. He was "a gentleman of good property, in Northampton and Warwickshire," says Keightly, "descended from the minister of Richard III., and had been brought up a Catholic; but he deserted that religion, plunged into all sorts of excesses, and ran through his patrimony. He then (1598) returned to his old religion, and, making up for his apostasy by zeal, became a fanatic, and engaged in all the treasons and conspiracies which agitated the latter years of Elizabeth.

"He now conceived the diabolical project of blowing up the Parliament-house with gunpowder. This design he communicated in Lent, 1604, to John Wright and Thomas Winter, two Catholic gentlemen of good character, family, and fortune. The latter hesitated at first, but his scruples soon gave way, and he went over to the Netherlands on a double mission; the one was to try to induce the Constable of Castile, who was coming over to conclude the peace, to make some stipulations in favor of the Catholics; the other to engage in the plot some gentleman of courage and of military knowledge and experience. Finding that the Court of Spain would not hazard the peace which was so necessary to it, on their account, he proceeded to execute the other part of his commission; and the person on whom he fixed was one Guy Fawkes, a man of good family in Yorkshire, who, having spent his little property, had entered the Spanish service. If we may credit Father Greenway, the associate and panegyrist of the conspirators, Fawkes was 'a man of great piety, of exemplary temperance, of mild and cheerful demeanor, an enemy of broils and disputes, a faithful friend, and remarkable for his punctual attendance upon religious observances'—in a word, a fanatic in whose eyes religion justified every deed. Though this high-wrought character is doubtless beyond the truth, there seems on the other hand to be no ground for regarding Fawkes as a mere vulgar ruffian.

"On the night of the 11th of December, Catesby and his associates entered the house in Westminster, well supplied with mining tools, and with hard eggs and baked meats for their support. They began to mine the wall of three yards in thickness between theirs and the Parliament-house. Fawkes stood sentinel while the others wrought. They spread the matter which they extracted in the day over the garden at night, and not one of them ever went out of the house, or even into the upper part of it, lest they might be seen. They wrought without ceasing till Christmas-eve, when Fawkes brought them intelligence that Parliament was further prorogued till October. They then agreed to separate till after the holidays, when they would resume their labors.

In February they renewed their labors in the mine, and they had pierced half way through the wall, when they suddenly, as we are assured, heard the tolling of a bell within the wall under the Parliament-house; they stopped and listened; Fawkes was called down, and he also heard it. On sprinkling the place, however, with holy water, the mysterious sound ceased; it was frequently renewed. but the same remedy always proved efficacious, and it at length ceased altogether. One day they heard a rushing noise over their heads; they thought they were discovered, but Fawkes, on inquiry, found that it was made by a man of the name of Bright, who was selling off his coals from a cellar under the House of Lords, in order to remove. They resolved at once to take the cellar, for, exclusive of the labor, they found the water now coming in on them. The cellar was taken in Percy's name also; twenty barrels of powder were conveyed to it from the house in Lambeth, their iron tools and large stones were put into the barrels with it, in order to give more efficacy to the explosion, and the whole was covered with billets and fagots; and lumber and empty bottles were scattered through the cellar. They then closed it up, placing marks withinside of the door, that they might be able to ascertain if any one should enter it during their absence. Having sent Fawkes to Flanders to inform Sir William Stanley and other English officers of the project, and try to obtain foreign aid, they separated for the summer. In the autumn, Sir Edmund Baynham was sent to Rome, as the agent of the conspirators, with whose designs it is likely he was acquainted. As it was necessary to have horses and arms ready, Catesby pretended that he was commissioned to raise a troop of horse for the Spanish service, and he had thus a pretext for collecting arms, &c., at his own house, and at that of Grant; and several Catholic gentlemen undertaking to join him as volunteers, he directed them to prepare their arms, and to be ready when called on. He and Percy now thought it necessary to associate some gentlemen of wealth, in order to obtain the requisite funds; and they fixed on Sir Everard Digby, of Rutlandshire, Ambrose

Rookwood, of Suffolk, and Francis Tresham, of Northamptonshire; the two first, who were weak bigots, but virtuous men, hesitated at first, but finally joined cordially in the project; the last, a man of indifferent character, was only admitted on account of his wealth, and Catesby, it is said, had always a mistrust of him.

"Parliament being finally appointed to meet on the 5th of November, the conspirators made their final arrangements. Fawkes was to fire the mine, by means of a slow match, which would take a quarter of an hour to reach the powder; and as soon as he had lighted it, he was to hasten and get aboard a small vessel which was ready in the river, and carry the news over to Flanders. Digby was on that day to assemble a number of the Catholic gentry, under pretext of a hunting-party, at Dunchurch, in Warwickshire; and as soon as they heard of the blow being struck, they were to send a party to seize the Princess Elizabeth, who was at Lord Harrington's, in that neighborhood, and she was to be proclaimed in case Winter should fail in the part assigned him, of securing one of her brothers.

"There was one point which had been disputed from the beginning, namely, how to act with respect to the Catholic nobles. Catesby, it would seem, had little scruple about destroying them with the rest, but the majority were for saving their friends and relations. Tresham, in particular, was most earnest to save his brothers-in-law, the Lords Stourton and Mounteagle. It was finally agreed that no express notice should be given, but that various pretexts should be employed to induce their friends to stay away. This, however, did not content Tresham, and some days after he urged on Catesby and Percy that notice should be given to Lord Mounteagle; and on their hesitating, he hinted that he should not be ready with the money he had promised, and proposed that the catastrophe should be put off till the closing of the Parliament. His arguments, however, proved ineffectual.

"On the 26th of October, Lord Mounteagle went and supped at his house at Hoxton, where he had not been for a month before. At supper a letter was handed him by a page, who said he had received it from a strange man in the street.

It was anonymous. By his lordship's direction, a gentleman named Ward read it aloud. It desired him to make some excuse for not attending Parliament, 'for God and man,' it said, 'hath concurred to punish the wickedness of this time,' with sundry other mysterious hints. Lord Mounteagle took it that very evening to Lord Salisbury, at Whitehall, who showed it to some other lords of the council; and it was decided that nothing should be done till the king's return from Royston, where he was hunting.

"Next day (31st) the king returned to London; a council was held the following day on the subject of the letter, and James himself is said to have divined its secret meaning.* It was determined to search the cellar, but not till Monday, the 4th. On that day, the Lord Chamberlain, Lord Mounteagle, and others, went to the Parliament-house. They found Fawkes in the cellar, but they made no remark, and that night, Sir Thomas Knevett, a magistrate, was sent to the place with his assistants; he met Fawkes as he was stepping out of the door, and arrested him, and on searching the cellar, thirty-six barrels of powder were discovered. Fawkes was brought before the council, where he avowed and gloried in his design, but refused to name his accomplices; he was then committed to the Tower.

"Fawkes was at first sullen, but on the 8th of November he made a full confession, concealing, however, the names of his associates, whom, however, next day he named to Lord Salisbury. It is highly probable that, according to custom, the rack had been applied to him.

"In the whole course of history, an instance more demonstrative of the baleful effects of a false sense of religion on the mind and heart is not to be found than this plot. A more horrible design never was conceived; yet those who engaged in it were mostly men of mild manners, correct lives, and independent fortunes—all, we may say, actuated by no ignoble motive, but firmly believing that they were doing good service to God. 'I am satisfied,' said John Grant, on the day of his execution, 'that our project was so far from being sinful, that I rely on my merits in bearing a

---

* He might have done this, and yet Cecil have known the real fact already.

part of that noble action as an abundant satisfaction and expiation for all sins committed by me during the rest of my life.' 'Nothing grieves me,' said Robert Winter to Fawkes, 'but that there is not an apology made by some to justify our doing in this business; but our deaths will be a sufficient justification of it, and it is for God's cause.' It is said by Greenway, that as Rookwood was drawn to execution, his wife stood at an open window in the Strand, comforting him, and telling him 'to be of good courage, inasmuch as he suffered for a great and noble cause.' Of the truth of this, however, we are rather dubious; fear alone would, we apprehend, prevent her from giving utterance to such expressions."

During the revolutionary movements of the last century, no figure attracts more sympathy and interest among the actors in sanguinary scenes of unjustifiable violence, than that of Charlotte Corday, of Normandy, herself descended from the Norman nobility. She was masculine in the vigor of her intellect and acquaintance with political economy, but virtuous and modest in character. At first an advocate of the French Revolution, because she hailed it as the dawn of national liberty, the unprincipled and bloody aspect it soon assumed disheartened and alarmed her, until her single absorbing thought was the protection of whatever of freedom remained to France.

"Marat," records Madame Junot, "was at this period the ostensible chief of the mountain party, and the most sanguinary of its members. He was a most hideous deformity, both in mind and person; his lank and distorted features, covered with leprosy, and his vulgar and ferocious leer, were a true index of the passions which worked in his odious mind. A series of unparalleled atrocities had raised him to the highest power with his party; and though he professed to be merely passive in the revolutionary government, his word was law with the Convention, and his fiat irrevocable. In every thing relating to the acquisition of wealth he was incorruptible, and even gloried in his poverty. But the immense influence he had acquired turned his brain, and he gave full range to the evil propensities of his nature, now unchecked by any authority. He had formed principles of political faith in which, perhaps, he sincerely believed, but which were founded on his inherent love of blood, and his hatred of every human being who evinced talents or virtue above his fellow-men. The guillotine was not only the altar of the distorted thing he worshipped, under the name of Liberty, but it was also the instrument of his pleasures: for his highest gratification was the writhings of the victim who fell under his axe. Even Robespierre attempted to check this unquenchable thirst of human blood; but in vain; opposition only excited Marat to greater atrocities. With rage depicted in his livid features, and with the howl of a demoniac, he would loudly declare that rivers of blood could alone purify the land, and must, therefore, flow. In his paper, entitled 'L' Ami du Peuple,' he denounced all those whom he had doomed to death, and the guillotine spared none whom he designated.

"Charlotte Corday, having read his assertion in this journal, that three hundred thousand heads were requisite to consolidate the liberties of the French people, could not contain her feelings. Her cheeks flushed with indignation:—

"'What!' she exclaimed, 'is there not in the whole country a man bold enough to kill this monster?'

"Imagining that, if she could succeed in destroying Marat, the fall of his party must necessarily ensue, she determined to offer up her own life for the good of her country.

"She went to the Palais Royal, and bought a sharp-pointed carving-knife, with a black sheath. On her return to the hotel in which she lodged—Hotel de la Providence, Rue des Augustins—she made her preparation for the deed she intended to commit the next day. Having put her papers in order, she placed a certificate of her baptism in a red pocket-book, in order to take it with her, and thus establish her identity. This she did because she had resolved to make no attempt to escape, and was, therefore, certain she should leave Marat's house for the conciergerie, preparatory to her appearing before the revolutionary tribunal.

"Next morning, the 14th, taking with her the knife she

had purchased, and her red pocket-book, she proceeded to Marat's residence. The representative was ill, and could not be seen, and Charlotte's entreaties for admittance on the most urgent business were unavailing. She therefore withdrew, and wrote the following note, which she herself delivered to Marat's servant:—

"CITIZEN REPRESENTATIVE:—
"I am just arrived from Caen. Your well-known patriotism leads me to presume that you will be glad to be made acquainted with what is passing in that part of the Republic. I will call on you again, in the course of the day; have the goodness to give orders that I may be admitted, and grant me a few minutes' conversation. I have important secrets to reveal to you.
"CHARLOTTE CORDAY.

"At seven o'clock in the evening she returned, and reached Marat's antechamber; but the woman who waited on him refused to admit her to the monster's presence. Marat, however, who was in a bath in the next room, hearing the voice of a young girl, and little thinking she had come to deprive him of life, ordered that she should be shown in. Charlotte seated herself by the side of the bath. The conversation ran upon the disturbances in the department of Calvados; and Charlotte, fixing her eyes upon Marat's countenance, as if to scrutinize his most secret thoughts, pronounced the names of several of the Girondist deputies.

"'They shall soon be arrested,' he cried, with a howl of rage, 'and executed the same day.'

"He had scarcely uttered these words, when Charlotte's knife was buried in his bosom.

"'Help!' he cried; 'help! I am murdered.' He died immediately."

The very latest attempt at assassination was the fruitless aim of the weapon of death at the life of Alexander of Russia, whose details are still fresh in the minds of the civilized world—a madly rash endeavor to slay a monarch unrivaled in regard for popular rights, and in the admiration of his subjects, no less than of other nations. It revealed the slumbering hate of the aristocratic class, and the certainty that if a ruler's policy infringe upon time-honored exclusiveness, and proud but unrighteous distinctions, his life is in peril, along with that of the tyrant who exasperates, with better reason on their part, the outraged masses. This naturally brings me to the assassination of Abraham Lincoln, the purest patriot and wisest, most paternal ruler of any age.

I shall not discuss the political questions and resolutions whose issue was the election to the presidential chair of Abraham Lincoln, in the autumn of 1860. But to follow the conspiracy against his life from the beginning to the fearful end, I go back to the thwarted plot which followed that popular choice.

The statement made by a gentleman of Philadelphia, who was a prominent actor in the defeat of the deliberate and well-arranged plan to murder the President elect, will furnish an argument in behalf of the detective service, the strength of which is measured by the value of his useful life during more than four years. The narrative was substantially as follows:—

In the month of January, 1861, a gentleman, holding a position in this city which made him a proper agent to act on the information, was waited upon by a lady, who stated to him her suspicions or knowledge—whence derived we are not able to say—of a plot to assassinate Mr. Lincoln when on his way from his home, in Illinois, to Washington, to be inaugurated as President. The active parties, or some of them, in the business, were understood to be in Baltimore. At all events, the gentleman considered that the intelligence had sufficient foundation to make it his duty to satisfy himself whether it might be correct. He accordingly employed a detective officer, a man who had in his profession become notable for his sagacity and success, to go to Baltimore and adopt his own course to detect the parties to and plan of the conspiracy. The officer went to Baltimore, and opened an office as some sort of broker or agent, under an assumed name. Being supplied with needful funds, he made occasions to become acquainted with certain classes of secessionists, and by degrees was on free and easy terms with them. He took each man in his humor, dined and supped with some, gambled with others, 'treated,' and seconded dissipations in more ways than need be expressly stated, until he had secured enough of their confidence to be familiar with the particulars of their schemes. Meanwhile it had been ascertained that on the line of the Baltimore Railroad there were men engaged in military drilling. Several other detectives were employed by the chief to discover the purpose of those organizations; and, disguised as laborers or farm hands, they got themselves mustered in. One of the military companies proved to be loyal in its purpose; another, under pretense of being prepared to guard one or more of the bridges north of Baltimore, was designed for quite an opposite purpose. It will be remembered that some time before Mr. Lincoln set out from his home for Washington, his intended route thither was published. A part of the programme was that he should visit Harrisburg and Philadelphia. We believe that Mr. Lincoln was not advised especially of any personal danger until he was about to go to Harrisburg, and then, at the instance of the gentleman referred to, he was urged to proceed without delay to Washington. He replied, however, that he had promised the people of Harrisburg to answer their invitation, and he would do so if it cost him his life. He accordingly visited Harrisburg on the 22d of February, 1861. It was intended he should rest there that evening. But under the management of 'the gentleman,' another arrangement was effected. The night train from Philadelphia to Baltimore and Washington left at half-past ten o'clock in the evening. It was determined that Mr. Lincoln should go secretly by that train on the evening of the 23d; and to enable him to do so, a special train was provided to bring him secretly from Harrisburg to Philadelphia. After dark, in the former city, when it was presumed he had retired to his hotel, he accordingly took the special train, and came to Philadelphia. Meanwhile, in anticipation of his coming, 'the gentleman' had insured the detention of the Philadelphia and Baltimore train, under the pretense that a parcel of important documents for one of the departments in Washington must be dispatched by it, but which might not be ready until after the regular time of the starting of that train. By a similar representation, the connecting train from Baltimore to Washington was also detained. Owing to the late hour at which the special train left Harrisburg with Mr. Lincoln, it did not, as was anticipated, reach this city until after the usual Philadelphia and Baltimore time. Mr. Lincoln was accompanied by the officer who had been employed in Baltimore. A formidable bundle of old railroad reports had been made up in the office of the Philadelphia and Baltimore Company, which the officer, duly instructed, had charge of. On the arrival of the Harrisburg train, Mr. Lincoln took a carriage in waiting, and with his escort was driven to the depot at Broad and Prime Streets. The officer made some ostentatious bustle, arriving with his parcel for which the train was detained, and passing through the depot entered the cars, Mr. Lincoln in his company. As Mr. Lincoln passed through the gate, the man attending it remarked: 'Old fellow, it's well for you the train was detained to-night, or you wouldn't have gone in it.' No one aboard the train but the agent of the company and the officer knew of Mr. Lincoln's being in it. He was conducted to a sleeping car, and thus was kept out of the way of observation. To guard against any possible communication by telegraph at this time, the circuit was broken, to be united when it would be safe to do so. The plan of the conspirators was to break or burn one of the bridges north of Baltimore, at the time of Mr. Lincoln's anticipated approach, on the following day; and in the confusion incident to the stoppage of the train, to assassinate him in the cars. Hence the extra precaution above mentioned, regarding the telegraph. In due time the train with Mr. Lincoln reached Washington, and he being safe there, the officer, as previously instructed, sent a dispatch to 'the gentleman' that 'the parcel of documents had been delivered.' The public, and, above all, the conspirators, awoke on the morning of the 24th to be astonished with the intelligence that Mr. Lincoln had arrived in Washington. It may be well to mention here that the story of his disguise in a 'Scotch cap' and cloak, was untrue. He wore his ordinary traveling cap, and was in no sense of the word disguised.

His safe arrival in the Capital, the public receptions, and the joyful anticipations of the loyal people, succeeded the hours of unappreciated danger because generally unknown.

ASSASSINATION OF PRESIDENT LINCOLN.

The services of the remarkable man, during the war, have become familiar history to the humblest citizen.

April 11, 1865, the National Capital and the country were again jubilant over the closing victories of the conflict. The recently reinaugurated President was serenaded, and made congratulatory speeches amid the splendors of the evening illumination. Then came the 14th, with the commemorative flag-raising at Fort Sumter; and the 17th was set apart for a general expression of grateful joy.

But it was a day of darkness and woe, which has no parallel in national annals. The events which shrouded the land in this tearful gloom will be detailed in the account of the capture of the assassin, and his career in its relation to it.

There was a very extraordinary indifference in the mind of Mr. Lincoln in regard to threats of assassination, some of which I communicated to him. Several times I walked with him in the grounds of the White House, at a late hour of the evening, conversing upon such intelligence of the war as I had received. Whenever allusion was made to the intimations of cherished designs upon his life, he almost playfully listened, and apparently was unable to believe depravity could go so far as to destroy a friend of all the people, such as he felt himself to be. But the *risk* was taken, and the plotting was too successful against the victorious loyalty of the North.

About ten o'clock in the evening of April 14, 1865, while the play, "Our American Cousin," was progressing, a stranger, who proved to be John Wilkes Booth, an actor of some note, worked his way into the proscenium box, occupied by the presidential party, and leveling a pistol close behind the head of Mr. Lincoln, he fired, and the ball was lodged deep in the brain of the President. The assassin then drew a dirk, sprang from the box, flourishing the weapon aloft, and shouted, as he reached the stage, the motto upon the escutcheon of the State of Virginia, "*Sic Semper Tyrannis!*" He dashed across the stage, and before the audience could realize the real position of affairs, the murderer had mounted a fleet horse in waiting in an alley in the rear of the theatre, and galloping off, he escaped for a time.

The screams of Mrs. Lincoln first disclosed to the audience the fact that the President was shot, when all rose, many pressing toward the stage, and exclaiming, "Hang him! Hang him!" The excitement was of the wildest nature. Others rushed for the President's box, while others cried out, "Stand back! Give him fresh air!" and called for stimulants. It was not known at first where he was wounded, the most of those about him thinking that he was shot through the heart; but after opening his vest, and finding no wound in his breast, it was discovered that he was shot in the head, between the left ear and the centre of the back part of the head. In a few moments he was borne to a private house, Mr. Peterson's, just opposite the theatre, where the Surgeon-General, and several prominent physicians and surgeons were speedily summoned. Meanwhile the members of the Cabinet, with the exception of Secretary Seward, whose life had been attempted by an assassin at about the same hour with the President, assembled in the room where the Chief Magistrate of the nation lay dying.

Secretaries Stanton, Welles, Usher, McCulloch, Attorney-General Speed, and Assistant Secretaries Maunsell B. Field, of the Treasury, and Judge William T. Otto, of the Interior, together with Speaker Colfax, and several other prominent gentlemen were present. The scene was one of extraordinary solemnity. The history of the world does not furnish a parallel. Quiet, breathing away his life serenely, unconscious of all around, sensible to no pain, lay the great MAN of the nineteenth century, passing hence to that immortality which has been accorded by Providence to few of earthly mould.

All the long, weary night, the watchers stood by the couch of the dying President. From the moment when the fatal bullet entered his brain he never spoke, never evinced any consciousness, but, with closed eyes, rested in a repose which appeared to be the quiet of death. Mrs. Lincoln and Captain Robert Lincoln several times entered the chamber, but their grief was such that they tarried but a brief time, tender friends urging them to remain in the adjoining room.

Day dawned at length, and the tide of life ebbed more rapidly, and at twenty-two minutes past seven o'clock, on

LAST HOURS OF THE PRESIDENT.

the morning of Saturday, April 15, 1865, the President breathed his last, closing his eyes as if falling to sleep, and his countenance assuming an expression of perfect serenity. There were no indications of pain, and it was not known that he was dead until the gradually decreasing respiration ceased altogether.

The Rev. Dr. Gurley, pastor of the Presbyterian Church, in Washington, which Mr. Lincoln attended regularly with his family, immediately on its being ascertained that life was extinct, knelt at the bedside, and offered an impressive prayer, which was responded to by all present.

Dr. Gurley then proceeded to the front parlor, where Mrs. Lincoln, Captain Robert Lincoln, Mr. John Hay, the President's Private Secretary, and others were waiting, where he again offered prayer for the consolation of the family.

The following minutes, taken by Dr. Abbott, show the condition of the President throughout the night :--11 P. M., pulse 44 ; 11.05 P. M., pulse 45, and growing weaker ; 11.10 P. M., pulse 45 ; 11.15 P. M., pulse 42 ; 11.20 P. M., pulse 45, respiration 27 to 30 ; 11.25 P. M., pulse 42 ; 11.32 P. M., pulse 48 and full ; 11.40 P. M., pulse 45 ; 21.45 P. M., pulse 45, respiration 22 ; 12.08 A. M., respiration 22 ; 12.15 A. M., respiration 21, ecchymosis of both eyes ; 12.30 A. M., pulse 54 ; 12.32 A. M., pulse 60 ; 12.35 A. M., pulse 66 ; 12.40 A. M., pulse 69 ; right eye much swollen, and ecchymosed ; 12.45 A. M., pulse 70, respiration 27 ; 12.55 A. M., pulse 80, struggling motion of arms ; 1 A. M., pulse 86, respiration 30 ; 1.30 A. M., pulse 95, appearing easier ; 1.45 A. M., pulse 87, very quiet, respiration irregular, Mrs. Lincoln present ; 2.10 A. M., Mrs. Lincoln retired with Robert Lincoln to an adjoining room ; 2.30 A. M., the President is very quiet, pulse 54, respiration 28 ; 2.52 A. M., pulse 48, respiration 30 ; 3 A. M., visited again by Mrs. Lincoln ; 3.25 A. M., respiration 24, and regular ; 3.25 A. M., prayer by the Rev. Dr. Gurley ; 4 A. M., respiration 26, and regular ; 4.15 A. M., pulse 60, respiration 25 ; 5.50 A. M., respiration 28 and regular, sleeping ; 6 A. M., pulse failing, respiration 28 ; 6 30 A. M., still failing, and labored breathing ; 7 A. M. symptoms of immediate dissolution ; 7.22 A. M., death

Surrounding the death-bed of the President were Secretaries Stanton, Welles, Usher, Attorney-General Speed, Postmaster-General Dennison, M. T. Field, Assistant Secretary of the Treasury; Judge Otto, Assistant Secretary of Interior; General Halleck, General Meigs, Senator Sumner, F. R. Andrews, of New York; General Todd, of Dacotah; John Hay, Private Secretary; Governor Oglesby, of Illinois; General Farnsworth, Mr. and Miss Kenny, Miss Harris, Captain Robert Lincoln, son of the President, and Dr. E. W. Abbott, R. K. Stone, C. D. Gatch, Neal Hall, and Leiberman. Secretary McCulloch remained with the President until about 5 A. M., and Chief-Justice Chase, after several hours attendance during the night, returned again early in the morning,

A special Cabinet meeting was called immediately after the President's death, by Secretary Stanton, and held in the room where the corpse lay. Secretaries Stanton, Welles, and Usher, Postmaster-General Dennison, and Attorney-General Speed, were present.

After his death, a complete examination was made of the wound with the following result: The ball entered the skull midway between the left ear and the center of the back of the head, and passed nearly to the right eye. The ball and two loose fragments of lead were found in the brain. Singularly enough, both orbital roofs were fractured inwardly, properly from contre-coup. The tenacity of life was specially noticed by every surgeon in attendance. The brain was taken out, but a considerable portion of it had already escaped from the wound.

Ford's Theater, now converted into a museum of war relics, is situated on Tenth Street, just above E Street; a large edifice, built of brick, and plain in appearance. The four upper boxes were *the* boxes of the theatre, and very elegant and spacious.

The box which the President occupied, and which was known as "The President's Box," consisted of the two upper boxes on the right-hand side of the house as you face the stage, thrown into one. It was fitted up with great elegance and taste. The curtains were of fine lace and buff satin, the paper dark and figured, the carpet Turkey, the seats velvet, and the exterior ornamentations were lit up with a chaste chandelier suspended from the outside. A winding staircase led up to the lobbies which conducted to the box, and unless the arrangements were stringent, no decently dressed person would find much difficulty, probably, in entering after being opened for the ingress of the party. The house would hold probably between two and three thousand people.

There were two alleys at Ford's Theater. One led from the stage, along the east side of the theater, between the theatre and a refreshment saloon, and so out to Tenth Street. The alley was neatly paved, and boarded and papered on both sides. The entry to it from the stage was through a glass door, and the exit from it on to Tenth Street through a wooden one.

The other passage-way led from the back of the theatre to a small alley which communicated with Ninth and other streets, and conducted to a livery-stable locality. It was in this alley that the horse of the murderer was kept waiting.

The Tenth Street door would have been too public, and escape, even temporary, a matter of impossibility. But the escape by the alley leading from the back of the stage was comparatively safe.

There were two doors there, one used for the egress and ingress of the actors, and the other devoted to the accommodation of scenery and machinery. It was through the smaller one that the assassin made his exit.

On one occasion I carried to Mr. Lincoln two anonymous communications, in which he was threatened with assassination. In a laughing, joking manner, he remarked, "Well, Baker, what do they want to kill me for? If they kill me, they will run the risk of getting a worse man "

CHAPTER XXIV.

THE ASSASSINS CAPTURED.

Excitement around my Headquarters at Washington—The Chief Conspirator—A Graphic Narrative of his Arrest—His Burial—Desire for Relics from his Body—Hanging of the Conspirators.

ALONG with my own narrative, and that of other officers, I shall freely quote from sketches written at the time by others, and chiefly at my headquarters, around which the excitement attending the dreadful tragedy seemed to surge, like a felt but invisible tide, gathering strength every hour. To gratify, as far as possible to do so, the mournful curiosity of the people to learn the details of the affair, some correspondence directly from the centre of investigation and emotion was allowed. With this general explanation, there will be no further reference to the extracts; they will be indicated by their connection and the tone of narrative, and quite accurate in detail.

One of the writers, whose account of Booth's arrest may seem somewhat "sensational," and who sat in my office under unusual nervous excitement, created by the extraordinary circumstances, is now a foreign correspondent of a leading New York daily.

"John Wilkes Booth was the projector of the plot against the President, which culminated in the taking of that good man's life. He had rolled under his tongue the sweet paragraphs of Shakespeare referring to Brutus, as his father had so well, that the old man named one son Junius Brutus, and the other John Wilkes, after the wild English agitator, until it became his ambition, like the wicked Lorenzino de Medici, to stake his life upon one stroke for fame, the murder of a ruler obnoxious to the South.

"Booth shrank at first from murder until another and

less dangerous resolution failed. This was no less than the capture of the President's body, and its detention or transportation to the South. I do not rely for this assertion upon his sealed letter, where he avows it; there has been found upon a street within the city limits a house belonging to one Mrs. Greene, mined and furnished with underground apartments, furnished with manacles, and all the accessories to private imprisonment. Here the President, and as many as could be gagged and conveyed away with him, were to be concealed, in the event of failure to run them into the Confederacy. Owing to his failure to group around him as many men as he desired, Booth abandoned the project of kidnapping; but the house was discovered, as represented, ready to be blown up at a moment's notice.

"It was at this time that Booth devised his triumphal route through the South. The dramatic element seems to have been never lacking in his design, and with all his base purposes he never failed to consider some subsequent notoriety to be enjoyed. He therefore shipped, before the end of 1861, his theatrical wardrobe from Canada to Nassau. After the commission of his crime he intended to reclaim it, and 'star' through the South, drawing many, as much by his crime as his abilities.

"When Booth began, 'on his own responsibility,' to hunt for accomplices, he found his theory at fault. The bold men he had dreamed of refused to join him in the rash attempt at kidnapping the President, and were too conscientious to meditate murder. All those who presented themselves were military men, unwilling to be subordinate to a civilian and a mere play actor, and the mortified bravo found himself, therefore, compelled to sink to a petty rank in the plot or to make use of base and despicable assistants. His vanity found it easier to compound with the second alternative than the first

"Here began the first resolve, which, in its mere animal state, we may name courage. Booth found that a tragedy in real life could no more be enacted without greasy-faced and knock-kneed supernumeraries than upon the mimic stage. Your 'First Citizen,' who swings a stave for Marc Antony, and drinks hard porter behind the flies, is very like the bravo of real life, who murders between his cocktails at the nearest bar. Wilkes Booth had passed the ordeal of a garlicky green-room, and did not shrink from the broader and ranker green-room of real life. He assembled around him, one by one, the cut-throats at whom his soul would have revolted, except that he had become, by resolve, a cut-throat in himself.

"About this time certain gentlemen in Canada began to be unenviably known. I make no charges against those whom I do not know, but simply say that the Confederate agents, Jacob Thompson, Larry McDonald, Clement Clay, and some others, had already accomplished enough villainy to make Wilkes Booth, on the first of the present year, believe that he had but to seek an interview with them.

"He visited the provinces once certainly, and three times it is believed, stopping in Montreal at St. Lawrence Hall, and banking four hundred and fifty-five dollars odd at the Ontario Bank. This was his own money. I have myself seen his bank-book with the single entry of this amount. It was found in the room of Atzeroth at Kirkwood's Hotel.

"Some one or all of these agents furnished Booth with a murderer—the fellow Wood, or Payne, who stabbed Mr. Seward, and was caught at Mrs. Surratt's house in Washington. He was one of three Kentucky brothers, all outlaws, and had himself, it is believed, accompanied one of his brothers, who is known to have been at St. Albans on the day of the bank delivery. This Payne, besides being positively identified as the assassin of the Sewards, had no friends nor haunts in Washington. He was simply a dispatched murderer, and after the night of the crime struck northward for the frontier, instead of southward in the company of Booth. The proof of this will follow in the course of the article.

"Half applauded, half rebuffed by the rebel agents in Canada, Booth's impressions of his visit were just those which would whet him soonest for the tragedy. His vanity had been fed by the assurance that success depended upon himself alone, and that as he had the responsibility he would absorb the fame; and the method of correspondence was of that dark and mysterious shape which powerfully operated upon his dramatic temperament.

"What could please an actor, and the son of an actor, better than to mingle as a principal in a real conspiracy, the aims of which were pseudo-patriotic, and the ends so astounding, that at its coming the whole globe would reel. Booth reasoned that the ancient world would not feel more sensitively the death of Julius Cæsar, than the new the sudden taking off of Abraham Lincoln.

"And so he grew into the idea of murder. It became his business thought. It was his recreation and his study. He had not worked half so hard for histrionic success as for his terrible graduation into an assassin. He had fought often on the boards, and had seen men die in well-imitated horror, with flowing blood upon the keen sword's edge, and the strong stride of mimic victory with which he flourished his weapon at the closing of the curtain. He embraced conspiracy like an old diplomatist, and found in the woman and the spot subjects for emulation.

"Southeast of Washington stretches a tapering peninsula, composed of four fertile counties, which at the remote tip make Point Lookout, and do not contain any town within them of more than a few hundred inhabitants. Tobacco has ruined the land of these, and slavery has ruined the people. Yet in the beginning they were of that splendid stock of Calvert and Lord Baltimore, but retain to-day only the religion of the peaceful founder. I mention, as an exceptional and remarkable fact, that every conspirator in custody is by education a Catholic. These are loyal citizens elsewhere, but the western shore of Maryland is a noxious and pestilential place for patriotism.

"The country immediately outside of the District of Columbia, to the south, is named Prince George's, and the pleasantest village of this county, close to Washington, is called Surrattsville. This consists of a few cabins at a crossroad, surrounding a fine old hotel, the master whereof, giving the settlement his name, left the property to his wife, who for a long time carried it on with indifferent success. Having a son and several daughters, she moved to Washington soon after the beginning of the war, and left the tavern to a trusty friend—one John Lloyd. Surrattsville has gained nothing in patronage or business from the war, except that it became, at an early date, a rebel post-office. The great secret mail from Matthias Creek, Virginia, to Port Tobacco, struck Surrattsville, and thence headed off to the east of Washington, going meanderingly north. Of this post route Mrs. Surratt was a manageress; and John Lloyd, when he rented her hotel, assumed the responsibility of looking out for the mail, as well as the duty of making Mrs. Surratt at home when she chose to visit him.

"So Surrattsville, only ten miles from Washington, has been throughout the war a seat of conspiracy. It was like a suburb of Richmond, reaching quite up to the rival capital; and though the few Unionists on the peninsula knew its reputation well enough, nothing of the sort came out until after the murder.

"Treason never found a better agent than Mrs. Surratt. She was a large, masculine, self-possessed female, mistress of her house, and as lithe a rebel as Belle Boyd or Mrs. Greensborough. She had not the flippancy and menace of the first, nor the social power of the second; but the rebellion has found no fitter agent.

"At her country tavern and Washington home, Booth was made welcome, and there began the muttered murder against the nation and mankind.

"The acquaintance of Mrs. Surratt in Lower Maryland undoubtedly suggested to Booth the route of escape, and made him known to his subsequent accomplices. Last fall he visited the entire region, as far as Leonardstown, in St. Mary's County, professing to buy land, but really making himself informed upon the rebel post stations, with all the leading affiliations upon whom he could depend. At this time he bought a map, a fellow to which I have seen among Atzeroth's effects, published at Buffalo for the rebel government, and marking at hap-hazard all the Maryland villages, but without tracing the high-roads at all. The absence of these roads, it will be seen hereafter, very nearly misled Booth during his crippled flight.

"When Booth cast around him for assistants, he naturally selected those men whom he could control. The first that recommended himself was one Harold, a youth of inane and plastic character, carried away by the example of an actor, and full of execrable quotations, going to show that that he was an imitator of the master spirit, both in text and admiration. This Harold was a gunner, and therefore versed in arms; he had traversed the whole lower portion of Maryand, and was therefore a geographer as well as a tool. His friends lived at every farm-house between Washington and Leonardsville, and he was respectably enough connected, so as to make his association creditable as well as useful.

"Young Surratt does not appear to have been a puissant spirit in the scheme; indeed, all design and influence therein was absorbed by Mrs. Surratt and Booth. The latter was the head and heart of the plot; Mrs. Surratt was his anchor, and the rest of the boys were disciples to Iscariot and Jezebel. John Surratt, a youth of strong Southern physiognomy, beardless and lanky, knew of the murder and connived at it. 'Sam' Arnold and one McLaughlin were to have been parties to it, but backed out in the end. They all relied upon Mrs. Surratt, and took their 'cues' from Wilkes Booth.

"The conspiracy had its own time and kept its own counsel. Murder, except among the principals, was seldom mentioned except by genteel implication. But they all publicly agreed that Mr. Lincoln ought to be shot, and that the North was a race of fratricides. Much was said of Brutus, and Booth repeated heroic passages, to the delight of Harold, who learned them also, and wondered if he was not born to greatness.

"In this growing darkness, where all rehearsed coldhearted murder, Wilkes Booth grew great of stature. He had found a purpose consonant with his evil nature and bad influence over weak men; so he grew moodier, more vigilant, more plausible. By mien and temperament he was born to handle a stiletto. We have no face so markedly Italian; it would stand for Cæsar Borgia any day in the year. All the rest were swayed or persuaded by Booth; his schemes were three in order:—

"1st. To kidnap the President and Cabinet, and run them South or blow them up.

"2d. Kidnapping failed, to murder the President and the rest, and seek shelter in the Confederate capital.

"3d The rebellion failed, to be its avenger, and throw the country into consternation, while he escaped by the unfrequented parts of Maryland.

"When this last resolution had been made, the plot was both contracted and extended. There were made two distinct circles of confidants, those aware of the meditated murder, and those who might shrink from murder, though willing accessories for a lesser object. Two colleagues for blood were at once accepted, Payne and Atzeroth.

"The former I have sketched; he is believed to have visited Washington once before, at Booth's citation; for the murder was at first fixed for the day of inauguration. Atzeroth was a fellow of German descent, who had led a desperate life at Port Tobacco, where he was a house-painter. He had been a blockade-runner across the Potomac, and a mail-carrier. When Booth and Mrs. Surratt broke the design to him, with a suggestion that there was wealth in it, he embraced the offer at once, and bought a dirk and pistol. Payne also came from the North to Washington, and, as fate would have it, the President was announced to appear at Ford's Theater in public. Then the resolve of blood was reduced to a definite moment.

"On the night before the crime, Booth found one on whom he could rely. John Surratt was sent northward by his mother on Thursday. Sam Arnold and McLaughlin, each of whom was to kill a Cabinet officer, grew pigeon-livered and ran away. Harold, true to his partiality, lingered around Booth to the end; Atzeroth went so far as to take his knife and pistol to Kirkwood's, where President Johnson was stopping, and hid them under the bed. But either his courage failed, or a trifling accident deranged his plan. But Payne, a professional murderer, stood 'game, and fought his way over prostrate figures to the sick victim's bed. There was great confusion and terror among the tacit and rash conspirators on Thursday night. They had looked upon the plot as of a melodrama, and found to their horror that John Wilkes Booth meant to do murder.

"Six weeks before the murder, young John Surratt had

taken two splendid repeating carbines to Surrattsville, and told John Lloyd to secrete them. The latter made a hole in the wainscoting and suspended them from strings, so that they fell within the plastered wall of the room below. On the very afternoon of the murder, Mrs. Surratt was driven to Surrattsville, and she told John Lloyd to have the carbines ready, because they would be called for that night. Harold was made quartermaster, and hired the horses. He and Atzeroth were mounted between eight o'clock and the time of the murder, and riding about the streets together.

"The whole party was prepared for a long ride, as their spurs and gauntlets show. It may have been their design to ride in company to the Lower Potomac, and by their numbers exact subsistence and transportation.

"Lloyd, I may interpolate, ordered his wife, a few days before the murder, to go on a visit to Allen's Fresh. She says she does not know why she was so sent away, but swears that it is so. Harold, three weeks before the murder, visited Port Tobacco, and said that the next time the boys heard of him he would be in Spain; he added that with Spain there was no extradition treaty. He said at Surrattsville that he meant to make a barrel of money, or his neck would stretch.

"Atzeroth said that if he ever came to Port Tobacco again he would be rich enough to buy the whole place.

"Wilkes Booth told a friend to go to Ford's on Friday night and see the best acting in the world.

"At Ford's Theater, on Friday night, there were many standers in the neighborhood of the door, and along the dress circle in the direction of the private box where the President sat.

"The play went on pleasantly, though Mr. Wilkes Booth, an observer of the audience, visited the stage and took note of the position. His alleged associate, the stage-carpenter, then received quiet orders to clear the passage by the wings from the prompter's post to the stage door. All this time, Mr. Lincoln, in his family circle, unconscious of the death that crowded fast upon him, witnessed the pleasantry and smiled, and felt heartful of gentleness.

"Suddenly there was a murmur near the audience door, as of a man speaking above his bound. He said:—

"'Nine o'clock and forty-five minutes!'

"These words were reiterated from mouth to mouth until they passed the theater door, and were heard upon the sidewalk.

"Directly a voice cried, in the same slightly raised monotone—

"'Nine o'clock and fifty minutes!'

"This also passed from man to man, until it touched the street like a shudder.

"'Nine o'clock and fifty-five minutes!' said the same relentless voice, after the next interval, each of which narrowed to a lesser span the life of the good President.

"Ten o'clock here sounded, and conspiring echo said in reverberation—

"'Ten o'clock!'

"So, like a creeping thing, from lip to lip went—

"'Ten o'clock and five minutes!'

"An interval.

"'Ten o'clock and ten minutes!'

"At this instant Wilkes Booth appeared in the door of the theater, and the men who had repeated the time so faithfully and so ominously, scattered at his coming as at some warning phantom.

"All this is so dramatic that I fear to excite a laugh when I write it. But it is true and proven, and I do not say it, but report it.

"All evil deeds go wrong. While the click of the pistol, taking the President's life, went like a pang through the theater, Payne was spilling blood in Mr. Seward's house from threshold to sick-chamber. But Booth's broken leg delayed him or made him lose his general calmness, and he and Harold left Payne to his fate.

"I have not adverted to the hole bored with a gimlet in the entry door of Mr. Lincoln's box, and cut out with a penknife. The theory that the pistol-ball of Booth passed through this hole is now exploded. When Booth leaped from the box he strode straight across the stage by the footlights, reaching the prompter's post, which is immediately behind that private box opposite to Mr. Lincoln. From this box to the stage-door in the rear, the passage-way leads behind the ends of the scenes, and is generally either closed up by one or more withdrawn scenes, or so narrow that only by doubling and turning sidewise can one pass along. On this fearful night, however, the scenes were so adjusted to the murderer's design that he had a free aisle from the foot of the stage to the exit-door.

"Within fifteen minutes after the murder the wires were severed entirely round the city, excepting only a secret wire for Government uses, which leads to Old Point. I am told that by this wire the Government reached the fortifications around Washington, first telegraphing all the way to Old Point, and then back to the out-lying forts. This information comes to me from so many credible channels that I must concede it.

"Payne having, as he thought, made an end of Mr. Seward, which would have been the case but for Robinson, the nurse, mounted his horse, and attempted to find Booth. But the town was in alarm, and he galloped at once for the open country, taking, as he imagined, the proper road for the East Branch. He rode at a killing pace, and when near Port Lincoln, on the Baltimore pike, his horse threw him headlong. Afoot and bewildered, he resolved to return to the city, whose lights he could plainly see; but before doing so he concealed himself some time, and made some almost absurd efforts to disguise himself. Cutting a cross section from the woolen undershirt which covered his muscular arm, he made a rude cap of it, and threw away his bloody coat. This has since been found in the woods, and blood has been found also on his bosom and sleeves. He also spattered himself plentifully with mud and clay, and taking an abandoned pick from the deserted intrenchments near by, he struck out at once for Washington.

"By the providence which always attends murder, he reached Mrs. Surratt's door just as the officers of the Government were arresting her. They seized Payne at once, who had an awkward lie to urge in his defense—that he had come there to dig a trench. That night he dug a trench deep and broad enough for them both to lie in forever. They washed his hands, and found them soft and womanish; his pockets contained tooth and nail-brushes, and a delicate pocket-knife. All this apparel consorted ill with his assumed character.

"Coarse, and hard, and calm, Mrs. Surratt shut up her house after the murder, and waited with her daughters till the officers came. She was imperturbable, and rebuked her girls for weeping, and would have gone to jail like a statue, but that in her extremity Payne knocked at her door. He had come, he said, to dig a ditch for Mrs. Surratt, whom he very well knew. But Mrs. Surratt protested that she had never seen the man at all, and had no ditch to clean.

"'How fortunate, girls,' she said, 'that these officers are here; this man might have murdered us all.'

"Her effrontery stamps her as worthy of companionship with Booth. Payne has been identified by a lodger of Mrs. Surratt's as having twice visited the house, under the name of Wood.

"Atzeroth had a room almost directly over Vice-President Johnson's. He had all the materials to do murder, but lost spirit or opportunity. He ran away so hastily, that all his arms and baggage were discovered; a tremendous bowie knife and a Colt's cavalry revolver were found between the mattresses of his bed. Booth's coat was also found there, showing conspired flight in company, and in it three boxes of cartridges, a map of Maryland, gauntlets for riding, a spur, and a handkerchief marked with the name of Booth's mother —a mother's souvenir for a murderer's pocket.

"Atzeroth fled alone, and was found at the house of his uncle, in Montgomery County, Maryland. I do not know that any instrument of murder has ever made me thrill as when I drew his terrible bowie-knife from its sheath.

"I come now to the ride out of the city by the chief assassin and his dupe. Harold met Booth immediately after the crime in the next street, and they rode at a gallop past the Patent Office and over Capitol Hill.

"As they crossed the Eastern Branch at Uniontown, Booth gave his proper name to the officer at the bridge. This, which would seem to have been foolish, was, in reality, very shrewd. The officers believed that one of

Booth's accomplices had given this name in order to put them out of the real Booth's track. So they made efforts elsewhere, and Booth got a start. At midnight, precisely, the two horsemen stopped at Surrattsville, Booth remaining on his nag, while Harold descended and knocked lustily at the door. Lloyd, the landlord, came down at once, when Harold pushed past him into the bar, and obtained a bottle of whisky, some of which he gave to Booth immediately. While Booth was drinking, Harold went up stairs and brought down one of the carbines. Lloyd started to get the other, but Harold said :—

"'We don't want it; Booth has broken his leg, and can't carry it.'

"So the second carbine remained in the hall, where the officers afterward found it.

"As the two horsemen started to go off, Booth cried out to Lloyd:—

"'Don't you want to hear some news?'

"'I don't care much about it,' cried Lloyd, by his own account.

"'We have murdered,' said Booth, 'the President and Secretary of State.'

"And, with this horrible confession, Booth and Harold dashed away in the midnight, across Prince George's County.

"On Saturday, before sunrise, Booth and Harold, who had ridden all night without stopping elsewhere, reached the house of Dr. Mudd, three miles from Bryantown. They contracted with him, for twenty-five dollars in greenbacks, to set the broken leg. Harold, who knew Dr. Mudd, introduced Booth under another name, and stated that he had fallen from his horse during the night. The doctor remarked of Booth that he draped the lower part of his face while the leg was being set; he was silent, and in pain. Having no splints in the house, they split up an old-fashioned wooden band-box and prepared them. The doctor was assisted by an Englishman, who at the same time began to hew out a pair of crutches. The inferior bone of the left leg was broken vertically across, and, because vertically, it did not yield when the crippled man walked upon it.

"The riding boot of Booth had to be cut from his foot;

within were the words 'J. Wilkes.' The doctor says he did not notice these. The two men waited around the house all day, but toward evening they slipped their horses from the stable and rode away in the direction of Allen's Fresh.

"Below Ervantown run certain deep and slimy swamps. Along the belt of these Booth and Harold picked up a negro named Swan, who volunteered to show them the road for two dollars. They gave him five more to show them the route to Allen's Fresh; but really wished, as their actions intimated, to gain the house of one Sam Coxe, a notorious rebel, and probably well advised of the plot. They reached the house at midnight. It is a fine dwelling, one of the best in Maryland; and after hallooing for some time, Coxe came down to the door himself. As soon as he opened it, and beheld who the strangers were, he instantly blew out the candle he held in his hand, and, without a word, pulled them into the room, the negro remaining in the yard. The confederates remained in Coxe's house till 4 A. M., during which time the negro saw them eat and drink heartily; but when they reappeared they spoke in a loud tone, so that Swan could hear them, against the hospitality of Coxe. All this was meant to influence the darkey; but their motives were as apparent as their words. He conducted them three miles further on, when they told him that now they knew the way, and giving him five dollars more, making twelve in all, told him to go back.

"But when the negro, in the dusk of the morning, looked after them as he receded, he saw that both horses' heads were turned once more toward Coxe's, and it was this man, doubtless, who harbored the fugitives from Sunday to Thursday, aided, possibly, by such neighbors as the Wilsons and Adamses.

"At the point where Booth crossed the Potomac the shores are very shallow, and one must wade out some distance to where a boat will float. A white man came up here with a canoe on Friday, and tied it by a stone anchor. Between seven and eight o'clock it disappeared, and in the afternoon some men at work on Methxy Creek, in Virginia, saw Booth and Harold land, tie the boat's rope to a stone and fling it ashore, and strike at once across a ploughed field for

BOOTH AND HAROLD CROSSING THE POTOMAC.

King George Court House. Many folks entertained them, without doubt, but we positively hear of them next at Port Royal Ferry, and then at Garrett's farm.

"The few Unionists of Prince George's and Charles Counties, long persecuted and intimidated, came forward and gave important testimony.

"Among these was one Roby, a very fat and very zealous old gentleman, whose professions were as ample as his perspiration. He told the officers of the secret meetings for conspiracy's sake at Lloyd's Hotel, and although a very John Gilpin on horseback, rode here and there to his great loss of wind and repose, fastening fire coals upon the guilty or suspected.

"Lloyd was turned over to Mr. Cottingham, who had established a jail at Robytown; that night his house was searched, and Booth's carbine found hidden in the wall. Three days afterward, Lloyd himself confessed.

"The little party, under the untiring Lovett, examined all the farm-houses below Washington, resorting to many shrewd expedients, and taking note of the great swamps to the east of Port Tobacco; they reached Newport at last, and fastened tacit guilt upon many residents.

"Beyond Bryantown they overhauled the residence of Dr. Mudd, and found Booth's boots. This was before Lloyd confessed, and was the first positive trace the officers had that they were really close upon the assassins.

"I do not recall any thing more wild and startling than this vague and dangerous exploration of a dimly known, hostile, and ignorant country. To these few detectives we owe much of the subsequent successful precaution of the pursuit. They were the Hebrew spies.

"By this time the country was filling up with soldiers, but previously a second memorable detective party went out under the personal command of Major O'Bierne. It consisted, besides that officer, of Lee, D'Angelis, Callahan, Hoey, Bostwick, Hanover, Bevins, and McHenry, and embarked at Washington on a steam-tug for Chappell's Point. Here a military station had long been established for the prevention of blockade and mail running across the Potomac. It was commanded by Lieutenant Laverty, and garrisoned by sixty-five men. On Tuesday night Major O'Bierne's party reached this place, and soon afterward a telegraph station was established here by an invaluable man to the expedition, Captain Beckwith, General Grant's chief cipher operator, who tapped the Point Lookout wire, and placed the War Department within a moment's reach of the theater of events.

"Major O'Bierne's party started at once, over the worst road in the world, for Port Tobacco.

"If any place in the world is utterly given over to depravity, it is Port Tobacco. From this town, by a sinuous creek, there is flat-boat navigation to the Potomac, and across that river to Mattox Creek. Before the war, Port Tobacco was the seat of a tobacco aristocracy and a haunt of negro traders. It passed very naturally into a rebel post for blockade-runners and a rebel post-office general. Gambling, corner-fighting, and shooting matches were its lyceum education. Violence and ignorance had every suffrage in the town. Its people were smugglers, to all intents, and there was neither Bible nor geography to the whole region adjacent. Assassination was never very unpopular at Port Tobacco, and when its victim was a Northern President, it became quite heroic. A month before the murder, a provost-marshal near by was slain in his bed-chamber. For such a town and district, the detective police were the only effective missionaries.

"The hotel here is called the Brawner House; it has a bar in the nethermost cellar, and its patrons, carousing in that imperfect light, look like the denizens of some burglar's crib, talking robbery between their cups; its dining-room is dark and tumble-down, and the cuisine bears traces of Kaffir origin; a barbecue is nothing to a dinner there. The court-house of Port Tobacco is the most superfluous house in the place, except the church. It stands in the center of the town, in a square, and the dwellings lie about it closely, as if to throttle justice. Five hundred people exist in Port Tobacco; life there reminds me, in connection with the slimy river and the adjacent swamps, of the great reptile period of the world, when iguanodons, and pterodactyls, and plesiosauri ate each other.

"Into this abstract of Gomorrah the few detectives went

like angels who visited Lot. They pretended to be inquiring for friends, or to have business designs, and the first people they heard of were Harold and Atzeroth. The latter had visited Port Tobacco three weeks before the murder, and intimated at that time his design of fleeing the country. But everybody denied having seen him subsequent to the crime.

"Atzeroth had been in town just prior to the crime. He had been living with a widow woman, named Mrs. Wheeler, and she was immediately called upon by Major O'Bierne. He did not tell her what Atzeroth had done, but vaguely hinted that he had committed some terrible crime, and that since he had done her wrong, she could vindicate both herself and justice by telling his whereabouts. The woman admitted that Atzeroth had been her bane, but she loved him, and refused to betray him.

"His trunk was found in her garret, and in it the key to his paint shop in Port Tobacco. The latter was fruitlessly searched, but the probable whereabouts of Atzeroth in Montgomery County obtained, and Major O'Bierne telegraphing there immediately, the desperate fellow was found and locked up. A man named Crangle, who had succeeded Atzeroth in Mrs. Wheeler's pliable affections, was arrested at once and put in jail. A number of disloyal people were indicated or "spotted" as in no wise angry at the President's taking off, and for all such a provost prison was established.

"A few miles from Port Tobacco dwelt a solitary woman, who, when questioned, said that for many nights she had heard, after she had retired to bed, a man enter her cellar, and be there all night, departing before dawn. Major O'Bierne and the detectives ordered her to place a lamp in her window the next night she heard him enter; and at dark they established a cordon of armed officers around the place. At midnight punctually she exhibited the light, when the officers broke into the house and thoroughly searched it, without result. Yet the woman positively asserted that she had heard the man enter.

"It was afterward found that she was of diseased mind.

"By this time the military had come up in considerable

numbers, and Major O'Bierne was enabled to confer with Major Wait, of the Eighth Illinois.

"The major had pushed on, on Monday night, to Leonardstown, and pretty well overhauled that locality.

"It was at this time that preparations were made to hunt the swamps around Chapmantown, Bethtown, and Allen's Fresh. Booth had been entirely lost since his departure from Mudd's house, and it was believed that he had either pushed on for the Potomac or taken to the swamps. The officers sagaciously determined to follow him to the one, and to explore the other.

"The swamps tributary to the various branches of the Wicomico River, of which the chief feeder is Allen's Creek, bear various names, such as Jordan's Swamp, Atchall's Swamp, and Scrub Swamp. There are dense growths of dogwood, gum, and beech, planted in sluices of water and bog, and their width varies from a half mile to four miles, while their length is upward of sixteen miles. Frequent deep ponds dot this wilderness place, with here and there a stretch of dry soil, but no human being inhabits the malarious extent; even a hunted murderer would shrink from hiding there. Serpents and slimy lizards are the only living denizens; sometimes the coon takes refuge in this desert from the hounds, and in the soft mud a thousand odorous muskrats delve, and now and then a tremulous otter. But not even the hunted negro dare to fathom the treacherous clay, nor make himself a fellow of the slimy reptiles which reign absolute in this terrible solitude. Here the soldiers prepared to seek for the President's assassins, and no search of the kind has ever been so thorough and patient. The Shawnee, in his stronghold of despair in the heart of the Okeefenokee, would scarcely have changed homes with Wilkes Booth and David Harold, hiding in this inhuman country.

"The military forces deputed to pursue the fugitives were seven hundred men of the Eighth Illinois Cavalry, six hundred men of the Twenty-second Colored Troops, and one hundred men of the Sixteenth New York. These swept the swamps by detachments, the mass of them dismounted, with cavalry at the belts of clearings, interspersed with detectives at frequent intervals in the rear. They first formed a strong picket cordon entirely around the swamps, and then, drawn up in two orders of battle, advanced boldly into the bog by two lines of march. One party swept the swamps longitudinally, the other pushed straight across their smallest diameter.

"A similar march has not been made during the war; the soldiers were only a few paces apart, and in steady order they took the ground as it came, now plunging to their armpits in foul sluices of gangrened water, now hopelessly submerged in slime, now attacked by legions of wood-ticks, now tempting some unfaithful log or greenishly solid morass, and plunging to the tip of the skull in poisonous stagnation; the tree boughs rent their uniforms; they came out upon dry land many of them without a rag of garment, scratched, and gashed, and spent, repugnant to themselves, and disgusting to those who saw them; but not one trace of Booth or Harold was anywhere found. Wherever they might be, the swamps did not contain them.

"While all this was going on, a force started from Point Lookout, and swept the narrow necks of St. Mary's quite up to Medley's Neck. To complete the search in this part of the country, Colonel Wells and Major O'Bierne started, with a force of cavalry and infantry, for Chappell's Point. They took the entire peninsula, as before, and marched in close skirmish line across it, but without finding any thing of note. The manner of inclosing a house was by cavalry advances, which held all the avenues till mounted detectives came up. Many strange and ludicrous adventures occurred on each of these expeditions. While the forces were going up Cobb's Neck there was a counter force coming down from Allen's Fresh.

"Major O'Bierne started for Leonardstown with his detective force, and played off Laverty as Booth, and Hoey as Harold. These two advanced to farm-houses and gave their assumed names, asking at the same time for assistance and shelter. They were generally avoided, except by one man named Claggert, who told them they might hide in the woods behind his house. When Claggert was arrested, however, he stated that he meant to hide only to give them up. Whi on this adventure, a man who had heard of the reward came very near shooting Laverty. The ruse now became hazardous, and the detectives resumed their real characters.

"One Mills, a rebel mail-carrier, also arrested, saw Booth and Harold lurking along the river bank on Friday; he referred Major O'Bierne to one Claggert, a rebel, as having seen them also; but Claggert held his tongue and went to jail. On Saturday night, Major O'Bierne, thus assured, also crossed the Potomac with his detectives to Boone's farm, where the fugitives had landed. While collecting information here, a gunboat swung up the stream, and threatened to open fire on the party.

"It was now night, and all the party worn to the ground with long travel and want of sleep. Lieutenant Laverty's men went a short distance down the country and gave up, and Major O'Bierne, with a single man, pushed all night to King George's Court-House, and next day, Sunday, re-embarked for Chappell's Point. Hence he telegraphed his information, and asked permission to pursue, promising to catch the assassins before they reached Port Royal.

"This the department refused. Colonel Baker's men were delegated to make the pursuit with the able Lieutenant Doherty; and O'Bierne, who was the most active and successful spirit in the chase, returned to Washington, cheerful and contented."

No lapse of time, nor varied experience, can ever efface the memory of the hour at headquarters when the following was penned:—

"The face of Lafayette Baker, Colonel, and Chief of the Secret Service, overlooks me. He has played the most perilous parts of the war, and is the captor of the late President's murderer. The story that I am to tell you, as he and his trusty dependants told it to me, will be aptly commenced here, where the net was woven which took the dying life of Wilkes Booth.

"When the murdering occurred, Colonel Baker was absent from Washington. He returned on the third morning and was at once brought by Secretary Stanton to join the hue and cry against the escaped Booth. The sagacious detective learned that nearly ten thousand cavalry, and one-fourth

PLANNING THE CAPTURE OF BOOTH.

as many policemen, had been meantime scouring, without plan or compass, the whole territory of Southern Maryland. They were treading on each others' heels, and mixing up the thing so badly, that the best place for the culprits to have gone would have been in the very midst of their pursuers. Baker at once possessed himself of the little the War Department had learned, and started immediately to take the usual detective measures, till then neglected, of offering a reward, and getting out photographs of the suspected ones. He then dispatched a few chosen detectives to certain vital points, and awaited results.

"The first of these was the capture of Atzeroth. Others, like the taking of Dr. Mudd, simultaneously occurred. But the district suspected being remote from the railway routes, and broken by no telegraph station, the Colonel, to place himself nearer the theater of events, ordered an operator, with the necessary instrument, to tap the wire running to Point Lookout, near Chappell's Point, and send him prompt messages.

"The same steamer which took down the operator and two detectives, brought back one of the same detectives and a negro. This negro, taken to Colonel Baker's office, stated so positively that he had seen Booth and another man cross the Potomac in a fishing boat, while he was looking down upon them from a bank, that the Colonel was at first skeptical; but, when examined, the negro answered so readily and intelligently, recognizing the man from the photographs, that Baker knew at last that he had the true scent.

"Straightway he sent to General Hancock for twenty-five men, and while the order was going drew down his coast survey maps, with that quick detective intuition amounting almost to inspiration. He cast upon the probable route and destination of the refugees, as well as the point where he would soonest strike them. Booth, he knew, would not keep along the coast, with frequent deep rivers to cross, nor, indeed, in any direction east of Richmond, where he was liable at any time to cross our lines of occupation; nor, being lame, could he ride on horseback, so as to place himself very far westward of his point of debarkation in Virginia. But he would travel in a direct course from Bluff

Point, where he crossed to Eastern Maryland, and this would take him through Port Royal, on the Rappahannock River, in time to be intercepted by the outgoing cavalrymen.

"When, therefore, twenty-five men, under one Lieutenant Dogherty, arrived at his office doors, Baker placed the whole under control of his former Lieutenant-Colonel, E. J. Conger, and of his cousin, Lieutenant L. B. Baker—the first of Ohio, the last of New York—and bade them go with all dispatch to Belle Plain, on the Lower Potomac, there to disembark and scour the country faithfully around Port Royal, but not to return unless they captured their men.

"Quitting Washington at two o'clock P. M., on Monday, the detectives and cavalrymen disembarked at Belle Plain, on the border of Stafford County, at ten o'clock, in the darkness. Belle Plain is simply the nearest landing to Fredericksburg, seventy miles from Washington City, and located upon Potomac Creek. It is a wharf and warehouse merely, and here the steamer *John S. Ide* stopped and made fast, while the party galloped off in the darkness. Conger and Baker kept ahead, riding up to farm-houses and questioning the inmates, pretending to be in search of the Maryland gentlemen belonging to the party. But nobody had seen the parties described, and after a futile ride on the Fredericksburg road, they turned shortly to the east, and kept up their baffled inquiries all the way to Port Conway, on the Rappahannock.

"On Tuesday morning they presented themselves at the Port Royal Ferry, and inquired of the ferryman, while he was taking them over in squads of seven at a time, if he had seen any two such men. Continuing their inquiries at Port Royal, they found one Rollins, a fisherman, who referred them to a negro, named Lucas, as having driven two men a short distance toward Bowling Green, in a wagon. It was found that these men answered to the description, Booth having a crutch, as previously ascertained.

"The day before Booth and Harold had applied at Port Conway for the general ferry-boat, but the ferryman was then fishing, and would not desist for the inconsiderable fare of only two persons; but to their supposed good fortune a lot of Confederate cavalrymen just then came along, who threatened the ferryman with a shot in the head if he did not instantly bring across his craft and transport the entire party. These cavalrymen were of Moseby's disbanded command, returning from Fairfax Court House to their homes in Caroline County. Their captain was on his way to visit a sweetheart at Bowling Green, and he had so far taken Booth under his patronage, that when the latter was haggling with Lucas for a team, he offered both Booth and Harold the use of his horse to ride and walk alternately.

"This is the court house town of Caroline County, a small and scattered place, having within it an ancient tavern, no longer used for other than lodging purposes; but here they hauled from his bed the captain aforesaid, and bade him dress himself. As soon as he comprehended the matter, he became pallid, and eagerly narrated the facts in his possession. Booth, to his knowledge, was then lying at the house of one Garrett, which they had passed, and Harold had departed the existing day with the intention of rejoining him.

"Taking this captain along for a guide, the worn-out horsemen retraced their steps, though some were so haggard and wasted with travel that they had to be kicked into intelligence before they could climb to their saddles. The objects of the chase thus at hand, the detectives, full of sanguine purpose, hurried the cortege so well along, that by two o'clock early morning all halted at Garrett's gate. In the pale moonlight, three hundred yards from the main road, to the left, a plain, old farm-house looked grayly through the environing locusts. It was worn, and whitewashed, and two-storied, and its half-human windows glowered down upon the silent cavalrymen like watching owls, which stood as sentries over some horrible secret asleep within.

"Dimly seen behind, an old barn, high and weather beaten, faced the roadside gate, for the house itself lay to the left of its own lane; and nestling beneath the barn, a few long corn-cribs lay, with a cattle-shed at hand.

"In the dead stillness, Baker dismounted and forced the outer gate, Conger kept close behind him, and the horsemen followed cautiously. They made no noise in the soft clay, nor broke the all-foreboding silence anywhere, till the second gate swung open gratingly, yet even then nor hoarse nor nor shrill response came back, save distant croaking, as of frogs or owls, or the whiz of some passing night-hawk. So they surrounded the pleasant old homestead, each horseman, carbine in poise, adjusted under the grove of locusts, so as to inclose the dwelling with a circle of fire. After a pause, Baker rode to the kitchen door on the side, and dismounting, rapped and hallooed lustily. An old man, in drawers and night-shirt, hastily undrew the bolts, and stood on the threshold, peering shiveringly into the darkness.

"Baker seized him by the throat at once, and held a pistol to his ear.

"'Who is it that calls me?' cried the old man.

"'Where are the men who stay with you?' challenged Baker. 'If you prevaricate, you are a dead man!'

"The old fellow, who proved to be the head of the family, was so overawed and paralyzed that he stammered and shook and said not a word.

"'Go light a candle,' cried Baker, sternly, 'and be quick about it.'

"The trembling old man obeyed, and in a moment the imperfect rays flared upon his whitening hairs, and bluishly pallid face. Then the question was repeated, backed up by the glimmering pistol. 'Where are these men?'

"The old man held to the wall, and his knees smote each other. 'They are gone,' he said. 'We haven't got them in the house; I assure you that they are gone.'

"In the interim Conger had also entered, and while the household and its invaders were thus in weird tableau, a young man appeared, as if he had risen from the ground. The eyes of everybody turned upon him in a second; but, while he blanched, he did not lose loquacity. 'Father,' he said, 'we had better tell the truth about the matter. Those men whom you seek, gentlemen, are in the barn, I know. They went there to sleep.' Leaving one soldier to guard the old man—and the soldier was very glad of the job, as it relieved him of personal hazard in the approaching combat—all the rest, with cocked pistols at the young man's head, followed on to the barn. It lay a hundred yards from the house, the front barn-door facing the west gable, and was an

THE BARN—THE PROPOSAL AND REPLY.

old and spacious structure, with floors only a trifle above the ground level.

"The troops dismounted, were stationed at regular intervals around it, and ten yards distant at every point, four special guards placed to command the door, and all with weapons in supple preparation, while Baker and Conger went direct to the door. It had a padlock upon it, and the key of this Baker secured at once. In the interval of silence that ensued, the rustling of planks and straw was heard inside, as of persons rising from sleep.

"At the same moment Baker hailed:—

"'To the persons in this barn I have a proposal to make. We are about to send in to you the son of the man in whose custody you are found. Either surrender to him your arms, and then give yourself up, or we'll set fire to the place. We mean to take you both, or to have a bonfire and shooting-match.'

"No answer came to this of any kind. The lad, John M. Garrett, who was in deadly fear, was here pushed through the door by a sudden opening of it, and immediately Lieutenant Baker locked the door on the outside. The boy was heard to state his appeal in under tones. Booth replied:—

"'—— you. Get out of here. You have betrayed me.'

"At the same time he placed his hand in his pocket, as if for a pistol. A remonstrance followed; but the boy slipped on and over the reopened portal, reporting that his errand had failed, and that he dare not enter again. All this time the candle brought from the house to the barn was burning close beside the two detectives, rendering it easy for any one within to have shot them dead. This observed, the light was cautiously removed, and everybody took care to keep out of its reflection. By this time the crisis of the position was at hand; the cavalry exhibited very variable inclinations, some to run away, others to shoot Booth without a summons; but all excited and fitfully silent. At the house near by, the female folks were seen collected in the doorway, and the necessities of the case provoked prompt conclusions. The boy was placed at a remote point, and the summons repeated by Baker:—

"'You must surrender inside there! Give up your arms and appear; there's no chance for escape. We give you five minutes to make up your mind.'

"A bold, clarion reply came from within, so strong as to be heard at the house door:—

"'Who are you, and what do you want with us?'

"Baker again urged:—

"'We want you to deliver up your arms, and become our prisoners.'

"'But who are you?' hallooed the same strong voice.

"'That makes no difference; we know who you are, and we want you. We have here fifty men, armed with carbines and pistols. You cannot escape.'

"There was a long pause, and then Booth said:—

"'Captain, this is a hard case, I swear. Perhaps I am being taken by my own friends.'

"No reply from the detectives.

"'Well, give us a little time to consider.'

"'Very well; take time.'

"Here ensued a long and eventful pause. What thronging memories it brought to Booth we can only guess. In this little interval he made the resolve to die. But he was cool and steady to the end. Baker, after a lapse, hailed for the last time:—

"'Well, we have waited long enough; surrender your arms and come out, or we'll fire the barn.'

"Booth answered thus:—

"'I am but a cripple—a one-legged man. Withdraw your forces one hundred yards from the door, and I will come. Give me a chance for my life, captain. I will never be taken alive!'

"'We did not come here to fight, but to capture you. I say again appear, or the barn shall be fired.'

"Then, with a long breath, which could be heard outside, Booth cried, in sudden calmness, still invisible, as were to him his enemies:—

"'Well, then, my brave boys, prepare a stretcher for me!'

"There was a pause repeated, broken by low discussions within between Booth and his associate, the former saying, as if in answer to some remonstrance or appeal: "Get away from me. You are a —— coward, and mean to leave me in my distress; but go—go! I don't want you to stay—I won't have you stay!' Then he shouted aloud:—

"'There's a man inside who wants to surrender'

"'Let him come, if he will bring his arms.'

"Here Harold, rattling at the door, said: 'Let me out; open the door; I want to surrender.'

"'Hand out your arms, then.'

"'I have not got any'

"'You are the man who carried the carbine yesterday; bring it out!'

"'I haven't got any.'

"This was said in a whining tone, and with an almost visible shiver. Booth cried aloud at this hesitation:—

"'He hasn't got any arms; they are mine, and I have kept them.'

"'Well, he carried the carbine, and must bring it out.'

"'On the word and honor of a gentleman, he has no arms with him. They are mine, and I have got them.'

"At this time Harold was quite up to the door, within whispering distance of Baker. The latter told him to put out his hands to be handcuffed, at the same time drawing open the door a little distance. Harold thrust forth his hands, when Baker, seizing him, jerked him into the night, and straightway delivered him over to a deputation of cavalrymen. The fellow began to talk of his innocence, and plead so noisily, that Conger threatened to gag him, unless he ceased. Then Booth made his last appeal, in the same clear, unbroken voice:—

"'Captain, give me a chance. Draw off your men, and I will fight them singly. I could have killed you six times to-night, but I believe you to be a brave man, and would not murder you. Give a lame man a show.'

"It was too late for parley. All this time Booth's voice had sounded from the middle of the barn.

"Ere he ceased speaking, Colonel Conger slipped around to the rear, drew some loose straws through a crack, and lit a match upon them. They were dry and blazed up in an instant, carrying a sheet of smoke and flame through the

parted planks, and heaving in a twinkling a world of light
and heat upon the magazine within. The blaze lit up the
black recesses of the great barn, till every wasp's nest and
cobweb in the roof were luminous; flinging streaks of red
and violet across the tumbled farm gear in the corner,
ploughs, harrows, hoes, rakes, sugar-mills, and making
every separate grain in the high bin adjacent gleam like
a mote of precious gold. They tinged the beams, the upright columns, the barricades, where clover and timothy,
piled high, held toward the hot incendiary their separate
straws for the funeral pile. They bathed the murderer's
retreat in a beautiful illumination, and while in bold outline
his figure stood revealed, they rose like an impenetrable
wall to guard from sight the hated enemy who lit them.

"Behind the blaze, with his eye to a crack, Conger saw
Wilkes Booth standing upright upon a crutch. He likens
him at this instant to his brother Edwin, whom, he says, he
so much resembled that he believed, for the moment, the
whole pursuit to have been a mistake. At the gleam of the
fire, Wilkes dropped his crutch and carbine, and on both
hands crept to the spot to espy the incendiary and shoot him
dead. His eyes were lustrous, like fever, and swelled and
rolled in terrible beauty, while his teeth were fixed, and he
wore the expression of one in the calmness before frenzy. In
vain he peered, with vengeance in his look; the blaze that
made him visible concealed his enemy. A second he turned
glaring at the fire, as if to leap upon it and extinguish it, but
it had made such headway that this was a futile impulse, and
he dismissed it. As calmly as upon the battle-field a veteran
stands, amidst the hail of ball, and shell, and plunging iron,
Booth turned at a man's stride and pushed for the door, carbine in poise, and the last resolve of death, which we name
despair, sat on his high, bloodless forehead.

"As so he dashed, intent to expire not unaccompanied,
a disobedient sergeant, at an eyehole, drew upon him the
fatal bead. The barn was all glorious with conflagration,
and in the beautiful ruin this outlawed man strode like all
that we know of wicked valor, stern in the face of death. A
shock, a shout, a gathering up of his splendid figure, as if to
overtip the stature God gave him, and John Wilkes Booth

fell headlong to the floor, lying there in a heap, a little life remaining. But no.

"'He has shot himself,' cried Baker, unaware of the source of the report, and rushing in, he grasped his arm, to guard against any feint or strategy. A moment convinced him that further struggle with the prone flesh was useless. Booth did not move, nor breathe, nor gasp. Conger and the two sergeants now entered, and, taking up the body, they bore it in haste from the advancing flame, and laid it without upon the grass, all fresh with heavenly dew.

"'Water,' cried Conger; 'bring water.'

'When this was dashed into his face, he revived a moment, and stirred his lips. Baker put his ear close down and heard him say:—

"'Tell mother—and—die—for my country.'

"They lifted him again, the fire encroaching in hotness upon them, and placed him upon the porch before the dwelling.

"A mattress was brought down, on which they placed him, and propped his head, and gave him water and brandy. The women of the household, joined meantime by another son, who had been found in one of the corn-cribs, watching, as he said, to see that Booth and Harold did not steal the horses, were nervous, but prompt to do the dying man all kindnesses, although waved sternly back by the detectives. They dipped a rag in brandy and water, and this being put between Booth's teeth, he sucked it greedily. When he was able to articulate again, he muttered to Baker the same words, with an addenda:—

"'Tell mother I died for my country. I thought I did for the best.'

"Baker repeated this, saying at the same time, 'Booth, do I repeat it correctly?' Booth nodded his head.

"By this time the grayness of dawn was approaching; moving figures, inquisitively coming near, were to be seen distinctly, and the cocks began to crow gutturally, though the barn by this time was a hulk of blaze and ashes, sending toward the zenith a spiral line of dense smoke.

"The women became importunate at this time that the troops might be ordered to extinguish the fire, which was spreading toward their precious corn-cribs. Not even death could banish the call of interest. Soldiers were sent to put out the fire, and Booth, relieved of the bustle around him, drew near to death apace. Twice he was heard to say, 'Kill me—kill me!' His lips often moved, but could complete no appreciable sound. He made once a motion, which the quick eye of Conger understood to mean that his throat pained him. Conger put his finger there, when the dying man attempted to cough, but only caused the blood at his perforated neck to flow more lively. He bled very little, although shot quite through, beneath and behind the ears, his collar being severed on both sides.

"A soldier had been meanwhile dispatched for a doctor, but the route and return was quite six miles, and the sinner was sinking fast. Still the women made efforts to get to see him, but were always rebuffed, and all the brandy they could find was demanded by the assassin, who motioned for strong drink every two minutes. He made frequent desires to be turned over—not by speech, but by gesture—and he was alternately placed upon his back, belly, and side. His tremendous vitality evidenced itself almost miraculously. Now and then his heart would cease to throb, and his pulse would be as cold as a dead man's. Directly life would begin anew, the face would flush up effulgently, the eyes open and brighten, and soon relapsing, stillness reasserted, would again be dispossessed by the same magnificent triumph of man over mortality. Finally, the fussy little doctor arrived, in time to be useless. He probed the wound to see if the ball were not in it, and shook his head sagely, and talked learnedly.

"Just at his coming, Booth had asked to have his hands raised and shown him. They were so paralyzed that he did not know their location. When they were displayed, he muttered, with a sad lethargy, 'Useless—useless!' These were the last words he ever uttered.

"As he began to die, the sun rose and threw beams into all the tree-tops. It was at a man's height when the struggle of death twitched and lingered in the fading bravo's face. His jaw drew spasmodically and obliquely downward; his eyeballs rolled toward his feet, and began to swell; lividness, like a horrible shadow, fastened upon him, and with

a sort of gurgle, and sudden check, he stretched his feet, and threw his head back, and gave up the ghost.

"They sewed him up in a saddle-blanket. This was his shroud; too like a soldier's. Harold, meantime, had been tied to a tree, but was now released for the march. Colonel Conger pushed on immediately for Washington; the cortege was to follow. Booth's only arms were his carbine, knife, and two revolvers. They found about him bills of exchange, Canada money, and a diary. A venerable old negro living in the vicinity had the misfortune to possess a horse. This horse was the relic of former generations, and showed by his protruding ribs the general leanness of the land. He moved in an eccentric amble, and when put upon his speed was generally run backward. To this old negro's horse was harnessed a very shaky and absurd wagon, which rattled like approaching dissolution, and each part of it ran without any connection or correspondence with any other part. It had no tail-board, and its shafts were sharp as famine; and into this mimicry of a vehicle the murderer was to be sent to the Potomac River, while the man he had murdered was moving in state across the mourning continent. The old negro geared up his wagon by means of a set of fossil harness, and when it was backed to Garrett's porch, they laid within it the discolored corpse. The corpse was tied with ropes around the legs, and made fast to the wagon side.

"Harold's legs were tied to stirrups, and he was placed in the centre of four murderous-looking cavalrymen. The two sons of Garrett were also taken along, despite the sobs and petitions of the old folks and women, but the rebel captain who had given Booth a lift got off amid the night's agitations, and was not rearrested. So moved the cavalcade of retribution, with death in its midst, along the road to Port Royal. When the wagon started, Booth's wound, now scarcely dribbling, began to run anew. It fell through the crack of the wagon, and fell dripping upon the axle, and spotting the road with terrible wafers. It stained the planks and soaked the blankets; and the old negro, at a stoppage, dabbled his hands in it by mistake; he drew back instantly, with a shudder and stifled expletive, 'Gor-r-r, dat 'll never come off in de world; it's murderer's blood.' He wrung his hands, and looked imploringly at the officers, and shuddered again; 'Gor-r-r, I wouldn't have dat on me for tousand tousand dollars.'

"The progress of the team was slow, with frequent danger of shipwreck altogether, but toward noon the cortege filed through Port Royal, where the citizens came out to ask the matter, and why a man's body, covered with sombre blankets, was going by with so great escort. They were told that it was a wounded Confederate, and so held their tongues. The little ferry, again in requisition, took them over by squads, and they pushed from Port Conway to Belle Plain, which they reached in the middle of the afternoon. All the way the blood dribbled from the corpse in a slow, incessant, sanguine exudation. The old negro was niggardly dismissed with two paper dollars. The dead man untied and cast upon the vessel's deck, steam gotten up in a little while, and the broad Potomac shores saw this skeleton ship flit by, as the bloody sun threw gashes and blots of unhealthy light along the silver surface.

"All the way associate with the carcass went Harold, shuddering in so grim companionship, and in the awakened fears of his own approaching ordeal, beyond which it loomed already, the gossamer fabric of a scaffold. He tried to talk for his own exoneration, saying he had ridden as was his wont, beyond the East Branch, and returning found Booth wounded, who begged him to be his companion. Of his crime he knew nothing, so help him God, &c. But nobody listened to him. All interest of crime, courage, and retribution centered in the dead flesh at his feet. At Washington, high and low turned out to look on Booth. Only a few were permitted to see his corpse for purposes of recognition It was fairly preserved, though on one side of the face distorted, and looking blue like death, and wildly bandit-like, as if beaten by avenging winds.

"Finally, the Secretary of War, without instructions of any kind, committed to Colonel Lafayette C. Baker, of the Secret Service, the stark corpse of J. Wilkes Booth. The Secret Service never fulfilled its vocation more secretly. 'What have you done with the body?' said I to Baker. **That is known, he answered, 'to only one man living** beside myself. It is gone; I will not tell you where; the only man who knows is sworn to silence; never till the great trumpeter comes shall the grave of Booth be discovered.' And this is true. Last night, the 27th of April, a small rowboat received the carcass of the murderer; two men were in it; they carried the body off into the darkness, and out of that darkness it will never return; in the darkness, like his great crime, may it remain forever; impassable, invisible, nondescript, condemned to that worse than damnation—annihilation.

"The river bottom may ooze about it, laden with great shot and drowning manacles. The earth may have opened to give it that silence and forgiveness which man will never give to its memory. The fishes may swim around it, or the daisies grow white above it; but we shall never know. Mysterious, incomprehensible, unattainable, like the dim times through which we live, we think upon it as if we only dreamed in a perturbed fever; the assassin of a nation's head rests somewhere in the elements, and that is all; but if the indignant seas or the profaned turf shall ever vomit this corpse from their recesses, and it receives Christian burial from some one who does not recognize it, let the last words those decaying lips ever uttered be carved above them with a dagger, to tell the history of a young, and once promising life."

It is not improper to state, that only two persons on earth know where the body of Booth lies. Lieutenant Baker, on whose lap his dying head was laid, and myself, have the dark secret to keep. The night before the removal of the remains I was ordered, by the Secretary of War, to have them securely guarded, that no one might touch them; as "every hair of his head would be a valued relic to the sympathizers with the South in Washington." I had not had my clothes off for nearly two weeks, and was granted leave of absence from the vessel, on whose deck was lying the corpse of the assassin, covered with two blankets sewed together like a sack, completely concealing it. Upon my return, I was greatly surprised and indignant, to find persons of high position, and some of secession proclivities, around the dead body, the coarse shroud parted at the seam, and a lady at that moment cutting off a lock of the black, curled, and beautiful hair. I seized the fair hands, and, after a refusal to give me the relic, forcibly took it, and then cleared the deck, to the amazement and displeasure of some of the party.

At noon of that night, with my trusty lieutenant, a man of thoroughly Christian principles, I placed the body in a small boat, and we rowed away from the silent leviathan of Mars, which had borne the loathsome body to the nation's capital; with no watchful eye upon us, but that of Him who scattered above us the shining stars. It was a strange, wild hour on the calm Potomac; and yet, so great was my exhaustion and fatigue, that I fell to dozing with the oar in my hand, and the sack containing the assassin's corpse at my feet. Further I cannot go—it is best to let the curtain of unbroken secrecy and mystery remain between the burial and all human curiosity.

The diary kept by Booth after the murder of the President, to which I referred in connection with the giving of the personal effects of Booth to the Secretary of War, recorded the adventures of the fugitive; one of these was the killing of his horse in the tangled forest to avoid detection, and then sleeping between the animal's legs to get the warmth while it remained in the dead body, during the long hours of the horrible night. With the dawn, he dragged his own painful limbs along his untrodden path of flight from the apparently slow, but certain, grasp of avenging justice.

"On the 9th of July, 1865, at as early an hour as eight A. M.," says an eye-witness, "people commenced to wend their way down to the prison, and the boats to Alexandria, which ran close by the jail, were crowded all day by those who took the trip in hopes of catching a glimpse of the gallows, or of the execution, but it was all in vain. The only position outside of the jail that could be used as an observatory, was the large building upon the left side of the arsenal, which had about fifty spectators upon it, who had a good view of the whole.

"Between nine and ten o'clock in the morning the three ante-rooms of the prison, on the first floor, were thronged with army officers, principally of Hancock's corps, anxious

SECRET BURIAL OF BOOTH.

THE EXECUTION.

to get a view of the execution from the windows, from which
.ne scaffold could be plainly seen. The newspaper reporters
soon began to congregate there also, and in a few minutes
not less than a score were in attendance, waiting to pick up
the smallest item of interest. No newspaper man was allowed
to see the prisoners in their cells before they were led out to
execution, and General Hartranft was very decided on this
point.

"While waiting here for over two hours, the clergymen
passed in and out through the heavily riveted door leading
to the prisoners' cells, which creaked heavily on its hinges
as it swung to and fro, and the massive key was turned upon
the inner side with a heavy sound as a visitor was admitted
within its portals.

"Mrs. Surratt's daughter passed into the ante-room,
accompanied by a lady, who remained seated, while the
daughter rapidly entered the hall, and, passing through the
heavy door, is soon in the corridor where her mother is
incarcerated.

"Messrs. Cox, Doster, Aiken, and Clampitt, counsel for
the prisoners, are specially passed in for a short interview,
and in a few minutes they return again to the ante-rooms.
Time flies rapidly, and not a moment is to be lost. No useless words are to be spoken, but earnest terse sentences are
from necessity employed when conversing with the doomed
prisoners, whose lives are now measured by minutes.

"Aiken and Clampitt are both here. They walk impa-
tiently up and down the room, whispering a word to each
other as to the prospect of Mrs. Surratt's being reprieved
through the operations of the habeas corpus, which, Aiken
confidently tells us, has been granted by Justice Wylie, and
from which he anticipates favorable results. Strange infatu
ation! It was the last straw to which, like drowning men,
they clutched with the fond hope that it was to rescue their
client from her imminent peril.

"Atzeroth passed the night previous to the execution
without any particular manifestations. He prayed and cried
alternately, but made no other noise that attracted the
attention of his keeper. On the morning of the execution

he sat most of the time on the floor of his cell in his shirt sleeves.

"He was attended by a lady dressed in deep black, who carried a prayer-book, and who seemed more exercised in spirit than the prisoner himself. Who the lady was could not be ascertained. She left him at half-past twelve o'clock, and exhibited great emotion at parting.

"During the afternoon Atzeroth was greatly composed, and spent part of the time in earnest conversation with his spiritual adviser, Rev. Mr. Butler, of St. Paul's Lutheran Church, Washington. He occupied cell No. 151 on the ground floor, which was directly in view of the yard, where he could see the gathering crowd and soldiery, although he could not see the scaffold. He sat in the corner of his cell on his bed, and when his spiritual adviser would go out for a few minutes and leave his Testament in his hands, his eyes would be dropped to it in a moment, and occasionally wander with a wild look toward the open window in front of his cell.

"He wore nothing but a white linen shirt and a gray pair of pants. The long irons upon his hands, which he had worn during the trial, were not removed.

"Atzeroth made a partial confession to the Rev. Mr Butler, a few hours before his execution. He stated that he took a room at the Kirkwood House on Thursday afternoon, and was engaged in endeavoring to get a pass to Richmond. He then heard the President was to be taken to the theater and there to be captured. He said he understood that Booth was to rent the theater for the purpose of carrying out the plot to capture the President. He stated that Harold brought the pistol and knife to the Kirkwood House, and that he (Atzeroth) had nothing to do with the attempted assassination of Andrew Johnson.

"Booth intended that Harold should assassinate Johnson, and he wanted him (Atzeroth) to back him up and give him courage. Booth thought that Harold had more pluck than Atzeroth.

"He alluded to the meeting at the restaurant about the middle of March He said Booth, Harold, Payne, Arnold, and himself were present, and it was then concerted that Mr. Lincoln should be captured and taken to Richmond.

"They heard that Lincoln was to visit a camp near Washington, and the plan was that they should proceed there and capture the coach and horses containing Lincoln, and run him through Prince George' County and Old Fields to G. B. There they were to leave the coach and horses and place the President in a buggy which Harold would have on hand, and thus convey him to a boat to be in readiness, and run him by some means to Richmond. He denies that he was in favor of assassinating Lincoln, but was willing to assist in his capture.

"He stated, however, that he knew Lincoln was to be assassinated about half-past eight o'clock on the evening of the occurrence, but was afraid to make it known, as he feared Booth would kill him if he did so.

"He said that slavery caused his sympathies to be with the South. He had heard a sermon preached which stated that a curse on the negro race had turned them black. He always hated the negroes, and thought they should be kept in ignorance.

"Booth had promised him that if their plan succeeded for the capture of Lincoln they should all be rich men, and they would become great. The prisoners would all be exchanged, and the independence of the South would be recognized, and their cause be triumphant. He had never received any money as yet.

"The crowd increases. Reporters are scribbling industriously. A suppressed whisper is audible all over the room and the hall as the hour draws nearer, and the preparations begin to be more demonstrative.

"The rumbling sound of the trap, as it falls in the course of the experiments which are being made to test it, and to prevent any unfortunate accident occurring at the critical moment, is heard through the windows, and all eyes are involuntarily turned in that direction, for curiosity is excited to the highest pitch to view the operations of the fatal machinery. There are two or three pictorial papers represented. One calmly makes a drawing of the scaffold for the next issue of his paper, and thus the hours till noon passed away.

"The bustle increases. Officers are running to and fro, calling for orderlies and giving orders. General Hartranft is trying to answer twenty questions at once from as many different persons. The sentry in the hall is becoming angry because the crowd will keep intruding on his beat, when suddenly a buggy at the door announces the arrival of General Hancock.

"He enters the room hurriedly, takes General Hartranft aside, and a few words pass between them in a low tone, to which Hartranft nods acquiescence; then, in a louder voice, Hancock says: 'Get ready, General; I want to have every thing put in readiness as soon as possible.' This was the signal for the interviews of the clergymen, relatives, and friends of the prisoners to cease, and for the doomed to prepare for execution.

"The bustle increases. Mr. Aiken approaches General Hancock, and a few minutes' conversation passes between them. Aiken's countenance changes perceptibly at General Hancock's words. The reason is plain; there is no hope for Mrs. Surratt. The habeas corpus movement, from which he expected so much, has failed; and Aiken, in a voice tremulous with emotion, said to me: 'Mrs. Surratt will be hung.'

"The bright hopes he had cherished had all vanished, and the dreadful truth stood before him in all its horror Clampitt, too, till General Hancock arrived, indulged in the hope that the habeas corpus would effect a respite for three or four days.

"Three or four of Harold's sisters, all in one chorus of weeping, come through the prison-door into the hall. They had left their brother and spoken to him the last words, and heard his voice for the last time.

"At fifteen minutes after one o'clock, General Hartranft blandly informs the 'press gang' to be in readiness for the prison-doors to be opened, when they can pass into the prison-yard, from whence a good view of the procession can be obtained as it passes by to the scaffold. About 11 A. M., the prison-yard was thrown open to those having passes, and about fifty entered. The first object in view was the scaffold.

THE EXECUTION.

which was erected at the northeast corner of the penitentiary yard, and consisted of a simple wooden structure, of very primitive appearance, faced about due west. The platform was elevated about twelve feet from the ground, and was about twenty feet square. Attached to the main platform were the drops, &c., two in number, on which the criminals stood. At the moment of execution, these drops were connected with the main platform, by means of large hinges, four to each drop.

"The drops were supported by a post, which rested on a heavy piece of timber placed on the ground, and so arranged that two soldiers stationed at the rear of the scaffold instantaneously detached the two supports from their positions by means of pressing two poles, which occupied a horizontal position, the action of which dislodged the props of the scaffold and permitted the drops to fall.

"The gallows proper was divided into two parts by means of a perpendicular piece of timber, resting on the platform, and reaching up to the cross-beam of the gallows. Two ropes hung on either side of the piece of timber mentioned. They were wound around the cross-beam, and contained large knots and nooses at the lower end. The platform was ascended by means of a flight of steps, thirteen in number, erected at the rear of the scaffold, and guarded on either side by a railing, which also extended around the platform. The platform was sustained by nine heavy uprights, about which rose the two heavy pieces of timber which supported the cross-beam and constituted the gallows. The entire platform was capable of holding conveniently about thirty people, and was about half full at the time of the execution.

"The executioners were all fine stalwart specimens of Union soldiers, and did their work well. The rope was furnished from the navy yard, and was one and a half inches in circumference, and composed of twenty strands.

"The graves were dug close to the scaffold, and next to the prison wall. They were four in number, and were about three feet and a half deep, in a dry, clayey soil, and about seven feet long and three wide. Four pine boxes, similar to those used for packing guns in, stood between the graves and the scaffold. These were for coffins, both being in full view of the prisoners as they emerged from their cells, and before them until they commenced the dreadful ascent of those thirteen steps.

"About a thousand soldiers were in the yard and upon the high wall around it, which is wide enough for sentries to patrol it. The sun's rays made it very oppressive, and the walls kept off the little breeze that was stirring. There was no shade, and men huddled together along the walls and around the pump to discuss with one another the prospect of a reprieve or delay for Mrs. Surratt. But few hoped for it, though some were induced by Mrs. Surratt's councel to believe she would not be hanged to-day. When one of them came out and saw the four ropes hanging from the beam, he exclaimed to one of the soldiers: 'My God! they are not going to hang all four, are they?'

"But there are times when it is mercy to hang criminals, and that time was drawing nigh, it seemed, for those who have been used for years to apologizing for the Rebellion, and its damning acts, to be brought to believe that any crime is to be punished. Of such material were the prisoner's counsel.

"The drops, at 11:30, are tried with three hundred pound weights upon them, to see if they will work. One falls all right; one hangs part way down, and the hatchet and saw were brought into play. The next time they were all right. The rattle echoes around the walls; it reaches the prisoners' cells close by, and penetrates their inmost recesses. All is quiet in the yard, save the scuffle of the military, and the passing to and fro of a few civilians.

"At 12:40, four arm-chairs are brought out and placed upon the scaffold, and the moving around of General Hart ranft indicates the drawing near of the time. The news paper correspondents and reporters are admitted to a position about thirty feet from the gallows, and about one o'clock and ten minutes, the heavy door in front of the cells is swung upon its hinges for the hundredth time within an hour, and a few reporters, with General Hancock, pass in and through to the yard, and the big door closes with a slam behind them. All take positions to get a good view. General Hancock for the last time takes a survey of the preparations, and being satisfied that every thing is ready, he re-enters the prison building, and in a few minutes the solemn procession marched down the steps of the back door and into the yard.

"Mrs. Surratt cast her eyes upward upon the scaffold, for a few moments, with a look of curiosity, combined with dread. One glimpse, and her eyes fell to the ground, and she walked along mechanically, her head drooping, and if she had not been supported would have fallen.

"She ascended the scaffold, and was led to an arm-chair, in which she was seated. An umbrella was held over her by the two holy fathers, to protect her from the sun, whose rays shot down like the blasts from a fiery furnace. She was attired in a black bombazine dress, black alpaca bonnet, with black veil, which she wore over her face till she was seated on the chair. During the reading of the order for the execution, by General Hartranft, the priests held a small crucifix before her, which she kissed fervently several times.

"She first looked around at the scene before her, then closed her eyes and seemed engaged in silent prayer. The reading and the announcement of the clergymen in behalf of the other prisoners having been made, Colonel McCall, assisted by the other officers, proceeded to remove her bonnet, pinion her elbows, and tie strips of cotton stuff around her dress below the knees. This done, the rope was placed around her neck and her face covered with a white cap reaching down to the shoulders.

"When they were pinioning her arms, she turned her head, and made some remarks to the officers in a low tone, which could not be heard. It appeared they had tied her elbows too tight, for they slackened the bandage slightly, and then awaited the final order. All the prisoners were prepared thus at the same time, and the preparations of each were completed at about the same moment, so that when Mrs. Surratt was thus pinioned, she stood scarcely ten seconds, supported by those standing near her, when General Hartranft gave the signal, by clapping his hands twice, for both drops to fall, and as soon as the second and last signal was given, both fell, and Mrs. Surratt, with a jerk, fell to the full length of the rope. She was leaning over when the drop fell, and this gave a swinging motion to her body, which lasted several minutes before it assumed a perpendicular position. Her death was instantaneous; she died without a struggle. The only muscular movement discernible was a slight contraction of the left arm, which she seemed to try to disengage from behind her as the drop fell.

"After being suspended thirty minutes, she was cut down, and placed in a square wooden box or coffin, in the clothes in which she died, and was interred in the prison yard. The rope made a clean cut around her neck, fully an inch in diameter, which was black and discolored with bruised blood. The cap was not taken off her face, and she was laid in the coffin with it on, and thus has passed away from the face of the earth Mary E. Surratt. Her body, it is understood, will be given to her family for burial.

"Payne died as he has lived, at least as he has done since his arrest, bold, calm, and thoroughly composed. The only tremor exhibited by this extraordinary man during the terrible ordeal of the execution was an involuntary vibration of the muscles of his legs after the fatal drop fell. He was next in order to Mrs. Surratt in the procession of the criminals from their cells to the place of execution.

"He was supported on one side by his spiritual adviser, and on the other by a soldier, although he needed no such assistance, for he walked erect and upright, and retained the peculiar piercing expression of the eye that has ever characterized him. He was dressed in a blue flannel shirt, and pants of the same material. His brawny neck was entirely exposed, and he wore a new straw hat. He ascended the steps leading to the scaffold with the greatest ease, and took his seat on the drop with as much *sang froid* as though he was sitting down to dinner.

"Once or twice he addressed a few words in an undertone to persons close by him, and occasionally glanced at the array of soldiers and civilians spread out before him. A puff of wind blew off his hat, and he instantly turned around to see where it went to. When it was recovered and handed to him, he intimated by gesturing that he no longer required it, and it was laid aside.

"During the reading of the sentence by General Hartranft, just previous to the execution, he calmly listened, and once or twice glanced upward at the gallows, as if inspecting its construction. He submitted to the process of binding his limbs very quietly, and watched the operation with attention.

"His spiritual adviser, Rev. Dr. Gillette, advanced, a few minutes previous to the execution, and made some remarks in Payne's behalf. He thanked the different officials for the attention and kindness bestowed on Payne, and exhorted the criminal in a few impassioned words to give his entire thoughts to his future state. Payne stood immovable as a statue when the drop fell. Although next to Harold, who died the hardest, he exhibited more bodily contortions than the others while suspended. While the noose was being adjusted to his neck, Payne raised his head, and evidently desired to assist the executioner in that delicate operation.

"Probably no one of the criminals felt as great a dread of the terrible ordeal through which they were to pass as young Harold. From the time he left his cell until his soul was sent into the presence of the Almighty, he exhibited the greatest emotion, and seemed to thoroughly realize his wretched condition. His face wore an indefinable expression of anguish, and at times he trembled violently. He seemed to desire to engage in conversation with those around him while sitting in the chair awaiting execution, and his spiritual adviser, Rev. Mr. Old, was assiduous in his attentions to the wretched man.

"Harold was dressed in a black cloth coat and light pants, and wore a white shirt without any collar; he wore also a black slouch hat, which he retained on his head until it was removed to make room for the white cap. At times he looked wildly around, and his face had a haggard, anxious, inquiring expression. When the drop fell, he exhibited more tenacity of life than any of the others, and he endeavored several times to draw himself up as if for the purpose of relieving himself from the rope by which he was suspended.

"Atzeroth ascended the steps of the scaffold without difficulty, and took his seat at the south end of the drop without exhibiting any particular emotion. He was dressed in a dark gray coat and pants, and black vest and white linen shirt, without any collar; on his feet he wore a pair of woolen slippers and socks. He sat in such a position that he could see the profiles of his fellow-prisoners, and he had his hands pinioned behind him. He wore no hat, had a white handkerchief placed over his head with a tuft of hair protruding from it and spreading over his forehead.

"Directly behind him stood his spiritual adviser, who held an umbrella over him to keep off the burning rays of the sun. During the reading of the sentence by General Hartranft, he kept perfectly quiet, but his face wore an expression of unutterable woe, and he listened attentively. He wore a thin moustache and small goatee, and his face was pale and sallow. Once, and once only, he glanced around at the assembled throng, and occassionally muttered incoherent sentences, but he talked, while on the scaffold, to no one immediately around him.

"Just before his execution, his spiritual adviser, Mr. Butler, advanced and stated that Atzeroth desired to return his sincere thanks to General Hartranft and the other officials for their many acts of kindness extended toward him. He then called on God to forgive George Atzeroth, reminded him that while the wages of sin were death, that whomsoever placed their hope in the Lord Jesus Christ were not forgotten. He hoped that God would grant him a full and free forgiveness, and ended by saying: 'May the Lord God have mercy on you, and grant you his peace.'

"The handkerchief was then taken from his head, and he stood up, facing the assembled audience, directly alongside of the instrument of his death. His knees slightly trembled, and his legs were bent forward. He stood for a few moments the very embodiment of wretchedness, and then spoke a few words in an undertone to General Hartranft, after which he shook hands with his spiritual adviser and a few others near him; while he was being secured with bands, tied around his legs and arms, he kept muttering to himself, as if engaged in silent prayer.

"Suddenly he broke forth with the words, 'Gentlemen, beware who you—' and then stopped, as if with emotion; as the white cap was being placed over his head he said, 'Good-bye, gentlemen; may we all meet in the other world. God

THE EXECUTION.   345

take me now.' He muttered something loud enough for those close by him to hear, just as the drop fell, evidently not anticipating such an event at that moment. He died without apparent pain, and his neck must have been instantly broken.

"After hanging a few seconds, his stomach heaved considerably, and subsequently his legs quivered a little. His death appeared to be the easiest of any of the criminals, with the exception of Mrs. Surratt, who did not apparently suffer at all. After hanging half an hour, Atzeroth's body was taken down, it being the first one lowered, and an examination made by Surgeons Otis, Woodward, and Porter.

"About half-past eight o'clock this morning, Miss Surratt, accompanied by a female friend, again visited the White House, having been there last evening for the purpose of obtaining an interview with the President. President Johnson having given orders that he would receive no one to-day, the door-keeper stopped Miss Surratt at the foot of the steps leading up to the President's office, and would not permit her to proceed further. She then asked permission to see General Mussey, the President's Military Secretary, who promptly answered the summons, and came down stairs where Miss Surratt was standing.

"As soon as the General made his appearance, Miss Surratt threw herself upon her knees before him, catching him by the coat, with loud sobs and streaming eyes, implored him to assist her in obtaining a hearing with the President.

"General Mussey, in as tender a manner as possible, informed Miss Surratt that he could not comply with her request, as President Johnson's orders were imperative, and he would receive no one.

"Upon General Mussey's returning to his office, Miss Surratt threw herself upon the stair steps, where she remained a considerable length of time, sobbing aloud in the greatest anguish, protesting her mother's innocence, and imploring every one who came near her to intercede in her mother's behalf. While thus weeping, she declared her mother was too good and kind to be guilty of the enormous crime of which she was convicted, and asserted that if her mother was put to death she wished to die also

"The scene was heart-rending, and many of those who witnessed it, including a number of hardy soldiers, were moved to tears. Miss Surratt, having become quiet, was finally persuaded to take a seat in the East Room, and here she remained for several hours, jumping up from her seat each time the front door of the mansion was opened, evidently in hopes of seeing some one enter who could be of service to her in obtaining the desired interview with the President, or that they were the bearers of good news to her.

"Two of Harold's sisters, dressed in full mourning and heavily veiled, made their appearance at the White House shortly after Miss Surratt, for the purpose of interceding with the President in behalf of their brother. Failing to see the President, they addressed a note to Mrs. Johnson, and expressed a hope that she would not turn a deaf ear to their pleadings. Mrs. Johnson being quite sick, it was thought expedient by the ushers not to deliver the note, when, as a last expedient, the ladies asked permission to forward a note to Mrs. Patterson, the President's daughter, which privilege was not granted, as Mrs. Patterson was also quite indisposed.

"Payne, during the night, slept well for about three hours, the other portion of the night being spent in conversation with Rev. Dr. Gillette, of the First Baptist Church, who offered his services as soon as he was informed of the sentence. Payne, without showing any particular emotion, paid close attention to the advice of Dr. Gillette. Up to ten o'clock this morning, no relations or friends had been to see Payne.

"Atzeroth was very nervous throughout the night, and did not sleep, although he made several attempts. His brother was to see him yesterday afternoon, and again this morning. His aged mother, who arrived during the night, was also present. The meeting of the condemned man and his mother was very affecting, and moved some of the officers of the prison, who have become used to trying scenes, to tears.

"Rev. Dr. Butler, of the Lutheran Church, was sent for last night, and has been all night ministering to Atzeroth. **Harold was visited yesterday by Rev. Mr. Olds, of Christ**

EXECUTION OF THE ASSASSINS.

Episcopal Church, and five of his sisters, and this morning the minister and the entire family of seven sisters were present with him. Harold slept very well several hours during the night.

"Miss Surratt was with her mother several hours last night, as also Rev. Fathers Wiget and Walter, and Mr. Brophy, who were also present this morning. She slept very little, if any, and required considerable attention, suffering with cramps and pains the entire night, caused by her nervousness. The breakfast was sent to the prisoners at the usual hour this morning, but none eat, excepting Payne, who ate heartily.

"About three thousand troops were employed in guarding the building and its surroundings.

"The execution ground was a large square inclosure, called the Old Penitentiary jail yard, directly south of the Old Penitentiary building. It comprises probably three acres of ground, surrounded by a brick wall, about twenty feet in height.

"This wall is capped with white stone and surmounted with iron stakes and ropes, to prevent the guard from falling off while patrolling the tops of the wall. The Sixth Regiment Veteran Volunteers were formed on the summit of the wall during the execution, and they presented quite a picturesque appearance in their elevated position.

"The gallows occupied a position in the angle of the inclosure formed by the east wall and the Penitentiary building on the north. The First Regiment Veteran Volunteers were posted around the gallows, two sides being formed by the east wall and the Penitentiary building.

"The spectators, about two hundred in number, were congregated directly in front of the gallows, the soldiers forming a barrier between them and the place of execution. The criminals were led to the scaffold from a small door about one hundred feet from the place of execution. But for a small projection that runs south of the Penitentiary building, the gallows would be in plain view of the prisoners' cells, which are all on the first floor of the building.

"It was a noticeable incident of the execution that scarcely any Government officials or citizens were present, the spectators being nearly all connected with the trial in some capacity, or else representatives of the press.

"By permission of the authorities, the daughter of Mrs. Surratt passed the night previous to the execution with her mother, in her cell. The entire interview was of a very affecting character. The daughter remained with her mother until a short time before the execution, and when the time came for separation the screams of anguish that burst from the poor girl could be distinctly heard all over the execution ground.

"During the morning the daughter proceeded to the Metropolitan Hotel, and sought an interview with General Hancock. Finding him, she implored him in pitiable accents to get a reprieve for her mother. The general, of course, had no power to grant or obtain such a favor, and so informed the distressed girl, in as gentle a manner as possible.

"General Hancock, with the kindness that always characterizes his actions apart from the stern duties of his noble profession, did his best to assuage the mental anguish of the grief-stricken girl.

"The alleged important after-discovered testimony which Aiken, counsel for Mrs. Surratt, stated would prove her innocence, was submitted to Judge Advocate-General Holt, and, after a careful examination, he failed to discover any thing in it having a bearing on the case. This was communicated to the President, and doubtless induced him to decline to interfere in the execution of Mrs. Surratt.

"The residence of Mrs. Surratt, on H Street, north, near Sixth, remained closed after the announcement of her fate had become known.

"In the evening but a single dim light shone from one of the rooms, while within the house all was as quiet as death up to about eight o'clock, at which hour Miss Annie E. Surratt, who had been in constant attendance upon her mother, drove up to the door in a hack, accompanied by a gentleman.

"She appeared to be perfectly crushed with grief, and as she alighted from the carriage some ladies standing near were moved to tears of sympathy with the unfortunate girl whose every look and action betrayed her anguish.

"Miss Surratt, after gaining admittance to the house, fainted several times, causing great bustle and excitement among the inmates, who were untiring in their efforts to console the almost heart-broken young lady.

"From early in the evening until a late hour at night, hundreds of persons, old and young, male and female, visited the vicinity of Mrs. Surratt's residence, stopping upon the opposite side of the street, glancing over with anxious and inquiring eyes upon the house in which the conspirators met, commenting upon the fate of the doomed woman, and the circumstances connected therewith.

"During the evening not less than five hundred persons visited the spot."

CHAPTER XXV.

THE DETECTIVE POLICE AND THE ARREST OF THE ASSASSINS.

Personal Relations to President Lincoln—His Kindness and Confidence—My Order to Pursue the Conspirators—Results—Statements of Subordinates and Others.

I SHALL now proceed to give a brief official history of my connection with the arrest of the assassins of the President. For some weeks previous to the assassination I had been on duty in New York, engaged in making investigations with reference to frauds committed in the recruiting service. On Saturday morning, April 15, while in my room at the Astor House, having just risen to dress, Lieutenant L. C. Baker, who had come on from Washington the evening previous, rushed into my room and announced the fact that President Lincoln had been assassinated. This announcement called to my mind at once the various communications containing threats of assassination that had for nearly two years been received. The last advices from Washington, received early on Saturday morning, simply announced that the President still lived, but no hopes were entertained of his recovery. The feeling of indignation and sadness exhibited by my whole force, then on duty in New York, when I announced to them the fact, I have never seen equaled. We had all learned to love the President as a father. Amid all our scenes of trial, through the prejudice of loyal citizens and the passion of enemies of the Republic, and of detected criminals, we had received the kindest treatment from Mr. Lincoln. Whenever he was plied with charges against the bureau, he vindicated its character, and affirmed it to be one of the necessary institutions of the civil war.

He never hastily accepted the opinion of the highest in position, nor in a single instance arraigned the national police for its action, however loud the clamor of the victims of its argus-eyed vigilance.

INTENSE EXCITEMENT IN WASHINGTON. 353

At twelve o'clock on Saturday, April 15, I received the following dispatch from the Secretary of War:—

WASHINGTON, *April* 15. 1865.

Colonel L. C. BAKER:—
Come here immediately and see if you can find the murderer of the President.

EDWIN M. STANTON, Secretary of War.

No train left New York by which I could reach Washington before the following morning. On Sunday morning, April 16, I arrived in Washington. My interview with the Secretary of War was a sad one. As I entered the Secretary's office, and he recognized me, he turned away to hide his tears. He remarked—"Well, Baker, they have now performed what they have long threatened to do; they have killed the President. You must go to work. My whole dependence is upon you."

I made some inquiries with reference to what had been done toward the capture of the assassins, and ascertained that no direct clue even had been obtained, beyond the simple conceded fact that J. Wilkes Booth was the assassin of the President.

The popular excitement in Washington was fearfully intense. For the time the gigantic crime, and the arrest of the criminals, put into the background of interest the crisis of National affairs and the ordinary business of life. Every face which did not bear the affected anxiety or indifference of Southern sympathy, had the gloomy, mournful aspect of inexpressible, bewildering horror and grief.

The practical duties which engaged the exhausting labors of my bureau, and the results that followed, between the **murder of the President and the capture of Booth**, are narrated truthfully in the paper addressed to the Secretary of War:—

WASHINGTON CITY, *July* 7, 1866.

On the morning of April 15, 1865, while on duty in New York City, under orders from the War Department to investigate certain frauds in connection with the secret service, I first heard of the assassination of President Lincoln, and attempts to assassinate the Secretary of State. On the afternoon of the day before referred to, I received a telegram from the Secretary of War, direct.

War, to learn the particulars of the assassination, and what measures had been adopted to secure the capture of the assassins. I could learn but little beyond the simple fact that J. Wilkes Booth was the supposed assassin, and that Harrold was his accomplice. I asked if any photographs of the supposed assassins, or descriptions of their persons, had been secured or published. To my surprise I learned that nothing of the kind had been done; during the afternoon of Sunday rumors were freely circulated throughout the city connecting the name of John Surratt and others with the assassination. I immediately secured pictures of those mentioned above, and on Monday the 17th had them copied, with a full and accurate description of each assassin printed in a circular, in which I offered a reward of *Ten Thousand Dollars*. These, with their photographs and descriptions, I dispatched to a number of detective agents in all parts of the country. I also mailed large numbers to different localities. These photographs and descriptions were the first ever published or circulated. At this time it was almost impossible to obtain any information of a reliable character; the unparalleled atrocity of this terrible event, and the fact that the assassins had for the time being escaped, had seemingly paralyzed the entire community. The local detective force of New York, Philadelphia, Boston, Baltimore, and other cities, had arrived, and, with the entire military force of this department, had reported to General Augur, whose headquarters were in Washington. On Monday, April 18th, or Tuesday following, I dispatched six men of my force into Lower Maryland. After being absent four or five days, they returned, unsuccessful, toward the end of the week succeeding the assassination.

No reliable information having been obtained, so far as I knew, concerning the whereabouts of the assassins, and having become thoroughly convinced that Booth and Harrold had passed into Lower Maryland *via* Anacosta or Navy Yard Bridge, within an hour after the assassination, and being aware that nearly every rod of ground in Lower Maryland must have been repeatedly passed over by the great number of persons engaged in the search, I finally decided, in my own mind, that Booth and Harrold must have crossed the river into Virginia. After crossing they could not go toward Richmond or down the Potomac, as the Federal troops were then in possession of that entire section of country; the only possible way left open for escape was to take a south-western course, in order to reach the mountains of Tennessee or Kentucky, where such aid could be secured as would insure their ultimate escape from the country. On examining the map, I ascertained where the principal crossings of the Rappahannock were located. On Sunday morning, April 23, I asked Major Eckert to furnish me with a competent telegraph operator, and necessary apparatus, with the intention of opening an office at Port Tobacco. This request was complied with, as indicated by the note appended:—

OFFICE UNITED STATES MILITARY TELEGRAPH,
WAR DEPARTMENT, WASHINGTON, D. C., *April* 23, 1865.

COLONEL BAKER:—

This will introduce to you Mr. Beckwith, a cipher operator, of great scouting experience, who may be of great service to you, in addition to his telegraphing.

I also send with him Mr. Cheney, a repair man, to make speedy connections wherever it may be found necessary. Please furnish him a side-arm.

Yours truly,

Thos. F. Eckert.

Mr. Beckwith was sent to me on Sunday afternoon. This operator, with two of my detective agents, Hubbard and Woodall, left Washington on Sunday afternoon or evening, on board the steamer *Keyport*. They did not reach the landing at Port Tobacco until nearly morning on Monday. There was brought to my headquarters a colored man, who I was informed had important information respecting the assassins. On questioning the colored man, I found he had seen two men, answering the description of Booth and Harrold, entering a small boat in the vicinity of Swan's Point. After a series of questions propounded and answered by this colored man, giving a description of the assassins, I was surprised to learn from him that he had three days previously communicated precisely the same information to some soldier-men (as he expressed it) then engaged in searching for the assassins, but that the soldier-men called him a damned black, lying nigger, and did not believe his story. This information, with my preconceived theory as to the movements of the assassins, decided my course. I wrote a note to Major-General Hancock, then in command of this Department, requesting him to send me a detachment of twenty-five cavalry, under charge of a competent, discreet, and reliable officer, to report at my headquarters for duty as soon as possible. I then called Lieutenant-Colonel Conger and Lieutenant L. B. Baker, formerly of my regiment (the First District Cavalry), and informed them that I had information concerning Booth and Harrold, and spreading a map of Virginia on my table, with a pencil I marked out the point where I supposed the assassins crossed, and their course after crossing the ferry at Port Conway. I then remarked, "I will give you the cavalry, and don't come back without them, for they are certainly in that vicinity." About one o'clock, or soon after (the precise time I cannot now recollect), a squad of cavalry rode up in front of my headquarters; the officer in command dismounted, and entered the office and inquired, "Is this Colonel Baker's headquarters?" Some one standing by said "Yes." I then said, "I am Colonel Baker." The officer said, "I am ordered to report to you." I asked the officer his name. He replied, "Lieutenant Dougherty." I asked, "What cavalry have you got?" He replied, "A detachment from the Sixteenth New York Cavalry." I called Lieutenant Dougherty to where Conger and Baker were standing, and said, "Lieutenant, you will act under the orders and direction of these two men," referring to Conger and Baker. "You are going after Booth, and have got the only reliable information concerning his whereabouts." Some further conversation occurred respecting the cavalry, rations, forage, transportation, &c. As I intended and did place the control and management of the expedition solely and exclusively under my own men, I did not deem it necessary to give Lieutenant Dougherty any instructions whatever, and only called to my assistance the military to protect my men in the execution of my orders and instructions. This had usually been the practice in my bureau for two or three years previously. The unsettled condition of affairs in the section of Virginia to be visited by the expedition made it necessary that a military force should accompany it, otherwise my plans for the capture of the assassins could and would have been much more promptly and satisfactorily carried out and consummated by my detectives—for Booth would have been brought to Washington *alive*.

The expedition left Washington on the afternoon of Monday, April 24. The facts of the capture, killing of Booth, &c., having been detailed by those directly connected with and actual participators in the same, I shall conclude my statement by briefly referring to what occurred after the capture. On Wednesday, April 26, about 5 o'clock P. M., Colonel Conger arrived at my headquarters with the first information respecting the result of the capture of the assassins. I immediately took him to the house of the Secretary of War, when he detailed briefly the facts of the pursuit, capture, and killing of Booth, &c., at the same time handing to the Secretary of War the effects, or articles, taken from the dead body of Booth. By direction of the Secretary of War, with Colonel Conger, I went immediately to Alexandria, to intercept and take charge of the prisoner Harrold, and the dead body of Booth, which since the capture had been in charge of Lieutenant Baker. About 12 o'clock, the steamer *Ide*, with the assassins, arrived at Alexandria. I went on board, and took charge of the management and disposition of the prisoner Harrold and body of Booth. It is a well-known fact, with few exceptions, that as soon as it was publicly known that the assassins were captured, those that had been the most persistent in forcing their claims before the committee appointed to investigate the matter, entirely ceased and abandoned all efforts to procure, or even assist in procuring, the requisite proofs to convict the assassins. I desire to state positively that the information that prompted me to send the expedition to Port Conway was not, in any way, shape, or manner, derived from the War Department, or from any information or intimation furnished by any one connected with the search for the assassins. I neither saw nor knew the contents of any telegrams, letter, or memorandums, referring in the slightest manner to the fact that the murderers had crossed the Potomac River. I desire further to state that the information before referred to in this statement, and my belief and preconceived theory as to the intended movement of the assassins, was the sole and only incentive that prompted the sending out of the expedition which resulted so successfully. My honest conviction is, and it is the opinion repeatedly expressed by those in authority, that, had not this expedition reached the Garrett Farm as they did, on Wednesday morning, before daylight, Booth and Harrold would have escaped entirely.

Respectfully submitted,
L. C. BAKER,
Late Brig.-Gen., and Pro.-Mar. War Department.

It is well known among the authorities at Washington, that the preliminary steps and investigations, with reference to the assassination, had already been taken, before my arrival there, at General Augur's headquarters. A commission, consisting of Colonel Wells, Colonel Foster, and Colonel Alcott, was then in session, and all information, from whatever sources derived, was laid before this commission. The enormity of the crime committed by the assassins, and the anxiety of the public for their arrest, had divested my mind entirely of any thing like rivalry in the investigations going on. I was willing, and indeed anxious, to work and cooperate with any officer or officers in the prosecution of this investigation. I was even willing to place myself under the advice, counsel, and direction of any officer, whether military or civil. Accordingly, I repaired to General Augur's headquarters, and asked some questions with regard to the information already obtained. I was informed that neither my services nor the services of my force were required; that a positive clue had been obtained as to who the assassins were, and their whereabouts. After making some further inquiries, to all of which I received either evasive or insulting replies, I determined to set on foot an investigation under my own direction. With this view, I immediately obtained photographs of the supposed assassins, and had a large number of them copied, which I sent in all directions. I believe the first clue obtained as to the assassins was derived from a man named Fletcher, employed in the livery stable of Mr. Naylor, in Washington. Harrold had, on the afternoon previous to the evening of the assassination, hired a horse at Mr. Naylor's stable. Mr. Naylor, fearing that Harrold would run away with the horse, had sent Fletcher to watch him. The evidence of Fletcher, given before the commission on the trial of the assassins, shows that he went to the Navy Yard bridge. The bridge being guarded by a military force, and having no pass, he could not cross; but he learned that two suspicious characters had just crossed on horseback. He returned to General Augur's headquarters about one o'clock on Saturday morning, and reported the fact. Here begins the first series of blunders in this attempted search for the assassins. Fletcher's statement was entirely disregarded. No steps were taken by those in possession of this information to follow up the clue thus given until sixteen hours afterward. This delay enabled the assassins to get entirely beyond the reach of those sent in pursuit. On Sunday, at ten o'clock, I received the following information:—

BALTIMORE, *April* 16, 1865.

The following information has just been received from Polk Gardner, a lad who left Upper Marlborough, Prince George County, on Friday night, to come here to see his father, who is dying. On the road, about four miles from Washington, he met a man on a roan horse, who inquired the way to Upper Marlborough, and whether he had seen a man riding rapidly in that direction. About two miles from Washington he met another man, on a bay horse, who also inquired the road to Upper Marlborough, and asked him if he had seen a man riding in that direction. The last named then rode on rapidly. This occurred at eleven o'clock, or a little later.

The steamer *Commerce* left here yesterday morning at six o'clock, without passengers, but with a guard and shrewd officer, with orders to make her usual trip and take in all passengers that presented themselves, and then secure them and bring them all here. As she goes to Upper Marlborough, stopping at Benedict and other places, it is not unlikely that the guilty parties may be caught.

I immediately sent for Polk Gardner, and had his statement taken. The description given of the horses—to wit, one bay and one roan—corresponded exactly with the description furnished by Fletcher of the horses hired from Naylor's stable. This, with Fletcher's statement, furnished to my mind conclusive evidence that the assassins had gone in the direction of Lower Maryland.

It is proper to state, in this connection, that a large military force, consisting of a whole brigade of infantry and over one thousand cavalry, together with over two hundred detectives and citizens, had gone into Lower Maryland. My force being small at the time, many of them being engaged in the Western States in pursuit of criminals, I sent a small detachment of detectives with photographs and circulars into Lower Maryland. They were absent four or five days, and returned with no clue to the assassins. The community were becoming impatient at the delay in the capture of the assassins, and beginning to fear that they would finally escape. On Sunday morning, the 23d of April, I sent the following note to Major-General Hancock:—

WAR DEPARTMENT, WASHINGTON CITY, *April* 24, 1865.

Major-General HANCOCK, United States Army:—

GENERAL—I am directed by the Secretary of War to apply to you for a

THE PURSUIT BEGUN.

small cavalry force of twenty-five (25) men, well mounted, to be commanded by a reliable and discreet commissioned officer.

Can you furnish them? and if so, will you please direct the officer commanding the squad to report to me with the men at No. 217 Pennsylvania Avenue, opposite Willard's Hotel, at once?

I am, Sir, your obedient servant,
(Signed) L. C. BAKER,
Colonel, and Agent War Department.

Official:
DUNCAN S. WALKER, A. A. General.

In response to this communication, the cavalry arrived at my headquarters. I immediately called into my private office two of my detective officers—Colonel Conger and Lieutenant Baker—and informed them that I had information that Booth and Harrold had crossed the Potomac, at the same time pointing out with a pencil the place on a map where they had crossed, and where I believed they would be found. Lieutenant Dougherty, of the Sixteenth New York Cavalry, who commanded this squad, was introduced to Colonel Conger and Lieutenant Baker, with the following remark:—"You are going in pursuit of the assassins. You have the latest reliable information concerning them. You will act under the orders of Colonel Conger."

I then dispatched a messenger to the quartermaster at Sixth Street wharf, with a request to furnish a boat as soon as possible, to take a squad of cavalry down the Potomac. The messenger returned, bringing the following communication from Captain Allen, the quartermaster:—

ASSISTANT QUARTERMASTER'S OFFICE,
RIVER TRANSPORTATION, SIXTH STREET WHARF,
WASHINGTON, D. C., *April* 22, 1865.

Colonel L. C. BAKER, Agent War Department:—

SIR—I have the honor to inform you that I will have a boat ready for you at four P. M. this day.

Very respectfully, your obedient servant,
A. S. ALLEN,
Captain and Assistant Quartermaster.

The expedition left Washington on board the steamer *Ide*, about four o'clock. The facts and incidents connected with the pursuit and capture of the assassins, from this time until the body of Booth was returned to Washington, and placed in my possession, I will leave to be detailed by Colonel Conger and Lieutenant Baker:—

WASHINGTON, D. C., *December* 24, 1866.

To the Hon. E. M. STANTON, Secretary of War:—

SIR—Under General Order No. 164, in reference to the rewards offered by the Secretary of War for the apprehension of Booth and Harrold, the assassins of the late President, E. J. Conger, late a lieutenant-colonel, and L. B. Baker, late a lieutenant, beg to submit the following narrative of the events of that service:—

They were important actors in the pursuit and capture of those parties, and themselves did, and saw others do, every thing that went to make up that enterprise, from its inception in the brain of its projector and master-spirit, until the bodies of the two fugitives, living and dead, were delivered into the hands of the Department of War; and it is that this narrative may, in some degree, help to the proper appreciation of the services of the parties to whose hands the chief of the Detective Bureau committed the execution of his plans.

General Baker, under the orders of the Department, reported at Washington for duty Sunday morning, April 16th. He was accompanied by Lieutenant Baker, and joined by Colonel Conger the Monday following. Both of these gentlemen, then private citizens, were taken into service by General Baker, and assigned, under his immediate orders, to the special duty of the subject of this statement.

Upon the arrival of General Baker, he found the entire field occupied by a numerous corps of detectives, whom the importance of the service and the calls of the Government had assembled from various points, and in whose hands seemed to be all the various sources of information, and the clues to all that was known or suspected, then at command.

He found, upon approaching these parties, that they were unwilling to impart to him their information, receive him into confidence, and share with him their counsels; and with such slender information as was then in the personal possession of the Secretary of War, the chief of the Military Bureau was obliged to take the case up from the beginning; and after the field had been gone over and gleaned by other hands and the footprints of the assassins effaced or lost.

It was an accepted fact that Booth was the immediate assassin of the President, and that Harrold was his accomplice, and shared his flight or place of concealment.

A careful analysis of all that could be ascertained satisfied General Baker that these parties had fled, and would probably attempt to escape across the Lower Potomac; and his first efforts were directed to securing the accurate likenesses of Booth and Harrold, as well as of others, and a full and minute description of their persons. These likenesses were taken, and printed—the first and only ones issued of these parties—he caused to be extensively circulated in every direction likely to be taken by the fugitives; in particular

GENERAL BAKER AT WORK.

Lieutenant Baker was detailed, with five or six active and reliable men, to traverse Lower Maryland and distribute them. He was also to examine and note every possible indication of the presence of the parties, or other suspected persons, from which labor he returned the Saturday following, having explored the whole region unsuccessfully, while the chief remained at headquarters, with Colonel Conger and other assistants, constantly, anxiously, and exhaustively collating and exploring every outside rumor, theory, and source of information that sleepless labor, vigilance, and experienced sagacity could compass.

It is out of place here, perhaps, to refer to the weight of indignant and impotent grief that was added to a nation's sorrow for its loss, as the conviction settled upon the hearts of men that the murderers had escaped—that the resources and ingenuity of the police of the nation, aroused by a huge crime, and made active by the temptation of a great money reward, were baffled.

While this feeling was hardening into certainty, the energy and determination of the chief of the military detectives were preparing more effective efforts.

On Monday, the 24th, General Baker, steady in the opinion he had formed, sent one of his men, Theodore Woodall, with a telegraph operator, into Lower Maryland with his instruments, to be attached to the wire at given points, and thus enable him to communicate, without loss of time, with that region. Woodall, while on this duty, fell in with ——————, an old negro, whose statement so impressed him, that, instead of sending it by telegraph to Washington, he took and delivered him bodily to his superior.

The examination of the colored man satisfied General Baker that he had at last struck the trail of the fleeing murderers. That they had crossed the Potomac, near Matthews Point, on Saturday night, the 22d of April, and that Booth was lame.

A hasty interview with the Secretary of War, and Colonel Conger was sent with a note from General Baker to General Hancock for a commissioned officer and twenty-five cavalry, to report immediately to General Baker, for duty under his command, while Lieutenant Baker made the necessary arrangements with the Quartermaster's Department for transportation down the Potomac. Upon their return from these duties, General Baker fully explained to them the information on which he was acting, and, with the aid of a map, pointed out with care the place of Booth and Harrold's crossing and their probable course and plans, and told them he was about to send them in pursuit; that they were to have full charge of the expedition, and that the cavalry force would go, subject to their orders; that the expedition was to start the moment it could be got ready. It was to go down to Belle Plains, and, if there was no dock for landing at that point, to go to Aquia Creek, and if the dock had been destroyed there, that the horses must be made to take the water, for in no event must they go below; once on land, they must act on their own judgment and discretion; that they must, if possible, discover the trail of Booth and Harrold, and, once upon it, must push forward to their capture over all obstacles; that the cavalry would go with nothing but their arms, and men and horses must not be spared; that he knew Conger and Lieutenant Baker, and had entire confidence in their judgment, sagacity, and courage, and committed the enterprise fully to them.

About two P. M. of the 24th, Lieutenant Dougherty of the Sixteenth New York Cavalry, reported to General Baker for orders, and was by him introduced to Colonel Conger and Lieutenant Baker; General Baker told him that he was to be sent with him in pursuit of Booth and Harrold; that they had full information and instructions as to the service, and would have the direction of it, and he must render them all the assistance in his power. No other or farther orders were given by General Baker to Lieutenant Dougherty, nor were explanations made to him about the service by General Baker, nor by Colonel Conger nor Lieutenant Baker.

The party left Washington about sundown on the evening of the 24th, on steamer *Ide;* arrived at Belle Plains about ten in the evening and landed. Colonel Conger, while in service, having been the senior of Lieutenant Baker in the same cavalry regiment, and of large experience, by tacit consent as between them, took the main direction of affairs when present. In his absence, Lieutenant Baker was the acknowledged director of the expedition.

Colonel Conger refused to have an advanced guard, but himself and Lieutenant Baker took the lead. At the divergence of the roads, a mile and a half from the river, the party took that which led to the Rappahannock. Conger went to almost every house they passed during the night. He called himself Boyd, a brother of the Maryland Boyd, who had been killed. Said his party were rebels, trying to avoid the Union soldiers and escape into the interior. That they had been scattered, and he had lost some of his companions, one of whom was lame, and they were anxious to learn of his whereabouts, &c. He inquired who had crossed the Rappahannock, and where; and the location of all the crossings, whether by ferry or ford; also about all the doctors, as they supposed Booth would seek the aid of some of them. Nothing was learned during the night. Daylight disclosed the character of the party, and changed the tactics of the leaders.

The party arrived, without incident or information bearing on the service, at Point Conway on the Rappahannock, opposite Port Royal, about twelve o'clock, when they halted for thirty minutes.

While resting here, Lieutenant Baker went to the ferry, near which he fell in with a man who gave his name as Rollins. A conversation ensued, in which Lieutenant Baker showed him the likeness of Booth, which Rollins recognized as one of the party who crossed the day before, except that that man had no *moustache.* He also recognized the likeness of Harrold. Colonel Conger was sent for, and took Rollins's statement, now on file in the Judge-Advocate-General's office. The substance was, that Booth and Harrold arrived there the day before, late in the afternoon, in an old wagon driven by a negro, and wanted to go on. Booth was lame, and would give him, Rollins, ten dollars in gold to take them on to Bowling Green, fifteen miles toward Orange Court House. Meantime three rebels came up on horseback, Bainbridge, Ruggles, and Jett, who had a conversation with Booth and Harrold, and agreed to help them on, and did so. As some of that party resided at Bowl

HALF-WAY HOUSE—BOWLING GREEN.

ing Green, it was supposed that Booth and Harrold would be taken there by them. Rollins was willing to go as a guide for Conger and Baker, and was put under arrest to save appearances.

The expedition was ferried over the river with as little delay as possib'e, and pickets posted to prevent any parties leaving Port Royal till the party was again in motion. After passing the river a short distance, two men were discovered on horseback, as if observing the party, to whom Conger and Baker gave chase. After pursuing them about two miles, they plunged into the woods and disappeared.

The command reached the "Half-way House," so-called, a solitary building, about nine in the evening. The occupants, four or five young women, raised and kept up such a clamor, that Conger's and Baker's inquiries were a "pursuit of knowledge under difficulties," until one of them said that they were looking for a party that had committed an outrage on a girl, which led to their being told that a party of five men, describing them, with three horses, had called there the day before and taken drinks, and that they all came back but one. The supposition was that Booth, the principal, had been left at Bowling Green. Once more in the saddle, horses exhausted, and men weary, hungry, and sleepy, the command pushed forward, and reached Bowling Green between eleven and twelve o'clock.

The one hotel, where Booth might be, a large, rambling, utterly silent and dark building, was surrounded by the dismounted cavalry, and a vain effort made to arouse the inmates, if occupants it had.

A negro finally conducted Colonel Conger to a shanty in the rear, where another negro told him that a woman and her daughter occupied the tavern, and that Jett was there also.

Colonel Conger entered the house and found his way to Jett's room and arrested him, when he was joined by Baker and Lieutenant Dougherty. Jett was alarmed, wanted to see the commander of the party, and was referred to Colonel Conger. Baker and Lieutenant Dougherty withdrew, when Jett said he knew what Colonel Conger wanted; he wanted Booth and Harrold, and he, Jett, could take him and show him where they were.

He wanted assurances of personal safety, and Colonel Conger gave them. Jett dressed, and on joining Lieutenant Baker, he told them, Conger and Baker, that Booth and Harrold were about three miles from Port Royal, at Garrett's. And on being told that the party had just passed along there, he was disconcerted, for he had supposed that they came from Richmond, and found that their coming from Port Royal had frightened Booth and Harrold away, as it had.

Upon remounting the party, it was found that one or two of the men had straggled, and two or three others were left to look them up. The object of the return was not made known to Lieutenant Dougherty until near Garrett's house.

The party reached the lane that led from the road to Garrett's house about two A. M., of the 20th. During the time that Conger and Baker were exploring the way to the house, the men had dismounted, thrown themselves on the ground, and gone to sleep; and it was with much exertion that they were aroused and got in motion again. The house was surrounded, and, in response to the summons of Lieutenant Baker, the elder Garrett appeared, struck a light, and said, in reply to Baker's inquiry, that the two men had gone off into the woods. At the approach of Colonel Conger, a son of Garrett's came up and said the men were in the barn, and offered to show them where they were. The party proceeded to the barn, Lieutenant Baker with a lighted candle, and having the young Garrett in custody.

The barn, with the buildings near it, were as promptly and effectually surrounded as the condition and discipline of the command would permit.

The barn, as it was called, was in fact an old tobacco-house, perhaps sixty feet square, weather-boarded, with large doors in the middle of the front side, and in one of which was a smaller door; a barn, a shed, with other buildings, were near this building. Colonel Conger and Lieutenant Dougherty placed the dismounted soldiers about the buildings, while Lieutenant Baker with young Garrett approached the door with the candle, when young Garrett remembered that the door was locked on the outside. Another young Garrett then came up and was sent by Baker for the key. When the key arrived, Lieutenant Baker in a loud voice said to Garrett, "Go in and tell the men to come out and surrender." He said he was afraid; the men were armed with pistols and carbines, and would shoot him. Lieutenant Baker, then addressing the parties inside, said, "We are going to send in the men in whose custody you are to demand your arms and surrender." Baker then unlocked the door, and Garrett, in much trepidation, went in; and Baker heard a mumbled conversation inside, Booth finally saying, "Get out of here or I will shoot you. Damn you, you have betrayed me," and Garrett came back much frightened, and was let out, saying that Booth was going to shoot him, and "You may burn the barn." Something had been before said about burning the barn, partly to alarm Booth and Harrold, and as one of the means that might ultimately be resorted to, to which young Garrett had objected.

In the mean time, it had occurred to Conger and Baker, that in the event of an attempt to escape by Booth and Harrold at the door, and which would bring on a general contest, that it would be very likely to draw the fire of the soldiers nearest, which would endanger them quite as much as it would Booth and Harrold, and as a precaution for their own safety, they removed all the soldiers from the front of the building, and all whose posts were such as to command a view of the area immediately about the door.

Colonel Conger also found on his rounds one man who refused to do duty, because he was without arms—took none with him, but was supplied with a pistol on the ground. It was also found necessary to place a rail or pole, or some other object, on the ground, to indicate to each man his position, and they were ordered by Colonel Conger, personally, not to leave their posts on any pretext whatever without orders. Lieutenant Dougherty was most of the time, in the early part of the affair, at the barn, and took a position under an open shed, not far from the building; and there consulted about burning the barn. Colonel Conger had ordered one of the young Garretts to deposit a quantity of brush against an angle of the barn, but at a point where he did not intend to fire it, and for the purpose of distracting the attention of Booth, and to mislead him.

Understanding what Garrett was doing, Booth threatened to shoot him if he did not desist. He also twice offered to Lieutenant Baker that if he would withdraw his men fifty yards he would come out and fight him.

Harrold finally came to the door, offered to surrender, and Lieutenant Baker opened it, took him by the hands, pulled him out, called Lieutenant Dougherty and turned him over to him.

As a more effective means to insure the capture of Booth, it was finally determined to set the building on fire. There was on the floor a quantity of litter, thrown in a loose pile against one side near an angle. From an opening at this Colonel Conger drew out some straw, twisted it, set it on fire, and instantly the whole mass was in flames. Under the eye of Colonel Conger, Booth immediately approached the fire, with a carbine in both hands, as if to fire, and cast his eye up and down the opening between the boards, but with the intense light between him and the opening, and the darkness without, it was impossible for him to see any thing outside. He paused, dropped his hands, his head fell, as if in thought, and he then turned and went toward the door. Colonel Conger immediately started around the building, to reach the same point, when, on his way, he heard a pistol-shot, and upon going round he found Lieutenant Baker standing over the body of Booth, near the center of the building, and where he obviously had been in no position to injure anybody. Colonel Conger at first supposed, and so said, that Booth had shot himself.

At the moment of firing the barn, Lieutenant Baker opened the door, and saw Booth just as he turned from the fire, when he dropped his crutch, and came with a rapid, halting walk, toward the door; when within twelve or fifteen feet of the door, with his carbine in his hand, he received the shot, and fell. Baker rushed to him, seized him by the arm, and was there found by Conger. Lieutenant Baker saw that the shot was from some one outside, and remarked to Conger that "the man who fired it should go back to Washington under arrest."

Sergeant Boston Corbitt, who fired the shot, had been placed by Colonel Conger about thirty feet from the barn, with orders not to leave his post on any pretext. Yet he did leave it, and approach the barn, when without order, pretext or excuse, he shot Booth.

The communications from the party of Conger and Baker, to Booth and Harrold, in the barn, were made entirely through Lieutenant Baker. It is believed that no other one of the party addressed them. Much more passed between them than is stated above. Among other things, Booth said to Baker, whom he addressed as "Captain," "I could have shot you five or six times, but I believe you to be a brave and honorable man, and I will not hurt you."

To the offers of Booth to come out and fight, Lieutenant Baker replied that "we did not come to fight you but to capture you."

The few words and incoherent mutterings of the dying Booth are of no value in this narrative. Nor does it seem requisite to correct and contradict, to any great extent, the statements of some of the parties present, as to the details of the transaction, and their own part in it. Lieutenant Dougherty was the mere commander of the soldiers, under Colonel Conger or Lieutenant Baker, the former of whom often gave orders directly to them. At the barn, Lieutenant Dougherty took no part in the communications with Booth and Harrold, and was absent from the door when Booth was shot.

As soon after the termination of the affair as possible, Colonel Conger, in possession of Booth's diary, papers, &c., started for Washington, where he reported to General Baker, about four P. M. of the 26th, leaving Lieutenant Baker with the body of Booth, and Harrold under arrest, under the escort of Lieutenant Dougherty and the cavalry, to make their slower way back, which was accomplished with little delay, the party arriving before daylight of the 27th.

On Wednesday afternoon, April 26th, about five o'clock, Colonel Conger came to my headquarters, and, in a low whisper, announced the capture of Booth and Harrold, adding that the former was shot. It is not often that I am unbalanced by tidings of any sort; but I sprang to my feet, and across the room, and felt like raising a shout of joy over the triumph of justice, and the relief to millions of burdened hearts which would attend the tidings over the land. I immediately called for a carriage, took Colonel Conger with me, and drove to the house of the Secretary of War. He had been very despondent regarding the capture, and had often spoken of the disgrace it would be if the base assassins should escape. When I entered the room he was lying upon a sofa. I had in my hand Booth's two pistols, his belt, knife, and compass — the latter all covered with tallow, where he had held the light up at night, to see in what direction he was going—his pipe, and his diary. I rushed into the room, and said, "We have got Booth." Secretary Stanton was distinguished during the whole war for his coolness, but I had never seen such an exhibition of it in my life as at that time. He put his hands over his eyes, and lay for nearly a moment without saying a word. Then he got up and put on his coat very coolly. In the mean time I had laid on his table all the effects that had been taken from Booth. He asked where he was captured. I said, "Near Port Conway, beyond the Rappahannock in Virginia. Here are the things found on Booth's body." Colo-

nel Conger gave the Secretary a brief statement of the capture. The Secretary directed me to take a boat and go to Alexandria and meet the boat that was bringing the body up. Accordingly I proceeded to Alexandria, and at twenty minutes to eleven o'clock the steamer *Ide*, having on board the assassin Harrold and the dead body of Booth, with Lieutenant Baker in charge, arrived. The Secretary had directed that the boat conveying the assassins should go directly to the Navy Yard, and that the prisoner Harrold and the body of Booth should be placed on board a gunboat, as will be shown by the following order:—

WAR DEPARTMENT, WASHINGTON CITY, *April* 26, 1865.
To the Commandant of the Washington Navy Yard:—

Let Colonel Baker come into the Navy Yard wharf and alongside the ironclad to place one or two prisoners on board.

EDWIN M. STANTON, Secretary of War.

We proceeded to the Navy Yard, and at the dead hour of the night disembarked our prisoner, put him in double irons, and confined him in the hold of the vessel, where a number of other prisoners, arrested for their supposed connection with the assassination, had been already some days confined. The body of Booth was placed on deck, in charge of a marine guard. It had been securely sewed up in a blanket before it left the Garrett farm. On the following morning a *post-mortem* examination was held, in order to the proper identification of the body. Dr. May, a physician of Washington, who had some two years before removed a tumor from Booth's neck, was called in as a witness. The scar of this tumor was readily found by Dr. May, and his testimony, with that of six or seven others, as to the identification, placed the question of indentity beyond all cavil. Afterward Dr. Barnes, the Surgeon-General of the United States Army, with an assistant, cut from Booth's neck a section of the spine through which the ball passed. This section is now on exhibition at the Government Medical Museum at Washington. This was the only mutilation of J. Wilkes Booth that ever occurred, notwithstanding the numerous reports that his head was cut off and sent to Europe or Canada. On Thursday, the 27th, I was sent for by the Secretary of War, and directed to make a disposition of the body of Booth. In compliance with these instructions, with the assistance of Lieutenant L. B. Baker, I disposed of the body, as related on another page, and also the circumstances connected with the trial of the assassins.

CHAPTER XXVI.

LETTERS ON THE ASSASSINATION.

Jacob Thompson—Volunteer Suggestions respecting the Assassin's Hiding-Places before his Death, and the Disposal of his Remains afterward—Threats of more Assassinations—A Mysterious Letter—J. H. Surratt.

I SHALL now copy a few of the many letters from different parts of the North, called forth by the exciting tragedy at our capital, the most of which were addressed to the Secretary of War, and by him placed in my hands. Their chief value and interest arises from the expressions of feeling they furnish, and the manifold suggestions respecting the discovery and disposal of the homicide.

The first communication relates to Jacob Thompson, for whose arrest subsequently a reward of $25,000 was offered.

HARTFORD, CONNECTICUT, *April* 18, 1865.

Hon. E. M. STANTON, Secretary of War, Washington:—

DEAR SIR—I was yesterday told a story, by a young man from New York, implicating one George Thompson, a companion of Booth, and, I believe, an actor in Laura Keene's Theatre, in the assassination of the President and Secretary Seward; will write further about it if you think advisable. Hoping this may be serviceable in discovering the guilty assassin,

I am, very respectfully, yours,

WM. O.

Temple Street.

HARTFORD, CONNECTICUT, *April* 18, 1865.

W. O. SUMNER, JR.:—

States that he has been told a story implicating one George Thompson, a companion of Booth, in the murder of President Lincoln.

WAR DEPARTMENT, WASHINGTON, *April* 22, 1865.

Respectfully referred to Colonel L. C. Baker, Agent, &c., for his information, action, and report.

By order of the Secretary of War,

H. S. BURNETT, Judge-Advocate.

The indorsement on the back of the next letter will explain its import.

BUFFALO, NEW YORK, *April* 18, 1865.

Hon. E. M. STANTON, Secretary of War, Washington, D. C.:—

MY DEAR SIR—Business has called me to Toronto, C. W., several times within the past two months, and while there I have seen and heard some things, knowledge of which may be of service to the Government.

About five weeks since I saw at the Queen's Hotel, at Toronto, a letter written by the late John Y. Beale just previous to his execution, which, after speaking of his mock trial, unjust sentence, the judicial murder that was to be perpetrated by his execution, &c., called upon Jacob Thompson to vindicate his character before his countrymen of the South, and expressed his belief that his death would be speedily and terribly avenged. The letter itself was addressed to Colonel J. Thompson, Confederate Commissioner at Toronto, but the superscription upon the envelope (which was in a different handwriting from the body of the letter) read simply, J. Thompson, Toronto, Canada. This circumstance caused it to be delivered to a Mr. Thompson for whom it was not intended. I was permitted to peruse but not to copy the letter. I was informed at that time that the friends of Beale were banded together for the double purpose of avenging his death and aiding the Rebel Government. I have heard the same statement repeated many times since, and have frequently been told by citizens of Toronto, that some great mischief was being plotted by Beale's friends and other refugees in Canada. More than a month General Dix's name was mentioned in my hearing in connection with the threatened vengeance. I regarded all such stories as idle tales unworthy of notice, consequently I never repeated them. Last Friday evening, while sitting in the office of the Queen's Hotel, I overheard a conversation between some persons sitting near me, which convinced me that the plan to assassinate the President was known to some at least of the refugees in Canada. The party was mourning over the late rebel reverses; commenting also upon the execution of Beale, the extradition of Burley, the discharge of the raiders, &c.; after which they endeavored to cheer themselves after this fashion: "We'll make the damned Yankees howl yet." "I'll wager, boys, that we'll get better news in forty-eight hours." "I reckon, by God, that Jeff. Davis will live as long as Abe Lincoln." "Old Abe won't hang Davis." "We'll have something from Washington that will make people stare." "Won't the damned Yankees curse us more than ever." I do not pretend to give the exact language of any of the parties, but expressions like those above quoted were of frequent occurrence during the conversation. I took very little notice of the party. Their words at the time appeared to me to be simply profane and vulgar, implying idle threats which could never be executed. Some of the party had evidently been drinking freely. They were all strangers to me. The next morning (Saturday, April 15), when I received the news of the assassination, I could not help feeling that the party I had heard the night before were implicated in the act. I met two of them in company with Ben Young, and one or two others of the St. Alban's raiders, on Saturday, in the bar-room of the Queen's. One remarked, "Good news for us this morning," and another, "Damn well done, but not quite enough of it." And as they raised their glasses, one of them said, "Here's to Andy Johnson's turn next," which was replied to, "Yes, damn his soul." On relating this circumstance to Hon. E. G. Spaulding and others, they were of opinion that I should communicate them to your Department. For my own part, I beg to refer to Hon. Ira Harris, of the Senate, and Hon. John A. Griswold, of the House.

I am, my dear Sir, very truly yours, G. S. O.

Mr. O. is a respectable lawyer in this city, and his statements are entitled to credit.

E. G. G.,
Buffalo, N. Y.

From G. S. O.

April 18, 1865.

To Secretary of War:—

States that while at Toronto, C. W., five weeks ago, he saw a letter written by John Y. Beale to Colonel Jacob Thompson, Confederate Commissioner at Toronto, expressing, among other things, his belief that his death would be speedily and terribly revenged. Was informed that the friends of Beale were banded to avenge his death. Respectfully referred to Colonel Baker for his information.

H. S. BURNETT,
Judge-Advocate, &c.

I received several missives like the following :—

BLODGET MILLS, N. Y., *April* 19, 1865.

Colonel L. O. BAKER, Agent of War Department at Washington:—

DEAR SIR—I have been engaged with different traveling companies for some eight or ten years. I know the habits of them pretty well. I used to be acquainted with J. Wilkes Booth. I don't think there is a theatre or circus company of any note but what I am more or less acquainted with. I am so well acquainted with that class of people that I think I could be of some use in tracking him out. If I had the means I should have been after him before now. I am at your service if you think I can be of any use to you.

From your obedient servant,

S. D. S.

P. S.—I could find out things from that class of people that those unacquainted with them could not so readily.

S. D. S.

Astrologists and spiritualists offered the Government the benefit of their prophetic gifts :—

LAFAYETTE, IND., *April* 23, 1865.

Mr. E. M. S.:—

DEAR SIR—I wish to say a few words to you in regard to the whereabouts of Booth, who now lays concealed in a house in the State of Virginia, near the town of Middleburg, a little northeast of the Town House, one story, cottage style, roof very steep, back of the house high hills, in front a garden laid out into squares. The man of the house is tall and straight, of sandy complexion and sore eyes. If I had means to go to the south part of the State to consult with a friend of mine, I think that we could draw a diagram of the exact location and send to you, but I am poor. I have had thieves caught through my way of telling things. I have been put in prison for telling the same, and life threatened also. If you should think this of any importance, please answer. If I can get means to go and see my friend, w will send you a correct diagram of the house and place of concealment. It won't cost much to try. Sir, please not mention this to no one but you friends. You may not have any faith in this, but *try*.

Yours truly,

H. F.

Threats of additional assassination followed the murder of Mr. Lincoln:—

TANNER, CANADA, *April* 20, 1865.

To ANDREW JOHNSON, President of United States, or other authority:—

With certainty I state to you that John A. Payne and thirteen others are sworn to murder Andrew Johnson, E. M. Stanton, and L. S. Fisher, within thirty days from 23d April, 1865. The arrangements are all made and in progress of execution. I do not know where John A. Payne is now; he was at Montreal and Tanner, Canada, when this plot was projected. His brother (name I do not recollect) is also implicated. Seven of the plotters are at Washington, four at Bedford, Bedford Co., Penn., and the thirteenth is with Payne. These are plain facts. Do not reveal this, but arrest John A. Payne and his brother. Yours truly,

JOHN P. H. HALL,

Of Tanner, Canada

I send this to Detroit to avoid suspicion.

PHILADELPHIA, *April* 20, 1865.

To Hon. W. H. SEWARD:—

You may survive the fatal blow which I aimed at your throat, but know, thou most *cruel, cunning*, and *remorseless man*, that *sooner* or *later* you will fall by the *very hand* which assaulted you last Friday night, and now pens these calm, solemn words.

MOOREHEAD CITY, NORTH CAROLINA, *May* 5, 1865.

Hon. WM. H. SEWARD, Secretary of State:—

SIR—Inclosed you will find a letter which I found floating in the river by the new Government wharf, at this place, on the evening of the 2d instant. It was not until late last night that I succeeded in learning its purport, it being in cipher. Having learned its nature, I lose no time in transmitting it to you, as one concerned. I send also a copy of the letter as I translate it. It is easy to perceive that the first word is Washington; the second, April; the fourth, Dear; and the fifth, John. Having ascertained that much, I had

out little difficulty in making out the remainder. The letter, evidently, had not been opened when thrown in the river. I think the fiend was here awaiting the arrival of General Sherman, and, on learning the General had gone to Wilmington, and feeling himself pressed by the detectives, threw it overboard.
Respectfully yours,

CHAS. DENET.

P. S.—If the letter should lead to any thing of importance, so that it would be necessary that I should be seen, I can be found at 126 South H Street, between 6th and 4½. I am at present engaged in the Construction Corps, Railroad Department, at this place. Will be in Washington in a few days.

CHAS. DENET.

[COPY.]

Translation of the Cipher Letter.

WASHINGTON, *April* 15, 1865.

DEAR JOHN—I am happy to inform you that Pet. has done his work well. He is safe and Old Abe is in hell. Now, sir, all eyes are on you—you must bring Sherman. Grant is in the hands of Old Gray ere this. Red Shoes showed lack of nerve in Seward's case, but fell back in good order. Johnson must come, Old Crook has him in charge. Mind well that brother's oath and you will have no difficulty; all will be safe, and enjoy the fruit of our labors. We had a large meeting last night—all were bent on carrying out the programme to the letter. The rails are laid for safe exit. Old—always behind—lost the pass at City Point. Now, I say again, the lives of our brave officers, and the life of the South, depend upon the carrying this programme into effect. No. 2 will give you this. It is ordered no more letters shall be sent by mail. When you write, sign no real name, and send by some of our friends who are coming home. We want you to write us how the news was received there. We received great encouragement from all quarters. I hope there will be no getting weak in the knees. I was in Baltimore yesterday. Pet. has not got there yet. Your folks are well, and have heard from you. Don't lose your nerve.

O. B.
No. FIVE.

A few brief communications are taken at random, which need no words of introduction, but will be readily understood and appreciated.

McHENRY HOUSE, MEADVILLE, PENNSYLVANIA, *April* 25, 1865.

Hon. E. M. STANTON, Secretary of War, Washington, D. C.:—

SIR—Recent dispatches, referring to a former and futile attempt upon the life of the late Abraham Lincoln, by poison, have induced me to write you regarding a circumstance occurring at this hotel, where I have been cashier for a year and a half. Some time ago the following words were observed to have been scratched upon a pane of glass in room No. 22 of this house, evidently done with a diamond: "Abe Lincoln departed this life August 13, 1864, by the effects of poison." I give this just as it appears upon the glass. In view of recent events, it was deemed best to take the pane of glass out and preserve it, and we have it safe. As to the date of the writing, we cannot determine. It was noticed some months ago by the housekeeper, but was not thought particularly of until after the assassination, being considered a freak of some individual who was probably partially intoxicated. My theory now is, that the words were written in prophecy or bravado by some villain who was in the plot, and that they were written before the date mentioned, August 13th. As to who was the writer, we can, of course, give no definite information. J. Wilkes Booth was here several times during last summer and fall, on his way to and from the oil regions. He was here upon the 10th, and again upon the 29th of June, 1864, but does not appear to have been assigned to that room, still he may have been in it in company with others who did occupy it. Upon the 10th the room was assigned to W. H. Crowell and J. C. Ford, of Irvine, Pennsylvania; and upon the 29th, to R. E. Glass and J. W. King, of New York. Should you consider the matter of sufficient importance to desire it, I will give you a list of the persons occupying the room in question for a long time preceding the above date, as you may request.

With a hearty desire to do all in my power to bring to light and to punishment the author of this terrible crime,

I remain, very respectfully,

Your obedient servant,

S. D. PAGE.

BOSTON, *April* 18, 1865.

DEAR SIR—As I am willing to do all in my power to aid in the arrest of the assassin Booth, perhaps the following may be of service to you, as I have considerable confidence in my information, which I will let you know about at some future time. Go through Mass. Avenue to 8th Street near the market to house No. 61, in the rear. Mrs. Caroline or Angeline Wright lives or stays there, and Booth is secreted there. He goes out in the disguise of a negro, and also did before the assassination. He hides up stairs in a concealed closet, which would be difficult to find, unless carefully looked after, as there is a slide or panel. He jumped off his horse after the crime was committed, another man taking his place, to avoid suspicion. The house may be No. 84, and may possibly be some other avenue, but on 8th street, or near the corner. I am just and honest about this matter, but dare not give my name for fear I may be arrested; but should this give any information to you I shall probably know it.

Yours, H———.

ST. CLAIRSVILLE, OHIO, *April* 26, 1865.

To Hon. E. M. STANTON:—

Believing in the efficacy of prayer, and earnestly desiring that the assassin of our beloved President be brought to justice, I clearly dreamed that the assassin was in a man's house by the name of Cromwell, at Reading, Pennsylvania. I am no believer in Spiritualism or fanaticism of any kind, I am a matter-of-fact woman, but for the intelligence I prayed fervently; take it for what it is worth, but I desire that it never be made public. I feel it to be a duty to give my name, but a delicacy prevents me from so doing.

Yours truly,
ST. CLAIRSVILLE, BELMONT Co., OHIO.

BUFFALO, *April* 25, 1865.

Hon. Secretary of War:—

SIR—I crave your pardon for troubling you again with what some folks call foolishness, and perhaps you have no faith in. I have called several times on the person I mentioned to you since I wrote you; she still insists that the assassin is hid in the same place where he first went, and it is not three miles from the theater; she thinks he is clothed in female attire, and is making arrangements to go off on a large boat. I think it would be well to examine every female, young or old, that wants a pass to leave the city, and especially if their destination is Europe. You are aware, I presume, that a person of his profession can adapt themselves to any disguise. Do not let your disbelief in fortune-telling prevent you from using this as a means of information to bring the assassin to justice, for I have faith to believe he is concealed in a house of that description. You will forgive me for troubling you when you know how much we loved our late President.

Your humble servant,
MERCY.

83 Tenth Street.

The indignation of all classes of loyal people, which will deepen in its tone of condemnation and scorn around the nameless, unknown grave of the assassin, with the years of all coming time, is illustrated in the curious and varied correspondence copied below. Patriotism and religion entered alike into the absorbing interest of the exciting national experience during the spring of 1865.

To the Editor of the Chronicle:—

As any thing pertaining to Booth since his infamous deed (the murder of our noble, beloved President, Abraham Lincoln, who is lamented by all, and above all by the soldiers, as a kind, generous Father departed) possesses an interest to the great reading public, I, a soldier, relate the following incident, as showing how persistent and unchangeable the wretch has been in his treason since the outbreak of the Rebellion. At the commencement of the war, when black-browed and defiant treason stretched out 'ts impious hand, red with murder, to tear in pieces the Constitution, to which the millions of the North clung, as to their sheet-anchor of hope, J. Wilkes Booth was playing an engagement at the little Gayety Theatre, Albany, N. Y., which city, when startled from its propriety by the news of the unholy attack on Sumter, attested in action, more eloquent than words, its love for the old flag, by displaying it from every roof and window. Booth at that time openly and boldly avowed his admiration for the rebels and their deeds, which he characterized as the most heroic of modern times, and boasted loudly that the Southern leaders knew how to defend their rights, and would not submit to oppression.

So vehement and incautious was he in his expressions that the people became incensed, and, threatening him with popular violence, compelled his hasty departure from the city he had too long polluted with his presence. Before leaving, however, he attempted the life of a lady who, for the one or two past seasons, has been an established favorite at Mrs. John Wood's Olympic Theatre, New York City, with whom he (Booth) had a *liaison*, as was thought by many, more intimate than honorable; and conceiving, as I suppose, that she, with a profusion truly regal, showered her charms and blandishments on other suitors, he, in a fit of insane jealousy, entered her room at deep midnight and struck her with a dagger in the side. She, who could find no pleasure in becoming a martyr, merely for fun, turned upon him with the fury of a tigress, and in turn wounded him. Would to God that the dagger of the actress, to quote Carlyle, "had intervened fatally," and saved the wretch from the black, gigantic crime that was impending over his guilty head, and the nation from the universal grief which now shrouds it with the funereal gloom of the grave, and which has excited among the good Blue Coats of the army an indignant, piercing anguish, that goes far beyond all power of description in words.

A. D. Doty,
Carver U. S. General Hospital, Washington, D. C.

STATE OF MARYLAND, WASHINGTON COUNTY, *to wit:*

On this 2d day of March, 1865, before me, the subscriber, one of the Justices of the Peace of the State of Maryland in and for Washington County, personally appeared G. Y., and after being duly sworn according to law, doth depose and say, that he was in the clothing-store of John D. Reamer about three weeks since, and he heard Mr. John D. Reamer, in conversation with William Gabriel, say that there was in Canada from England fifty thousand men and that there would be in a short time fifty thousand more. He was then asked by Gabriel what that meant, and in answer he said he did not know, but we would find it out in a short time, and said that there was one hundred thousand dollars made up now for a man to kill Abraham Lincoln, and that the man wanted the one-half in hand and the balance when the deed was done. He was asked the question by Gabriel who the man was that was to do the act, and was answered by Reamer that that was not yet known, and by the 1st day of April next we would have Lincoln out of his seat. And further this deponent saith not. Sworn before

J. W. Cook, J. P.

I hereby certify that the above is a true copy of the original.

J. W. Cook, J. P.

Hon. E. M. Stanton:—

DEAR SIR—Thinking that any information tending to bring the actors and accomplices connected with the late lamentable occurrences in Washington to the bar of justice would be acceptable to your Government, I am induced to give the following particulars relative to a young man who came into our village some three days subsequent to the assassination of Mr. Lincoln, and whom I am inclined to believe is the Mr. Surratt spoken of in your paper as having escaped to this province. He is a young man of twenty-four or twenty-six years of age, five feet ten inches, perhaps six feet in height, black hair, parted behind, rather inclined to curl, lower jaw very large and deep, body small, legs disproportionately lengthy, figure good, bearing soldierly. His eyes are rather small and black. He had a moustache of a light brown when he came here, but dyed black since; no whiskers. His complexion is very fine. He is stopping with a Dr. Merritt, an escaped secessionist, who came here in December last, and who has always, when speaking of your Government and late Chief Magistrate, expressed himself in terms of unrelenting bitterness and hostility. It is currently reported in our village that, when the news of the assassination of Mr. Lincoln came in, he fairly danced with joy upon the street. From what I have seen of the man, I should be quite prepared to believe him capable of offering his house as a rendezvous for such creatures as the St. Alban's raiders (of whose doings he seems to have had some foreknowledge) and the villains who have lately thrown your country into mourning. I send inclosed an advertisement published by Dr. Merritt upon his arrival here, in which you will perceive he professes to have been on somewhat intimate terms with your present Chief Magistrate, President Johnson.

"J. B. MERRITT, M. D., would very respectfully notify the citizens of Ayr and surrounding country, that he has taken the good-will and practice of the late David Caw, M. D., and William Caw, and will be found at the office lately occupied by them in Ayr, on and after the 1st of December.

" With seventeen years' experience in the treatment of diseases, he feels justified in claiming a share of the public patronage.
"AYR, *November* 17, 1864."

" PERSONAL.—We direct the attention of our readers to the cards of Drs. William Caw, and J. B. Merritt, in another part of this issue, the former being about to retire in favor of the latter. Mr. Merritt comes to Ayr with the best of recommendations both as a medical practitioner and a gentleman. We have copies in our possession of quite a number of very flattering testimonials from some of the leading citizens of Knoxville, Tennessee, where Mr. M. formerly practiced. They include the names of Thomas A. R. Nelson, M. C., John Netherland, ex-Gov., W. G. Brownlow, Editor 'Knoxville Whig,' and one from the Governor of the State of Tennessee, which we give in full:—

[Copy.]
STATE OF TENNESSEE, EXECUTIVE CHAMBER,
NASHVILLE, *August* 10, 1864.

I have been intimately acquainted with Dr. J. B. Merritt for a long time, he having been my family physician for a number of years. It affords me great pleasure to commend him as a first-class physician, and as a gentleman entitled to every degree of public confidence.
(Signed) ANDREW JOHNSON, Governor.

Before taking the step I have done by writing the above, I consulted a most intelligent and efficient magistrate, a resident of this place, upon the matter, and he unhesitatingly indorsed the propriety of my communicating with you, and, like me, would be only too happy in being in any degree instrumental in bringing any of those villains, whether raiders or assassins, to the bar of justice.

By communicating with Robert Wyllie, Esq., J. P., or with me, if it be thought advisable, any information that you may desire in addition to the above, if possible to give it, will be most cheerfully forwarded to you.

Dr. T. J. Reid, one of your officers, at present on duty in the Findlay Hospital, Washington, can give you all needed information as to our village, its whereabouts, Robert Wyllie, Esq., and your correspondent.

Sincerely regretting that conduct so barbarous as the assassination of your departed President and the attempted assassination of your Secretary of State should have been witnessed in your midst to call for a communication of this character,

I am, Sir, your obt.,

G. W. BINGHAM, M. D.

AYR, COUNTY WATERLOO, CANADA WEST,
April 25, 1865.

YORK, PA., May 9, 1864.

Col. L. C. BAKER:—

SIR—I had the honor to suggest to you, at one time, that I thought Booth was secreted in underground apartments in the city, and that he might attempt to escape in the disguise of a female. Subsequent developments demonstrated that I was right in regard to the underground apartment, but wrong as to Booth. It was another one of the conspirators that was secreted there at the time. As to the disguise, I suppose, that was subsequently attempted—not by Booth, of course, but by another.

There is a point, I think, connected with the plot, which, if the Judge-Advocate could draw out of any of the prisoners or witnesses would make a stronger case, viz., the plan and canvass of the practicability of escaping from the city in a balloon, which I think they had at one time.

I submit to your consideration the following opinions or points: That quite a number of persons, cognizant of and connected with the conspiracy, are still at large; that they have a headquarters still, where they meet, and plan, and advise; that said headquarters are probably in some back office or rooms in the city, unknown to the authorities; and that their chief conspirator, plotter, adviser, and arch-devil, at present, is a sly, cunning, quiet, long-headed shoemaker or cobbler, who works upon his bench, and plots crime unsuspected.

Very respectfully, your obedient servant,

E. MATTOCKS.

CITY OF NEW YORK, April 28, 1865.

Hon. E. M. STANTON:—

SIR—The body of the assassin Booth should have no place on American soil. What State, county, or town, would consent to give him a burying-place? None but his sympathizers, and they should not be allowed to have it.

I would suggest that an inquest in full be had, and a full and complete perpetual history be made of all the circumstances, with the verdict of universal condemnation be pronounced upon him, a copy of which to be put in a bottle, and, with Booth, be sunk in the ocean, in the deepest part thereof, to be food for reptiles, and to inform future posterity of his infamy.

Your obedient servant,
LEANDER FOX.

128 HUDSON STREET.

To Hon. Mr. STANTON:—

I am glad to read this morning that the Booths are being searched and arrested, but oh, be vigilant; let not the cellar nor the housetop escape notice, let not the darkey that washes dishes nor old lady who knits in her easy chair fail to be looked in the face, for with them it is nothing but play to perform what has so long been rehearsed. Perhaps he is in bed, with the cap and nightgown of a female, feigning sickness. Let all things be done.

Arrest Edwin Booth also; it will do no harm, for I think he and his mother are very near to the murderer. O please, for the sake of the honor and safety of people in general, do pass a law punishable with death for either sex to wear the other's apparel. Without this all villains will run rampant through this fair land, and none will be safe. The utmost severity is needed in this trying hour, and if it is not done, others more inferior will trample all law under foot.

When going to the funeral of our loved President, I was asked by my neighbor if I was going to a circus.

May God grant your search may not be in vain, for we are filled with those that rejoice in our midst, and none more so than those who have grown rich in this bloody war.

In haste,
JUSTICE.

NEW YORK, *April* 27, 1865.

CLEVELAND, OHIO, *April* 27, 1865.

The Hon. the Secretary of War, Washington:—

SIR—Allow me to suggest that the skeleton of the assassin Booth be preserved and placed in appropriate receptacle, in order the more fully to perpetuate his infamy and be "a terror to evil doers."

I am, Sir, yours with the utmost respect,
J. B. GRIBBLE.

PHILADELPHIA, *April* 27, 1865.

To Secretary STANTON:—

RESPECTED SIR—Has the theater been examined critically by an architect or a practical builder. They could best detect any hiding-place formed by double floors, angular ceilings or roofs, partitions, or the straightening of crooked walls; also private communications with adjoining houses.

The hired horse, spurs, and rider may have been to blind. If newspapers

contained the likeness and description of the murderer, the colored man South as well as the whole North might be detectives. May God give you success With great respect,
I remain yours,

R. T. K.

N. B.—There is scarcely a house in this city but is so built that five or ten men could not be concealed in it. None but a builder perhaps could detect the place. If it was thought proper to examine, I would suggest that a small dog should be with them.

An Englishman in Montreal, who, previous to the murder of Mr. Lincoln, had sympathized strongly with the South, and associated with their agents in Canada, and has been fully posted in their movements, said that the assassination was too much for him, and stated that he knew that during the 20th of April the Southern agents heard from the party that murdered the President, and they expected him to arrive in Montreal within forty-eight hours—not sure that it was Booth, but one closely connected with assassination, if not the principal—that he is sure he will have him in thirty minutes after arrival—that he will probably arrive *via* Troy and Burlington, or W. R. Junction, but most likely by Ohio Central.

This information was given by said Englishman to Alderman Lyman of this city (Montreal), by Lyman to Mr. Cheney, an American, brother of the Expressman, Cheney & Co.; and Cheney came to St. Alban's and gave it to Governor Smith.

Honorable EDWIN M. STANTON:—

HONORED AND DEAR SIR—In the disposal of the remains of the assassin of President Lincoln, I would suggest the following: Let his body be inclosed in a sack of shoddy, and carried out to sea, beyond soundings, thrown overboard, there to remain to death and hell give up their *dead*.

Very respectfully yours,

JOHN McLAUGHLIN.

FRANKLIN ROAD, PHILADELPHIA,
April 29, 1865.

A few days after the assassination, the subjoined mysterious letter was picked up in Ford's Theatre, which as a relic of the times is put on record, with another anonymous epistle of different tone, which fell into my hands:

PHILADELPHIA, *Thursday Night.*

DEAR SIR—You are hereby notified that your presence in Philadelphia is obnoxious to the "Knights of the Blue Gauntlet," and that at a general convocation held this night, beneath the folds of the "Starry Banner," it was determined to notify you of the fact, and to give you ten days from date to place yourself without the pale of our jurisdiction. Beware, the Lapwing is on your track—the Moccasin lies hungry in your path—the true "Knights of the Blue Gauntlet" are not triflers. ******

To L. CARLAND, Actor, &c., 814 Market street.

Oh! What a joke.

Secesh & Co. have treated your honorable body with one of their latest Lincoln jokes. Wilkes Booth & Co. are under a thousand obligations for the pass you have, in your hour of great gratification, granted an intimate friend of his. Your military as well as detective force is not worth powder and lead to kill them. We thank you, honorable Sirs, with sincerity, for your official stupidity, and shall, through a different channel, enable you to patronize the vendors of crape in a wholesome way. Know then, all the rewards you may hereafter offer is of no avail, and further, that we will have the gratification to publish our friends safely at your expense. Oh! what an immense joke. How are you, base, foul Yankee trash. Signed for over ten thousand sworn and tried friends in the District of Columbia. Think of that, base tyrants, and tremble.

A WASHINGTONIAN.

The papers transmitted here were forwarded to me, with the handkerchief referred to in them, and have at least a single point of special interest. They show how near the son of the female assassin, himself deserving the halter, came to sharing this fate with his mother. The statements also underrate the instinctive vigilance of the quickened thought of the people, making otherwise ordinary events significant, and often detective, when a great crime has been committed.

MONTREAL, *April* 27, 1865.

Colonel L. C. BAKER:—

DEAR SIR—I have seen Governor Smith of Vermont, and from him obtained all the facts in relation to the information he obtained from this city. Inclosed you will please find a copy. While in Burlington I obtained a white linen handkerchief, which was dropped in the Vermont Central Depot, on Thursday evening, April 20, by one of three strange men who slept in depot all Thursday night. These men came from steamer *Canada*, Captain Flagg. She was very late that evening; did not connect with the train north (Montreal), which leaves at seven o'clock, P. M. They came into the depot between seven and a half and eight o'clock, after the night watchmen came on duty. They bad no baggage; not even a bundle. They were all rather poorly dressed, looked rather hard, worn-out, tired. The night watchman, C. H. B., is a sharp, intelligent fellow. He asked them which way they were going; they said, to Montreal. He told them that they could not go that night. They knew that. He wanted to know if they did not want to go to a hotel. They said no, that they were going to stay in the depot. They did not appear to have much of any thing to do with one another, or any thing to say to one another. They took separate seats around the room, curled themselves up, and went to sleep. They remained quiet all night. About four o'clock A. M., B. woke them up to take the train, which they did. After the train left, B. saw what he supposed some dirty cloth on the floor about the place where one of them slept. He picked this material up, thinking that it would do to wipe his lantern with. While handling the stuff, he found that he had got two very dirty pocket-handkerchiefs. They had tobacco juice all over them. While looking his prize over, he found the name of J. H. Surratt, No. 2, on the corner of one of the handkerchiefs. The other was unmarked. He took them home. His mother, with whom he lives, was away, attending to a sick brother, and did not return until Saturday morning. The brother died on Tuesday evening, the night these men remained in the depot. B. got his mother to wash the handkerchiefs, which she did on Saturday morning. During Saturday, P. M., B. went to the city and told this circumstance of his finding the handkerchiefs. Detective G. C. heard of it, and got the handkerchief from B., and I got the handkerchief from C. Inclosed, you will find that—B. said one of the men was tall, and the others short. He fully identifies the likeness of Surratt as being one of the men. I then found the conductor that ran the train from Burlington to Essex Junction. The baggage man ran the train up that Friday morning, the 21st. He was very sick when I called on him. He had some recollection of three men whom he found in the depot, and he, too, fully identifies Surratt's picture as being that of one of the men who went up with him. I next found the conductor who ran the through train to St. Alban's, Vermont. His name is O. T. Hobart, a very gentlemanly and intelligent man, belongs to the Vermont Central Railroad. His trip ends at St. Alban's, Vermont, on Tuesdays and Fridays. He gives this description of two men who got on his train at Essex Junction, Vermont: One very tall man, over six feet, and a short man, not much over five feet. This was on Friday morning, April 21, 5.05 o'clock, A. M., he being twenty-five minutes late that morning. These two men had no money to pay their fare with, so they said. Their story was, they were Canadians, had been to New York city to work. These two and another man roomed together, they worked together, got paid off together. During the night, after being paid off, the third man got up, rifled their pockets, and made off with all their money. They were penniless; could get money when they got home; would do so, and would then pay him. They had a description of the man who had robbed them, which was a copy of one they gave to some New York detective, whom they named. The conductor had a good deal of talk with the tall one; the other would not say any thing. He went to them three or four times, for he thought they had money, but was on the beat. The tall one offered his coat as security. Conductor told them that they were able-bodied men, and ought not to be traveling without money to pay their way. They did not want to go any further than St. Alban's, as they would be going away from home to continue on toward St. John's, C. E. Here is his story— one very tall man, six feet one inch, or more (being taller than the conductor, who is five feet eleven and a half inches), broad shoulders, otherwise slim, traight as an arrow; did not look like a laborer, although dressed rather poor; had on a loose sack-coat, colored; cassimere shirt, all one color; collar some turned over; an old spotted scarf, long, which hung down and was held by the vest, which was light color, buttoned half way up, old style; light-colored pants, being loose, had the appearance of having no suspenders on; had on a light-colored, tight-fitting skull-cap. His entire outfit was rather dusty, dirty, and seedy. His hair was black as jet and straight; no beard, nor the appearance of any; was young, not more than twenty-one or twenty-two. He left the train at St. Alban's. The other man was a good deal shorter, not much over five feet, thick set, short neck, full face, sandy complexion, thin sandy chin whiskers or goatee, light in quantity; no other beard. He wore a soft black felt hat, very dusty; dark-colored sack-coat, either black-brown or blue; light-colored pants; reddish-colored flannel shirt. Did not see any vest, as he had his coat buttoned up. He done but little talking—had not much to say for himself, let the tall man do that. The great object of both was to get *home* to *Canada*. He got off the train at St. Alban's. C. S. H. boards at the Mansion Hotel at St. Alban's, and as he was going into the house he saw these two men coming down the street toward the house. He watched them for a few minutes. They turned the corner going toward the depot again, but they did not take the cars again. He fully identifies Surratt's picture as the tall one; the other is not known. He says he should know Surratt at any place or anywhere. They seemed determined to ride on the platform. E. pulled them both in by the collar, saying if they rode with him they must do so inside, which they did, keeping close to the door all the time. H. said after he got to bed he could not go to sleep for nearly two hours, thinking about those fellows. He felt as if they had *beat* him, and that they were very likely a pair of the assassins. He spoke to some friend about the matter, and gave vent to his suspicions. He thought no more of them until I spoke to him on the subject. I never saw such looseness in the police business as they have up here. All these lines are regular highways for men or women of e true Southern style. They have no more fears of passing through along e northern border of Vermont or New York than though the territory was Dixie. C., the only one of the six men sent to Richmond to get the raiders' commissions who succeeded in getting through to Canada, came boldly into St. Alban's, registered his name in full from Richmond, Va., carelessly remarking that St. Alban's was a tough place for a man to come to from Richmond, Va. None molested him; he got into Canada safe with his papers. The Provost-Marshal at A. says that he never had any instructions as to what were his duties or his powers, only to arrest deserters and forward them to New Haven, Conn. He says he don't know that he has the power to arrest or search anybody, and if he had ever arrested anybody, he should have arrested them under the very stringent vagrant law passed by Vermont. I asked him if the commission of captain and provost-marshal made only a town constable of him. He said he did not know any thing of the duties or powers of the Provost-Marshal's office. He has always been a rank "copperhead" Democrat, but is a brother-in-law of Governor Smith; so last fall he went the "Reb." ticket and got appointed Provost-Marshal. He has just gone out to Kansas City on *bis.* or *pleasure*. There is a young major Post Commandant, who has four companies of vets. here, with some ten or twelve officers, but two privates are allowed to examine trains alone. The major says that he supposed such duties belonged to the Provost-Marshal. Then again, the Governor assumes some little powers in small details. Power and authority seem to clash—don't work together. As a consequence, nothing is done by any of them until too late. Noted rebels pass there every week or two to New York and back. A Miss M. came up on Saturday last. She goes back and forth at will, no doubt carrying letters and dispatches. There are several men who do the same. The conductors know them; but there is no Provost-Marshal or other officer who seems to have the power or inclination to arrest and search any of these parties. There is hardly a doubt but that Surratt and one or two others are in this province; who the others are I cannot tell—may be persons who are not known to fame as yet. Inclosed I send you a likeness of one of the Paynes, of whom there are seven brothers, all Kentuckians. Three are said to be in South America, one in jail at St. Alban's, and the others here, as you have a Payne, may be one of these brothers. The picture is marked on the back. If of no use, please send it back to the owner, Mr. Samuel Williams, Secretary of Civil and Military Affairs, St. Alban's, Vt I have placed those pictures in the hands of the Provost-Marshal, American consul, &c. Shall go down to Richmond, C. E., Three Rivers, Quebec, Point Levi, then through Upper Canada. Any orders or instructions by letter or by telegraph can find me, directed to the care of S. S. Potter, Esq., American Consul-General, Montreal, C. E. Shall drop any information I can get. I am going out into what are called the townships, that portion of Canada East bordering on Maine, New York, and Vermont north. Many rebels are in there. Young Saunders is out there now, together with others. Potterfield, a dangerous rebel, is making preparations to go to Nashville, Tenn.; ought not to be allowed. Towbridge, another, who ran a vessel-load of slaves into Mobile (the Wanderer), was convicted and sentenced to Clinton State Prison, but escaped from the officers, has gone to Detroit under some protection got by E., who says he is a cousin (cozzen, I guess).

I am respectfully, &c.,

G. A. G.

HEADQUARTERS UNITED STATES BARRACKS, }
ST. ALBAN'S, VERMONT, *April* 30, 1865. }

MAJOR—One week ago last Thursday night three men slept in the R. & B. Depot, Burlington, Vermont. They came in late at night by boat, and inquired for the first train for Montreal, and took it, coming as far as St. Alban's, Vermont, when they took stage to Franklin, Vermont, and thence off out into Canada. A detective from Colonel Baker's force was through this place last Tuesday, and he exhibited a handkerchief with Surratt's name upon it, which was found in the depot during the day, Friday, following the Thursday night these men slept in the building. These men, or two in particular, were noticed by the conductor on their way to St. Alban's and when the photographs of Surratt were shown him he said at once that they fully answered to one of the men who were on his train the Friday morning spoken of. He also said the photograph of Harrold answered well for another of the men. The detective was very sure, from his tracings, that Harrold and Surratt had passed through here on the day in question. Later developments have proved him mistaken as to Harrold. I had men who passed over every train, and the men saw these men, took notice of them, &c., but they did not answer to the description which they had of men they were ordered to arrest, consequently did not arrest them. I have traced these men, two of them, into Canada; they live in Broom, have been South, are deserters from our army, and, upon the whole, desperate fellows. This circumstance, then, is all that is worth noticing. These men are from the South, and I suppose there is little doubt that one of them dropped the handkerchief in question. Now, in view of the place they have come from, and the handkerchief, what is the circumstance worth? The two men I have followed into Canada are both known in the town where they were found, and neither of them Surratt or Harrold. But still what did they have Surratt's handkerchief for, &c.? I was told this man could be found any time in Swatebury or Broom. What action shall be taken? Can money expended in searching for these men be recovered?

I have the honor to be,
Very respectfully,
Your obedient servant,
J. GROUT, Jr.,
Major First Regiment F. C. Commanding Post.

To Major AUSTIN, Military Commander, Brattleboro, Vt.

DEPARTMENT OF THE EAST, NEW YORK, *May* 8, 1865.

Major-General J. A. DIX, Commanding:—

Refers communication from Major J. Grout, Jr., dated at St. Alban's, Canada West, relative to two suspicious characters who appear to be implicated in the Harrold and Surratt conspiracy.

Colonel BURNETT.

HEADQUARTERS, DEPARTMENT OF THE EAST,
NEW YORK CITY, *May* 8, 1865.

Respectfully referred to the Adjutant-General, United States Army.

JOHN A. DIX,
Major-General Commanding.

Respectfully forwarded to headquarters Department of the East, New York.

FR. AUSTIN,
Major U. S. A., Military Commander.

BRATTLEBORO, VERMONT, *May* 1, 1865.

WAR DEPARTMENT, *May* 9, 1865.
Respectfully referred to Colonel L. C. Baker, Agent War Department.
H. S. BURNETT,
Brevet Colonel, Judge-Advocate.

The following letters, written a year earlier, of a more domestic nature, will make a fitting and rather amusing accompaniment to the story of the handkerchief:—

SURRATTSVILLE, MARYLAND, *December* 16, 1863.

Miss BELL SEAMAN:—

DEAR COUSIN—"To live, is to learn," which has been fully verified by the contents of your *rather surprising* letter. I must confess, my dear Cousin, tha. your letter was short, sweet, and to the point. *Unkindness* is something, Cousin Bell, I have never yet been willfully guilty of, yet no doubt you construed my letter to that effect. "Judge ye not, and ye shall not be judged," is a wise maxim, and one to which I always well look. "Look before you leap."

"Satisfied in my conclusions," is the sentence in which you find so much fault. Well, *ma chère* Cousin, to explain those four words, it is necessary to retrace our steps to a certain letter you wrote me, which contained something about "having more principle than to hold an office under a Government you pretend to despise." In fact, you concluded that I was a hot-headed *rebel*, one belonging to the horned tribe, for they tell me they have horns, and that I ought not to hold an office under this *E pluribus busted up Union*, consequently my being superseded, "satisfied you in your conclusion." Is it not so, my dear Cousin? Do tell me, won't you? I sincerely hope now, Cousin, that you are really satisfied in your conclusions about my meaning.

Anna started for Steubenville, Ohio, last Monday week, and has arrived safely, but I believe lost her trunk. I arrived from Washington a few hours ago, and found your letter awaiting me. I have *proved* my *loyalty*, so that it cannot be doubted, and will regain my office as P. M. Joy is mine! Cousin Bell, I expect you think I am a hard case. Without doubt I am the crossest. most ill-contrived being that ever was. Just ask Anna, when you see her, for a description of your Cousin.

Pardon my *conclusion*, but I am getting really sleepy. It is now ten o'clock, an hour after my bed-time, for I go by the old saying, "Early to bed, and early to rise, makes a man healthy, wealthy, and wise." Ma sends her love to you and family. Write soon, as nothing gives me greater pleasure than to receive a letter from you.

Your Cousin,
J. HARRISON SURRATT.

SURRATT'S VILLA, MARYLAND, *August* 1, 1864.

MY DEAR COUSIN BELL—You ask me if we have warm weather in Maryland, My Maryland. If you have it to such a degree as you represent it, up North, what must it be in our hot-headed South? Yes, Coz, if we had you down here we would soon convert you into "sugar," and then use you to sweeten our dispositions. You know 'tis the extremely hot weather that makes us "Rebs" so savage, cruel, and disagreeable. Yes, Cousin Bell, it is so warm that we can neither eat, sleep, sit down, stand up, walk about, and in fact, to sum the whole in a nutshell, it is too warm to do any thing.

So you think I have a great deal of assurance. I am sorry to say you are the first one that ever told me so. On the contrary, I am a very bashful, and perfectly unsophisticated youth. As every thing pleases you, I am overjoyed to know that you are pleased with me, as very few young ladies take a fancy to me. I am really delighted. You have told me more than ever woman dared to tell. Coz. Bell, you ask me why I do not get married? Simply because I can find no one who will have me. Often have they vowed, yes. But—

"This record will forever stand—
Woman, thy vows are traced in sand."—BYRON.

If you know of any lovely angel, in human form, desirous of a "matrimonial correspondence," just tell her to indite a few lines to your humble Cousin, and I can assure her she will not be sorry for it.

August 10*th*.—Well, Coz., I have just been on a visit of a week's duration. It always takes me about two weeks to write a letter. Ma and Anna are sitting in the hall enjoying the evening breeze, whilst I am sitting over my desk, almost cracking my brain in order to find something to fill up these pages, for, Cousin Bell, you must have perceived, long before this, that I am a poor letter writer. I had almost forgotten to tell you that I called on your friend, Mr Wm. Underwood, at the Carver Hospital. He has nearly recovered from his wound, though it has not yet quite healed. He intended going home in a week or two, and perhaps he may be there now, as it has been over a week since I saw him.

Have you heard from your Uncle James lately? There has been some very hard fighting out West recently, and you know, Cousin Bell, that the foe has very little regard where he directs his bullets. May God preserve him, and grant that he may see the end of this unholy war without harm. At what time does your vacation arrive? Doubtless you look forward to that time with a great deal of impatience.

I am very sorry to think that it is your intention to become an old maid. The horrible creatures! curses upon society! a perfect plague! always meddling with affairs that do not concern them! This is my opinion of old maids. I express it to you, because you have not yet arrived at that state of misery and despair. They are looked upon down our way as unnatural beings—something forsaken by God, man, and devil. So beware! Coz., I met a gentleman from Washington County, Pennsylvania, by the name of Stevenson, who is very well acquainted with the name of Surratt—so he says. Do you know any thing of him? He is a very nice man, and a perfect gentleman. Have you heard any thing of the Rebel Captain, I have not heard from him for some time?

Really, I must bring my tiresome letter to a close. Every thing looks like starvation. Very encouraging, is it not? I hope you will answer soon, as nothing gives me greater pleasure than to receive a letter from you. Cousin Bell, I am not prone to flatter, so you must believe what I say. Ma and Anna send their love to you. I wish you knew Ma, I know you would like her. Neither of us is like her. My brother resembles her very much. He is the best looking of the family. That is saying a good deal for myself. Excuse this miserable scrawl, as I have to dip my pen in the stand at every word. Anna has just commenced playing the "Hindoo Mother." I would advise you to get it. It is really beautiful. Good-by. I hope to see you before many months.

Your Cousin,
J. HARRISON SURRATT.

"To whom shall we Grant the Meade of praise?" Ha! ha!

OFFICE OF THE COMMISSARY-GENERAL OF PRISONERS,
WASHINGTON, D. C., February 6, 1865.

MISS BELL SEAMAN:—

DEAR COUSIN—I received your letter, and not being quite so selfish as you are, I will answer it, in what I call a reasonable time. I am happy to say we are all well, and in fine spirits.

We have been looking for you to come on with a great deal of impatience. Do come, won't you? Just to think, I have never yet seen one of my cousins. But never fear, I will probably see you all sooner than you expect. Next week I leave for Europe. Yes, I am going to leave this detested country, and I think, perhaps, I may give you all a call as I go to New York. Do not be surprised, Cousin Bell, when you see your hopeful Cousin. Truly you may be surprised.

I have an invitation to a party, to come off next Tuesday night. Anna and myself intend going, and expect to enjoy ourselves very much. I have been to a great many this winter, so that they are beginning to get common; but as this is something extra, I looked forward with a great deal of impatience. I wish you were, in order that I might have the pleasure of introducing you to regular country hoe-down. I know you would enjoy it.

There is no news of importance, save the burning of the Smithsonian Institute, which, of course, you have heard of. His Excellency Jefferson Davis and Old Abe Lincoln couldn't agree, as sensible persons knew beforehand; and now I hope people are satisfied, and hope they will make up their minds to fight it out to the bitter end.

"Show no quarter." That's "my motto."

Cousin Bell, try and answer me in a few days at least, as I would like very much to hear from you before I leave home for good. I do not know what to think of our mutual Miss Kate Brady. Byron justly remarks—

"This record will forever stand—
Woman, thy vows are traced in sand."

I have just taken a peep in the parlor. Would you like to know what I saw there? Well, Ma was sitting on the sofa, nodding first to one chair, then to another, next the piano. Anna sitting in corner, dreaming, I expect, of J. W. Booth. Well, who is J. W. Booth? She can answer the question. Miss

Fitzpatrick playing with her favorite cat—a good sign of an old maid—the detested old creatures. Miss Dean fixing her hair, which is filled with rats and mice.

But hark: the door-bell rings, and Mr. J. W. Booth is announced. And listen to the scamperings of the ———. Such brushing and fixing.

Cousin Bell, I am afraid to read this nonsense over, so, consequently, you must excuse all misdemeanors. We all send love to you and family Tell Cousin Sam. I think he might write me at least a few lines.

Your Cousin,
J. Harrison Surratt,
541 H Street, between 6 and 7 Streets.

During my visits to the prisoners, before their execution, Mrs. Surratt confessed to me her complicity with the conspirators so far as the intended abduction was concerned, but affirmed that she reluctantly yielded to the urging of Booth in aiding the plot of assassination. He insisted that her oath of fidelity bound her to see the fatal end of the conspiracy.

CHAPTER XXVII.

ATTEMPTED SUICIDE OF WIRZ.

My Connection with the Imprisonment of Wirz and Jeff. Davis—Vigilance in Guarding the Prisoner—Mrs. Wirz visits her Husband—He desires a Call—The Interview—Attempted Suicide.

POOR Wirz, the German prisoner, keeper at Andersonville, has a place and a name in the history of the American conflict, imperishable as that of Jefferson Davis, and no more and no less enviable. He is only the willing servant, in war's cruelest work, of the master spirit of the revolt, who richly deserves the disgraceful doom of the wretched victim of the gallows, to whom no mercy was extended. Not alone by the surviving victims of his barbarity will Wirz be held in remembrance, but by all the loyal people of the land, who watched with intense interest the progress of his trial. Soon as it became evident that the testimony against this disciple of Nero was sufficiently strong to convict him, there were rebel emissaries who, fearing a confession from his lips, which would implicate Jefferson Davis and others in the guilt of his crimes, desired and determined, if possible, to bring the trial to a speedy close. Wirz himself had several times intimated that, if convicted, he would make a statement of all the facts connected with his administration of the Andersonville prison, which would show conclusively that he acted under the direct orders of Davis and General Winder.

I had taken no part in Wirz's trial, most of the evidence having been procured by military officers then on duty a the South. During the last days of the trial, Mrs. Wirz appeared in Washington, and desired an interview with her husband. The Secretary of War had directed the officer in command of the prison to exercise the utmost caution in

GENERAL BAKER FOILS WIRZ'S ATTEMPT AT SUICIDE.

respect to the prisoner. It was feared that he would commit suicide. Orders were issued not to allow any interview to be had with him under any pretense whatever. He was to be kept entirely secluded from the other prisoners, and only visited by the clergy and his counsel. Mrs. Wirz applied to me for permission to see him. She claimed that she desired only to administer to his comfort, as far as possible, and had no objection to the interview taking place in the presence of an officer of the Government. Wirz sent me a request to visit him, and accordingly I repaired to his apartment in the "Old Capitol." During the conversation, he expressed earnest desire to see his wife, when I reminded him that the orders of the Secretary prohibited such interviews. His anxiety was so great, that I stated the prisoner's request to Mr. Stanton, who consented to a meeting in my presence, with no communications in their own language between them. He then gave me the following order:

WAR DEPARTMENT, ADJUTANT-GENERAL'S OFFICE,
WASHINGTON, *November* 9, 1865.

Major-General AUGUR, commanding Department of Washington :—

GENERAL—Henry Wirz has sent a request to General L. C. Baker to visit him. The Secretary of War desires that the authority be given General Baker.

I am, very respectfully, your obedient servant,
E. D. TOWNSEND,
Assistant Acting Adjutant-General.

With this document I procured a permit, and requested Mrs. Wirz to be at the prison at four o'clock that day. The interview took place, and I shall never forget the first meeting between Wirz and his wife. She exhibited the most stoical indifference, and simply said, "How are you, Wirz?" Instead of embracing him, as would naturally have been expected under the circumstances, she sat down in a chair in front of him, and looked at the doomed man a moment, and then gave utterance to the most vindictive words against the Government, in which he joined. Instead of talking of their family affairs, the unfortunate position in which Wirz was placed, and the probability of his execution, she took occasion to denounce Colonel Chipman, Judge-Advocate of the commission before whom Wirz was being tried, and the witnesses as perjurers, and in the most threatening manner defied the Government to carry the findings of the commission into execution. This interview finally closed in their making an appointment for another.

The conduct of Wirz and his wife was to my mind very suspicious. I did not conceive that such indifference was natural under the circumstances, and determined to watch their next interview very closely. It came in due time, and was very similar to the first one. Mrs. Wirz sat in front of her husband, and I took a position where I could casually observe the movements of each. Mrs. Wirz took from her hand a glove, inside of which I noticed she had a small package; what it was I could not tell. The interview was short, as both were conscious that I was observing every movement. At the third interview the same thing was repeated. As we all rose to go to the door leading to the hall, Wirz walking first, Mrs. Wirz next, and myself at the rear, she for the first time approached him, when they embraced and put their lips up to kiss each other. I watched the motion, and perceived that she was conveying something from her mouth to his. I sprang forward in an instant, caught him by the throat, and threw him on the floor. He raised a pill from his throat, brought it within his teeth, crushed it and spit out. I picked it up and found it to be a small round piece of strychnine inclosed in a piece of oiled silk. Upon this discovery I informed Mrs. Wirz that she could have no more interviews with her husband. She was compelled, therefore, to leave him to his fate. My next step was to inform the Assistant Secretary of War and Judge Holt of the singular occurrence. I also showed to the former the strychnine pill. On the day of the prisoner's execution, I related the poison scene to a reporter of a New York paper. It was given to the public by him. The copperhead press immediately opened their artillery of abuse, making me the target of bitterest attack. The whole statement was pronounced a fabrication, while it was verified entirely by Louis Skade, the counsel of Wirz, and by Mrs. Wirz. It is a fact, which should make the loyal men of the land reflect deeply, that these reckless detractors of the administration of Mr. Lincoln, and all who aided him in checking the insane revolt, who defended the vilest actors in the drama of rebellion, are to-day the friends of Mr. Johnson and his "policy." No reflective patriotic mind can exclude the doubt whether the infamous keeper of the Andersonville prison pen would have been executed at all had the merited fate been delayed a few months longer, until the change in the tone of the Presidential feeling toward rebels, whom he had so warmly condemned and warned that their treason must be made "odious" for all coming time. It is more sad and stinging to know this, for those of us who necessarily were familiar with the character and deeds of the brutal servants of Davis and his counselors and commanders. I could narrate horrors which would stir the indignation of the coolest loyal heart, that were openly or silently approved by the Confederate Government; and yet we are asked to be charitable and conciliatory toward men who hated with the venom of a Nero our slain President and our "boys in blue," and have only changed from power to wreak their vengeance to weakness that can do no more than nurse a disarmed disloyalty. If it is true, in the words of the song, that John Brown's soul is marching on! it is equally a reality that the souls of Booth and Wirz are still marching stealthily on through the streets of the cities and over the plantation plains of the "sunny South."

ACTUAL BURIAL-PLACE OF BOOTH.

In compliance with a promise made in the Prospectus of this work, as well as to gratify public curiosity, and, if possible, forever put at rest the many absurd and foolish rumors in circulation concerning the final disposition of the remains of the assassin, J. Wilkes Booth, I submit the following facts —

In order to establish the identity of the body of the assassin beyond al question, the Secretary of War directed me to summon a number of witnesses residing in the city of Washington, who had previously known the murderer. Some two years previous to the assassination of the President, Booth had had a *tumor* or *carbuncle* cut from his neck by a surgeon. On inquiry, I ascertained that Dr. May, a well-known and very skillful surgeon, of twenty-five years' practice in Washington, had performed the operation.

Accordingly I called on Dr. May, who, before seeing the body, minutely described the exact locality of the tumor, the nature and date of the operation, &c. After being sworn, he pointed to the *scar* on the neck, which was then plainly visible. *Five* other witnesses were examined, all of whom had known the assassin intimately for years. The various newspaper accounts, referring to the *mutilation* of Booth's body, are equally absurd. General Barnes, Surgeon-General U. S. A., was on board the gun-boat where the post-mortem examination was held, with his assistants. General Barnes cut from Booth's neck about two inches of the *spinal* column through which the ball had passed; this piece of bone, which is now on exhibition in the Government Medical Museum, in Washington, is the only relic of the assassin's body above ground, and this is the only mutilation of the remains that ever occurred. Immediately after the conclusion of the examination, the Secretary of War gave orders as to the disposition of the body, which had become very offensive, owing to the condition in which it had remained after death; the leg, broken in jumping from the box to the stage, was much discolored and swollen, the blood from the wound having saturated his under-clothing. With the assistance of Lieut. L. B. Baker, I took the body from the gun-boat direct to the old Penitentiary, adjoining the Arsenal grounds. The building had not been used as a prison for some years previously. The Ordnance Department had filled the ground-floor cells with fixed ammunition—one of the largest of these cells was selected as the burial-place of Booth—the ammunition was removed, a large flat stone lifted from its place, and a rude grave dug; the body was dropped in, the grave filled up, the stone replaced, and there rests to this hour all that remained of John **Wilkes Booth.**

www.ingramcontent.com/pod-product-compliance
Lightning Source LLC
Chambersburg PA
CBHW032014220426
43664CB00006B/240